A Geopolitics of Academic Writing

Pittsburgh Series in Composition, Literacy, and Culture

David Bartholomae and Jean Ferguson Carr, Editors

A. Suresh Canagarajah

A Geopolitics of Academic Writing

University of Pittsburgh Press

Published by the University of Pittsburgh Press, Pittsburgh, Pa., 15260

Copyright © 2002, University of Pittsburgh Press

All rights reserved

Manufactured in the United States of America

Printed on acid-free paper

10 9 8 7 6 5 4 3 2 1

ISBN 0-8229-4187-2

LIBRARY OF CONGRESS CATALOGING-IN-PUBLICATION DATA

Canagarajah, A. Suresh.

   A geopolitics of academic writing / A. Suresh Canagarajah.

      p. cm. — (Pittsburgh series in composition, literacy, and culture)

   Includes bibliographical references and index.

   ISBN 0-8229-5794-9 (alk. paper)

   1. Scholarly publishing—Political aspects. 2. Scholarly publishing—
Political aspects—Developing countries. 3. Academic writing—Political
aspects. 4. Academic writing—Political aspects—Developing countries.
5. Communication in learning and scholarship—Political aspects.
6. Communication in learning and scholarship—Political aspects—
Developing countries.

   I. Title. II. Series

z286.s37c36 2002

070.5—dc21

2002008025

For A. J.

and colleagues at the University of Jaffna

Contents

Acknowledgments

This book is indeed multivocal. Apart from the different voices from the periphery that I attempt to represent, there are others from diverse communities that emerged through the process of researching and writing this book.

Without my colleagues at the University of Jaffna who shared their views, texts, and research, this book would not be possible. Many other of their writings were hunted down from long-forgotten local publications to build up my argument. R. Shriganeshan and A. J. Canagaratne went further to read different versions of this manuscript and comment on them.

Here in the United States, Deborah Brandt (University of Wisconsin–Madison) first understood the need to give space for this argument and did so in *Written Communication,* which she continues to edit. Later, as I developed this work into a book, she provided useful suggestions on sections of the manuscript as a reviewer for the University of Pittsburgh Press, together with Alpana Sharma (University of Nebraska–Lincoln) and another reviewer who wishes to remain anonymous. I also thank Niels Aaboe, Editorial Director of the University of Pittsburgh Press, and David Bartholomae and Jean Ferguson Carr, editors of the Pittsburgh Series in Composition, Literacy, and Culture, for their support.

Dwight Atkinson (Temple University, Japan) enters into this book in numerous ways. As a rigorous and perceptive student of the sociohistory of research writing, he has provoked my thinking on the implications of his work for periphery scholars. I was also successful in imposing upon him to read this manuscript. A scrupulous and patient peer-reviewer, he challenged me to examine my statements through his endless scribbles throughout the manuscript. Ilona Leki (University of Tennessee–Knoxville) too extended her expertise in academic literacy, offering suggestions for revision. I must of course take responsibility for my own obstinacy and weaknesses that account for the limitations in this book.

My wife, Nanthini, daughters, Lavannya and Nivedhana, and son, Wiroshan (whose birth six months before the completion of this manuscript fortunately slowed down my writing and provided some invigorating time for reflection), continue to accommodate my life in scholarship and activism.

A Geopolitics of Academic Writing

The Problem

"In China, a Spectacular Trove of Dinosaur Fossils Is Found" triumphantly proclaims the front-page headline of the *New York Times* of 25 April 1997. Datelined from Philadelphia the previous day, the first paragraph states: "An international team of paleontologists announced today that a fabulous trove of dinosaur fossils had been discovered in a remote region of northeast China." This international team is later introduced as comprising four members from American universities and another from a German university. Going by the journalistic penchant for immediacy and timeliness, readers might interpret the finding to have been made very recently, by this team. But it is after reading several more paragraphs that we find that the discovery had actually been made by the Chinese much earlier. The cause of the present announcement, it transpires, is simply the fact that the team of Western scientists had just returned from a visit to the site. The report was inspired by the meeting of the Academy of Natural Sciences the previous day in Philadelphia, where the paleontologists had reported the outcome of their visit. When we read even more closely, we find that Western scholars had got wind of the discovery about seven months before the Philadelphia conference, during a scholarly meeting in New York City. The discovery had been made by a Chinese farmer. The date he discovered the site is not given anywhere in the report. His name is also not given. The names of the members of the international team and their university affiliations are, on the other hand, cited very prominently.

The point to note about this report is not that the role of the West since the dinosaur fossils' belated discovery gets a lot of prominence. This is after all to be expected. A newspaper published in the United States for a readership primarily based here will narrate events from that standpoint. Therefore, the persons and events in the remote Third World location are

1

eclipsed by the Western academics and their activities. More troubling is
the impression created by the report that the Western intellectuals should
get sole or primary credit for the fossil discovery. When the newspaper
claims that "the spectacular trove was not announced until today" there are
many questions that arise in our minds. Announced *by* whom? *To* whom?
Certainly, the Chinese must have been aware for a long time of the discovery they had made in their own backyard. The unqualified manner in
which that statement is made reveals that its intent is to claim nothing less
than global relevance. The whole world is claimed to know about the fossils after the announcement at the Philadelphia conference. It is as if the
finding is real only when the West gets to know about it. It is at that point
that the discovery is recognized as a "fact" and constitutes legitimate
knowledge. Whatever preceded that point is pushed into oblivion.

The Chinese characters in this drama are no strangers to struggles over
the ownership of knowledge. A still closer reading of the report suggests
that the farmer himself understood the significance of what he had discovered. He had divided the fossils into two portions and sold them to
two rival Chinese universities. He had evidently had an insight into such
matters as the marketability of intellectual products, the competition for
ownership, and power struggles over knowledge. The Chinese faculty
members of the rival universities had also been theorizing about the find,
producing their own explanatory paradigms in competition with each
other. But little did they realize that beyond their local politics of knowledge, there was a greater power with far superior resources waiting to
pounce on their discovery. They would soon realize the reality of imperialism in knowledge construction, with the contest for the fossils and their
interpretation played out at the international level.

When Western scholars first heard about the find at the meeting of the
Society for Vertebrate Paleontology in New York, they responded in a pre-
dictable way. They concluded that their presence was immediately needed
in China. They quickly arranged for what they called a "reconnaissance
trip"—which ominously suggests an impending attack and continuous
engagement in the site. No sooner had they returned from their trip than
the team members announced their own hypothesis about the find. While
the Chinese believed that the chicken-sized dinosaur was a primitive non-
feathered relative of the earliest known true bird, the Western team dis-
agreed with this interpretation. It debunked the paradigm produced by the

Chinese scholars by positing a different chronology of dinosaur evolution. Needless to say, the news report devotes much space to explaining with considerable sympathy the hypothesis of the Western team.

Though I don't have the expertise to arbitrate that interpretive conflict here, the attitudes displayed by the Western scholars and media need to be criticized. The ease with which they overrode the local knowledge of the Chinese scientists on their find on their own soil is striking. The knowledge gained through the process of gathering data in the local context pales in significance next to the interpretation produced at a second remove (typically miles away in alien institutional or laboratory settings) by the foreign team. This displays a common Western assumption that though the Third World may have the data, it takes Western academics to theorize about it (Franco 1988; Loomba 1994). Third World communities are treated as if they don't have the know-how and theoretical sophistication to transform their raw material into valid knowledge. It also follows that, for the West (and the *New York Times*), it is not the context relating to the discovery and maintenance of the raw material that is important but the theoretical constructs generated from it. Predictably, the background behind the discovery of the fossils is given short shrift in the report, while the theoretical activity is given maximum attention.

To the credit of the Academy of Natural Sciences, it must be noted that it invited a Chinese national to be present (perhaps as a token) in Philadelphia when a contract was signed to jointly study the site. The news report in fact concludes with this statement by Dr. Ji Quiang: "This locality we have just begun to look at is not only a Chinese treasure, it is a global treasure." These are liberal sentiments that should be music to the ears of Western academics. It is not surprising that the report concludes with this statement. But the irony in an earlier statement by Dr. Quiang appears to be lost on the reporter and the international team. "I look forward to a wonderful cooperative project with American and *other* international paleontologists," says Dr. Quiang (emphasis added). He thus differentiates American researchers—who dominated both the so-called international team that visited the site and the contract-signing ceremony—from "other international paleontologists." Dr. Quiang seems to be calling for greater involvement from these "other" paleontologists in order to make the enterprise truly global. The composition of the "international team" that visited China was heavily (80 percent) American.

(Even the single member from the German university served to make the team only Western and not necessarily international in the widest possible sense.) This hasty dubbing of any of their intellectual involvement as "international" reveals certain other problematic attitudes of Western/American scholarly communities. Perhaps this indicates a myopic attitude that whatever activity they are involved in is of international/global significance. Perhaps the scholars are arrogating to themselves the right to speak for the whole world because of their presumed intellectual superiority.

Many of these impressions from the news report were confirmed that morning in my English as a Second Language (ESL) class (dominated, ironically, by Chinese students) during our daily discussion of the *New York Times* for reading-comprehension purposes. The students assumed that it was the American team that had made the discovery; that the hypothesis of the American team was superior to the one put forward by the local scholars; and that there was sincere international cooperation in the study of the site. The students also lauded the true intellectual commitment of the Western academics, who acted decisively and efficiently to make known to the rest of the world a find whose significance and import lay unrecognized in the rural hinterlands of China. We cannot blame such uncritical interpretations on superficial reading strategies or linguistic incompetence. There are many factors in the construction of this report that may encourage such impressions even among competent readers.

Consider first the textual strategies displayed in the report. Note such crucial features as the headline and introduction for what is said—and what is omitted. Recollect the conclusion that foregrounds the Chinese scholar's statement that the fossils would be everyone's property. Observe the texture of the report, which is replete with details of the Western scholars and institutions but contains almost nothing of the dates, names, or activities of the Chinese. We could also do a fine-grained analysis of the syntactic structures employed in the report—such as the passive construction in the headline and introduction, which allows for the omission of the agent (thus leaving vague who really made the discovery of the fossils). Furthermore, we must remember the power of the print media to establish "truth." When something appears in print it is widely construed as constituting publicly acknowledged facts in a manner that oral communication cannot. Even if the Chinese farmers and scholars had been talking about these fossils for years, the information would exist in the realm of hearsay, folk knowledge, and myth until it entered print. What is in print is accorded the status of verified knowledge. Through the media report, the Western scholars are able to achieve recognition for the discovery, while the oral knowledge of the Chinese farmers remains suppressed.

We must also take note here of the power of the written medium to transmit information to the global community. Those who enjoy the academic infrastructure that allows them to publish have an advantage in the dissemination and construction of knowledge. This is not a simple matter of having printing presses to publish one's scholarly activities and news. The community also needs ancillary technological facilities for speedy gathering and dissemination of information, marketing networks for global distribution, and relatively low-cost publishing for universal consumption. The advantages enjoyed by Western communities—in terms of technology, marketing infrastructure, and communication networks—enable them to appropriate the knowledge and findings of other communities while glorifying their own achievements. The Chinese scholars—like others in the periphery—obviously lack the means to represent their findings and knowledge effectively to the international community in a timely and effective fashion. Furthermore, the institutional organization and economic strength of the West enable it to act efficiently regarding the fossil discovery. It enjoys the means to get a team of researchers ready, to organize their travel to the site, to fund the team's subsistence, to arrange conferences of international scale to publicize their claims, to support the participation of the Chinese (and other international) scholars, and to initiate research on the site that may demand huge amounts of capital and equipment. If the Chinese scholars had enjoyed similar resources, they would have developed their interpretation and publicized their discovery much earlier to the global community. They would have also possessed the power to orchestrate the whole research enterprise under their own leadership. They would have thus been able to present the discovery in a manner favoring their community's interests, knowledge, and values.

This simple example of the processes involved in knowledge construction introduces some of the issues I wish to discuss in this book. The appropriation of Third World knowledge by Western academic institutions in the name of international scientific enterprise, the ways in which any raw data that might be found in the Third World have to undergo theorization/interpretation by the West to pass into the accepted stock of knowledge, the role of written communication in defining knowledge in public and transnational terms, the place of publishing/academic networks in serving the Western hegemony of knowledge, and how through all this the local knowledge of the Third World is marginalized—these form the nexus of issues that will be discussed in the chapters to follow.

I wish to explore these themes in the specialized domain of academic writing in research journals. This mode of writing is quite central to the practice of knowledge construction in the academy and plays a significant role in the leadership of Western communities in scholarship. In analyzing the composing and publishing processes of research articles in this book, I will make an argument that is very simple to formulate but difficult to substantiate. The argument features the following claims: academic writing holds a central place in the process of constructing, disseminating, and legitimizing knowledge; however, for discursive and material reasons, Third World scholars experience exclusion from academic publishing and communication; therefore the knowledge of Third World communities is marginalized or appropriated by the West, while the knowledge of Western communities is legitimated and reproduced; and as part of this process, academic writing/publishing plays a role in the material and ideological hegemony of the West. The many complicating details in this argument will be fleshed out as we proceed.

This book is organized around the different types of conventions governing academic writing. I broadly distinguish between *communicative conventions* and *social conventions*—both of which will be demonstrated to have different levels of influence on academic discourse. Under the former, I differentiate *textual* conventions and *publishing* conventions. Textual conventions are related to matters of language, style, tone, and structure that characterize academic texts. Publishing conventions are the procedural requirements of academic journals, such as the protocol for submitting papers, revisions, and proofs; the nature of interaction between authors and editorial committees; the format of the copy text; bibliographical and documentation conventions; the particular weight and quality of the paper; and the manuscript copies and postage required. Social conventions are the rituals, regulations, and relationships governing the interaction of members of the academic community as they engage in knowledge production and communication. Each of these levels of convention, then, helps us move from the product of writing to the process and to the larger social contexts of text production/reception. In assuming that all of these types of conventions have implications for academic discourse, I adopt a flexible attitude to the definition of discourse. I treat *discourse* as referring to genres of thinking/communicating/interacting that are influenced by concomitant forms of sociolinguistic conventions, ideological complexes, and knowledge paradigms. Through this inclusive definition I attempt to side step some of the hair-splitting debates today in the human and social sciences on the meaning of this now clichéd construct (Canagarajah 1999; Kress 1985; MacDonell 1986).

In the first chapter, I widen the context of academic literacy by locating the place of research articles in the intellectual and material inequalities between the *center* (referred to above as the West) and *periphery* (typically communities colonized by European intervention, referred to above as the Third World). The following two chapters introduce the theoretical constructs that help conduct this inquiry. I move on in the fourth chapter to describe the textual conventions that distinguish the writing of center and periphery scholars. In the fifth, I explore the publishing conventions established by center editorial circles and the ways in which periphery scholars attempt to meet such requirements in the context of limited resources. In dealing with the social conventions of disciplinary communities in the periphery in the sixth chapter, I present their academic culture from the "inside," while also exploring how it works as both a cause and a consequence of their exclusion from the publishing practices and networks of the center. In the seventh chapter, I consider the implications of this publishing inequality between the center and periphery communities for the politics of knowledge construction at the global level. Finally, in the eighth chapter, I suggest ways in which both center and periphery academic communities can productively refashion the nature of their relationship by accommodating multiple modes of literacy and textual practices. Such a relationship, based on respect for the local knowledge of each community, would serve to democratize academic communication and knowledge production.

But before we proceed further, I must acknowledge the peculiar contexts relating to this inquiry and the ways they shape this book. I explore in the next section, "The Project," the ironies of my positionality as a periphery scholar now working in (and writing from) the center, making a case on behalf of my former colleagues through the very channels of their intellectual domination.

The Project

With the simmering ethnic conflict between Tamil and Sinhalese communities taking a violent turn in 1983, many areas in Sri Lanka experienced the destruction of the meager technological facilities we had previously enjoyed. In Jaffna (where I lived while teaching at the local university), power supply was disrupted, as cables and power stations had sustained heavy damage during the fighting. Fuel, too, was banned by the state, as much of the region was controlled by the rebel militia. At night, students crowded around the streetlamps set up by the Red Cross with the aid of small power generators. We, being the teachers, were too embarrassed to fight for space with our students to read our Derrida or Foucault under streetlights. Instead, we used oil lamps fueled by kerosene purchased in the black market. When kerosene was not readily available, we used all kinds of other oil produced from local vegetation. This could be burned only for a limited number of hours, as it was very expensive. Our reading/writing had to compete with other household needs (such as cooking) to determine how much oil could be sacrificed for academic pursuits. Many of us worked when the sun was up and closed our books or drafts at nightfall.

Furthermore, communication facilities such as telephones, telegrams, fax, and electronic mail were not available because of the power cut. For the same reason, computer facilities were not accessible. Mass media such as radio and television did not function normally in Jaffna. Mail was delivered from outside the region once every three or four months by the Red Cross and other organizations as a humanitarian gesture. The delivery was further delayed because military forces of both sides screened mail for seditious matter. The effects of such scrutiny were evident when letters were delivered damaged and mutilated. Many were the times when the local postal agency issued a general invitation to the public to sift through the scraps in their sorting room to identify any letter that might belong to us. Under such conditions, it was only belatedly that we would come to know that Foucault had expired or that there had been an important international conference on postcolonial literature held in our own capital city. By the time we received calls for fellowships or conference participation, the deadlines for application would have long passed. There was also a ban on published literature from outside by both the government and the rebels (in order to restrict propaganda against themselves). So it was unthinkable to get Chomsky's newest book or the latest scholarly journals. While the few journals that the university library subscribed to would appear as late as three or four years after publication, many others had to be read only on a rare annual visit to the capital city, where the libraries of the British Council or American Center were located.

Moreover, there was a shortage of stationery, as it was banned by the government out of fear that rebels might use it for propaganda publications. So we came up with many ingenious methods to keep writing and printing. Since ruled notebooks were permitted for the use of students, most news pamphlets and scholarly proceedings were printed on such paper. Often, used paper was recycled—some of my first drafts and outlines were written on the blank reverse sides of printed paper. The extent of later revisions depended on the amount of paper one could find. Also, travel outside the region was restricted by both the government (in order to prevent infiltration by rebels) and the rebel militia (in order to prevent deserters and turncoats). The first and only scholarly conference I attempted to attend was that of Modern South Asian Studies in Berlin. After getting through all the red tape—the necessary clearance from the local militia, the Ministry of Education of the Sri Lankan government, and the German embassy—and the difficulties of reaching the airport in the capital city, I arrived at the conference on the evening of the last day of the proceedings, just as most scholars were leaving for home. Missing my own presentation was the least of my disappointments.

We can imagine the barriers such conditions can create to receiving the latest research information, negotiating our manuscripts for publication, and interacting with the international scholarly community. Despite these conditions, teaching and research of a high quality were and even now are conducted by a motivated band of academics—as reported in a series of articles in the *Chronicle of Higher Education* (Dube 1995a, 1995b). Being one of the six major universities on the island, and admitting a limited number of students based on highly competitive examinations, the University of Jaffna (hereafter UJ) could not afford to close down. In fact, UJ grants postgraduate degrees in certain disciplines, and faculty members engage in both research and teaching. The academics at UJ aim to conduct rigorous research of a high order, considering the difficulties as a fact of everyday life. Graduate students typed and retyped their theses on rickety typewriters after many painstaking handwritten drafts to meet the deadline. Faculty members wrote fascinating abstracts and papers for scholarly presentations, even though they could produce only shoddily printed copies.

Context

I would like to explore the practices of academic literacy and publishing in a context-sensitive manner, with all the peculiarity and uniqueness pertaining to what was at that time my setting. I am not too anxious to generalize these features to all periphery communities. Jaffna appears to present a worst-case scenario for academic work. It was perhaps the extremity of the conditions there that made me sensitive to the inequalities in academic work and brought into relief the differences in literacy practices. However, it must be noted that there are many scholars in other Asian, African, and South American communities who are working in conditions that approximate such economic underdevelopment, technological backwardness, and political instability (Gibbs 1995; Muchiri et al. 1995). The differences are mostly of degree and not kind. So, for example, political unrest has recently affected the functioning of universities in Zaire, Tanzania, and Kenya (Muchiri et al. 1995); economic recession has hampered new acquisitions in university libraries in Addis Ababa, sub-Saharan Africa, and Latin America (Gibbs 1995); technological limitations and lack of access to the information highway are bemoaned by academics in the West Indies and India (Gibbs 1995). Some of the disadvantages described above apply also to the periphery *within* the center—the marginalized, off-networked, and poorly facilitated institutions in technologically advanced nations (Murray 2000).

This book is largely based on my own and my colleagues' experiences in getting our scholarly work published in mainstream journals from an underdeveloped region. My academic experience at UJ for more than a decade (until recently, when I moved to New York) provided valuable firsthand insights into the scholarly practices of that community. I have conducted ethnographic/sociolinguistic studies in Jaffna in a variety of social sites (Canagarajah 1993b, 1994a, 1995c, 1995d)—with the literate conventions and discursive practices of the academic community featuring importantly in my research. I hope to generate important questions pertaining to the publishing prospects of periphery scholars through a close analysis of this sharply focused context.

Though I claim to represent scholars from the type of background described above, my critical insights are enabled by my work experience in some American university settings as well. My membership in the academic communities of the center and the periphery has oriented me to the differences in literacy practices of both circles and provided a peculiar "double vision" that informs the discussion in this book. I have had the good fortune to shuttle between both communities and live in each for extended periods of time. After joining the faculty of UJ in 1984, I came to the United States on leave granted by the university for my doctoral research. While doing graduate studies, I taught composition, literature, and ethnic studies at two different universities (in Ohio and Texas). Returning to Sri Lanka in 1990, I continued to teach and research at UJ in the midst of the intensified ethnic fighting described earlier. I relocated to New York in 1994 to join the faculty of the City University of New York. Through all this experience, in a sense, I have moved between sites of immense contrast—primitively rural and sophisticatedly urban; pathetically poor and prodigally opulent; technologically deprived and high tech; in short, the margins and the center of publishing/academic networks. Participating intimately in the activities of both communities has helped me understand the inside workings of knowledge production and publishing in these contexts. This process of shuttling between locations has also served to defamiliarize the academic cultures of *both* the center and the periphery.

It is easy to assert the advantages of this "double vision" (Bhabha 1994). But let me quickly acknowledge that there are also some tensions that are hard to resolve. It is because I moved to the center that I am able to publish about the scholarly deprivation and exclusion I suffered while teaching at UJ, but in the process of moving my status has changed, calling into question my ability to represent my periphery colleagues. In fact, a majority of them cannot and will not read this book that attempts to speak for them. There are other ironies that pervade this project. While complaining about the exclusion of periphery scholars from mainstream publishing networks, I am continuing to find avenues in the center to publish their story. Protesting against the ways in which center publishing circles appropriate if not distort periphery knowledge, I am managing to articulate oppositional messages through their very channels. Before I narrate below how I negotiate these tensions, I wish to first establish that my paradoxical stances represent quite well my thesis in this book.

I believe that it is a necessary evil that periphery scholars should use center publications even to resist their dominance. Given the power, spread, and currency of center publications, it is foolhardy not to use them to further periphery knowledge and interests. Since these are the established channels of academic communication, we cannot help but use them even for oppositional purposes. Furthermore, periphery scholars need to negotiate their interests and knowledge with center scholarship. This is important for challenging the limitations of mainstream knowledge, disseminating periphery knowledge effectively, and eventually contributing to the enrichment and democratization of international relations (as I will explain in chapter 8).

However, negotiating with the discourses and conventions of center publishing/research circles to bring out an oppositional perspective from the periphery is not an easy or straightforward process. One has to be sensitive to the conflicting values and interests motivating this negotiation. This is a case of tightrope walking, including the possibility that one may lose one's balance and fall to one side or the other. The process can also have mixed results—sounding unnecessarily hostile to center scholars and condescending to periphery readers. I want to narrate below how I have personally negotiated these challenges as I have continued to study and write on this subject. In a sense, I have to explain how I practice what I preach in this book! Perhaps my experience will serve as an example to my periphery colleagues of the challenges involved in negotiating center publishing/research conventions to represent local interests.

Research in Crisis Situations

I began to experience the inequalities in publishing most intensely when I returned to Sri Lanka from postgraduate work in the United

States. Though I faced a lot of difficulties in conducting research and writing, these matters could not be addressed in the articles I wrote. In a few instances, in order to explain the discursive differences in my work, I mentioned in a paragraph or two the problems of periphery scholars in conducting research and publishing according to center requirements. But, eventually, I had to omit these statements in the final drafts as reviewers felt that they were irrelevant to the focus of my paper. One set of reviewers felt that this kind of background information was too personal to suit the detachment and impersonality of academic articles. On another occasion, when I proposed to include a chapter on the publishing problems of local teachers in my first book dealing with center/periphery differences in English language teaching (ELT) (Canagarajah 1999), the reviewers advised me that this was unrelated to the research/pedagogical issues that the book should be dealing with. It is understandable that a self-reflective exploration of these procedural concerns might be construed as damaging the objectivity of research reporting. However, such publishing assumptions and practices place hurdles in the way of addressing the concerns relating to different contexts of knowledge production. This is perhaps another example of how mainstream academic conventions may serve to keep hidden (and perhaps reproduce) geopolitical inequalities.

Deciding that I have to address publishing problems through a full-fledged study in its own right, rather than appending such concerns to papers on other subjects, I planned out a research project. Although it wasn't clear to me at the time in what disciplinary framework I should conduct this study, I assumed that I would at least make a contribution to political economy, specifically the world systems perspective (Wallerstein 1991). I therefore read the literature on center/periphery relations and planned on showing how academic publishing is implicated in geopolitical inequalities. Having undertaken an ethnography of writing practices of minority students in an academic context in the United States for my doctoral research, I considered myself well prepared to do this study using similar methods. The empirical research was to focus on the UJ academic community, yielding both microsocial (i.e., linguistic, rhetorical) and macrosocial data on literacy practices. My plan was quite elaborate:

- to observe a few chosen scholars through their drafting and revising stages as they prepared a paper for a journal;
- to compare multiple drafts to understand the composing process;

- to hold text-based interviews with authors on their rhetorical choices;
- to collect the correspondence with editors and referees as local scholars engaged in publishing;
- to record scholarly interactions in the UJ university community for sociolinguistic analysis;
- to do an ethnography of literate practices in the university community;
- and to explore the institutional policies and attitudes of academic publishing and their implications for the literate life of local scholars.

As I began to identify the subjects for my longitudinal study, I confronted the type of practical problems I was going to continually face in conducting this research in periphery settings. There were not many scholars involved in publishing in mainstream journals. The few who were interested faced other problems in this unsettled community. A promising scholar who began discussing his plans for writing a journal paper with me had to abandon his project when he had to flee from his home. He lost the few pages of the manuscript he had started writing. This was similar to my own experience as I struggled to find the time and the space to concentrate on research writing. I then modified my plan to include scholars who were writing for local newspapers and magazines, in order to study their writing practices. But I found that many didn't have a consistent pattern of work. They might start a few paragraphs, forget about the project for a few months as they found themselves preoccupied with other domestic needs, write a few more paragraphs, then abandon the project altogether, and so on. With almost no pressure to get published, the composing process was indefinite and infrequent. It was also difficult to schedule appointments for interviews. Some found the study an irrelevant, even heartless preoccupation when there was hunger, scarcity, and heavy bombardment being experienced in the region. In a few cases, where I did manage to schedule someone to interview, we had to abandon the meeting in the middle of a bombing raid or some other emergency.

Apart from the problems of finding suitable subjects and scheduling interviews, I also faced difficulties in obtaining and using the necessary equipment. There was no electricity available in the region to run any audiovisual equipment. Although I had a pocket tape recorder, I found that batteries too were banned by the government in order to deprive the nationalist militants of any kind of power supply. (It was good that I had already ruled out the temptation to videotape some of the scholarly interactions in seminars and meetings.) More complicated was the danger that those who carried tape recorders could be suspected of being informants for one militant faction or the other. Furthermore, I didn't have Xeroxing facilities to make copies of the drafts written by my colleagues. Due to the limited printing facilities, I also had to cancel my plans to distribute a lengthy questionnaire to all my colleagues, inquiring about their literacy practices.

Soon I was facing a dilemma. One couldn't do respectable research when even the basic facilities were unavailable. It also appeared that research in a community that was undergoing what seemed to be an atypical situation wouldn't be accepted as constituting valid data or the basis for acceptable generalizations for other communities. I seriously contemplated abandoning this project. But there were a few considerations that suggested that this was not a good alternative. First, the seemingly atypical living conditions in Jaffna had fast become a fact of life for the people there. A generation of students had grown up in this condition of social instability, economic deprivation, and technological backwardness. This situation had become quite "normal" for them. (At the time of writing this book, about eight years after my research in Jaffna, the situation hasn't improved radically there—though there is relative quiet, as the government controls much of the region.) Second, it appeared to me from the information I could gather from other periphery communities that such conditions of work and life were not unusual. Third, these atypical or crisis-ridden contexts are important for their own sakes. They demystify the scholarly norms and bring into relief the conventions taken for granted in everyday academic life. Finally, if our story had to be suppressed simply because we didn't have the conditions and resources to undertake "empirically valid" research, then this is a form of silencing that would indirectly suit center interests.

I therefore decided to adopt a less rigid plan of obtaining whatever information I could get about the literate life of my colleagues as opportunities presented themselves. Even though it appeared that I might never get this project published in mainstream circles, I continued to document the problem for its own sake. At least it would satisfy my personal interest in the subject and fulfill my commitment to my community (helping create a better awareness of the social process of writing among my colleagues). Among the low-tech methods I could use to obtain data were the following: I adopted "participant observation" to gradually detach myself from the literacy events in the academic community and analyze their practices and conventions (Geertz 1983; Hornberger 1994). Although I couldn't audio- or videotape the interactions, I could take ample handwritten notes on the events. Of course, not all the notes were taken *during* the events. In some cases, I would reflect on significant statements of my colleagues or some unusual interactions to reconstruct the behavior and words from memory at a later time. It was customary for me at the end of the day at the university to light the lamp at home, take my notebook, revisit some of the interesting literacy events that had occurred on that day (which I had made a mental note to record later even as they occurred), and write them up. As for interviews, I spoke to colleagues informally in an unscheduled manner in the faculty common room, the streets, or department lounges. I already had the set of questions I wanted to ask about their literacy practices; only the opportunities and the setting had to be negotiated. Another convenient source of data that I carefully collected was the articles published by colleagues in local scholarly journals and popular media. I also collected for a textual analysis samples of other texts (monographs distributed in local seminars, locally published books, editorial correspondence, and administrative correspondence) from our everyday academic life.

When I moved back to the United States in 1994, I faced a conflict. The Red Cross, which ran a ship to transport refugees from Jaffna, held a policy that only two pieces of baggage were allowed per family. I had to ask myself how much and which of my data I should bring with me out of Jaffna. I negotiated with my family to include some of the most important texts, audiocassettes, and notebooks among the other necessities required for my four-year-old daughter and a six-month-old infant.

After starting to teach in New York City, I still lacked the confidence to make use of my data. My audience, too, had changed: I was no longer writing to educate my local colleagues but to challenge the center-based academic communities. To address the mainstream audience required a suitable entry point into its conversation. My increasing familiarity with mainstream center-based discourses gradually suggested ways in which I could use them for my advantage. Postmodernist discourses, which challenge traditional empirical/positivistic research approaches, were opening up new possibilities in academic inquiry. The usual dichotomies such as data/interpretation, informant/researcher, objective/subjective, disinterested/ideological didn't hold as much water anymore. Accordingly, new research methods and orientations were being proposed. I now had the opportunity to read research reports that were more personal and narrative. The justification by feminist and ethnic scholars of the place of narrative in research introduced me to new possibilities in presentation (Belcher 1999; Clandinin and Connelly 1991; Daniell 1999). Holloway and Jefferson (1997) talk of the biographical-interpretive method, whereby researchers elicit the experiences of their subjects in all their unanalyzed richness and complexity. Schenke (1991) develops an empathetic method for tapping the suppressed painful memories among her immigrant students in order to motivate them for literacy and language learning. Such developments presented the possibility that simply narrating the frustrating experiencing of my colleagues in their publishing life would produce fresh insights on academic literacy.

More significantly, I was now inspired to narrate my own publishing experience in Jaffna as part of my research. After all, this was a rich source of data that would add a significant dimension to my argument. In addition, rather than holding my own insights and experiences in abeyance when discussing the data (for the sake of objectivity), employing them actively to read into the texts, behavior, and practices of my colleagues would enable richer interpretive possibilities. Furthermore, there was increasing openness to using diaries, personal experiences, and other forms of self-reflective information as data in educational research (Bailey and Ochsner 1983; Ross and Buehler 1994). Such developments also gave me the confidence to use the sources of data I had myself gathered from memory recall. It now appeared to me that the observations I had jotted down under lamplight in my journal in Jaffna could be treated as important data. In fact, I began to engage in further disciplined introspection regarding my publishing experience in Jaffna from the defamiliarizing distance of my new location. The detachment of time and space, and the heuristic potential provided by the different literacy culture here in the center, enabled me to add to the notes I had brought with me. In doing all this, I took care—partly out of fear of the traditional positivistic modes of research—to be balanced, rigorous, and disciplined, in addition to being curious, imaginative, and introspective. There were strong ethical values that motivated this research—not only the burning desire to articulate the inequalities experienced by my colleagues but the drive to encourage more democratic literacy practices and intercommunity participation in knowledge construction.

A more dramatic influence on the direction of my project was the possibility of richer library research. I now had the advantage of reading about the experiences of other periphery scholars—an activity that gave me the impression that the experiences in Jaffna were not that atypical (Muchiri et al. 1995, Gibbs 1995). At least I now had the opportunity to make some connections with other periphery communities and read my data from Jaffna in the light of this scholarship. The emerging literature convinced me of the urgency of this problem and inspired me to take steps toward publishing an account of my experience. (That I had to come to the center in order to learn about other periphery communities is an irony easily explained by the publishing resources of the center.) Furthermore, my reading enabled me to reformulate my assumptions and objectives. My own field of composition (whose literature I will document later) showed that there were conversations here on the politics of academic literacy and the sociology of knowledge that I could enter in order to present the case for periphery scholars. This strand of research enabled me to see that the body of texts I had collected for analysis didn't need to be stretched unreasonably to make an argument on political economy. The texts could be analyzed closely in a linguistic sense to understand their social and rhetorical construction. In other words, I could merge the concerns of microlevel textual issues and macrolevel geopolitical interests in insightful ways. Thus I began asking new questions from the data I had with me.

Particularly exciting to me was the way I resolved a problem about using the texts I wanted to treat as my data. It bothered me that these texts were not collected according to the plan I had for full-blown ethnographic research. Therefore, I was reluctant to use them in my initial papers on this subject (Canagarajah 1996b). But John Swales's (1998) neologism for a method he was using for his description of disciplinary literacies in a center university gave me the confidence to use my body of texts. His method—an interpretation of texts in the light of ethnographic information—is called *textography*. He defines this as "something more than a disembodied textual or discoursal analysis, but something less than a full ethnographic account" (Swales 1998, 1). It occurred to me that I could still do a discourse analysis of these texts in light of the informal, culture-sensitive observations and interviews I had conducted at UJ. In chapter 4 of this book I present an analysis of my colleagues' articles in the context of the cultural and material influences shaping literacy in Jaffna.

After completing the final draft of this book, I came across another construct from the publication of my close friend and colleague Dwight Atkinson that helps justify the very unconventional array of data sources and analytical approaches used in my discussion. *Rhetorical analysis* is the label Atkinson (1999) uses, borrowing it from Bazerman's (1988, 3, n. 1) earlier definition of a type of analysis that situates texts in sociohistorical context and uses interpretive frameworks from different disciplines. Atkinson elaborates that this mode of analysis is eclectic, multidisciplinary, contextual, bottom-up, and genre sensitive. Focusing on texts and literacy practices, I too marshal social and historical information to complement my analysis.

If all this gives the sense that my research was still continuing, and that significant analytical directions were (and are) being taken here in the center rather than in the periphery, then this is ironically true. In fact, more significant changes in approach were to follow. After initial publication in a journal, the interaction this opened up with center referees and other periphery scholars added considerably to reshaping my orientation. I also had the advantage of getting more reactions from my own UJ colleagues (surprisingly critical) to what I was doing here in the West with their information and experiences. E-mail correspondence with other enthusiastic periphery scholars made me strengthen some of my claims. On the other hand, the cynicism of some center-based scholars made me move even further away from the deterministic and polarized center/periphery perspective I had adopted. I became more sensitive to the reality of cultural hybridity, rhetorical borrowing, and ideological negotiation in different communities. This theoretical flexibility didn't mean that I lost sight of power differences in geopolitical life. The influence from my periphery colleagues was too strong for that.

I won't be surprised if the methods informing this study trouble some readers, notwithstanding contemporary scholarship that complicates the status of empirical research methods. In some of my early journal submissions and my recent attempts to seek a publisher for this book, referees have had questions about the validity and reliability of my unconventional mix of data and research practices. I can only invoke Prior's (1998) use of Pickering's (1995) notion of the "mangle of practice" as a final explanation of my approach here. After a painstaking ethnography of the enculturation practices of scholars in disciplinary discourse, Prior points out the place of contingent factors (relating to unique contexts, personal dispositions, relationships, and unexpected developments in the course of research) in complicating and altering the direction of his inquiry. Even in the center, the seamless coherence of research reporting masks the struggles and fissures of research work, which considerably shape the findings of the scholar. It is time now to acknowledge—and celebrate—the role of these contingent factors in research. My research, too, shows the marks of mangled practice. But I don't have to be so defensive as to blame this solely on the atypical research situation in war-torn Jaffna. Prior inspires me to argue that mangled practice is in fact characteristic of *all* research conditions—including those of center scholars who are armed with sophisticated instruments, generous grants, and a relatively stable research environment.

Negotiating Conflicting Rhetorics

In the past, the preceding discussion would have been sufficient to establish the rationale for this book. But now we know that the representation of any research or academic inquiry is considerably mediated by the rhetorical processes of writing and publishing. Research findings cannot stand unaffected by textual forms of knowledge dissemination. Especially in a book that argues that periphery-based knowledge is often appropriated or suppressed by the publishing practices of the center, I have to explain my struggles with "packaging" this story in relation to the dominant rhetorical conventions.

It was after I moved to the United States in 1994 that I enjoyed resources for composing and access to the publishing houses to negotiate my work into print. I now came to know under what disciplinary framework this subject should be addressed and which journal would welcome my project. I became familiar with the publications of ethnographers of disciplinary communication, like Knorr-Cetina (1981) and Latour and Woolgar (1979), and the related work of those in my own hybrid field of composition/ELT, such as Myers (1990), Bazerman (1988), and Swales (1990) on

academic writing. Though it might have been sufficient to simply extend
the application of their constructs to the special case of periphery scholars,
I found this insufficient to make my publication "newsworthy" (Berkenkotter and Huckin 1995, chapter 2). A more significant "story," I found,
concerned the material constraints on writing, which I then called *nondis-*
cursive conventions (Canagarajah 1996b). The case I was interested in making
was that though many in composition research had given voice to the discursive differences in the writing of periphery/bilingual scholars, few had
considered the nondiscursive constraints.

In choosing a journal for my paper, it occurred to me that most journals in composition, rhetoric, and linguistics were too restricted in their
orientation to the internal structure of the text. My research seemed to focus too much on the practices that fall *outside* the bounds of the text. I was
talking about geopolitical and material issues of literacy in the age of discourse. *Written Communication,* however, appeared to show sufficient openness to different foci and approaches to writing research. So I stated in my
covering letter:

> I am pleased to read in your editorial policy statement that "no worthy topic
> related to writing is beyond the scope of the journal." This paper is some-
> what unconventional for journals on rhetoric and composition. I am dealing
> here with what I have termed "nondiscursive constraints" on academic pub-
> lishing (for want of better words). . . . I am again happy to note in your pol-
> icy statement that "published articles will continue to represent a wide range
> of methodologies." This paper is not intended as full-blown research, but as a
> preliminary investigation that will motivate scholars to conduct systematic
> research.

One can detect my diffidence in discussing issues that are not central to the
disciplinary discourse. I am also apologetic about research that may not be
perceived as systematic. But it is thus that I opened up a space for my story.

The title of my first draft was "'Non-discursive' Requirements in Academic Publishing, Western Hegemony of the Publishing Industry, and
Challenges for Periphery Scholars: A Rather Personal Account." The subjective framing of the paper sounds too bold, in retrospect. The explicit political tone may also be a bit too frank about my ideological motives. I display no attempt to finesse my political stance. The paper begins as follows.

> Getting something published in an academic journal does not depend on
> having original ideas, conducting rigorous research, possessing an encyclope-

dic knowledge of academic discourses, or having the dexterity of expression to employ academic turns of speech. Getting published depends on having the technological and economic resources to meet the conventions and practices of the publishing industry. At least this is the growing realization of scholars from the Third World who attempt to publish their work in scholarly journals. . . . The implications of these publishing practices, as I will show, are profoundly connected to the politics of scholarship and the geopolitical hegemony of the developed nations.

I narrate below my experiences from Sri Lanka in attempting to get my scholarly work published in Western journals. I will quote from correspondence from editors and referees to illustrate the expected practices of publishing and their perspectives on the attempts of Third World scholars. . . . To place this narrative in context we must understand the social context of the publishing industry and Third World academic institutions.

In retrospect, it is striking that there is no literature review or explicit creation of a disciplinary niche, in the commonly accepted tradition of introductions in research articles (Swales 1990). It is also evident that I am framing the paper as a personal narrative. Before beginning the narrative, however, I take care to set the social and publishing context necessary to understand my experience in publishing from Jaffna. I also make an attempt to show the significance of the subject and its centrality for the general scholarly community.

I was surprised to find that the paper received positive reviews from the referees. There was also a commitment from the editors to publish the paper after revisions. The challenge for me now was to negotiate the changes requested. It occurred to me then that it was an accepted convention of publishing to revise the paper to the satisfaction of the referees. What I didn't fully appreciate at that point was that these textual changes made in dialogue with center-based referees would entail considerable changes in my discourse and ideological stance. I give below a few excerpts from remarks of the reviewers to suggest their attitudes and the types of change requested. Admittedly, this is a partial representation of the feedback, as there were many supportive comments. (Perhaps I downplayed the compliments and focused only on the perceived limitations).

Referee #1: "The author's concerns are serious, important, and ought to be brought before the readers of WC. I have a number of problems with the essay as currently written, however. At the surface it reads a bit rambling and repetitious, and at times more complaining than analytical. So at the least, this needs a helpful round of editing. But I have more serious questions that may lead to more fundamental solutions."

Referee #2: "I believe that academic disciplines do work by constraining that work and arguments they consider. Linguistics, for instance, in all its forms, has a very limited view of language. That is how they move on and produce what they consider to be new knowledge. They do not need to consider all views as a matter of right and justice—they need to consider contributions that extend knowledge in a way that fits with their disciplinary missions. . . . I could offer a lot of sociology of science to support these assumptions. But you don't have to agree with me—you just have to see it is a big argument that is not going to be resolved in the space of this paper, and avoid assuming that all right thinking readers agree with your generalizations."

Referee #3: "This submission is a highly readable (for the most part) and somewhat impassioned (for the most part) essay attacking western academic gate keeping practices. . . . I personally think the paper would be greatly strengthened if the author were more aware of the fact that he/she is not alone in voicing these kinds of concern . . . [offers some references]. This is a pretty strong statement and probably needs hedging."[1]

In hindsight, I see many of these comments as suggesting the typical objections one can have against a more personal, narrative, contextually grounded mode of research reporting. The first referee was asking me to make my argument more explicit and my presentation more analytical. The more indirect and embedded form of my argumentation also earns the censure that the paper is not tightly organized. The referees also see a need for a more polemical approach. While the first referee poses a set of questions for me to argue against, the second referee argues with me directly and suggests that I adopt a less certain/absolute tone. The third referee seems to be damning me with faint praise as he or she comments on the impassioned writing. His or her request that I use more hedging devices also suggests the need to concede more and strike a balanced/neutral position. They all seem to agree that I have to become more objective. Many of my claims relating to the political nature of knowledge production have to be established more carefully for a skeptical center-based audience. In order to show that my experiences are not atypical, I have to use references and citations to generalize my claims. The referees themselves provide additional literature to suggest that I place my argument in the context of the publications by center-based scholars that have already appeared on this subject.

In the revised version for publication, my new title suggests the changes that have taken place in my discourse: "'Non-discursive' Requirements in Academic Publishing, Material Resources of Periphery Scholars, and the Politics of Knowledge Production." The reference to "Western hegemony" in my previous title, which would have caused the referees to find my tone whiny and shrill, is now omitted. The title is now less accusing of Western scholars. It also indicates that I am now adopting a relatively more detached stance. My opening paragraph shows the shifts in my positioning.

> Occasional news reports—like the one in a recent issue of *Scientific American* (Gibbs, 1995)—remind scholars in the western hemisphere that their Third World colleagues experience exclusion from "mainstream" scholarly publications which are overwhelmingly published from North American and Western European locations in the English language. The discursive reasons for this exclusion can be understood by employing some of the constructs already developed in composition theory and applied linguistics. . . . Robert Kaplan (1966, 1976) opened an inquiry into the manner in which the written texts of non-native scholars will display differences in structure from the preferred rhetoric and thought patterns of Anglo-American academic culture. While Kaplan's contrastive rhetoric was somewhat stereotyped and deterministic, recent scholars have moved much closer to the diverse genres of academic writing to empirically study the multiple discourses of non-native scholars (Clyne, 1987; Connor, 1996; Eggington, 1987; Hinds, 1990; Mauranen, 1993; Purves, 1988; Swales, 1990). . . . What is sometimes not well understood is the way the "nondiscursive" conventions of the publishing industry also function to exclude Third World scholars from scholarly journals. These are the supposedly commonplace or practical requirements of academic publishing which are not treated as having implications for the language, content or style of the writing—requirements such as the format of the copy text; bibliographical and documentation conventions; the particular weight and quality of the paper; the copies and postage required; the procedures for submitting revisions and proofs; and the nature of interaction between authors and editorial committees. These conventions assume the availability of certain material requirements—such as technological, communicational and economic resources—which cannot be taken for granted in the case of Third World scholars.

I now begin with a citation (the only one I could find—from a popular journal—and suggested by a referee) in order to ground my argument in published material on this subject. Then I go on to do a bit of disciplinary niche creation by invoking the field of contrastive rhetoric. It in fact constitutes a literature review of sorts. Though this field doesn't relate directly to my subject in this paper, it allows me to enter the disciplinary conversation at least obliquely. This reference also strikes a polemical tone that I sustain throughout the essay—influenced perhaps by the adversarial stance of my referees. To satisfy the concerns of the reviewers that I become more analytical and explicit, I define the notion of "nondiscursive conventions" more carefully at the end of the first paragraph. Though the narrative structure is retained for the greater part of the paper, it is modified by other features typical of academic discourse. As we can see, the introduction now falls more in line with the established opening "moves" of research articles.

With the above revisions I considered myself to have negotiated the personal and public, the narrative and the analytical, the center-based and the periphery-based more satisfactorily (at least for the taste of the center-based readership). I understood this as the usual process of rhetorical adjustment, balancing, and complexity deriving from negotiating with one's referees. The changes were rewarded by overwhelmingly supportive comments from many liberal Anglo-American scholars and periphery scholars studying/residing in the center after the publication of the paper. There were also E-mails from scholars in Venezuela and India congratulating me for broaching the subject. What I didn't expect was the way in which my discourse may have been moving away from the perspectives and orientations of my colleagues at home. Since *Written Communication* is not received by the UJ library and is not read by any scholar I know in Sri Lanka, I mailed an offprint to my former colleagues. This was quickly circulated among the faculty members there and read avidly. Surprisingly, their reception was very critical. Apparently, I hadn't fully understood the significance of my changes at the time of revision. Consider the views of one of my students, Shriganeshan, who is presently a lecturer at the University College in Vavuniya. He provides his own views as well as his understanding of the opinion of some members of the UJ faculty in his E-mail.

The power of oral culture and knowledge production in face to face discussion prevailing in the Jaffna academic society is placed for analysis. However the data you used to substantiate your arguments caused different negative religious-biased echoes and psychological (inferioty) complexities among people concerned. For example the scholarly presentation on Saiva Sithantha. Your mention about the use of Positivism and detachment in reasearch and the scholars of sixties' unawareness of latest developments due to non-availability of Journals was misinterpreted. The spirit is not recognised.

Personally I feel that you have made use of your observation with proof to formulate your concept as the Westerns do on cultural anthoropological research. The war situation in Jaffna made academic atmosphere worse because of non-availability of research Journals, stationery items and electricity and delay in mail service.

Your protest against discrimination done by Western editors to periphery scholars to exclude them from scholarly Journals because of not maintaining expected conventions and regulations of publication practices is well commended. (Personal communication, 8 April 1997)[2]

Aside from the cursory compliments, Shriganeshan voices some important criticisms. As he is a former student of mine, he is being somewhat cautious and oblique in his censure. It appears that my references to the influence of Saivite religious sentiments in the local academic discourse have hurt some of my UJ colleagues. My efforts to show the differences in the local academic culture and the material deprivations that create limitations for the local scholars have created the wrong effect back home. The paper could have sounded condescending to the local faculty, implying that they didn't measure up to the academic standards of the center. It is for this reason that Shriganeshan is defensive in reiterating that it is the war situation that has affected the productivity of UJ faculty. His enigmatic comment that "you have made use of your observation with proof to formulate your concept as the Westerns do on cultural anthropological research" should be understood as an insinuation that my paper is from a center-based perspective, using Western research methods to explain the local situation.

My mentor, Mr. Canagaratne, whom everyone calls A. J., took this criticism further in a handwritten letter to me. Not fettered by the unequal relationship that Shriganeshan experiences, A. J. deconstructs the hidden assumptions and motivations in my paper.

I delayed commenting about your article as I wanted to read it a second time. When I first read the article I got the impression that despite your explicit disclaimers there was an underlying (unconscious) assumption that only publication in a prestigious First World journal would confer academic cachet on Third World scholars. I'm afraid a second reading confirmed this impression. I'm sure you'll be horrified by this and you'd consciously reject this insidious internalization of colonialism. But at times the Ego is powerless against the Id. It goes without saying that you've mastered the discursive conventions. What you need to do further is to master any lurking vestiges of internalised colonialism in the unconscious. I'm afraid some of our talented young scholars are succumbing to the lures of western academic fashions. . . . I'm beginning to wonder whether there isn't a new and more sophisticated version of Orientalism in vogue in the Western academy in particular. The East was once acclaimed for being exotic. Now the acclaim is for Third World scholars, preferably young, who can reproduce (without too much criticism) the fashionable discourses and drop the correct names. This way radical scholars and critics in the West can salve their consciences while business goes on as usual. (Personal communication, 3 June 1997)

Certainly my paper has been read in a different way in the periphery than it was by those based in the center. It is quite understandable that even periphery scholars who move to the center can eventually reach a point where their perspective differs from that of their colleagues in the periphery and get absorbed into center-based ways of thinking. The key statement in A. J.'s letter is the telling understatement, "It goes without saying that you've mastered the discursive conventions." While this was the very condition for getting the paper published in the first place, A. J. considers this to have diluted my perspective—perhaps unconsciously—with colonial discourses. He is probably right to see that there is a subtext to my paper (beneath the "explicit disclaimers") constituting the "lurking vestiges of internalised colonialism." He goes on to charge that eventually these kinds of protest (conducted in terms of discursive developments and literate conventions in the center) represent ways in which the center mutes opposition or appropriates it to carry on its hegemonic purposes.

A. J.'s comments alert us to the dangers involved in voicing an opposition to the hegemony of center publishing/academic networks through their very channels. Needless to say, such pitfalls are always present in the efforts of periphery scholars who attempt to write about knowledge oppositional to the center through mainstream journals. With the changes in my discourse during the revision, my ideological positioning had also changed. The clear standpoint adopted earlier through the personal/narrative discourse, grounded in periphery communities, has shifted in my move to be more objective, qualified, and discipline-based. Neutrality and detachment, appreciated by the center referees, are suspicious to my UJ colleagues. The audience for my story (i.e., those from the center—as periphery scholars couldn't have even read this paper, being cut off from mainstream journals) has also shaped my discourse considerably. Though it is a truism that one should negotiate one's footing in terms of the publishing context/audience, that this involves ideological compromises is not always acknowledged. Note how my refusal to adopt any of the suggestions provided by the referees would have created a negative identity for me (as stubborn, dogmatic, and unprofessional) and damaged my chances of telling my story to the audience that really matters. (After all, periphery scholars know these problems well, and they don't have the resources to change this hegemony, as center scholars do.)

A. J.'s response is also an indictment of the work going on in the name of the periphery in the center. In fact, periphery scholars who have access to mainstream journals indulge in similar processes of exploitation of intellectual property as their center counterparts do. I myself use the writings of those like A. J. in little-known local journals in this book (see chapter 6). Since I have better access to mainstream journals now, I have an advantage in ransacking the available stock of periphery knowledge to earn academic credit for myself. In my other academic publications, again, I have freely borrowed from the insights and information generated in oral interactions at UJ. The weak sense of intellectual property existing in oral communities permits me to borrow ideas with impunity to boost my own academic credentials. (And, yes, by publishing on the views and experiences of my students and colleagues in Sri Lanka I have earned my tenure in an American institution!)

There is little achieved by defending myself to show in what ways I have differed from center-based discourses or how my intentions are anti-imperialistic in this book. Though it is migrant scholars like me who can create an understanding between these separate academic worlds, some compromises have to be made in the process. And it has to be acknowledged that I cannot pretend to speak authentically for the periphery. (What is the "authentic" periphery perspective anyway?) Mine is only one perspective on the problem. Furthermore, I am a complex subject constituted by center and periphery discourses (a mixture aggravated after moving to the center for my professional life). Therefore I cannot claim to speak fully for all periphery professionals. I am sure that another periphery scholar may present this subject matter in significantly different ways. But, eventually, it is hard for other periphery professionals too to claim to be able to represent the periphery consensus on the issue. I can imagine many monolingual scholars in the periphery who will say that even those who are still based in the periphery (like A. J. and Shriganeshan) do not represent their perspective. Their bilinguality, exposure to English literature/ writing, and awareness of Western scholarship will be pointed to as features providing them a subjectivity and discourse that are in subtle ways different from those of monolingual scholars. In the final analysis, we are all hybrid subjects, and our ability to represent an ideological position or community's interests is a relational matter.

Of course, one can ask whether it is necessary to talk about periphery concerns in center-based mainstream publications. Isn't it self-defeating for one to discuss reforming the publishing hegemony in the very pages of the journals that allegedly conduct such hegemony? What motivations would such fora have for voicing these concerns that appear to undercut the rationale behind their own power? What compromises should periphery authors make to fit into the discourses and framework preferred by these fora to articulate their views? While all these fears are justified, it is necessary for periphery scholars to infiltrate these publishing channels if real changes are to be achieved. Getting their arguments sidetracked into marginal or peripheral journals would only serve to further ghettoize and silence periphery knowledge. The mainstream publishing fora wield a real power in terms of reach, significance, and status that cannot be ignored if changes are to be wrought in the global knowledge-production industry. Refusing to publish in center-based fora and treating local publications as sufficient may constitute a blissful state of ignorance and isolation that will only let center scholars exercise their hegemony unchallenged. With periphery scholars absent, center scholars will continue to construct knowledge on periphery realities as well.

The type of struggle I am undertaking through the publication of this book is somewhat paradoxical. I am attempting to fight the master in his own court. There are well-known historical precedents for how the disempowered have used the internal contradictions, gaps, loopholes, and niches in the structures of the dominant groups to initiate a resistance from the inside (Goffman 1961; Scott 1985). Similarly, I am seeking spaces in the dominant publishing structure to articulate the experiences of periphery scholars. In this respect, the term *resistance,* as used throughout this book, needs clarification. Resistance, as I use it, is a constructive and creative notion that theorizes how the disempowered may reconstruct discourses and structures for fairer representation (Canagarajah 1999). It is not a totally destructive practice of *rejecting* the established structure, a vengeful exercise of *replacing* it with another, or the idealistic attempt to *eradicate* power in all forms. The project rather is to *reconstitute* discourses and structures in progressively more inclusive, ethical, and democratic terms.

I must acknowledge that one has to be wary of the agencies of power manipulating and of appropriating these modes of resistance for their advantage. My periphery colleagues articulate the challenges facing minority scholars who indulge in this paradoxical form of struggle. The way out is to negotiate one's stance with ideological sensitivity. We should appropriate the multiple discourses constituting the publishing domain for a fair representation of our interests, with a clarity regarding our ideological motivations and our social location. Articulating local knowledge to the global community through the established academic conventions calls for creative communicative strategies. As I will demonstrate in the final chapter, one has to negotiate with the dominant conventions to explore the extent to which they can be "re-formed" to suit one's purposes, interests, and messages. I believe I have grown wiser from the criticisms of my periphery colleagues and center reviewers so that I can now negotiate more effectively the ideological and discursive challenges in writing this book. I have attempted to employ the strengths I bring from my periphery discourses even as I have used a hegemonic language (English) and literate conventions (academic) to talk about periphery concerns. The periodic narrative sections, the self-reflexive commentary, and the unabashed personal voice are interspersed with documented detached analysis to achieve a hybrid textuality in this book.

But, as in any project of multivocal presentation, there are ambiguities in discourse, audience, and objectives in this book. Shriganeshan is still unrelenting in his criticism of what he sees as traces of condescending treatment of local scholars, though he is glad that somebody is articulating their problems (as expressed in his E-mail message of 23 January 2001, after he read this very manuscript). My center colleague Dwight Atkinson, on the other hand, has displayed his exasperation with what he sees as sweeping statements, belated evidence for important claims, lack of rigor in documenting sources, and looseness of organization, in his comments in the margin of this manuscript. Ironically, these are some of the features I identify in chapter 4 as characterizing the discourse of my periphery colleagues, deriving from local literacies that are unappreciated by outsiders. (At least from this criticism my periphery identity emerges as undeniable, however closely I may have participated in center discourses these past few years!)

Regarding questions about my audience and objectives, my answer is that I am deliberately straddling both center and periphery communities. While mainly arguing with center scholarly communities for reform in publishing conventions, I am indirectly demonstrating to periphery scholars ways they can negotiate the dominant conventions in their favor (as they cannot expect change to come solely from the center). While this book constitutes only one approximation of the conflicting discourses to make a case for more democratic practices in academic communication, I hope it provokes my periphery colleagues to engage in rhetorical experimentation that would better negotiate the academic discourses to make a space for their voices in the international fora. Through such processes of mediation, negotiation, and even argument, center and periphery scholars may establish mutually enriching scholarly discourses and more ethical knowledge-construction practices.

1. Contextualizing Academic Writing

In order to build more adequate models, then, literacy researchers must move away from modeling academic literacy as a single coherent practice that works itself out primarily in the spatial dimension of participants' representations. In these representations, virtual authors are presented as professionalized agents moving with rational purpose toward the progress of the community. Real authors, however, eat, go to the bathroom, worry about their career, and get interrupted by the noise in the street. Academic texts never acknowledge these human aspects of their real authors for to do so would jeopardize their claim to timeless truth. But researchers of academic literacy cannot afford to make the same mistake. Instead, we must make efforts to gather data on how participants' texts, representations, and activities change over time, and then we must look at the relationship among these temporal changes. In this analysis, we need to be prepared to see divergences and incoherencies as well as seamless wholes, and we must equip ourselves theoretically to explore their functionality within a larger framework of practice.—Cheryl Geisler, *Academic Literacy and the Nature of Expertise*

I focus in this book on a type of academic writing called the research article (RA). These are articles usually refereed by respected scholars in the field before getting published in specialized academic journals. Among the different genres of academic writing practiced (e.g., abstracts, book reviews, grant proposals, research prospectuses, dissertations, textbooks, and research monographs), the RA holds an important place in knowledge construction. For a variety of reasons, the most typical product of a scholarly study is its published article (Swales 1990, 93–95). The short length and narrow scope of the article enable researchers to try out sections of their research or stages of their evolving hypotheses before developing books out of their fully fledged theories. In fact, in some fields, like high-energy physics, no books are produced whatsoever (Traweek 1988). There is consensus among recognized scholars in the academy that the journal article is the primary mode of validating their research findings (Rymer 1988). The piece of research is not considered complete until it is made available to the relevant disciplinary community through its journals. Its very appearance in print is an indication of the research's legitimacy and worth. It is through such a process that knowledge claims are substantiated and established. In this sense, refereed journals are the gatekeepers of knowledge in each discipline. Cognizant of the status of the RA, the academic community depends on refereed journals for legitimate new knowledge across fields. Therefore it is understandable that one's scholarly worth is estimated according to the number of RAs one manages to get published. Through RAs scholars secure academic prestige and promotion. For many members of the academy, the RA is the primary goal of their career and work. For these reasons, the RA has an important place in academic culture and everyday scholarly life.

It is not surprising that, given their importance, research journals have been increasing in number lately. The growth of journals to about 70,000 in science and technology alone (Moravcsik 1982) and 100,000 for all disciplines (Garfield 1978) produces an average of 5,000,000 articles per year, according to Swales (1990, 95). This quantitative magnitude makes the RA "a gargantuan genre" and "the standard product of the knowledge-manufacturing industries" (Swales 1990, 95). We must also note here the proliferation of new disciplines and the increasing specialization of fields within each discipline. Almost every school of specialization within a field has its journal to propagate its own new knowledge. Journals solidify the emerging disciplinary community and provide it with cohesion, identity, and status, apart from serving to gatekeep membership and knowledge.

This increase in the avenues for publication should not, however, suggest that the publishing field is getting more democratized. Ways of controlling what is published have also been increasing in number and sophistication. Bazerman's (1987) chronicle of the growth of the American Psychological Association (APA) publication manual from six and a half pages in 1929 to two hundred pages in 1983 indicates how the policies and requirements of journals have become highly elaborate. These policies have served to define publication conventions more rigidly and formulaically, making them consistent with the dominant discourses in the discipline. These conventions now control the content that can get published, excluding writing that doesn't share the brand of discourse that is currently accepted in a field. It is important to note therefore that such requirements and conventions are not merely matters of form but integral to the knowledge that gets represented in the writing. Furthermore, they are "not simply passive reflectors of trends but also quiet instigators of policy" (Swales 1990, 93). Whatever functional rationale these conventions may be motivated by (and even if they are arbitrary to begin with), they are eventually reified and sanctioned by the journals themselves. Authors actively collaborate with the journal editors and reviewers as they shape their articles to meet the conventions and requirements of the journal (Myers 1985). Implicit in such publishing practices is the realization that articles don't get published only because of their content but also because they have been presented in such a way that they conform to the conventions of communication established by the journal or disciplinary community. These elaborate requirements also indicate that the RA is not "some fixed and inexorable inscription of reality—but rather an end product that has been specifically shaped and negotiated in the author's efforts to obtain acceptance" (Swales 1990, 93; see also Knorr-Cetina 1981; Myers 1990). New knowledge thus gets established in accordance with the requirements and conventions set by these journals.

If publishing conventions have such gatekeeping potential for knowledge construction, they raise concerns about the hidden interests they may harbor. From this perspective, the fact that they are set by scholars of narrow cultural/linguistic groups, and the fact that the journals themselves are based in narrowly circumscribed regions of the developed world, appear troubling. Such biased conventions can have dire implications for the research and intellectual contributions of minority communities. To begin with, the anglophone grip on the publishing industry is well documented. Garfield (1983) points out that 80 percent of the world's scientific publication is written in English. Baldauf (1986) surveyed journals devoted to cross-cultural psychology between 1978 to 1982 to discover an English-medium publication percentage of 97 percent. Comparing their 1981 data with the findings of a previous study of 1965, Baldauf and Jernudd (1983) find a striking and consistent advance made by the English language. Even in such fields as tropical agriculture, where one would expect less anglophone/Western-hemispheric domination, Arvanitis and Chatelin (1988) find that English accounted for 75 percent of the publications, followed by French (10 percent), Portuguese (7 percent) and Spanish (5 percent).

Interestingly, even the databases that produce the above statistics are located in the West and focus only on academic publications emanating from Western locations. Such indices as the Science Citation Index (SCI) of the Institute of Scientific Information (ISI) overwhelmingly represent journals based in the West, encouraging the perception (perhaps unwittingly) that these are the journals that matter in the profession. This practice further serves to promote the global importance of these journals. The ISI, in a research project sponsored to appraise its own practices in representing periphery research in the SCI, found that it might be underrepresenting valuable research from these communities by a factor of two (Moravcsik 1985). Arvanitis and Chatelin (1988) reveal that though Brazil publishes 149 scientific periodicals, only 4 are currently included in the SCI. They summarize the results of their count by stating that "one cannot be surprised to learn that the US produces 40% of the international production and receives 60% of the citations, or that 80% of the world scientific production is written in English" (1988, 114).

There is a similar partiality in the databases of RA abstracts. Though Baldauf and Jernudd (1983) begin one of their useful studies by assuming that the journal *Aquatic Sciences and Fisheries Abstracts* may have more democratic documenting practices because it is sponsored by the international organization UNESCO and it abstracts studies from a wide variety of languages and sources, they are surprised by the results of their analysis. English is the most important language of publication, accounting for about 75 percent of all articles abstracted, with French (5.5 percent) and Spanish (4 percent) coming in a distant second and third. Such unfair and unbalanced abstracting practices show the importance of English publications in the eyes of international agencies. Journals in other languages, published in other locations, lose their visibility and respect by getting left out of these indices and abstract databases. Such unfair practices also demonstrate how research and knowledge from outside North America, represented in non-English languages, may not be visible or accessible to mainstream disciplinary communities.

It is possible to argue that whatever location a journal is published from, contributions of merit could come from all over the world. But there is, in fact, a significant pattern of underrepresentation of scholars from the non-Western world. In research on journals in the health sciences and economics, Swales finds that only 20 percent of the writers are non-native speakers of English. Of the 117 locations he traced for these writers, only 21 were in the periphery—among which 5 were from Israel, "where the data is particularly suspect because of the large amount of US-Israeli academic traffic" (1985, 98). In my own discipline of second language teaching, the editor of the *TESOL Quarterly* shared with me recently that in 1994, 1995, and 1996 the contributions by non-native or periphery scholars numbered four, two, and two, respectively, out of an average of twenty-one articles each year (Sandra McKay, personal communication, 14 March 1997). Thus the already poor representation of periphery scholars in academic journals appears to have been becoming even poorer. Furthermore, Baldauf and Jernudd (1983) find in their study on fisheries publications that 80 percent of the articles originated in countries where English is the official or national language. Two-thirds of the remaining papers originated from international conventions or multinational organizations. The rest—or 6 percent—were submitted from locations where English is a foreign language—but few of these were outside Western Europe or Japan, which enjoy access to advanced technological and communication facilities. Even in regional areas of specialty such as tropical agriculture Arvanitis and Chatelin (1988) find that only one half of the publications come from the southern hemisphere. Even these few are mostly written in English.

Perhaps the representation of knowledge production can be widened by journals published in English but emanating from non-Western geographical locations. But such journals are accorded secondary status to the journals in the West. As is widely known in my field, these publications, like the *RELC Journal* (based in the Regional English Language Center in Singapore and devoted to English language teaching) or the *International Journal of Dravidian Linguistics* (based in India and devoted to studies on the Dravidian family of languages), do not enjoy the prestige accorded to journals in the West even if they have token Western scholars on their editorial boards. The mere outward appearance of the journals is considered enough to indicate their second-class status: the lower-quality paper, printing, and graphics are taken to indicate inferior content by many readers. The distribution of these journals is again mainly limited to local readers in the periphery. It is widely known that the papers published in such journals (of both periphery and Western scholars) are those usually rejected by Western journals or of scholars lacking access to Western journals. Even among periphery scholars these journals hold such low prestige that before submitting something to the *RELC Journal,* for example, a periphery scholar would usually attempt to publish in the *TESOL Quarterly.* Similarly, a scholar in Dravidian linguistics would prefer to publish in *Language* or *Language in Society* rather than in the *International Journal of Dravidian Linguistics.* It is especially troubling that such a situation characterizes even research of regional interest, such as describing the social life of Dravidian languages or analyzing local pedagogical practices. Swales (1990) points out that there are some exemplary academic communities, like that of Brazilian scholars, that prefer to publish in their own language in their local journals. But such examples are rare. The hegemony of Western academic journals is so complete that the superiority ascribed to them has been somewhat internalized by periphery scholars themselves.

Given such inequalities in the publishing domain, it is ironic that many of the journals based in North American/West European locations, with an editorial board of predominantly Western scholars (sometimes displaying a rare token periphery scholar based in a Western academic institution) and publishing mostly the work of their colleagues for a readership primarily consisting of their own academic circles, label themselves "international journals." Perhaps this indicates a bloated perception of their importance—the belief that whatever appears in their pages is of global significance. Perhaps the motivation is more sinister—to thrust the knowledge produced in the pages of these journals on other communities as universally relevant and valid.

Social Context

The patterns of inequality in publishing gain tremendous significance when considered from a wider vantage point. I endeavor to explore in this book how the advantages of Western scholars and their journals are attributable to material, political, and cultural sources of power. In turn, the knowledge constructed in these journals contributes to their ideological hegemony and sustains their material advantages. Therefore I wish to consider academic literacy in the framework of geopolitical relationships.

The asymmetrical relations between the center and periphery help frame the salient features of contemporary geopolitical realities. Though a significant tradition of work in developing this perspective stretches from economist Gundar Frank (1969), it is the model outlined by social theorist Immanuel Wallerstein (1974, 1991)—who coined the label *world systems perspective*—that enjoys the widest currency. According to this model, in the contemporary capital- and market-based global social system, superior economic and technological resources provide the center an edge over periphery communities. The raw material and markets in the periphery are exploited to maintain the dominant status of the industrially developed West. The market economy and industrialization sustain themselves by the underdevelopment of periphery communities. Through the processes of production, accumulation, and division of labor the capitalist world economy integrates communities beyond national borders for its expansion. It is by maintaining the periphery status of the underdeveloped communities that the capitalist countries can remain in the center of an interlocked global system of capitalism. The center yokes other communities in more than economic terms. Communication, entertainment, transport, industry, and technology are diverse other channels that make the periphery dependent on the center. The material advantage the center enjoys enables it to function as the nucleus in these other domains too.

There is considerable explanatory power achieved in looking at social life through the center/periphery framework. We begin to see conflicts at the local level as connected to struggles for power and resources at the global level. Consequently, political and economic realities are seen as not simply contained within the traditional boundaries of the nation-state. They are paradoxically both much larger and smaller than that. However, a consideration of the academic and discursive concerns, as described earlier, is difficult to undertake according to this framework. Such concerns are too messy to be accommodated by a mostly structuralist and economistic center/periphery model. While Wallerstein's paradigm prioritizes the economic bases of the center/periphery division, an analysis of the way in which other domains of life interact with material life calls for models that give importance to noneconomic concerns. Even Anthony Giddens's (1990) multifaceted model, which includes (in addition to Wallerstein's world capitalist economy) a political dimension (the nation-state system), a military dimension (the world military order), and a production dimension (the international division of labor), fails to do justice to the diverse domains that participate in constructing the world system. We need to consider therefore the work of other scholars who have attempted to theorize center domination from more complex perspectives.

Johann Galtung (1971, 1980) develops a multidimensional model that posits a greater role for values and ideologies in this domination. Unlike Giddens, Galtung includes more channels of center domination. Similarly, while Wallerstein prioritizes the economic dimension of domination, Galtung gives equal importance to multiple channels of center influence. In an interlocking/cyclical process, the politico-economic domination sustains other domains of superiority of the center, including the cultural and the intellectual, while these other domains strengthen the politico-economic domination. As powerful producers of mass media, information, popular culture, and education are based in center nations, the Western communities hold the advantage of spreading their values and ideologies to the periphery communities through these channels. Galtung insightfully mentions that whereas the colonialism of the seventeenth century was effected through military means, in later periods imperialist domination has been achieved through the more subtle imposition of values and ideologies. In other words, while the imperialism of the past was conducted through guns, the imperialism of the present is achieved through ideas. Such a perspective encourages us to consider knowledge and ideas as playing as significant a role in the dominance of the center as its material/economic influences.

Galtung's model also accommodates the possibility of multiple centers and multiple peripheries existing within the unequal world system. There are marginalized communities within the center (subordinate ethnic, class, and gender groups and institutions) that are made to serve the interests of the dominant groups in their own societies. Similarly, there are elite groups in the periphery that sustain their relative dominance by aligning with center elites and suppressing the minority and marginalized groups in their own local communities. An elite social group that dominates intranationally (in a periphery community) often gains its power by sharing the values, culture, and social relations of the international elite (in the center). Through the elite groups in the periphery, the center dominates these communities. This is a very effective form of hegemony as the center doesn't have to impose its values and power directly, but through a group of natives who act as its agents. This model thus allows for a dynamic process of center dominance that doesn't have to be imposed unilaterally from the center. Such a perspective accounts, paradoxically, for ways in which the periphery may participate in its own domination.

How education may function as a vehicle for center dominance needs to be analyzed carefully given the concerns of this book. Although Galtung accommodates the manner in which educational and intellectual activities serve an imperialistic agenda, he treats them only as an instance of cultural imperialism. However, educational imperialism needs to be considered as a construct in its own right. The celebrated African scholar Ngugi wa Thiong'o (1983) forcefully articulates the ways in which the educational domain may serve the purposes of center dominance. He asserts that it is primarily through education that the physically absent agents of Western imperialism have continued their hegemony in the periphery after decolonization (from the 1940s to the 1970s). Functioning as the intellectual center, the West trains periphery scholars in its institutes, sponsors expertise and scholarship, sends aid for educational purposes, and gives teaching materials and published literature to periphery communities. Through these channels, content knowledge and pedagogies of the center enter into local classrooms. These supposedly altruistic services thus play a part in spreading the Western orientation to life and values.

Another domain that Galtung's model accommodates but fails to explore explicitly is the imperialism of language. The English language—native to some of the Western communities—also serves to yoke the world system under the leadership of the center. Coining the term *linguicism* to denote language-based discrimination (analogous to *racism* or *sexism*), Phillipson (1992) traces how domination over other languages has served to justify, exert, and augment the politico-economic hegemony of English. It is for nonlinguistic reasons that English holds a preeminent position among global languages. Its worldwide spread, currency, and influence provide material and ideological advantages to native English communities (Pennycook 1994). The English language thus becomes a very effective vehicle for spreading center values globally and for providing Western institutions access to the periphery. The status of the English language also plays an important part in boosting the prestige of academic journals published in English and the dominance of Anglo-American academic communities. The access to transnational academic communities makes it attractive for international scholars to get their research published in

English. As English displaces Latin as the universal language of the intellect in the contemporary world, its ability to reproduce center values globally has also increased in similar fashion.

However, when we combine these different forms of imperialism, we arrive at a very complex and untidy picture of geopolitical dominance. For example, there are non-English communities (e.g., France and Germany) that also partake in the ideological dominance of the center by virtue of favored Eurocentric values. How does the imperialism of English relate to their languages and the power of their speech communities? Then there are communities like Japan and Korea that may not have the military dominance and political power of the European powers but that enjoy a measure of economic and industrial development that surpasses that of the Western nations from time to time. How does their economic power relate to center dominance? Even in matters of cultural life, the non-Western world is displaying a hunger for traditionally Western cultural practices and artifacts that exceeds the interest of the center. Note that the construction of skyscrapers, the formation of megalopolises, and other trappings of urban culture are more prevalent in Asia than in the West today (Appadurai 1994). On the other hand, while the West is turning to alternative medicine, natural diets, and meditation practices that were traditionally nurtured by Eastern cultures, the periphery seems to be turning to industrial products as the panacea for its ills. Things get even murkier when we consider the complicated interplay between dominance and resistance, or globalization and factionalism (Barber 1995). For example, the more the center exerts its drive for global homogenization, the more there is a paradoxical fracturing of communities (even in the West, as displayed by rightist militia groups), with diverse communities beginning to stress their cultural uniqueness and striving for political autonomy.

Such ironies and paradoxes in the cultural nexus of center/periphery relations call for a more complex formulation of geopolitical realities. Arjun Appadurai (1994) therefore constructs a dynamic model of a world system that assumes disjuncture as a constitutive principle. Appadurai takes into account the fact that power in each domain—of economics, politics, and culture—doesn't always correspond in a one-to-one fashion. In other words, economic superiority doesn't necessarily mean that the country will also be powerful in political and cultural terms. Though there are different axes of power and relative dominance in different domains, we shouldn't rule out some broad overlaps and linkages in the exercise of power. Therefore, Appadurai argues: "In order for the theory of global cultural interactions predicated on disjunctive flows to have any force greater than that of a mechanical metaphor, it will have to move into something like a human version of the theory that some scientists are calling 'chaos theory.' That is, we will need to ask how these complex, overlapping, fractal shapes constitute not a simple, stable (even if large-scale) system, but to ask what its dynamics are" (1994, 337). Though Appadurai doesn't offer a neat model suitable for our purposes, his articulation of the difficulties serves to warn us about making easy generalizations. Appadurai argues that the path toward a model lies in adopting a "radically context-dependent" approach (1994, 337). He also states that however complex the factors involved in center/periphery relations, the inequalities in this relationship should not be simply disregarded. Power difference should be treated as a fundamental condition of center/periphery relations.

I use the center/periphery framework in relative terms here, sensitive also to the context-bound nature of these constructs. The center and periphery are not monoliths that always correspond in every domain of consideration. The terms are fluid, and the status of specific communities may change according to the domain we are considering. For example, Scandinavian countries may share certain economic forms of superiority with the United States but claim inequality when it comes to linguistic and academic relations (Mauranen 1993b). In fact, we have to be open to the reality that there are peripheries within the center (e.g., rural communities and marginalized ethnic groups in the United States) and centers within the periphery (e.g., culturally elite and economically powerful circles in Asia, Africa, and Latin America). However, power flows in subtle ways through these disjunct domains, and we cannot deny that there are academic linkages between the United States, Scandinavian countries, and the periphery elite that sustain certain forms of cultural dominance. At any rate, we can use the center/periphery construct with certainty only in specific domains of consideration—and in this book we have to consider how this framework enables us to talk about the geopolitics of publishing and knowledge production.[1]

How the hegemony of the center is exercised through academic publishing in this complex nexus of geopolitical relationships has to be explored with depth in each specific academic community in terms of the factors dominant in that setting. First, we must situate academic literacy in the macrostructure of center/periphery relations. Academic publishing both gains from and complements the politico-economic dominance of the Anglo-American communities in complex ways. Based in the West, the publishing houses and academic societies enjoy the infrastructure and resources to publish conveniently and profitably. The technological sophistication, communication facilities, economic strength, and marketing networks of the center help the academic publishing enterprise in no small way. The resulting publications have thus attained a position where they can function as norm-enforcing institutions and academic clearinghouses for research work in the different disciplines. Periphery scholars are compelled to get published in such journals to validate the respectability of their work, disseminate their findings effectively to the academic channels that matter in their profession, and participate in knowledge construction. However, publishing according to the conventions and terms set by the center academic communities influences in no small way the representation of periphery knowledge. The publishing requirements, epistemological paradigms, and communicative conventions established by the center shape the knowledge that gets constructed through these journals. Such knowledge serves the interests of the center more than the periphery. The journals thereby disseminate partisan knowledge globally.

To localize our analysis further, we have to examine how geopolitical inequalities in academic publishing are instantiated in concrete academic settings in order to understand the *structuration* of hegemony (Giddens 1990). The settings and communities that I study are unique in their own way. But the patterns of relationship generated by this discussion can be fruitfully applied to other communities as well. Furthermore, however messy the politics of center/periphery relations, and however variable the conditions in different academic communities, this complexity should not be used as an excuse for explaining away the reality of power and domination. If anything, this analytical untidiness only goes to show that the mechanisms of power are subtle and pervasive—that power can achieve its ends even through disjunct domains and structures of social life.

Disciplinary Context

The subject of this book can be addressed in terms of diverse disciplines and research orientations, ranging from the most microlevel linguistic concerns of academic writing to macrolevel considerations relating to the political-economy of literacy. It is important therefore to demarcate the academic fields influencing my exploration.

The key term in the title—*academic writing*—suggests the main area of scholarship invoked in this book. The term enjoys currency among teachers and researchers of composition. Though used largely in the developmental sense of helping college students acquire proficiency in expository writing, the construct has also inspired the description of academic discourse conventions and literacy practices (Atkinson 1999; Bazerman 1988; Bizzell 1992; Geisler 1994; Myers 1990). Curiously, this pedagogical and research activity remains very much a North American enterprise (see, for reasons, Muchiri et al. 1995). In Europe, Asia, South America, and Africa the teaching of academic writing is not done in a systematic or institutionalized manner. Though I draw from the work of compositionists to discuss the conventions of periphery disciplinary communities and their academic writing, I focus on the actual writing done by professionals in such periphery institutional contexts. In an indirect compliment to the field of composition, I show why periphery scholars have to be concerned about the developing knowledge on academic writing. The marginalization of their scholarship may result partly from *not* taking the practice of academic writing seriously.

Another field that informs the study of academic writing is constituted by second language teachers. These professionals are engaged in work falling into disciplines like applied linguistics, English for Academic and Specific Purposes (EAP/ESP), and bilingual literacy. Since the primary area for work of these scholarly groups is the teaching of academic literacy to non-native students, they have studied the conventions and processes of writing in a comparative sense. Developing a keen sensitivity to issues in contrastive linguistics and contrastive rhetoric, they have formulated a stock of knowledge on how different linguistic and cultural groups construct texts (Connor 1996; Fox 1994; Purves 1988; Swales 1990). Such an orientation will prove useful for studying the discursive differences of periphery scholars.

Needless to say, the constructs of these circles will have to be considerably expanded and, in some cases, critically reformulated to help explore academic writing from a geopolitical perspective. Crucial notions for composition scholars—like discourse conventions, discourse communities, and literate practices—will have to be reinterpreted in order to develop this orientation. In situating these constructs in a geopolitical context, I will have to provide a more material, historical, and critical reading of them. It is such an orientation that will enable me to provide the unusual perspective on literacy I envision for this book. The place of material resources as a cause and consequence of written knowledge, the nondiscursive conventions and requirements in the practice of academic writing, the constitutive role of conflict in the work of academic communities, the multimodal nature of writing, and the social and political functions of academic texts are issues that will be given a more complex treatment in my discussion to follow in the next chapter.

A perspective on academic literacy that is indigenous to the periphery and influenced by postcolonial theoretical perspectives will challenge some of the excesses deriving from what are called the "ludic" poststructuralist/postmodernist approaches dominant in composition circles today. These approaches narrow down the context of language and texts and adopt a playful attitude to the multiple meanings generated by linguistic signs, to the point that they fail to address the harsh political and material concerns periphery scholars are painfully aware of (Canagarajah 1999). Moreover, although literacy studies on ESL students in Western educational institutions abound, it is dangerous to generalize such findings to characterize non-English writing conventions and non-Western discourses. Analyzing the writing practices of professionals and advanced scholars in their own languages and academic contexts is a more productive angle of research. The writing practices of periphery professionals will of course generate fresh insights into the developmental challenges of students from non-English communities in the acquisition of academic literacy.

Another area of scholarship that influences this book is symbolized by an imposing term that recurs in the text, *knowledge production*. There is increasing sensitivity to the connection between writing and knowledge these days. Accompanying this development is a questioning of the nature, functions, and construction of knowledge. It is now commonly assumed that we cannot take the dominant methods and constructs of knowledge for granted. The processes by which we form knowledge are being critically interrogated (Scheurich and Young 1997). It is no longer accepted that intellectual activity is a search for the final answers on the laws governing life and that this can be achieved by the transcendent human mind if only the inquiry is conducted without any distorting influences from social, cultural, and personal factors. What we might call the social-constructionist paradigm (influential in schools like the sociology of knowledge and the history of science) has helped describe the ways in which intellectual activity is a communal enterprise that is considerably influenced by material/historical factors (Hess 1995; Knorr-Cetina 1981; Kuhn 1962). Related to this critical orientation to epistemology these days is the awareness that language is central to our processes of inquiry (Foucault 1972). Language is not simply a medium to communicate knowledge but is itself constitutive of knowledge. It is from the perspective of these developments that writing and literacy become integral to knowledge production.

A troubling outcome of this epistemological critique is the realization that the dominant methods and practices of knowledge construction are partisan and partial to certain social groups. That the constructs sanctioned in educational research and pedagogy are loaded with the values and ideologies of dominant class, race, and gender groups has been examined in relation to different domains of school life (Apple 1986; Bourdieu and Passeron 1977; Giroux 1992). What may be termed critical pedagogy and political approaches to education have explored the ways in which the practices of mainstream schooling reproduce the ideologies and social relations of the dominant groups in areas like curriculum, pedagogy, and teaching material. The educational site is perceived as serving the interests of the dominant groups and institutions in sustaining an unequal social order. At the same time, how marginalized student communities may resist such ideological thrusts is also being explored. Teachers themselves are also exploring ways in which schooling can validate the knowledge of minorities, empower them, and educate them for the critical transformation of society. To make the educational domain a more democratic site is the common goal motivating the writing of this book.

Deriving from the work described above, my inquiry delves into the ways in which research paradigms and theoretical constructs in the academy are informed by the values and interests of European and American communities. The reasons for this intellectual domination lie in historical and political realities that will be outlined in the next chapter. Spearheading this line of inquiry is the emerging work of postcolonial thinkers.

These scholars are exploring the ways in which colonial and imperialist history has served to represent the knowledge, experience, and traditions of non-Western communities (Guha and Spivak 1988; Said 1993; Spivak 1990). Deconstructing the interests motivating the dominant forms of knowledge, postcolonial scholars are articulating the modes of local knowledge deriving from their own communities. But few in these circles have explored the ways in which the Euro-American dominance of intellectual inquiry is sustained and reproduced in the domain of academic writing and publishing. Empowering periphery knowledge may also involve critically intervening in the academic writing/publishing process. It is this thin but significant link in the process of knowledge production that I hope to examine as a contribution to the burgeoning scholarship of postcolonial thinkers.

The fact that I am highlighting two broad areas of work—academic writing and knowledge production—should not be taken to mean that I don't borrow from other relevant fields—like cultural studies, political economy, and sociology. We must not forget the other operative word in the title of this book—"geopolitics." By situating the exploration of writing and knowledge in the broadest possible historical and political contexts I invoke an interdisciplinary framework. Models of ideological reproduction and resistance, the discourse analysis of text and talk, traditions of orality and literacy, the sociolinguistics of bilingual/bicultural communication, and sociological approaches to group and interpersonal interaction are some of the areas that will inform the discussion in the following pages.

The Framework

The vast geopolitical setting and epistemological line of inquiry assumed in this project can become quite unwieldy in a monograph of limited proportions. The scope of analysis has to be carefully delimited to make the exploration more manageable. I have thus restricted my analysis in the following ways. First, it is difficult to analyze the journals of all academic disciplines to explore how publishing conventions affect scholarly interaction at the widest levels. Therefore, while I use information from many disciplines to suggest the general relevance of my argument, I will conduct a close analysis of the journals in the family of fields I know best. These are the fields generally related to applied linguistic science, such as ELT, sociolinguistics, discourse analysis, and written communication. These disciplines lie at the crossroads of the humanities and social sciences, providing a multidisciplinary scope of relevance to my discussion. Furthermore, some of the fields in the human and social sciences require more study of their literate practices and disciplinary discourses. Geisler (1994), who describes the literacy practices of scholars in philosophy, argues that the humanities are perhaps the least explored in research on academic writing. It is true that writing from the physical and biological sciences is relatively better discussed (Bazerman 1988; Myers 1990). Geisler also states that the disciplinary communities in the humanities were the last to institutionalize/professionalize themselves and, in many cases, are yet to develop a strong community identity or disciplinary consciousness. Similarly, certain social scientific fields have not yet evolved a strong discursive identity. Bazerman (1988) has analyzed the publishing conventions in political science and psychology to show how their respective discourses jostle inconsistently and clumsily with those of natural scientific fields. Trying to ape the more established scientific discourses, and disregarding their own unique traditions and focus, these emergent fields display much instability in their professional status. The emergent and unsettled nature of their discourses makes some of the humanistic and social scientific fields interesting to explore.

Furthermore, I will focus on those journals published in the English language, although the publishing practices I critique may characterize journals published in other colonial languages (e.g., German, French). One doesn't have to apologize for studying journals published in English. It is clear from the statistics cited earlier that these journals hold the most important place in the knowledge-construction industry in the academy. Furthermore, in order to show the relevance of my argument for all academic communities in the periphery, I need in-depth information on the publishing practices of Asian, African, and Latin American scholars. Periphery communities represent a range of languages and cultures that cannot be realistically covered in a single project. While I draw from available published information on these communities, I have to ground my exploration in the academic community I am "native" to—that based in the University of Jaffna, Sri Lanka. Focusing on the modes of academic literacy practiced there, I will consider interactions in the vernacular and other bilingual modes to examine how scholars there shape their English literacy.

Conclusion

I must emphasize that it is not geographical extensiveness or numerical plenitude that I muster to prove my argument. There are few periphery scholars publishing in mainstream journals who can be treated as "subjects" for quantitative research on publishing practices and attitudes. The others have never attempted to publish academically, are publishing in vernacular/nonacademic journals, or have stopped publishing after returning from postgraduate research abroad. Furthermore, since the exclusion of periphery scholars from Western academic publications is widely experienced but rarely expressed, there is little published material to cite/survey on this issue. This absence is an integral part of the syndrome—that is, the exclusion of periphery scholars from international publications also prevents their problems from being voiced. As far as statistical and demographic surveys are concerned, the pioneering work of American theoretical physicist Michael Moravcsik (1985) has served to demonstrate conclusively the global inequalities in knowledge production and dissemination. What is attempted in this book is what Moravcsik and other center-based scholars have not been able to achieve—a close analysis of texts and events in the practice of periphery knowledge construction with ethnographic sensitivity to the perspectives of local communities. As a sociolinguist, my interest is in a fine-grained analysis of language and discourse as they structure academic communication and interaction. Also, as I have argued above, there is a theoretical need to explore the microsocial instantiations of geopolitical inequalities in concrete academic settings in order to complement the macrosocial critiques of center/periphery relations.

2. Communities of Knowledge Construction

> Where the combined legacy of everyday tropes for, and structuralist theories of, discourse and society has encouraged us to imagine disciplines as autonomous objects existing in detemporalized space, as territories to be mapped or systems to be diagrammed, sociohistoric theories point toward an image of disciplines as open networks, forged through relational activity that intermingles personal, interpersonal, institutional, and sociocultural histories.
> —Paul Prior, *Writing/Disciplinarity*

The audience for the meeting convened by what is called the Academic Forum at the University of Jaffna has gathered in large numbers and with unusual excitement. A paper entitled "Accounting for the Name and Prestige of Panditamani"— written in Tamil by a senior professor in linguistics—has been circulated to the audience prior to the meeting.[1] The paper explores the life and work of a respected local *pundit* who was posthumously granted an honorary doctorate by the university.[2] The reason for the excitement is that this paper is considered a follow-up to one that the author presented earlier on the *pundit*. That paper created controversy in the local community, as the general public saw in it an attempt to denigrate the *pundit* and his tradition of indigenous scholarship.[3] There were heated discussions about that paper in the local media, with many readers accusing the university professor of prejudice against the *pundit*. The present paper has been submitted as a revision of the earlier thesis, with the author painting a very positive picture of the *pundit's* achievements and claiming to base his views on new, objective, and more complete data.

Following the conventions of the Academic Forum, the author orally introduces the thrust of his presentation before the audience debates the paper statement by statement. He first reminds the audience of what he perceives as the principles behind scientific research—especially objectivity, fidelity to the data, and rigor of analysis. In doing so, he closely follows the introduction of his written text. This opening turns out to be strategic, as it justifies the present revisions in the author's position toward his subject. To reinforce this claim that his revised position is motivated by fidelity to science, he also reminds the audience about the difficulties he had to go through in getting unbiased documents relating to the revered savant. However, one can't avoid the impression that the principles of scientific objectivity are asserted in a manner bordering on fetishism. This is all the more glaring at a time when mainstream academic communities (in the center) are likely to make such positivistic and empiricist claims in more qualified terms (if they would make them at all). As the seminar progresses, many sources of epistemological tension get played out in the forum. These tensions generate multiple ironies relating to the nature and function of the scientific claims made by the author.

Consider first the *pundit's* own status in the competing epistemological traditions. His title *(pundit)* derives from the mastery of texts defined as intellectual according to indigenous forms of scholarship. This tradition cultivates a respect for religion, ancient canonical texts, and the authority of the ancients and a commitment to preserving this knowledge. Memorization, exegesis, and apologetics are valued activities in this intellectual enterprise. The author's use of empirical science to praise a practitioner of traditional/religious scholarship is replete with irony. However, the author doesn't show any discomfort about this clash of competing epistemologies.

The disciplinary orientation of the paper also displays some tensions with the scientific discourse the author claims to represent. The author's treatment of the subject is vaguely biographical and doesn't seem to fall into any academically recognized discipline—for example, history, literature, or his own area of linguistics. The paper is structured in a narrative style, with subsections dealing with the *pundit's* achievements in widely differing areas of inquiry. The *pundit* is presented as having mastered science, Hinduism, English literature, vernacular literature, philosophy, and much more. Perhaps the image developed of the *pundit* as a *sakala kalaa vallavan* (a master of all arts) is itself motivated by indigenous cultural norms. Furthermore, there is no claim of a disciplined methodology employed to research this subject. In some respects, the paper sounds like a panegyric, paying tribute to the accomplishments of a famous person.

The way the *pundit* is represented reveals certain questionable interests that motivate the author's position on the subject. In his concluding section, the author presents the *pundit* as holding significance primarily to the Jaffna Tamil Saiva society (where the *pundit* comes from).[4] In a multiethnic community consisting of scholars from Hindu, Christian, and Muslim religions, in addition to regional and caste affiliations, the author's representation has tremendous ideological implications. Some members of the audience therefore question the interests of the author in presenting the significance of the *pundit* in this manner. Though the author doesn't acknowledge his social location during the presentation, he himself comes from the Jaffna Tamil Saiva community, which constitutes the hegemonical cultural tradition in the local society. Despite the claims of disinterested objectivity then, the presentation appears to be in fact shaped by partisan interests and values.

Even the social and historical contexts influence the representation of the *pundit*. Since the author's previous publication on this subject, the local society has seen considerable social and ideological changes. The militant linguistic nationalism of the local community has inspired the creation of a de facto separate state. The nationalism spawned by resistance against the rival Sinhala community has snowballed into a general reaction against Western values and foreign cultures. Ideologies that value a return to traditional culture, linguistic purity, religious fundamentalism, and the lifestyle of the past have greater appeal. This ideological pressure may well have motivated the scholar's reinterpretation, which now turns out to be less critical and detached toward the indigenous tradition represented by the *pundit* than his previous presentation.

Moreover, the principles of objectivity and detachment claimed in the paper come into conflict with the whole tenor of the meeting and the ethos of the local audience. The discussion becomes very personal, passionate, and even explosive as the various interest groups in the audience (composed along religious, regional, and ideological lines) clash among themselves and with the author. The audience is unforgiving, despite the author's changes in his presentation. Some point out that the revision seems to have been hastily done by the author, with inadequate evidence, simply to save face. Others try to discover ulterior motives for this revised presentation, cynically speculating that the author is trying to curry favor with the powers that be by sounding nationalist. They question the interests motivating this representation of the *pundit* and the agenda of the author. The author's attempt to enforce scientific objectivity falls on deaf ears as the audience becomes increasingly shrill, combative, and emotional. Some wonder at this point whether the author's commitment to positivistic modes of inquiry is an attempt to declare all questions about interests, ideologies, and contexts irrelevant to his presentation. But one thing is clear: the audience itself is not ready to suppress these concerns in the name of disinterested inquiry.

Finally, tensions at a different level shouldn't be missed here. It is interesting that the indigenous traditions of knowledge are celebrated in the portals of a university that has historically been associated with nontraditional (modernist) approaches to knowledge. It is indeed ironic that the *pundit* should be honored in a modern-day university. The university thus turns out to be a site containing hybrid traditions of knowledge and communication—even though some leading members of the faculty (including the author) attempt to deny this diversity by upholding the universal principles of positivistic science and Enlightenment thinking. Furthermore, the relationship between these epistemological traditions is characterized by conflict. There is an attempt to achieve power and hegemony for one tradition over the other—motivated no doubt by the relative status of the groups espousing each tradition. The representation of the life and work of the *pundit* is, interestingly, dependent on the outcome of this process of power struggle. Knowledge about the *pundit* is therefore not "out there" to be claimed by those with proper data and a scientific disposition, as claimed by the author himself—but is being constantly reconstructed in negotiation with the shifting ideologies of the interest groups in the community.

Competing Intellectual Traditions

Such tensions in the different orientations to academic inquiry problematize the nature of knowledge. How do we relate to the diverse forms of knowing represented by the different communities in this academic speech event? The tradition of scientific positivism—which presently enjoys a near-universal status as the paradigmatic way of conducting academic inquiry, though it has declined considerably in power since its high point about fifty years back—would treat some of the other approaches represented above as inferior to its own or as simply irrational.[5] The dominant orientation of the members of the audience at UJ—which treats knowledge as interested, value-ridden, contextual, and personal—displays all the features that the Enlightenment tradition stereotypically considers as distorting knowledge. The types of tensions displayed in the above interaction may not be visible to those belonging to the scientific tradition. They would simply consider the audience to be asking the wrong questions. There is no tension for them in the event because whatever inquiry deviates from the Enlightenment tradition cannot be considered as constituting a valid orientation to knowledge. The Enlightenment tradition considers knowledge to be so decontextualized, transcendental, "pure," and value-free that any consideration of knowledge as being influenced by contexts, interests, and ideologies would be summarily dismissed (Bajaj 1990). Similarly, knowledge is considered universal, so that any question of inequality or bias or vested interests to favor a specific community or interest group would be treated as irrelevant. From this viewpoint, if such interests do happen to motivate any intellectual work, it is simply bad scholarship. Positivist scientists might perhaps fault the author for not more rigorously applying empirical lines of inquiry and for failing to follow through on the epistemological assumptions that he committed himself to.

But in the evolving post-Enlightenment tradition of defining knowledge, diverse forms of conducting inquiry (as displayed in the literacy event described above) are treated with more significance. Multiple influences in the construction of knowledge are also acknowledged. The assumptions motivating the post-Enlightenment or postmodernist perspective can be summarized in the following ways.[6]

Knowledge is *constructed*. Knowledge does not occur by itself. It doesn't imprint itself on the empty minds of passive subjects (as Locke's tabula rasa would have us believe). It is put together by members of the community in terms of the interests and values that matter to them. There is an active process of construction by human agents according to the contextual conditions existing in the community. We realize that there is nothing given or obvious or self-evident about the knowledge on the *pundit*. It is being constantly negotiated and reconstructed by scholars in terms of the changing social context.

Knowledge construction is *collaborative*. It is a social activity done by human agents in collaboration with others through everyday processes of interaction. The knowledge produced by the author on the *pundit* is shaped by many others—in other words, by the new data made available to him by fresh informants; by the challenge posed to his earlier paper by his critics; by the knowledge produced by previous scholars who have written on this subject; and by the comments made by the audience during his latest presentation. Knowledge is not created by the solitary activity of an individual.

Knowledge construction is *contextual*. Material, historical, and social conditions governing the community's life and experience shape its knowledge. In addition to the contextual influences noted above, consider how the following features would influence the author's perspective on the subject: the social positions of the author, the *pundit,* and the members of the audience; the ideological shifts in the community; and the recent changes in local political and social conditions. This context leads to a dynamic process of periodic knowledge reconstruction according to the changing conditions, interests, and values of the community. There is thus a strong connection between context and knowledge, as the community produces the type of knowledge that proves useful to explain, understand, and manage its conditions of existence.

Knowledge construction is *value-ridden*. The cultural traditions and practices of the community play a part in interpreting social and natural phenomena. The interests, values, beliefs, feelings, and imaginations of the subjects do play a role in the shape knowledge takes as it is constructed. The fact that the *pundit* is worthy of academic inquiry, the evidence accounting for his greatness, the sources that are valued in understanding his status, and the way his scholarly image is represented—all these are culturally motivated. Of course, for those from Western communities the scholarly stature of a figure is represented in a different way. They may not consider the *pundit* worthy of any serious attention. It is unrealistic, therefore, to imagine that such "subjective" aspects can be excluded in knowledge construction.

Knowledge is *discursive*. Knowledge is constructed by and through language. This is because language mediates our perception and interpretation of life. At a microlevel, the interactions between members of a community who engage in knowledge production take place through talk. Since language embodies the values of that community, it not only functions as a *medium* for knowledge construction but shapes knowledge actively. While talk about the *pundit* in Tamil comes loaded with positive values, it will be awkward to talk about the same subject in English, as it is informed by a different epistemological background. Note that terms like *sakala kalaa vallavan* encapsulate the achievements of traditional scholars in the local community and make it possible to readily talk about their feats with approbation. (In fact, in this book, the very representation in English of the speech event that took place at the Academic Forum may sound badly translated and distorted to members of the UJ community.) Furthermore, what transpires in the talk in the forum now embodies the latest knowledge on the *pundit* and would provide the framework and "language" for future discussions on the subject.

While the above orientation to knowledge construction may appear unproblematic in the light of a single community, it has controversial implications when we consider the relationship between different communities. Each community struggles not only to maintain its own knowledge (which best suits its interests) but also to thrust itself on other groups in order to legitimize its knowledge as universally valid. This gives birth to intergroup conflict. Needless to say, each community's knowledge tradition would appear correct to itself and, therefore, superior to those of others. The hegemony of one group's knowledge tradition over others can be explained by the ulterior motive of monopolizing available material and cultural resources. Note in the speech event cited above how the different caste, regional, and religious groups hold different understandings of the *pundit*. The differences are shaped by the interests of each group. The representation of the *pundit* as a contributor to the Saiva, Vellala caste, Jaffna Tamil, tradition provokes the questioning by other groups at the forum. Since it is this group that is dominant in the local society, it is natural that it appropriates leading historical figures to build its own status. The other groups would attempt to broaden the significance of the *pundit* to include their groups or deny his significance altogether. There is also implied here a conflict at a transnational level. The local scholars are studying and glorifying the work of the *pundit* as a way of celebrating their indigenous intellectual traditions and scholarship. This activity can even take the paradoxical strategy of using Western epistemological traditions/methods to boost local knowledge—as occurs in this instance. But those who believe that the Enlightenment tradition should hold universal sway can be expected to scoff at this scholarship on the *pundit*. For them the subject as well as the type of research conducted would be of no consequence. The conflicts underlying the proceedings of the Academic Forum at UJ bring us to the most powerful notion that motivates this book—*knowledge as interested* and, therefore, ideological.

We must realize that, just like any other intellectual tradition, Enlightenment science also cannot stand free of social construction, contextual influence, and ideological interests. It too is a discourse that is shaped by contexts and values. Note how the use of empirical claims of analysis by the author above is motivated by certain personal agendas. Scientific principles claiming disinterested inquiry thus function to suppress alternate readings of the presentation by the audience and perhaps to downplay the author's own motivations influencing his interpretation. Therefore, in a paradoxical sense, disinterested positivism serves ideological interests. Similarly, we have to be open to the possibility that Enlightenment principles can work to enable the West to further its hegemony. There are many important critical works available now that demonstrate how this domination has been exercised in recent history (Hess 1995, 18–86; Nandy 1990). Though Ashis Nandy and the Indian contributors to his *Science, Hegemony, and Violence* would consider such imperialistic practices as part of a hidden and conscious agenda of the West, this also derives discursively (by virtue of science being a discourse that needs to further the interests of its community and exert its hegemony for its survival).

What is emerging from the postmodernist perspective on knowledge is the realization that the principles of empiricism, objectivity, rationalism, positivism, and detached inquiry that characterize scientific scholarship are not the only "correct," universally valid, or superior way of attaining knowledge. This approach to inquiry is based on the values and interests of communities based on European ancestry (Huff 1993). They can in fact be traced to a time when contextual and historical conditions favored the construction of such an epistemological orientation. The scientific movement was helped, enhanced, and/or initiated by parallel sociopolitical developments like industrialization/urbanization (Merton 1970), (Protestant) reformation (Jacob 1976), capitalism (Hessen 1971), nationalism (Porter 1995), and colonialism (Adas 1989). While not denying the fact that there are subtle variations and changes in the intellectual traditions of the communities across the European and American continents, the scientific principles can still be accommodated within a broad paradigm that has an identity and interests aligned to the center. The imposition of this world-view on knowledge on a global scale, and the suppression of other forms of knowledge in periphery communities, have been attributed to the con-tinuing technological, economic, and political expansion of the center. The fact that many communities across the globe see this worldview as su-perior (including some university faculty members in remote Jaffna) only attests to the effectiveness with which it has become internalized, sanc-tioned, and institutionalized.

The complicity of empirical science with the colonial enterprise is of special concern for periphery communities (Adas 1989; Alvarez 1990). The technological superiority of the West—both helping and helped by sci-ence—provided the military power and resources for it to colonize the Asian, African, and South American communities. The scientifically ad-vanced West believed that it was the "white man's burden" to spread its message of Enlightenment and scientific revolution to the East—which had different epistemological traditions. The Enlightenment was believed to be a universally applicable project, not a cultural product of the West— one produced by a Judeo-Christian worldview based on individualism, detachment from and control over nature, a teleological view of time, and the celebration of reason (Merton 1970). But this altruistic mission did not rule out the search for more raw materials for the West's industry and more markets in which to sell its unrestrained production of goods. Colo-nialism thus boosted capitalist industry and economy. Scholars like Hess (1995) and Nandy (1990) document how multinational corporations are still exploiting the natural resources and cultures of the periphery for their production goals even after decolonization. The scientific worldview has now gained approval globally as all communities have become integrated into a vast network of market economy and industrial production in the contemporary world order (Lunn 1982; Larsen 1990; Giddens 1990). Al-though science would claim to be apolitical, then, it both complements and benefits from a favorable set of sociopolitical, material, and historical conditions.

This picture of how social conditions and the formation of Enlighten-ment science come together to promote the hegemony of Western civi-lization and its knowledge tradition might sound too sweeping and sim-plistic to be credible. Needless to say, the details of the science connection and the subtle permutations and dynamics in the construction of the Enlightenment worldview have been worked out through research in diverse geographical sites, social institutions, and academic disciplines (see, e.g., Harwood 1993; Traweek 1988; Turkle 1978). This thrust for power doesn't have to be blamed on the intentional and manipulative activity of specific historical agents. Power works subtly through a network of institutions and discourses. It is not even the case that science developed as a revolutionary movement at the expense of other ideologies. Not only was the development gradual, but other ideologies existed alongside science and continue to do so (Atkinson 1999, 167–70; Hess 1995, 88). Though "metanarratives" of this nature, which generalize historical and philosophical movements across time and space, are now deplored, there is some value in identifying broad currents for critical purposes. At least, we shouldn't go to the other extreme of localizing movements to such an extent that their geopolitical implications are lost. Anyhow, this survey of Western science is rendered here only as a backdrop to the geopolitics of publishing, not for its own sake. As far as the scope of this book is concerned, the ways in which the publishing industry complements the intellectual dominance of the West are what matter.

In fact, a post-Enlightenment orientation to knowledge attributes controversial significance to the part played by writing/publishing in intellectual activities. Texts mediate, shape, construct, and represent knowledge (as exemplified in the research on the role of writing in diverse academic disciplines by Atkinson 1999; Bazerman 1988; Berkenkotter and Huckin 1995; Gilbert and Mulkay 1984; Myers 1990; and Knorr-Cetina 1981). According to the Enlightenment perspective, knowledge is supposed to precede the writing of it in texts—and therefore stand free of factors of language and communication. The texts are supposed to be passive instruments or neutral media to communicate preconstructed information (Killingsworth and Gilbertson 1992). But in the theoretical position adopted here, the relationship between texts and knowledge is conceived in more dynamic terms. We will therefore explore the following aspects in this connection: how texts construct and constitute knowledge; how the values of the Western intellectual traditions are reflected in the conventions and practices of academic communities and their communication; how mainstream journals and their publishing practices are congenial to the interests of center knowledge while proving recalcitrant to periphery discourses; and how academic writing/publishing functions as an important means of legitimating and reproducing center knowledge.

Understanding Discourse Communities

If knowledge is community specific, and the linguistic interactions of the community mediate and constitute that knowledge, we must understand the role of *discourse communities*. A discourse community is a unit at a varying level of magnitude—ranging from theoretical schools within each discipline (such as structuralists, transformationalists, and critical linguists in the field of linguistics) to the disciplinary groups in a single academic institution (such as physicists, sociologists, and linguists at UJ) and even to the whole of the center as a discourse community (which collaborates in the construction of epistemological paradigms that suit its interests). It is a remarkably fertile term that enables us to go beyond traditional domains like "disciplines" and to connect intellectual activities to larger communities beyond national/state boundaries. It provides an important means of attaining both a micro- and macrolevel perspective on the creation, management, and dissemination of knowledge by enabling us to analyze the activity and functions of the discourse community in the context of its geopolitical implications. Fields such as composition, education, the sociology of knowledge, philosophy, and cultural studies are some of the disciplinary groups that actively employ this construct.

Though this construct is useful in being paradoxically both very broad and very discrete, for the same reason it has also been employed loosely. Also, for leading to the perception of communities as too structured, homogeneous, and self-contained, the construct has been treated as deficient by those in fields like composition and education (Harris 1989; Herzberg 1986; Prior 1998). Before I use this term to explore the activities of disciplinary communities from a geopolitical perspective, I have to raise some problematic functions and implications of this construct that need reconsideration. I find it useful to redefine the term for my purposes rather than constructing neologisms that add to the confusing set of alternatives that are coming up.[7]

A natural starting point for understanding discourse communities is their connection to the linguistic notion of the speech community, with which they have at least an analogical relationship. This perspective is important for this book, as I am interested in considering how disciplinary circles interact with speech communities. But the definition of a speech community is also by no means settled. There is a gradual deepening in the complexity of the term as it has been used over time. The speech community has been defined as a homogeneous collective based on a shared *language* (Hockett 1958); as regular speech *interaction* (Bloomfield 1933); as shared *uses* of the code, including its norms and conventions (Hymes 1972; Bauman and Sherzer 1974); and as a solidarity attained through shared *attitudes* toward the language (Labov 1972). As we can see, the term *speech community* is now associated less with objective constructs like language systems and more with microsocial processes of values and attitudes. However, all these definitions overlook diversity and conflict within the speech community, forcing Pratt (1987) to consider such communities as "linguistic utopias."

While the notion of a speech community tries to capture the ways in which language serves to constitute a community through its communicative and symbolic potential, there are other features that it does not share with a discourse community. To begin with, some of the differences have to do with differences in the definitions of language and discourse. Even the most ideologically sensitive sociolinguist would go only so far as acknowledging the notion of language as a regulative and pragmatic grammar system. From this perspective, there is a core abstract system of language separate from values and social context. The functional dimension of language in the social context is considered to have its own rules of communicative competence, distinct from a formalistic linguistic competence (Hymes 1972; Labov 1972). But the notion of discourse defines language as an intrinsically material, social, and ideological symbol system. According to discourse theorists, language develops in social practice and functions semiotically to interpret life and make meaning for the community (Kress 1985; Fairclough 1995). It isn't just a value-free system or passive instrument. Thus, unlike speech communities, discourse communities hold shared ways of understanding social and material life, in addition to shared uses of language. It is by using these discourses and becoming subjects of these communities that people become social beings. This is because discourse encodes the forms of knowledge and ideology held in common by the community. The notion of discourse also materializes and politicizes language radically. Speech communities are not defined in terms of knowledge and ideology, as language is not directly linked to such constructs by sociolinguistic schools influenced by structuralist/formalist orientations.[8]

Furthermore, while the system of language is defined synchronically by most linguists, discourse is situated in historical context. Therefore, in keeping with the changing historical experiences of the community, its ways of looking at the world also change, with corresponding changes in its language. These discursive changes in turn initiate developments in social life. So while speech communities are conceived in relatively more permanent terms (based on impersonal and immutable factors such as geography, gender, age, and ethnicity) discourse communities are evolving, thus displaying more mobility. It is also implied that human agents have more initiative in the formation and management of discourse communities, unlike in speech communities, where (at least in one's native or primary speech community) one usually gains membership by birth, adoption, or incorporation. In this sense, the discourse community is more dynamic and accommodates human agency.

The diachronic orientation of discourses enables us to conceive how the heterogeneous dialects, registers, and styles of a specific language can constitute different discourse communities over time. Such discourse communities are not only social groups (e.g., Blacks, Hispanics, Jews) but also institutions (e.g., educational, state, religious) and specialized collectivities (e.g., artists, scientists, biologists). In this sense, the notion of a discourse community also readily explains our membership in multiple communities, defined in more particular and discrete ways than more homogeneously defined speech communities. In fact, discourse communities have a built-in tendency to break down into specialized subgroupings. Since there are many such discourses in society, representing different social groups and institutions, we can be simultaneously members of different discourse communities. Though we can be members of multiple discourse communities, our membership will be unequally stratified according to access to the required codes.

Speech communities may also be somewhat limited in geographical terms, compared to discourse communities. Deriving from the linguistic tradition that gives primacy to speech, the definitions of the speech community assume an interaction that is primarily oral. But discourse communities may interact through various other symbol systems—including, most importantly, writing. Ideally, a community that interacts through writing can go beyond spatio-temporal boundaries (Faigley 1985). A journal produced by a disciplinary community situated in the West, for example, may be read by a scholar in the Tamil speech community, 20,000 miles away, ten years after publication. Even through such disjointed interaction the scholar might consider him- or herself as belonging to that disciplinary community. We can imagine how the interaction and constitution of discourse communities can be even more complex if communication takes place through digital and electronic media. Therefore, a discourse community is more expansive and fluid than a speech community.[9]

Using this perspective to understand the discourse community, we can discern finer distinctions within the sociolinguistic speech community. The discourse community cuts across speech communities: physicists from France, Korea, and Sri Lanka could belong to the same discourse community, though they may belong to three different speech communities. On the other hand, within the same speech community there could be many discourse communities: thus there are specialized groups such as physicists, philosophers, and poets within the Jaffna Tamil speech community.

Such an orientation raises certain difficult questions about the intra- and intergroup relations of the discourse community. To focus on intragroup constitution first, we can consider Swales's (1990) definition of discourse community. He lists the following as characteristics of the discourse community (24–27):

1. A discourse community has a broadly agreed set of common public goals.

2. A discourse community has mechanisms of intercommunication among its members.

3. A discourse community uses its participatory mechanisms primarily to provide information and feedback.

4. A discourse community utilizes and hence possesses one or more genres in the communicative furtherance of its aims.

5. In addition to owning genres, a discourse community has acquired some specific lexis.

6. A discourse community has a threshold level of members with a suitable degree of content and discoursal expertise.

The definition broadly identifies some of the mechanisms necessary to ensure channels of communication between members as they work collaboratively on common interests. But such definitions have a bias toward cohesion and harmony. They don't consider sources of internal tension in the community. They also have a bias toward a post-hoc orientation, perceiving the communities after they have been formed rather than considering the processes by which they come to be constituted. Although Swales is prepared to note in the last point that there are experts and novices within the community, he is looking at this only in terms of the apprenticeship of newcomers. Whether this division can also lead to conflict within the community needs to be addressed. Furthermore, how are the "threshold level" of membership and hierarchical positions decided? The dominant members would work out mechanisms and conventions to keep others in the margins or simply outside the group. In fact, what constitutes "relevant" knowledge, register, genres, conventions, and terminology for the community may be periodically redefined to provide an advantage to the experts. The distinction between experts and novices then can give rise to conflict and struggle.

Such forms of tension need not be dysfunctional to the discourse community. It is after all through the process of debate and consensus that discourse communities construct new knowledge, constantly revising their knowledge/ideological paradigms and moving toward deeper (or at least additional) levels of specialization. Questions arising from the limitations in existing paradigms generate opposition to the status quo. Debate ensues when members holding vested interests in the existing paradigm resist change. But the force of the questions and the persuasive strength of the critics (newcomers?) lead to the revision of the dominant framework and a change in the status quo. Such conflicts contribute to the sophistication and dynamism of knowledge construction as the new paradigms better reflect the changing experiences and interests of the community. A community without such creative tension will ossify and die (Bruffee 1983).

What additionally contributes to intracommunity tensions is the fact that members often enjoy affiliation in different discourse communities and engage in diverse interests. In interacting within one community, members bring with them the influences and interests they carry over from other multiple affiliations (Wenger 1998). This influence thus brings alternative perspectives that have oppositional potential. The Academic Forum at UJ, for example, comprises members with other regional, religious, and political interests in the larger speech community. It is not difficult to imagine ways in which the members of these other interest groups can have points of commonality that bring them together in the Academic Forum. But there are also sources of conflict in the values of the different communities. It is possible to imagine ways in which the discourses in these other communities can generate oppositional perspectives on the activity of the Academic Forum (as exemplified in the event discussed above). Therefore the intracommunity implications of members' intercommunity relations needs to be theorized in more depth.

To some extent, such tensions have been noted by scholars in rhetoric and composition (Faigley 1985; Bizzell 1992). But there is sometimes the limitation that their models contain these conflicts within a harmonious, unified community structure. Generally, these structuralist-influenced definitions of discourse community accommodate conflict within an overriding unity. Joseph Harris (1989) is correct to observe that the very label "community" is inappropriate for discursive interaction because it connotes an idyllic coexistence of parties with different interests, with the result that the full implications of conflict are ignored. A structuralist orientation also overlooks the historical life of communities—that is, how they are formed, build up, break, and diversify. Furthermore, the ways in which the discourse and activities of these communities relate to their material life is insufficiently theorized. I will, therefore, proceed to *materialize* and *historicize* discourse communities in greater depth to develop an orientation suitable to exploring the geopolitics of knowledge production in this book.

First, we need to understand the struggle between communities for hegemony. Because discourse communities are interested in expanding their sphere of influence by spreading their paradigms, they desire that new discourses be constructed only according to their own terms and conditions. For example, in a very broad sense, physicists from different countries or speech communities may belong to a single disciplinary community. But in order to preserve their vested interests, the members of Community A will attempt to suppress the status of Communities B and C. On the one hand, Community A needs Communities B and C to be connected to itself. This is because Community A would like its rivals to function in a subsidiary or dependent role. It is the fact that there are other groups that share its discourse that provides power and validity to Community A. This provides a wider currency to its discourse. But on the other hand, mechanisms have to be worked out to control the other groups—

both to contain their production of separate discourses and to restrict their material/political strength. Foucault's (1972) definition of "fraternities of discourse" captures the paradoxical generative and repressive functions of discourse communities quite well: "[Their] function is to preserve or to reproduce discourse, but in order that it should circulate within a closed community, according to strict regulations, without those in possession being dispossessed by this distribution" (225).

The hegemony of discourse communities results partly from their interest in material resources and influence. In fact, material resources are important for the knowledge-producing activity of disciplinary communities. Even such everyday functions as travel, equipment, conferences, and publishing require money. A disciplinary community that can draw from a robust economic infrastructure will certainly prosper in its activity. The dominance of the discourse of this community over the knowledge constructs of other communities will in turn contribute to its expanding material resources. Thus the knowledge produced ensures the material advantage of the community. To let any and every community generate knowledge is to lose this monopoly on economic resources. Often, therefore, the legitimation and dissemination of the discourse are aimed at preserving the material interests of that community. After all, as Bourdieu (1977) reminds us, linguistic and cultural capital plays no small role in the control of economic capital.

An insightful orientation to the material motivations of discourse communities is developed by Knorr-Cetina (1981) in *The Manufacture of Knowledge.* She labels the broad context in which academic communities engage in their work as *variable transscientific fields,* which she defines as "the locus of a perceived struggle for the imposition, expansion and monopolisation of what are best called *resource-relationships*" (83; emphasis in original). Disciplinary groups therefore struggle to turn everything into a resource of symbolic and material use in the competition for monopoly. The scholar him- or herself as well as the knowledge constructed can become a resource in a protracted process of appropriating everything for material purposes. If the new findings produced by the research are widely accepted, the scholar will earn more grants for research, hold patents on the products manufactured by using the findings, and finally gain more status in the academic world (as reflected in increased salary and promotions). The scholar's symbolic power (marked by his or her titles and designations) will in turn help to earn more grants and material resources to expand her research.

This competition is conceived in dynamic terms as cutting across ranks and statuses in the discourse community: while the supervisor may attempt to exploit the services of the research assistant to build his or her own reputation, the student will exploit the name of the supervisor when searching for employment. Furthermore, this competition for resources is *"a continuous and generally reciprocal accomplishment"* (Knorr-Cetina 1981, 86; emphasis in original). Unlike a relationship in which discrete products are exchanged at a specified value at a given time, resource relationships are dominated by what could happen in the future as well as what happened in the past, and by anticipated profits rather than a concrete flow of goods. Since what *counts* as a resource is itself at stake, scientists take care to build the value of their product in an ongoing manner. For this reason, scientists must be actively engaged in *building, solidifying,* and *expanding* resource relationships.

In the above orientation, note how the status of the intellectual product is defined by the ongoing involvement of the community in orchestrating its cumulative intellectual resources. This grounds knowledge construction in historical context. Similarly, the discourse community doesn't exist in a timeless vacuum. Its rules and activities in the past contribute to its present strength and future power. The specific relations, discourses, and practices characterizing its past activity contribute to its present ideological character. For example, the struggle for interpreting the *pundit's* life at UJ is motivated by competing intellectual traditions and changing social movements. Situating evolving discourses in the larger contexts of institutional, economic, and political histories will reveal much about the strategies taken by the community in achieving (or trying to achieve) its hegemony.

In a paradoxical way, therefore, disciplinary groups are communities based on conflict. Their "unity" is based on their shared antagonism deriving from the common desire to dominate material and intellectual resources. Not only is there ever-present conflict between communities, but there is conflict within the "community." Rather than focusing on shared common characteristics like language, values, knowledge, or genres of literacy for the constitution of the discourse community, we should focus on an open-ended and dynamically changing circle of scholars who have to respond constantly to the conflicts shaping their activity from within and outside their circle. This perspective thus brings into focus the manner in which the practices of these communities are shaped by the contingencies of changing relationships and resources. Discourse communities have to therefore live always with indeterminacy, heterogeneity, and conflict. Knorr-Cetina (1981) theorizes that the indeterminacy behind such a conceptualization of cognitive and social concerns is the driving force of knowledge production: "The issue is not to deplore the existence of indeterminacy, but to see it as constitutive for the increase of knowledge, as defined by an increase in contextually relevant complexity and variety" (91). Ways of controlling this intellectual indeterminacy will be motivated by the need to exercise control over resource relationships. Thus conflict enables knowledge construction. This is a complex explanation of the material motivations behind the activity of discourse communities.[10]

Paul Prior (1998) is therefore right to argue that we should think of discourse communities as organized in terms of activity rather than discourses. It is not common values or discourses but engagement in a focused activity that brings members together. This also makes the community open-ended, unlike the self-contained models of structuralist orientations. Subjects holding different values, purposes, and identities may temporarily come together in a discourse community to practice certain focused activities to further their interests. This perspective also draws attention to knowledge creation as a practice, and not one emanating from an object (e.g., a common core of language, discourse, or values). Discourse is a by-product, not the rationale, of the activity. Community activity (especially of knowledge creation through literate practices) is constantly reshaped in terms of tensions with other communities, institutions, and persons and changes in artifacts, practices, and resources. Calling this a "sociohistoric perspective," Prior situates the practices of disciplinary communities in historical and material context, making them thoroughly open to these influences.

For the purposes of this book, then, the notion of the discourse community is being used with the following understanding: discourse communities practice institutionalized genres of language that embody concomitant forms of knowledge and ideology; there is perpetual tension in the discourses of these communities, with established discourses being challenged and new discourses struggling for dominance; the community comprises privileged subjects and resisting/aspiring subjects with competing claims of knowledge; the discourse community is shaped by forms of conflict with other communities as much as by the focused activity unifying its own members; while certain communities can be interlinked or subsume one another, there is conflict between others; the power of the discourse community depends considerably on the way in which it draws from a solid material base and contributes to its further expansion; the character and functioning of the discourse community are shaped by its history of cumulative, ongoing struggles in knowledge production; such conflicts, contingencies, and interests are the engines of new knowledge/discourse creation.[11]

The explorations into the politics of publishing in this book will enable us to understand how discourse-community relations are instantiated in a focused domain of interaction. Publishing is but one of the many domains of academic life and intellectual activity where members from different communities come into conflict, collaboration, and negotiation. In the more intense forms of this interaction, members of different communities vie for page space within the covers of the same journal of a specific discipline. To orientate to this engagement, I will adopt the *contact zone perspective* proposed by Mary Louise Pratt (1991). The contact zone perspective enables us to envision educational domains as "social spaces where cultures meet, clash, and grapple with each other, often in contexts of highly asymmetrical relations of power, such as colonialism, slavery, or their aftermaths as they are lived out in many parts of the world today" (Pratt 1991, 34). Although such contact can be painful and damaging, as there is power inequality in these zones, it can also be productive. There are many alternate literate practices and genres of communication fashioned in these contexts by the marginalized to resist or renegotiate their unequal status and the denigration of their knowledge. New knowledge creation also results from the clash of competing interests, which can enlighten both the dominated and the dominating. We will treat academic publishing as a contact zone activity where discourse communities struggle for power and resources even as they engage in the shared enterprise of constructing knowledge in their respective disciplines.

In describing the UJ scholars as constituting a discourse community, I will look at them as a relatively independent body, characterized by certain values and practices, shaped partly in response to their unequal relationship with center disciplinary communities in the contact zones of academic interaction. Periphery communities can be described according to their intracommunity activities and practices—still keeping in mind that they are constantly being shaped by tensions with rival groups and changes in resources and discourses. Thus throughout the book I will also examine the many coping strategies and negotiating practices local scholars develop in their potentially creative and productive engagement with mainstream/center scholars. Some of the texts, genres, and discourses produced out of their interaction with other communities have the possibility of resisting and transforming geopolitical inequalities—even though they arise out of experiences of domination.

The Geopolitics of Disciplinary Communities

The adversarial/conflictual model of discourse communities developed above can help us consider many complex issues in the unequal relations between center and periphery academic communities in publishing and knowledge production. In what ways do academic communities in the center profit from and contribute to the material base of the larger communities they are situated in? In what ways does the history of colonialism and imperialism shape the past and present activity of the center and periphery academic communities? How are the discourses of center academic communities reproduced through the activity of periphery academic communities? Through what mechanisms are periphery disciplinary communities both integrated with and separated from the discourses and practices of the related center disciplinary communities? What are the various forms of disadvantage periphery scholars face in negotiating resource relationships in knowledge construction? Before exploring these questions in the following chapters, it is useful here to observe certain sites of conflict that scholars have already studied to reveal the transnational relations of discourse communities. I will paint the picture of these relations in broad strokes here, leaving the exploration of microsocial levels of academic conflict (especially in text construction) for later. Needless to say, the picture of geopolitics that emerges here is one of domination by the center; I will present subtle strategies of resistance from the periphery in later chapters.

The influences of imperialistic interests in knowledge production have been well exposed in the field of anthropology (Asad 1973; Hymes 1969).

We now know of the abortive efforts in the 1960s to tempt social scientists with grants in return for research that would help Latin American counterinsurgency operations (named Project Camelot). The charge in 1970 that ethnographic research in northern Thailand was employed in counterinsurgency efforts against communist groups in Indochina (referred to commonly as the Thai Affair) is a second case (Marcus and Fischer 1986, 35). Frances Saunders's (1999) *Cultural Cold War* draws together recently declassified documents to narrate the secret campaign in which some of the most vocal exponents of intellectual freedom in the West became instruments of the CIA as they channeled money, organized conferences, founded magazines, and mounted exhibitions around the world to spread the dominant American ideology. The post–cold war recruitment drive by the CIA for scholars with advanced degrees and "backgrounds in Central Eurasian, East Asian and Middle Eastern languages" is another blatant example of center scholars made to serve military/intelligence purposes (Weiner 1997). These are cases that show that the complicity of academics with the political interests of the center is not imaginary. When the funds and resources provided to these scholars help them to conduct supposedly disinterested research, such knowledge is materially and politically motivated.

This is in addition to the fact that the knowledge produced on native ways in remote villages helps Western marketing, media, and technology interests to develop products that are culturally and economically advantageous to them (Hess 1995). In many of these cases, funding and scholarship by even nongovernmental organizations in the West have had an important role to play. It is inevitable that funding agencies focus on the priorities of their communities, facilitating their own agendas through these projects. Similarly, scholarships given to Third World scholars can be shaped unwittingly by the disciplinary areas of interest in the center (Moravcsik 1985).

Less direct are the ways in which colonial political and historical realities have shaped the representation of knowledge relating to what the West has called the Orient. Edward Said (1978) has initiated an exploration into how this representation by the scholarly communities of the Enlightenment West constituted a discourse suited to their interests and values. This knowledge production paralleled the colonial intervention in these periphery communities—an intervention that enabled, aided, informed, and thus actively shaped this discourse. The West's political and military presence in the East provided these scholars a foothold for their scholarly activity in the first place. The knowledge they produced directly or indirectly helped the imperial agencies gain strategic insight into the practices of the indigenous communities for more effective rule. Even when the representation of the East is supposed to be complimentary, it is subtly distorted by the discourses of the West. For instance, dichotomies such as nature/civilization, myth/reason, and religion/science, used to explain the differences between the "Orient" and the "Occident," respectively, result from the dominant Enlightenment discourses of the time and affirm the civilized and superior status of the West. The orientalists may not always have been conscious of the ways in which their knowledge production was influenced by the needs and interests of imperial rule. Material and political contexts shaped the discourse in subtle and unconscious ways.

More surprisingly, even supposedly radical contemporary disciplinary schools—like feminism—have not been free of complicity with the material and political hegemony of center communities. Feminist scholars of color have recently critiqued the knowledge produced by center feminists about periphery women. Chandra Talpade Mohanty (1988), reviewing recent scholarly publications in the center, argues that supposedly positive images of Third World women, which are expected to counter the previous denigration of them as an oppressed group, are still one-sided and stereotypical. Images like those of the veiled woman, the powerful mother, the chaste virgin, and the obedient wife reduce the complexity of Third World women while propping up the sophistication of center women. In the very act of representing periphery women (defining, coding, and analyzing them) the agency and power of Western authors are realized. Periphery women are turned into objects of Western discourses who cannot speak for themselves. Mohanty argues that this act of scholarly representation is another way in which center/periphery relations are maintained. Ironically, even progressive academic discourses generated in the center are contaminated by questionable interests and influences and may have hegemonic consequences. This raises the paradoxical possibility that the very paradigm of multiculturalism, fashionable today in Western academic circles, cannot free itself from center ideological concerns—and may in fact serve center interests.

I wish to discuss at more length my own field of ELT, which is often treated as a pragmatic pedagogical activity of imparting value-free grammar to non-native speakers. The picture I offer of center/periphery relations in this field is based on available research and personal observation. How the theorization and professionalization of ELT have been shaped by past colonial and present neocolonial conditions has been documented by Pennycook (1994) and Phillipson (1992). During the colonial period, language teaching served the purpose of creating a native intelligentsia that would be faithful to the colonial administrators. Some of these educated locals made up the cadre of bureaucrats, who mediated the relationship between the colonists and natives. Such political functions and practices lie at the root of the instrumental and formalistic discourses dominating ELT and applied linguistics today. Phillipson interprets the later activities of agencies like the British Council and the Asia Foundation (which have had major roles in the growth of ELT) as motivated by cold war propaganda purposes. It was realized that, in the absence of direct political involvement after decolonization, language was a powerful ideological weapon to achieve similar colonial ends. Thereafter, Western academic institutions, cultural agencies, commercial enterprises, and government organizations have had a vested interest in adopting a narrowly apolitical, technocratic, and universalistic definition of language and teaching. The foundational discourses of this disciplinary community have thus been shaped by the ideological and material interests of the center.

If material motivations have historically shaped the discourses of ELT, its disciplinary practices have also helped boost the material resources of the profession. The assumption that their work is universal in relevance has led center-based ELT institutions to conduct language teaching according to the pedagogical practices and theoretical constructs available in the center, while ignoring the linguistic/educational/cultural traditions of periphery communities (Canagarajah 1999). This universalist discourse in the discipline has served the center interests well. Textbooks and materials produced according to center teaching conditions can be marketed in periphery communities without the need to suit periphery conditions (Canagarajah 1993a). A cadre of teachers from the center can travel all over the world to practice their expertise gained at home with little consideration of the needs of local communities. Teachers from the periphery are trained according to the pedagogical assumptions and constructs of the center (Govardhan, Nayar, and Sheorey 1999). Center expertise and knowledge are employed to influence language policy in other educational contexts through the consultants and agencies that visit communities far and wide (Holliday 1994). These practices boost the dominance of center-based ELT circles, expand their resources, and disseminate their preferred discourses globally. But the advantages go beyond the center professional circles. At a wider community level, we can imagine how these activities can help the center economically by generating foreign employment, the marketing of published material, and the development of trained personnel. More significant are the ideological advantages of professionals and texts from the center gaining access to periphery communities and spreading their dominant discourses.

The discourse of ELT gets reproduced in satellite disciplinary communities in the periphery through some interesting mechanisms. Though about 80 percent of the world's English language teachers are members of periphery communities, their professionalization and expertise are heavily dependent on the center (Widdowson 1994). There is a one-sided flow of discourses from the center to the periphery. With few material resources to carry out independent research or to disseminate local knowledge abroad, the expertise of the periphery applied-linguistics communities remains marginalized. Phillipson (1992, 223–67) catalogues the many practices of the center that limit the production of alternate knowledge based on periphery conditions. Funds are provided for sharing expertise, conducting teacher training, and developing textbooks but not for undertaking research work (especially by periphery scholars) in local contexts. Thus there is a marginalization of knowledge about periphery educational and cultural realities that could disturb the hegemony of the center. On the other hand, the resources that the center applied-linguistics community enjoys for conducting research and publications on the periphery enable it to arrogate the task of defining discourses to itself. In fact, center professionals often enjoy the privilege of theorizing the pedagogical realities of the periphery according to their preestablished frameworks and thus translate local experience to suit their interests.[12] The assumption that the periphery cannot research and theorize its own subjects and experiences, as it doesn't have the necessary technical know-how, is deeply ingrained in center scholarly circles. Moreover, trained in center institutions, selected foreign teachers get inducted into the center's discourses and spread them in their own communities. The paradigms of the periphery ELT community are then a derived discourse—not one that is manufactured according to its own needs in the local community. This creates tensions within periphery ELT circles. They are often torn between upholding center discourses in theory but conducting their practice according to local traditions and cultures. The periphery ELT circle thus turns out to be a hybrid community that is characterized by subtle tensions and disjunctures in relation to the patterns of the center (as I will illustrate in chapter 6). This can lead to its further marginalization and even greater inferiority in disciplinary status, as its inconsistencies can be treated as examples of novice status in the dominant discourses. (However, this partial integration into the "parent" disciplinary community and hybrid tendencies in the disciplinary discourse are not necessarily limiting; they have the *potential* for resistance and independent knowledge construction, as I will argue in chapter 8.)

What emerges from this macrosocial perspective on the disciplinary community of ELT is the following: it is largely center-based and supported in its enterprise by other institutions and agencies of the center; it is implicated in political and economic processes having a bearing on the larger geopolitical domination of the center; the material and ideological interests of the larger speech community influence the activities of the disciplinary community; the historical roots of ELT in the colonial experience have implications for the disciplinary discourses; and conflict with periphery disciplinary communities is managed in such a way that there is an exclusion of knowledge and discourses that can disturb the material and political interests tied to the "parent" community. The relationship between center and periphery should be explored in other disciplinary communities in the academy to discern the subtle mechanisms and processes by which geopolitical domination takes place.

Conclusion

Let us now return to the Academic Forum at UJ to situate the local drama enacted there in the wider geopolitical processes of knowledge construction. It is in the context of hegemony that we can explain why scientific positivism enjoys such prestige and value here despite the diverse local epistemological traditions that struggle for legitimacy. Ironically, at a time when there are emergent postmodern movements of critique against Enlightenment thinking in the West, it is the periphery that appears to give new life to the positivistic paradigm. If the periphery disciplinary communities are one step behind the intellectual fashions in the center, this too is advantageous to the Western scholarly communities. It ensures that the periphery will always be dependent on the intellectual developments of the center. The tensions within the periphery communities, torn uncertainly between different paradigms, lead to the instability of these communities. Their inconsistencies themselves can be used by the center to claim that their scholarship is half-baked, immature, or suspect. Only the periphery communities that are critically conscious will use these hybrid discourses as a resource—rather than a problem—to tap the benefits of the contact zone. They will creatively fashion their own intellectual paradigms rather than waiting for scholarly fashions to arrive belatedly from the center or seeking acceptance from the center.

If the geopolitical inequalities in knowledge production are recognized, the next step is to analyze the ways in which practices of academic literacy and publishing play an important role in reproducing this state of affairs. Though some of the periphery scholars discussed above (like Said and Mohanty) have helped develop an insightful critique of the interested nature of knowledge and disciplinary discourses, they do not consider the way in which publishing/writing practices are implicated in this process. The contention of this book is that academic literacy plays an important role in the inequalities of knowledge construction. Since research publications bear a gatekeeping role in establishing and disseminating knowledge, those who have access to this forum have an advantage in the knowledge-production industry. In fact, knowledge production is achieved through the production of texts. Since periphery communities have different conventions of text construction, do not enjoy the resources that enable participation in academic publishing, or practice an academic culture that devalues writing and publishing, they are disadvantaged. We must therefore turn now to issues related to academic literacy: What is the nature of literacy in center academic communities? What are the dominant conventions of academic writing and communication? What are the material and historical motivations for these conventions? How are periphery communities situated in relation to the literate cultures and practices of the center?

3. Conventions in Knowledge Construction

In every society the production of discourse is at once controlled, selected, organized and redistributed according to a certain number of procedures, whose role is to avert its powers and its dangers, to cope with chance events, to evade its ponderous, awesome materiality.—Michel Foucault, "The Discourse on Language"

Although the author of the paper on Panditamani adopts the position that an empirical approach assures an undistorted/direct access to reality, there are many conventions that mediate his presentation. In claiming greater accuracy and objectivity for his own depiction of the *pundit*'s life, the author overlooks the values brought in by the communicative conventions shaping his presentation.

Consider the conventions involved in getting to present this paper in the Academic Forum in the first place. Not everybody can call a meeting of the forum to give their lecture at any time they want. The scholar has to indicate his interest to the dean of the faculty. The dean constitutes the one-man committee that decides on the value of the presentation and the date and venue for the meeting. Before calling for a meeting, the dean takes responsibility for typing and Xeroxing the complete text of the presentation, nominates a moderator for the meeting, and distributes the paper to all the full-time faculty members. Though the dean generally accommodates a request to present (especially if it comes from a scholar of some standing in the community), there are times when the faculty feels that the presentation is unworthy of the forum. There was one recent occasion when a learned scholar from outside the university was permitted to make a presentation. Since his approach was influenced by traditional

religious discourses, a few faculty members were displeased. There was a
move by some faculty members after this to make the dean screen and
limit the presenters more rigorously. I will consider such regulations governing issues of access in knowledge construction (i.e., institutional procedures regulating who gets to present a paper, where, and how) in chapter 6.

Another dimension of discourse conventions relates to the interactions
constituting the literacy event. The meeting of the Academic Forum proceeds in the following fashion: the moderator first introduces the author
and reminds the audience of the rules of interaction; the author then gives
a brief preface to the paper, summarizing its main findings or objectives;
the discussion thereafter is based on each successive page of the paper. The
conventions of interaction are as follows: the moderator announces the
page of the paper that will be discussed and solicits questions from the audience; those interested indicate their intention by raising their hands; the
moderator assigns turns for each commentator; the moderator may disal-
low certain questions that may be construed as inappropriate; the author
answers the questions one by one. Trying to relate issues discussed on a
particular page to other sections in a nonlinear fashion is disallowed. Such
questions are construed as violating the rules of interaction established for
this forum.

Turning to the text now, there are particular conventions here too that
mark the Academic Forum as a distinct community. Though a range of
discourses is possible, depending on the purpose of the author, the paper
on Panditamani is written in a largely narrative structure. While there is an
introduction that reminds the audience of the prevailing scholarship on
the *pundit* and a conclusion that sums up his significance for the community, these sections are not written argumentatively to confront the views
of other scholars or schools. The central part of the paper adopts a chrono-
logical sequence in following the life and works of the *pundit*. The development is episodic, with considerable authorial involvement in the presentation of the subject. Such a text is different from the more analytical
and discipline-centered texts of other communities. Much of the polemic
and analysis in the forum occurs in the oral interactions occasioned by the
text, not in the paper itself.

The conventions I have described above are not written down anywhere; they are the unwritten rules of knowledge construction in the

Academic Forum. These are appropriately labeled conventions rather than rules or regulations, since they mostly develop informally and unconsciously through the process of continued social interaction. (This is not to deny that there are ad hoc impositions of rules in certain specialized academic circles.) Since conventions occupy an important place in the life of disciplinary communities, we have to understand their functions and constitution. Note first that these conventions are not just matters of text construction. They also relate to social interactions and institutional regulations. The textual conventions have implications for how interactions take place in the construction of knowledge. (For example, the episodic structuring of the text is amenable to the page-by-page discussion of the text in the forum proceedings.) The textual conventions are similarly influenced by the wider social values and cultural practices in the community. The peculiar narrative structuring of the text described above may be influenced by the preferred values and communicative practices in an orality-dominant community. A narrative, episodic, involved structuration facilitates easier understanding in face-to-face delivery, typical of oral interactions.

We also see that these conventions are matters not just of form but of content. According to traditional definitions, conventions are related to the form of texts, which are considered limited to the surface or outer shell that embodies the content. But as we know now, the medium is also the message. Conventions may shape the content in subtle and indirect ways. See, for example, that in this academic community accounting for the greatness of a charismatic savant qualifies as scientific research (recalling from the last chapter that the presenter claimed this status for his paper). There are conventions like this about what is acceptable subject matter and what can be said about a particular subject in a specific disciplinary circle. Moreover, the convention of discussing one page at a time in a sequential flow constrains the content in interesting ways. Because of this convention, the inconsistencies and conflicts the audience perceives between one section and another are disallowed. This makes possible a compartmentalized perspective on the *pundit*. The writer can get away with a representation that makes the *pundit* unique in each endeavor he undertook, without having to analyze his overall achievements or compare the relative strength of each. Similarly, the narrative flow and the suppression of explicit argumentation facilitate a perspective that is grounded fully in the local context, enabling a eulogistic presentation of the savant's charisma in the community. A different set of conventions (such as those that exist in refereed journals in the center) would have led to a different representation of the *pundit*.

What gives validity to the knowledge constructed is the community that stands behind its conventions. Conventions are peculiar to each community in line with its cultural practices and intellectual traditions, strongly influenced of course by its material and social history. Anyone wishing to participate in the life of the community has to adopt those conventions. So it is interesting that the nonacademic scholars from outside who are participating in the forum are adopting its conventions, though they may find them strange and even disagree with them. Even to challenge the legitimacy of the knowledge constructed on the *pundit,* they still have to employ (in this context) the conventions of the forum. They thus give life to these conventions. These conventions are therefore constitutive and definitive of the knowledge-making community. Not only do they help regulate the life of the community, but they also serve to define its very identity and existence. There is a circular and interdependent relationship here: communities construct conventions; conventions maintain the community. Every time these conventions are used, the community reproduces itself.

If there is such a vested interest in upholding the conventions, how is change possible? There are ways for the dominant groups to still be in control of the community, while accommodating changes in the conventions. In fact, the dominant circles can themselves change the conventions so that newcomers who have mastered the old conventions will again be at a disadvantage. There are of course other reasons why conventions change. Since there is a close connection between discourse and culture, changes in the social and cultural conditions of the community can lead to changes in the conventions. This is not to rule out the fact that changes in discourse can also lead to changes in the way the community is structured. The conventions of the Academic Forum were showing signs of changes at the end of my stay at UJ. For example, the professor who delivered the paper on the *pundit* wrote another paper on the status of bilingualism in the community (Suseendirarajah 1992). In this case, however, he chose to circulate it for reading among the faculty members and invited feedback/comments in writing. It was difficult to understand the reasons for the deviation from the usual practice. From the hints he gives in his brief preface, it appears that he wanted to limit the discussion to only those "interested" in this subject. Therefore, the paper was distributed only to the full-time faculty, and to a select few at that. We can see in this move an attempt to limit participation in knowledge construction. It is possible that the author found the increasing presence of the nonacademic audience and their unceremonious challenges a little too bothersome. But this deviation from the usual practice created considerable criticism from the junior faculty (some of whom had been left out of this discussion). We thus see how this attempted change of conventions is implicated in conflict and domination.

While scholars influenced by a positivistic orientation would deny that conventions play any significant role in the construction of knowledge, this chapter will demonstrate their importance. While such scholars would argue that the dominant conventions are the most logical or self-evidently appropriate for academic writing, we will explore their relative status in different communities and cultures. While they would insist that conventions are merely pragmatic tools for communication, we will unravel their ideological import. Such an exploration will help us appreciate the differences in the writing practices of periphery scholars and the inappropriateness of being judged according to center-based conventions.

Functions of Conventions

In order for interpersonal relations and communication to be conducted effectively it is necessary for members of the community to make a coordinated effort to adopt mutually agreeable procedures.[1] There is a well-articulated philosophical orientation that understands conventions as representing regularized solutions to commonly occurring coordination problems (Lewis 1969; Grice 1975). There should be mutual knowledge and reflexive awareness of these rules if the conventions are to be functional. The emphasis in this orientation is on the notion of conventions as a mechanism for harmonious relations. The model assumes goal-oriented, rational subjects bent on finding pragmatic means for achieving their ends. Consider the elaborate process of refereeing a paper for publication. The editor functions as an independent channel to refer the paper to two or three readers. Their anonymous response gives the editor an indication of the acceptability of the paper. The procedure is supposed to eliminate any biases in the decision-making process. The awareness that their identities are hidden gives the reviewers the confidence to express their evaluations frankly. The author is similarly expected to satisfy the reviewers, however prestigious the former's status may be in the eyes of the editor. Mutual knowledge of the conventions helps all three parties—writer, editor, and reviewers—to calculate their moves accordingly in order to arrive at potentially controversial and anxiety-causing decisions about publishability with equanimity and efficiency.[2]

Another perspective on conventions, the cognitive orientation, focuses on processing/production economy. From this perspective, the ready-made frames for genres of communication facilitate interaction by referencing the norms and practices that govern a particular communicative event. This cognitive orientation has been articulated forcibly by schema theorists—including those in the psycholinguistic and discourse-analytical traditions—who show how the scripts we hold in our minds tap the knowledge demanded in respective communicative situations (de Beaugrande and Dressler 1981). The fact that we have finite cognitive resources to employ for processing and producing information gives significance to the conventions that make thought and communication more manageable. Consider the way in which the well-established IMRD (Introduction/Method/Results/Discussion) structure of experimental articles facilitates reading and writing. This textual convention enables us to selectively focus on a specific part of the paper with expectations as to what we will find there, so that we can move between sections in a nonlinear way to seek the types of information we desire (Bazerman 1988). We can provide greater or less emphasis to the sections, according to our needs. In addition to being *schema-maintaining,* conventions can also function in *schema-enabling* ways (Gumperz 1982a; Bollinger 1964). That is, conventions can function as an indexing (or cueing) system that can activate other higher-level or parallel conventions and bring into play the required schema for that situation. Consider how a specific move in the introductory section of a paper can create an expectation of the related sequence of moves, as articulated by Swales's (1990) "creating a research space" (CARS) model. For example, step 3 in move 1—reviewing items of previous research—will create an expectation of the next move, establishing a niche, and the final move, occupying a niche.[3]

While the above functions are merely *regulative* of discourse, we must note that conventions also *constitute* discourse. This function points to the propositional dimension of conventions. Discourse conventions, from this point of view, assume specific ways of perceiving and representing reality. The conventions of each discourse community then become a record of the unique ways in which it orientates to social and material life. In this sense, conventions are semiotic systems. According to the poststructuralist perspective (which sometimes exaggerates the issue by making it too deterministic) it is not we who speak, but the discourse conventions that speak through us (Harland 1987). Implicit in this view is the notion that discourse conventions are not merely tools of communication; they are ways of thinking. It can be asserted that all knowledge making calls for conventions. The accepted rules, frameworks, and values function as a grid or as spectacles to make sense of life and phenomena. Conventions may then reconstruct our experience in significant ways, as we use them in reading or writing a paper. The requirement in the IMRD structure that the paper should move from methodology to data to interpretation assumes an inductive, empirical, and presumably positivistic orientation to doing research. The convention assumes that data and interpretation can be kept separate—a questionable notion according to many post-Enlightenment orientations to knowledge. Such values are actively brought into play as we read or write a paper employing the IMRD structure.

We are approaching here the ideological functions of discourse conventions. Consider what will happen to research that begins with the assumption that the scholar's theoretical background influences him or her to select specific types of data for analysis. In order to find publication in a journal that insists on the IMRD structure the scholar has to forcibly reconstruct the whole research experience according to the empirical way of representing research. Bazerman (1988) provides a similar example of articles in psychology, which continue to be written according to conventions popularized by the behaviorist school. As long as these conventions—stipulated by the APA style manual—continue to be used to construct academic papers, they counteract the newer paradigms of psychological analysis. Suppressing the emergent humanistic and holistic approaches, these conventions reproduce a positivistic and impersonal orientation to psychological life. Conventions are therefore not neutral, passive, pragmatic tools of thinking and talking. They come loaded with partisan social values and orientations to power. In this sense conventions not only enable thought but also suppress thought. Foucault (1972) draws attention to this suppressive function of conventions when he argues that "in every society the production of discourse is at once controlled, selected, organized and redistributed according to a certain number of procedures, whose role is to avert its powers and its dangers, to cope with chance events, to evade its ponderous, awesome materiality" (216).

Scholars who insist on communicating their alternative orientations to knowledge and invent newer conventions to represent their thinking may find their papers rejected by established journals. It is from this angle that we realize that conventions may not only create cohesion and solidarity within groups but also cause exclusion from them. Sharing certain sets of conventions is a way for community members to enjoy in-group membership, guard their knowledge, and keep those who do not control the conventions away from their material and social advantages. If anyone wants to lay a claim to these advantages then they have to first display these conventions and patterns of thought. It is for this reason that crossing discourse communities becomes a highly charged affair. We are asking new members to not only adopt these conventions but also conform to the related ways of understanding life. Adopting the alternate conventions leads the new members to accommodate the hegemony of the new discourse community. Furthermore, though conventions may be freely available to everyone, there are subtleties in the ways they are used. New members will be discriminated against for their unconfident or "accented" ways of using these conventions. Therefore they will always be marked as outsiders and provided marginal status in the community. If too many outsiders should master the conventions and use them fluently, there is always the option for the insiders of changing the rules of the game and adopting new conventions of communication.

Conventions are then a necessary evil. While we need them for conducting thought and communication, they enable us to do so only in a partial and partisan way. In the area of written communication then, textual conventions will have all these paradoxical possibilities. They are not just passive frameworks for channeling preconstructed knowledge but active mechanisms for imposing desired ways of thinking. They are not only ways of achieving textual coherence but instruments for filtering knowledge. They are not only rules of achieving harmonious communication but methods of gatekeeping. They are not just the medium but the message. This orientation to conventions has many implications for the geopolitics of academic writing and knowledge production. To ask periphery writers to conform to the textual conventions of center journals simply because this is the accepted mode of writing is to ask for much more than that. In adopting these conventions there is the possibility that the knowledge they wish to represent will be distorted, suppressed, or perhaps appropriated according to the terms set by the center. Their own voices and ethos are likely to be suppressed as they adopt a mode of communicating that is safe and comfortable for the center. In fact, as we all know, rigidly holding on to preestablished conventions is unhealthy to any community—whether in the center or the periphery. We should therefore adopt a paradoxical attitude of resisting conventions even as we communicate with them. We should creatively manipulate them for our needs and purposes. I will discuss later (in chapter 8) how we can take the dominant conventions of a community seriously while also subverting them for our purposes.

Contextualizing Writing Conventions

I wish to consider here how the dominant conventions in English academic writing arose in relation to specific social, cultural, and material conditions in the center communities. This discussion on the processes by which conventions are constructed and reformulated will enable us to realize the functional/pragmatic nature of writing conventions, as they are shaped by the contexts and purposes of their respective communicative situations. Conventions are, in effect, relative, variable, flexible, and contingent. This realization will perhaps help correct the aura conventions have of being universal, immutable, and natural. This is sometimes the assumption that motivates scholars as they conform unquestioningly to the dominant disciplinary conventions. Referees and editors also display a normative attitude in the way in which they treat the dominant publication conventions as sacrosanct. Matters are made worse by the fact that conventions are not self-evident and, therefore, don't invite critical reflection. Contextualizing conventions will impress upon us the need to accommodate diverse modes of academic communication according to changing conditions.

The contingent nature of conventions is not often recognized by the literate communities in the center because they have a long tradition of orientating to academic texts as autonomous—in other words, as physical objects that can stand free of the context and the writer to speak by themselves. This attitude of *autonomous textuality* is widely considered to have been developed by the Royal Society of London, as an extension of the literate tradition of classical culture (Atkinson 1999; Geisler 1994). In a sense, Greek literate culture culminated in seventeenth-century England with the essayistic genre treated as the norm for scholarly communication. The orientation to meaning as explicit and free-standing in the text found favorable soil in the contemporary positivistic ideology that treated scientific knowledge as universal, objective, and free of influences from the subject or the context. Geisler (1994) calls this assumption "the *myth* of autonomous texts" because writing and knowledge are in fact considerably shaped by their material and social contexts. That meaning is not influenced by textual conventions and that texts are not influenced by contextual forces are themselves cultural assumptions that are taken for granted by the center-based communities. This myth is ideological, as it promotes the textual representation of scholarly findings to unsuspecting audiences as value-free, self-evident, and unmediated.

We will revisit here some key moments in the development of the conventions of research writing in the center to understand their socially constructed nature. According to Shapin (1984), an important landmark in the development of many of the textual conventions practiced in the academy today is the seventeenth-century Royal Society of London, the first modern scientific society. Robert Boyle, a leading member of the society, promoted the experimental approach through his development of a suitable mode of written report. Boyle's writing conventions enabled him to cope with the material and social constraints he faced in legitimizing his approach to knowledge. The methodological accounts of research papers first gained considerable significance as Boyle had to enact the practice of *communal witnessing* of research. According to this practice, gentlemen of high standing in society signed their names attesting to the results observed at the end of an experiment. Boyle had to textually reconstruct the research context by describing in detail the expensive and delicate air pump that he had put together painstakingly for his experimental purposes. Since others couldn't be expected to construct the same mechanism, the writer had to give detailed information on the way that instrument was put together and the ways in which it functioned in the experiment. Through the methodology section, Boyle attempted to simulate the research process and facilitate a "virtual witnessing" for others in the scientific community.

Another strategy employed by Boyle to make his findings decisive amidst challenges by others is his matter-of-fact, categorical, self-evident discourse, which gives the impression of nature speaking for itself without human mediation. This matter-of-factness was calculated to silence debate and legitimize his findings at a time when no discernible disciplinary tradition had developed in science. In fact, the Royal Society was struggling to establish its authority at this time as the legitimate forum of knowledge construction. Boyle was especially concerned that ad hominem arguments (of the sort conducted by the rival scholastics of the time) should be avoided. The unwarranted confidence and quarrelsomeness characterizing the ethos of late scholasticism were what appeared inimical to empirical scientists. Therefore Boyle drew attention to the *object* of research through his unvarnished, concrete style of writing. Boyle thus invented a style that attempted to transcend debate and conflict—a rhetoric that paradoxically appeared free of any rhetorical influence.

Dwight Atkinson (1996)—who samples articles from the *Philosophical Transactions of the Royal Society (PT)* from 1675 to 1975 to show the multiple factors motivating rhetorical change through a period of three centuries—provides additional explanations for this disinterested rhetoric. He argues that this scholarly ethos was initially considerably influenced by the genteel form of life that was culturally dominant at that time in Europe. Atkinson (1996) states: "Early modern scientists and their apologists traded on this conventional social image of the gentleman for rhetorical purposes. In so doing, they hoped to gain for themselves its special claims to authority, disinterestedness, and moral rectitude—a borrowing all the more natural since most of these scientists were in fact gentlemen" (362). According to this perspective, we can infer that there was also a class motivation for this style of writing. In order to legitimize their knowledge, the dominant scientific circles tapped the cultural values of the elite social circles of that time.

In fact, a significant genre of writing of this period that died later was the report of research findings in the form of a letter to the editor of the *PT.* Since letter writing was considered a cultured activity suitable for discoursing on profound moral and philosophical matters, research writing too gained the same effect by cashing in on this genre. In effect, the article was a written version of genteel conversation. The use of second-person address in this genre contributes to a personal/direct style of writing in the RAs of this period. Compared to later scholarly discourse, Atkinson finds in the RAs of this period a more involved, author-centered rhetoric, manifested through the preponderant use of first- and second-person pronouns, expressions of affect, stance markers (such as hedges and possibility modals), and active-voice verbs. The first-person references and action verbs in this writing derive from the humility and modesty that the writer wants to construct in order to develop the gentlemanly ethos. They also put the author at the center of the events recounted. Interestingly, then, some of the important conventions of scientific writing were actively borrowed from the cultural ethos, communicative modes, and social practices dominant in the European community of this time.

When the social circumstances changed, with changes in the composition of the scholarly community, the strategies used by Boyle and his peers became somewhat ineffectual. New social conditions called for the development of alternate conventions (although, as Atkinson [1990] shows, the textual changes were gradual, often showing traces of previous discourses). Consider, for example, the impact of changes in material resources. As the production of experimental instruments became cheaper and research procedures became more standardized, it was not necessary to indulge in an extended narrative in the methodology section to enact the process of research. Therefore, methodology sections became very brief. A mere mention of the instrument's name or the type of procedure was sufficient to simulate the experiment for the reader. Similarly, with the development of a more structured tradition of disciplinary knowledge as we approach the present, different rhetorical strategies were required to legitimize research. It is now more important to situate research in the conceptual niches left in the discipline and engage with current knowledge to win acceptance for findings.

Atkinson (1996) attributes the gradual break from the genteel ethos to the development of a more organized and less individualistic empirical approach, as reflected in the more abstract and impersonal reporting conventions from the beginning of the nineteenth century. A pronounced change to an objective discourse is reflected in the increased appearance of passivizations and of nonanimate natural objects or phenomena as grammatical subjects or informational-structural topics in later RAs. The increased importance given to methods, controlled experimentation, and replication of previous research explains this rhetorical change. Contrary to expectations, however, impersonal writing is not motivated by empiricist/positivistic philosophies alone. Even this rhetoric is inscribed in social and cultural practices of the European society of this time. Atkinson (1996) places this development in the movement for democratic reform and social mobility, against the dominance of genteel society. Disciplined methods of inquiry and research became the new criteria for scholarly validation, diminishing the place of birth and breeding. These rhetorical changes were also motivated by changes in the academic community, to some extent. As scholars studying geology and astronomy broke away from the Royal Society to form their own disciplinary organizations, they ushered in the development of specialist journals and a heightened sense of disciplinary autonomy. With the "disciplining" of science into separate specialties, analysis was conducted in terms of well-defined research problems, in a somewhat more depersonalized manner.

The subsequent rhetorical change, involving a depreciation of impersonal methods sections and an emphasis on theoretical discourse, has been dated and explained variously. Researchers have identified this change as beginning around 1890 (Atkinson 1996), 1920 (Bazerman 1984), or 1944 (Berkenkotter and Huckin 1995). Atkinson ruminates on the possibility that a strong reaction against Darwinian research and the increasing standardization of research procedures could have partly caused this phenomenon. But the emergent anti-Enlightenment thinking that would culminate later in postmodernist research paradigms should also be noted in explaining this rhetorical change. Disenchantment with positivistic analytical approaches, new sensitivity to the problems of interpretation, a reflexive attitude toward the subjectivity of the researcher, and alertness to the philosophical/ideological baggage that comes with any research approach—these have all contributed to the emergent rhetoric of RAs. Even these philosophical changes are situated in social conflict. The questioning of positivistic approaches was considerably generated by minority community groups (e.g., environmentalists, women, traditional communities, periphery scholars) who experienced the suppression of their cultures and interests under the impersonal march of science (Hess 1995; Nandy 1990).

Having traced these past changes, it is important to realize that the RA is by no means a settled genre currently (if it has ever been at all). The story of RAs doesn't lead to a greater rhetorical uniformity; there is still a lot of splintering and diversification in academic culture. This then is not a narrative about a progression toward a superior and stable set of conventions; changes in social conditions still generate ongoing changes in RA conventions. An indication of this diversity is the phenomenal rise of newer disciplinary fields. Each discipline—and sometimes each specialized circle within each discipline—begins to practice its own variant of RAs. The level of professionalization of the circle and its evolving disciplinary tradition play an important role in the status and structure of RAs. Charles Bazerman (1984) and John Swales (1990) have conducted diachronic analyses of the RA in the twentieth century—the former in a major journal in experimental physics and the latter in a major journal in applied linguistics—to show how the evolving disciplinary discourse has impacted RA conventions.

Bazerman's (1984) survey of spectroscopic articles in the *Physical Review,* from its founding in 1893 to 1980, brings out many changes in the use of citations. In the early phase, though references were quite common (averaging about ten per article) they were rather general, relating broadly to the subject of the papers. By 1910, the number of references had been curtailed, and the few that were present were all recent and directly relevant to the research. In more recent articles, references have increased in number while maintaining their specificity of relevance. Also, citations are not restricted to the introductory section but distributed throughout the text so that every stage of the discussion relates to the relevant existing research. These changes are explained by the fact that there is a growing body of new research and by the fact that the findings are getting embedded into a well-integrated disciplinary tradition.

Bazerman's further observations in this article on the changes in syntactic and lexical features of spectroscopic RAs point as well to their growing rhetorical complexity. As relative clauses decline in frequency and noun clauses and subordinate clauses become more frequent, one gets the impression of a shift from description to explanation. Subjects of main clauses have become more abstract, as concrete subjects have given way to nouns of process or quality (such as *ionization* and *correlation*). Such changes show an advance in conceptualizing and theorizing the findings in the field. Nonverbal material also shows concomitant changes. The number of apparatus drawings and the number and size of tables decrease, while the amount and complexity of graphs and equations increase. In terms of organization, before 1950 only 50 percent of the articles were formally divided into titled sections, but after 1950 section headings become a regular feature. Moreover, until 1930 articles ended with a results section; in the articles after that date, discussion and conclusion sections become important and often follow the presentation of results. The latter sections have also increased in length and complexity, while methods and apparatus sections have declined. Such changes in the text structure accompany the increasing sophistication and disciplinary specialization of the scholarly community. They indicate an attempt to formalize the available stock of research information into generalized concepts and also to integrate emerging studies into a more unified framework. There is also an intensification of polemical stance, as the status of each new piece of research has to be established in relation to the existing findings. Needless to say, the greater effort at interpretive work contributes to the expansion of the discussion sections in the papers.

There are similar motivations for the development of the RA genre in applied linguistics, even though its academic culture and written discourse are different from those of physics. Swales's (1990) analysis of the first twenty years of the *TESOL Quarterly* shows how the RAs in ELT/applied linguistics reflect the evolving tradition of knowledge in the field. He observes the following developments:

- an increase in nontextual material (principally tables);
- an increase in references (from four in 1968 to thirty-four in 1986);
- a decline in the citation of books (especially textbooks) and an increase in the citation of articles;
- an increase in subsectioning of articles, coauthorship, and use of statistics;
- an increase in citing articles previously published in the very same journal.

These changes manifest a growing self-consciousness and professionalization among scholars of that discipline. To some extent then, regardless of differences in the disciplinary cultures of the fields concerned, RAs undergo a logic of development based on the level of professionalization in the discipline. These are *discipline-internal* motivations for rhetorical change, different from the *extra-academic* (i.e., social and material) motivations we considered earlier.

As knowledge production continues and new subdisciplines are formed, the newer disciplinary communities will invent writing strategies suitable to their needs and purposes. A more recent example of scholars reconstructing conventions suitable for their purposes comes from Danette Paul (1996). She illustrates how scholars promoting chaos theory wrote their initial articles in the 1980s to introduce their revolutionary ideas into scientific discourse. These writers used standard rhetorical moves in novel ways, and/or invented unusual moves, to create a context for their work. Although later articles conformed to standard rhetorical moves, once the discipline became more established, the earliest articles, which launched chaos theory, are the most successful in terms of reception by the scientific community despite their unconventional rhetoric.

A discourse strategy popular among the early writers on chaos theory was to make an *exemplar move*—that is, scientists used a classical equation of Newtonian physics to reveal chaotic behavior. Such equations and figures were used as exemplars central to the argument, both making the argument persuasive and functioning as a research site. This strategy provides unity to all the articles in this genre. In terms of the convention of embedding the current research in existing disciplinary discourse, Paul finds that the earliest writers worked hard to develop such a context for their novel ideas. They devoted more space and effort to the opening moves designed to catch the readers' attention and create a context for the new work. This strategy faded somewhat in the middle period, when the field had attracted sufficient attention and recognition. As a school forms a formidable community of its own, scholars attempt to draw diverse publications together and embed their specific study into the evolving literature in the discipline. In terms of space devoted to old information, the more established the audience, the less space devoted to creating a context by reminding readers of previous work and findings. But the effort and space given to introductions (and old information) peaked again in the third period, when younger scholars in diverse fields attempted to establish their work in terms of the previous developments in chaos theory. This renewed interest was motivated by the fact that chaos theory had become interdisciplinary, and writers had to remind each new audience they were addressing of initial developments. Paul's study thus provides another example of how the contexts and purposes of knowledge creation shape the changing conventions of the RA.

The diachronic orientation to RAs that I have reviewed here serves to deconstruct research-writing conventions. The inevitability or indispensability that accompanies the genres of writing enforced by dominant journals is thereby demythologized. We are made to realize that RA conventions are context bound. They are shaped by a variety of contingent factors. Some are discipline-internal factors: the state of professionalization, the status of the discipline, and the identity of the scholars in the field. Others are extra-academic: the availability of material resources, dominant cultural values in the community, and patterns of social relations in the larger society. More importantly, we find that these conventions are implicated in social conflict. Not only do certain conventions gain importance "naturally" because they belong to dominant social groups, but in some cases these are calculated to establish the knowledge of the dominant circles over others. We see how textual conventions played a role in the thrust for scholarly power by the members of the Royal Society over scholastics and by postmodernists over Enlightenment scholars.

There are many serious implications here for center-periphery relations in academic publishing. The dominant RA conventions should not be enforced without regard to the time, place, and purposes that shaped them. Conventions that have a unique tradition of development in a specific community cannot be sanctioned as the normative/universal form of writing for all communities. Center editors and reviewers who reject periphery papers based on these conventions are at best unwittingly fetishizing these genres or, at worst, colonizing others with their community's rhetorical and intellectual traditions. Conventions tend to take on a life and logic and validity of their own, and their spread throughout all communities serves to reproduce the values of the center and sponsor its global hegemony. Center editors who denigrate the peculiar conventions adopted in periphery RAs should ask what contextual features influence the writing of periphery scholars. Ironically, as I will demonstrate in the next chapter, many of the rhetorical strategies employed by periphery scholars are motivated by the same problems encountered by center scholars during the formative stages of their own disciplines—in other words, a lack of universal familiarity with expensive research instruments, being weakly integrated into the disciplinary community, or embarking on areas of research that don't have an established discourse or tradition in the field. The realization that the dominant conventions of the RA have been changing through history in response to differing imperatives should enable center scholars to be more understanding of the atypical conventions adopted by periphery scholars. Center scholars should be open to the possibility that conventions may continue to change, as they have already done many times before in history. They should be prepared to accommodate a plurality of rhetorics if a more inclusive platform is to be created for international knowledge creation.

Modalities in Knowledge Production

As we know, communities provide different statuses to orality and literacy in their communicative life, even though they are complexly interconnected in actual text production (Heath 1983; Tannen 1982; Olson and Torrance 1991). These differences bring different sets of values and conventions related to constructing knowledge. As we can see in the vignette at the opening of chapter 2, the paper on Panditamani is only a springboard for oral construction of knowledge on the subject. It is the oral interaction that holds primacy for this academic community. Therefore, while the Academic Forum functions similarly to other orality-dominant events like seminars and colloquia in contemporary academic communities in many ways, the literacy event brings into play a different set of rhetorical values and analytical orientations. As we saw, the construction of knowledge on the subject also takes routes strange to those in the center.

We must be careful, however, not to think that the orality-dominant practices of the Academic Forum display no logical reasoning processes. It has been widely claimed by cultural historians that the breakthrough to literacy from orality marks the shift to objective inquiry and thought processes that lie at the heart of modern science (see, e.g., Olson 1991). Before exploring the material and geopolitical implications of this dichotomy, we must recognize the biases involved in this hypothesis. First, orality and literacy don't *entail* any particular thought processes or social practices; they simply operate differently in different contexts. Orality-dominant communities display their own forms of metacognitive and rational discourses that form their intellectual tradition (Denny 1991; Feldman 1991). The everyday discourse of oral communities also has a logic of its own—which literate communities often find difficult to understand.

Sociolinguists have compared the preferred forms of coherence in text and talk in oral and literate communities to explain the differences (Michaels and Collins 1984; Kochman 1981; Tannen 1982). While the style of communication in each community has its own logic and validity, it is a fact of human history that literate ways of communicating and thinking dominate the modern urban/technocratic world order. This dominance has been enabled in part by the greater cultural and material resources held by center communities (Hess 1995; Huff 1993). The power difference cannot be blamed, therefore, on any inherent inferiority in oral communication itself or in the thought processes of oral communities.

The relativistic position on the equality of oral and literate practices shouldn't lead to a denial of the real advantages offered by literacy in modern life. Literate styles of communication are forms of cultural capital that help individuals succeed in the technological world today. The advantages of the relative portability, displacement, and permanence of written products provide literate communities a communicative possibility across generations—transcending time and space—that is of immense power. The ways in which printing transformed social life provide examples of the powers of literacy. While developing mass literacy, printing also developed a sense of community that went beyond the narrow boundaries of isolated societies. Benedict Anderson (1984) has noted the ways in which printing developed a sense of *nation* among scattered individuals. Many have started theorizing how the computer culture and the information superhighway have similarly served to construct "imagined communities" that transcend time and space (Warschauer 2000). Virtual reality and life in cyberspace offer communicative possibilities that are alien to many communities that lack the advantages of technology and literate culture (Murray 2000; Luke 2000).

The problem for periphery communities is not that they cannot cultivate literate modes of communicating (perhaps with some effort). But they don't have the material resources to develop these *uses* of literacy, nor do they have the desire to do so. In a sense, there are no purely oral communities today. Nearly everyone has a script and a tradition of literate communication. (It is for this reason that I am using relative terms like *orality-dominant* and *literacy-dominant* when I refer to these communities.) However, literacy is technology. The very use of pen and paper—or quilt and parchment—involves considerable technical capabilities of production. It is in this sense that literacy belongs to the haves. It is not a demo-cratic medium of communication. Consider how much material resources and economic and technological infrastructure is required to set up and own even primitive forms of printing presses. (There are not many of these in the periphery.) More resources than this are required to partici-pate in the computer revolution. So the global village that the information highway is supposed to construct is still far from realization. We see divi-sions and fissures that make the much-touted global oneness questionable. There is a big gap between the center and the periphery—even between the majority and minority groups in the center—in the possession and use of computers. According to one estimate, "In January 1995, nearly 98% of Internet hosts were located in the United States, Western Europe, Canada, Australia, and Japan. The presence on the Internet of much of Africa, Asia, and Latin America is nonexistent" (Faigley 1997, 39; see also Murray 2000 for related statistics). Though some periphery countries like India are con-nected to the Internet and display a remarkably sophisticated digital cul-ture today, these resources are not widely available to local people.

Moreover, such inequalities are perpetuated in the digital world itself. Doheny-Farina (1996) argues that while cyberspace unifies people at a certain level, the community developed is at best very selective. In fact, the language of cyberspace is to a large extent still English and related Western discourses. The symbols, codes, and conventions employed to conduct this communication are largely borrowed from the culture of the dominant communities (Selfe and Selfe 1994; Luke 2000). Cyberspace is therefore unequally stratified and is by no means a democratic space as has been claimed in the first flush of the computer revolution.

The more serious point is that even if computers are provided for every household in the periphery by a generous center donor (perhaps Bill Gates?), orality-dominant communities may not use them according to the ways of the center. For example, though the Tamil community, like other South Asian and Far Eastern groups, possesses a script and texts from two thousand years back, the uses to which it puts this literacy are differ-ent. Since oral forms of communication and thinking are still dominant, literacy is simply subservient to orality here. As I will illustrate in chapter 6, writing is used to record and preserve the more important oral texts. Sometimes writing is an aide-mémoire for oral interactions. Furthermore, literacy is practiced in ways analogous to oral modes of communication.

Narasimhan (1991) shows that the more dynamic collocation of symbols in spatial and spatio-temporal terms (as characteristic of many multimedia, gestalt, or postmodern ways of communicating today) is not cultivated or desired in many periphery communities. Texts are encoded and decoded in temporal sequence, much in the manner oral communication works. It is in these more subtle ways that the possibilities afforded by mass literacy and the computer revolution will still be most marked by inequality.

Literacy in Academia

In later chapters we will consider the literate practices of periphery academic communities and the implications these have for their participation in knowledge construction. But it is important to first remind ourselves of the way literacy functions in center academic communities.

The most important means by which academic communities conduct business is writing (Brodkey 1987). Scholars interact with each other primarily through print. In fact, they interact more often through written texts than through the oral medium. This is partly because a scholar's writing is accorded more authority and significance than his or her spoken word. Unless a scholar publishes his or her research or thinking, the work gains no recognition. The reference point for a scholar's status, value, and contribution is the written form of his or her work. Much of this may derive from the ideology of autonomous texts, discussed earlier, according to which the record of knowledge in written form is considered authentic and valid. The screening procedures adopted before knowledge gains textual form also contribute to its legitimacy and authority. The importance of writing in academia derives from the fact that the written version of knowledge is available across time and space for verification by the wider community of scientists. Thus a culture based on literate interactions and practices is treated by many scholars as the defining feature of academic life in the center (see, e.g., Brodkey 1987).

In fact, in many research institutions the production of texts takes precedence over other forms of material production. Latour and Woolgar (1979), in their observations at the Salk Institute, California, found that much more significant than the synthetic substances produced by the work of a lab is the writing generated there. In fact, the synthetics produced are not sold. More important for the scientists are the papers that can be produced through the observations resulting from the substances.

Furthermore, oral communication in the institute takes a secondary or subsidiary place to written activity. It is understandable that "almost without exception, every discussion and brief exchange observed in the laboratory centered around one or more items in the published literature" (1979, 52). There were other indirect manifestations of the importance of writing for the research center. Reams of observation reports and research records had to be written and read daily by all members. These were then developed into articles to be sent out to journals and books, providing access to other scholars. The lab was thus a site of text production, even though its overt purpose was the production of chemicals. As Latour and Woolgar (1979) observe, for these scientists, texts were not *papers* but *products* (49).

Writing organizes the work of scientists in many other ways. Rymer (1988) shows, through the ethnography of a professor of biochemistry at work, that writing a collaborative research paper was how he knew what everyone in the lab was doing on a daily basis. The writing project led by the professor helped organize and manage the work of the research team as its members went about their different tasks related to the research. The evolving text in fact marked for them the different stages of their ongoing research activity. Even if the members rarely had time to interact on a face-to-face, one-on-one level, the text provided a good forum for interaction. It thus helped focus the interaction between the members. Writing also helped the professor evaluate the work of his graduate students. He wrote his periodic evaluation reports based on how the students contributed to the evolving written document. This example suggests the way in which the RA constructs the roles, identity, and status of the individual scientists at work, transcending the mere bounds of the text. Writing both enables and controls social interaction during knowledge production. To a large extent then, the social organization of the lab and its research activity are constructed by the research paper. To put it provocatively, it is not the lab that produces the text but the text that produces the lab.

Such possibilities of literacy go beyond the domains of a research institute or lab. Freed from the need for face-to-face interaction, the members of the scholarly community can interact with each other across vast spans of space and time. It is quite possible for scholars who have never met each other to still consider themselves acquainted through the experience of reading each other's writing. We have all had the experience of forming an image of a scholar through his or her writing. We also develop a conception of the scholar's status in relation to the others in the scholarly circle in terms of his or her body of texts. We even grow into certain forms of relationship—as opponents or allies or collaborators—through the medium of print even if we have never met each other face to face. Needless to say, these identities, statuses, and relationships are sometimes "staged" in strategic ways in texts to favor our scholarly interests.[4]

We have to keep in mind that such social processes involved in writing influence knowledge construction. It is now acknowledged that writing does not come after the fact of research to merely record what transpired. In many cases, the paper comes before and along with the research (Myers 1990). For example, scholars often have their eyes set on the type of paper they will produce for a publication before getting started on their research. The RA will considerably shape the research experience. As the scholars write their paper, or plan the outlines of one, their research gets reconstructed/transformed according to this rhetorical context. For example, the need to disseminate findings through a specific journal would motivate writers to highlight or downplay certain aspects of their research to suit the dominant conventions, interests, scholarship, and styles preferred by that audience.

That the conventions and contexts of writing mediate scholarly knowledge in complex ways is now well articulated in ethnographies of science. For example, Gilbert and Mulkay (1984), analyzing how a controversy in biochemistry is discussed by its leading protagonists, find some interesting tensions between the personal and published positions of the authors. They find that the empiricist discourse that characterizes the public writing of the scholars masks the "contingent rhetoric" that they are prepared to discuss in personal interviews. While their research writing follows an impersonal discourse that represents findings as natural and inevitable, in personal discussions they "presented their actions and beliefs as heavily dependent on speculative insights, prior intellectual commitments, personal characteristics, indescribable skills, social ties and group membership" (Gilbert and Mulkay 1984, 56). These scholars are not lying in these papers. They are simply presenting the knowledge according to the appropriate conventions governing the public presentation of their findings. One account is not more true or real than the other. In fact, the "personal" position is equally mediated by other contingencies.

There are more dramatic tensions between the activity of research and the representation of it in writing. In a microanalysis of the various stages of evolution of a paper produced in a research center in Berkeley, Knorr-Cetina (1981) discovers how an incidental finding in the research gets written about as if it were the conscious and central research focus all along. The scientists report as if they were exploring precisely this particular problem when they designed the research in the first place. Many of us are familiar with this predicament. This writing strategy is justified on the grounds that the genre conventions of research writing have a problem-solution structure that demands that a finding be presented in this fashion. But there are further transformations that take place in subsequent revisions. Writers include more hedges in their syntax and tone down the triumphalist claims of their conclusions in deference to the opinions and reactions of the disciplinary community. In fact, studies by Dubois (1986) and Fahnestock (1986) show how the same research finding will be represented differently based on whether it is presented in a research journal or a popular magazine. In popular articles, there is a use of ordinary language, reduction of careful qualifications, and a desire to capture human interest. As a consequence, the research findings get represented as convincing facts of certainty, rather than as merely tentative or hypothetical. It is clear therefore that rhetorical, linguistic, and genre conventions of writing are not simply matters of textual form; they considerably shape the representation of knowledge.

Conclusion

We might summarize the implications of the above discussion for contemporary practices of academic knowledge construction in three simple (but provocative) propositions.

Knowledge is writing.
Knowledge is conventional.
Knowledge is contingent.

In fact, the first proposition explains the other two. The centrality of written representations of knowledge contributes in no small measure to the ways in which knowledge is shaped by genre conventions and other contextual contingencies. It is this orientation to knowledge that invites an understanding of the center/periphery differences in knowledge production. The ways in which the social and cultural contexts of these different communities enter into the production of knowledge now begin to assume importance. Similarly, the different orientations to literacy and publishing gain significance in the knowledge-producing activity of these communities. Insisting on knowledge as value-free, transcendental, and universalist, or treating academic discourse conventions as mere matters of form, or asserting the autonomy of texts to represent knowledge free of contextual and subjective influences—these are all ways of suppressing a clear understanding of center/periphery inequalities in knowledge production.

In order to pursue the theme of geopolitical inequalities in knowledge production, we will explore the following questions in the coming chapters.

What precise role does writing play in the academic cultures of periphery communities?

What other modes of knowledge production and dissemination are practiced in these communities?

How are the conventions of academic communication in periphery disciplinary communities different from those of center communities?

What discursive and communicative challenges do periphery academics face in adopting the textual conventions of the center?

In what ways do periphery experience and knowledge get reconstructed in the framework of center textual conventions?

4. Textual Conventions in Conflict

> One can take a pencil and trace lexical reiteration, pronoun reference, and other devices by which texts point back and forth and usually in at themselves. But tracing such structural patterns in language-on-its-own is like coming upon a scene of a party after it is over and everybody has gone home, being left to imagine from the remnants what the party must have been like.
> —Deborah Brandt, *Literacy as Involvement*

Raj knew that he had to finish writing the paper soon. When he first discovered the ways in which languages were alternated by local people to redefine their roles and relationships, he thought he had stumbled upon an original insight. He assumed that his social-constructionist perspective would challenge the dominant correlationist treatment of codeswitching. But since writing the introduction to his paper four months back, he had heard of at least three new books that had come out in North America developing a similar perspective.[1] He was now getting despondent, worrying that after all the hard work he was going to put into writing this paper, it might very well be rejected by mainstream sociolinguistic journals for being "old news" in the West.

The reasons why he hadn't written for four months were not lethargy or procrastination. When he fled from his village as the army marched in, he had accidentally left behind the sheaf of paper on which he was writing. From the cramped room in his cousin's house, where he was now staying with his wife and infant daughter, he had made many unsuccessful attempts to start working on the paper. But he could never write more than a few lines without being distracted. He had to search for food for his family in the daytime. He was particularly anxious about running out of milk for his infant daughter, as it was in short supply in the area. To make matters worse, the university staff had not been paid their salaries for some months now, as the government had restricted the flow of cash into regions where there was fighting. So even though he was still teaching, he had to give private tuition to students in the neighborhood in order to earn money. Apart from all this, the continuing power cut in the region prevented him from writing after dark. His intermittent work on the paper prevented him from developing his thoughts coherently, causing him to constantly revise the outline and goals he had set for himself in this writing project.

When his university closed for Christmas two months later, Raj made another more sustained attempt to work on the paper. Since he had lost the outline and notes he had written initially, he tried to reconstruct the paper from memory. Raj realized that it was necessary for him to write the introduction all over again, as he had now obtained some information about the new books on codeswitching. But he had merely read about these publications in a book review in the pages of a journal that a friend had managed to Xerox for him from the only American Center library in the country, located in the far-off capital city. Though he hoped to situate his research in relation to new knowledge in the discipline, he didn't have sufficient information to do this confidently. Perhaps he could pretend that he had read the books themselves. How could he cite the book review as his only source of the knowledge represented in the books? And what if the referees challenged him to engage more closely with the books in his discussion? Finally he decided to begin the paper with a brief announcement of what he was trying to do in this study, leaving out any citation of publications.

As he developed the paper, he realized that there were new points he could make on codeswitches he had observed. Perhaps because he had lost his original outline, or because of the long interval since he had conducted his study, he had gained fresh insights into his data. Thinking that these were the disguised blessings of working in an unstable environment, he decided that he would incorporate these new perspectives into his discussion as he went along. Although he planned on providing a sound summary of the evolving argument in the paper's concluding paragraph, he had a nagging suspicion that he wasn't giving enough clues for his readers to follow his line of thinking. But he justified his writing strategy by rationalizing that it was the reader's responsibility to participate in his intellectual journey. For this reason, he also ruled out the possibility of starting all over to adopt a more coherent approach that anticipated all his arguments.

Furthermore, stationery was in short supply. It was with some difficulty that he had managed to get writing paper from his office in the university (usually supplies are restricted to urgent institutional purposes). Getting more paper for another draft was out of the question. Even more difficult would be finding the time for another round of revisions. His inclination was to get his handwritten manuscript typed immediately by the department secretary (which would itself take a few weeks) and mail the paper soon. It would take yet another three months for the paper to reach the editor in the United States by mail. But it was with a huge sigh of relief that he reread his script once more and made some changes in vocabulary and syntax on the text itself before he turned it in for typing.

The Writing Scene

That was how I composed a paper that was published in the journal *Multilingua* in 1995 (Canagarajah 1995d). I find it more comfortable to narrate my experience with some detachment in the third person— through the fictional name "Raj." The paper was published after it was given a thorough revision, having been rejected by the first journal I sent it to. As one can guess from the narration above, the referees commented on the inappropriate lead-in, inadequate awareness of recent research, lack of coherence, lack of a unified focus, and sloppy editing.

The reason I find this composing experience important is because it is typical of the writing practices undertaken by my colleagues in Sri Lanka. The types of struggles we face in composing papers are missed by the think-aloud protocols constructed in the center to characterize the strategies of skilled and unskilled writers. The reports of the composing processes of many center scholars typically show them mulling over such intricate textual details as the placement of a comma or the choice of a single word for hours in undisturbed tranquility. Rymer's (1988) ethnography of a center scholar's composing strategies shows the intense level of engagement of the writer in the construction of the text. Periphery scholars, on the other hand, have to switch back and forth between pressing concerns of their everyday lives as they compose. Center composition researchers may perceive these distractions as characteristic of the writing processes of unskilled writers. But given the context in which periphery scholars work, this pattern of composing is inevitable. Perhaps some of these findings on skilled/unskilled writers are themselves products of research design. Observing writers in isolated clinical settings, limiting the definition of writing as an interaction between the mind and the text, these "think-aloud" protocols lose a lot of information from the larger social/material context. My approach in this chapter is to widen the writing context so that we can see how the writer has to switch radically between texts and contexts. (Paul Prior [1998] shows through his ethnographic research that such uneven composing processes are found in center scholars too—if we only had the eyes to see them.)

Among the many perspectives emerging from this widened context of writing activities is one focusing on the way in which material conditions influence the text. What have generally been described as characteristics of the composing process of ESL writers can be explained as influences from the context of their writing. Needless to say, descriptions of the composing processes of periphery writers often focus on deficiencies. Consider how Tony Silva (1993) sums up the findings from a large corpus of studies to depict the state of the art on ESL writers. Replete with phrases like "less effective" and "less productive" to describe the composing process of ESL writers, their differences from native writers are characterized in the following way.

"L2 writers did less planning, at the global and local levels" (661).

"L2 writers did less goal setting, global and local, and had more difficulty achieving these goals" (661).

"Organizing generated material in the L2 was more difficult" (661).

"Transcribing in the L2 was more laborious, less fluent, and less productive" (661).

"Pauses were more frequent, longer, and consumed more writing time" (662).

"L2 writers wrote at a slower rate and produced fewer words of written text" (662).

"L2 writing reportedly involved less reviewing" (662).

"There was evidence of less rereading of and reflecting on written texts" (662).

"L2 revision seemed to focus more on grammar" (662).

We must note that Silva is only summarizing current research and not providing an interpretation (though it is difficult to eschew one's own attitudes while writing about research). Silva also doesn't offer explanations for the practices characterizing L2 composing, as he is interested only in showing how it is different from L1 composing and why similar pedagogical or theoretical paradigms cannot be used for both groups of writers. But he does allude to both linguistic and cultural explanations—which are frequently invoked by compositionists to explain such differences. My contention here is that an ignored dimension of explanation—the material factor—should prove useful in understanding the characteristics listed above.[2]

If we consider the opening vignette again, we see how the material context shapes the type of writing practices described by Silva. For example, my plans—global and local—had to be constantly revised as I struggled with the problems of finding cash and food for my family. I had to start afresh each time there was some respite from the fighting. It was also difficult for me to generate and organize reference material because I didn't have complete access in my hometown to the books I needed for my paper. The brief book review I read created more problems than solutions for my writing. We can also understand why my transcribing process was more laborious, time consuming, and intermittent. I simply didn't get uninterrupted stretches of time to engage in writing or to approach my task with a calm and collected mind. Furthermore, the nature of the unsettled political context—which required people to be constantly alert to dangers from the fighting, to flee from the advancing battle zones, and to work in more than one job in order to survive the economic hardships—suggests that for those in the periphery the first draft is often the final product (assuming that we can fully complete even this). Local scholars also inevitably suppress the desire to revise and produce multiple drafts. The difficulties in obtaining writing paper permitted me only to correct the grammar in the first draft. It is possible that these writing strategies, developed under pressure from everyday living conditions, then become habitual. Both readers and writers in the periphery develop cultures of literacy that cope with the conditions existing in their communities.

Interestingly, I adopted the above strategies though I had myself practiced process-oriented strategies of writing (assumed by studies surveyed by Silva) in the United States before coming to Sri Lanka. I had even taught these strategies to students in universities in the United States. But given the working conditions in Sri Lanka, I had to make many uncomfortable adjustments in my writing process. The material condition thus places certain constraints on the writing process. We should of course be open to the possibility that with greater access to material resources the writing strategies of periphery scholars can change. (Back here in the United States now, this is the fourth revision of this chapter, which I word-process with effortless ease in a software program that corrects my grammar and spelling as I go on composing!)

It is from the above perspective that I am sometimes suspicious of culturalist and linguistic explanations for the writing practices of periphery scholars. These two explanations have been the dominant ones given by most scholars discussing the texts of non-English writers. The implication is there in the studies reviewed by Silva that the differences in composing strategies derive from the limited proficiency of the writers in the discourse practices of academic writers; this is a dominant hypothesis employed by researchers in second language acquisition (SLA) and applied linguistics. Contrastive rhetoric, a subfield in applied linguistics, has generated explanations based on the cultural backgrounds of writers (Kaplan 1966; Mauranen 1993a, 1993b; Connor 1996). Kaplan has shifted his position over the years on defining cultural differences in texts as deriving variably from the first language of the writers (1966), from their preferred patterns of thought (1976), or from their forms of socialization (1986). While studies from these perspectives have revealed differences in periphery writing, there are also some problems in the rationale motivating these studies.[3]

Though scholars in these traditions are careful to steer clear of overtly expressed biases, the linguistic explanation smacks of blaming the writers for a deficiency, and the culturalist paradigm benignly ghettoizes them under the guise of tolerating their differences. The attitude can be described as follows: periphery writers compose the way they do because they are still trying to develop proficiency in our language or because they have to make a shift from their culture to ours; we'll permit them to participate in our conversation when they develop the types of proficiency required. In this kind of reasoning, the onus is on the periphery writers; the center cannot be blamed for their exclusion. Under the guise of tolerant understanding, both explanations lead to justifying, or at least excusing, the exclusion of periphery writers from mainstream journals. But if we understand that many of the differences in the written product also result from the material conditions of the respective communities, we can perceive how some of these problems are implicated in geopolitical inequalities. We see above how the poverty, political instability, living conditions, and lack of scholarly support systems—along with other such matters of unequal distribution or access to resources—shape the different practices and outcomes of academic literacy.

This is not to say that the materialist perspective is to be used as the sole explanation in this chapter. It is possible to imagine how cultural practices, linguistic systems, and rhetorical traditions can be considerably influenced by material life. Thus, I wish to keep open other forms of explanation for what contributes to differences in periphery texts. The level of integration into the relevant disciplinary discourses, the peculiarities in epistemological traditions, and the sociolinguistic competence in modes of orality and literacy are other features that have to be taken into consideration in explaining the challenges confronting periphery scholars in writing for professional journals. I must stress, also, that the materialist explanation is not to be applied only to periphery writers. There are material influences in the writing of center scholars as well—in fact, in writing in general.[4] Nor do I want to enforce an environmental determinism here to imply that periphery writers can't negotiate the contextual problems they face for creative expression. Material conditions—even unfavorable ones —don't have to always pressure periphery writers to adopt a rhetoric of failure. In fact, writers develop many creative strategies to negotiate the contextual conditions for their purposes (as I will illustrate at the end of this chapter and later, in the concluding chapter of this book). I myself adopted many coping strategies and alternate discourses in order to publish in mainstream journals in sociolinguistics and applied linguistics from Jaffna.

To describe the textual conventions characterizing periphery academic writing below, I use a wider range of work than is usually found in studies in L2 composition or applied linguistics. Most of the studies in these fields sample the writing of periphery students rather than professionals. These studies also derive the "native discourse" of periphery communities from their writing in English. But this practice ignores the different levels of linguistic mediation involved. The English texts of non-native writers cannot be assumed to reflect their vernacular discourses. But center scholars who lack proficiency in periphery languages can't help but analyze texts written in their own language (i.e., English). The tendency is also there to essentialize writing styles irrespective of the different text types, contexts, and audiences involved (Kubota 1999). Therefore, the collection of texts I consider in the following discussion comes from at least three different contexts—those written in English for publication in mainstream/center journals, those written in English for the local community, and those written in Tamil for local publication. The texts are of different types—for example, those that were published, and those that were rejected; those written for distribution among select readers, and those used as a basis for formal oral presentation; those published as monographs, and those published as journal articles; and those that are different drafts of the same paper. An important point to realize about these writings is that periphery writers do switch discourses in recognition of the context of writing (a point that hasn't come out clearly in composition research that analyzes single texts from single writers). When we closely analyze the reasons for and directions of the switches, we can discover the discourses desired by the writers, the way they perceive the audience in each publishing context, and the constraints existing in the different contexts.

Structure of Research Articles

Before we analyze the articles of periphery scholars, it is necessary to understand how center scholars define the structure of the RA. Swales (1990) describes the genre using (as noted in chapter 3) the acronym IMRD (Introduction/Method/Results/Discussion). Since he claims to derive this structure from empirical research, his formulation enjoys considerable status. As the commonly practiced form of the RA in the academic community today, the model is also used widely to teach periphery/ESL students to compose in academic contexts. Instructors assume that center editors and referees take this structure as their frame of reference when they judge papers for publication. Although there are rhetorical variations in each discipline, the IMRD structure is still useful as a heuristic to understand the generic conventions of academic writing.

The structure and flow of the RA have been likened to the hourglass. The introduction is broad in the generality of concerns it deals with. The author situates his or her study in the overall research tradition and disci-

Table 4.1

Feature	*I*	*M*	*R*	*D*
Movement	outside-in	narrow	narrow	inside-out
Reporting statements	high	very low	low	high
Present tense	high	low	low	high
Past tense	fairly low	very high	very high	fairly low
Passive voice	low	high	variable	variable
Authorial comment	high	very low	very low	high

Adapted from Swales 1990, 137. Reprinted with the permission of Cambridge University Press.

plinary discourse. The methods and results sections then narrow down in the next stages to deal specifically with the author's study. The article broadens again in the discussion section as the implications and significance of the findings are situated in the widest possible context. The first two sections (introduction and method) are then mirror-imaged by the other two sections. Swales formulates his research findings on the linguistic and rhetorical differences between the sections in the manner shown in table 4.1.

Such observations have influenced many scholars to posit that I and D are complex, while M and R are simple. This is of course corroborated by ethnographers of writing who have observed that I and D take more rhetorical effort and time for construction, while M and R are rarely redrafted (Knorr-Cetina 1981).

Of the four sections of the RA, the most research has taken place on introductions. Calling the sequence of claims authors make in order to situate their research in the ongoing scholarly conversation "moves," Swales identifies three broad moves as characterizing this section. His CARS (creating a research space) model for the opening of RAs is formulated as shown in figure 4.1.

Swales goes on to make the strong claim that "the three moves occur at a high frequency in their assigned order" (1990, 145). When such a normative place is given to the structure of the introductory moves, any variations by periphery scholars will raise problematic questions. In fact, when

Swales analyzes an article by an ESL graduate student that fails to display its move 2 before its move 3, Swales considers this as deriving from the ineptitude of the writer and not as a reason to modify his model (1990, 158).

In regard to the methods section, Swales states that there is a tendency for this section to become a checklist of instruments and procedures well established in the discipline. Less effort is taken by the writer to work out textual coherence, and readers are expected to supply the inferences and cohesive links themselves. Swales finds this especially true of the physical sciences, where methodological rigor and appropriateness are taken for granted and research procedures are standardized relatively more than in other disciplines.

The conclusion of the RA is the other section that has featured much

Figure 4.1. CARS Model for a RA introductions

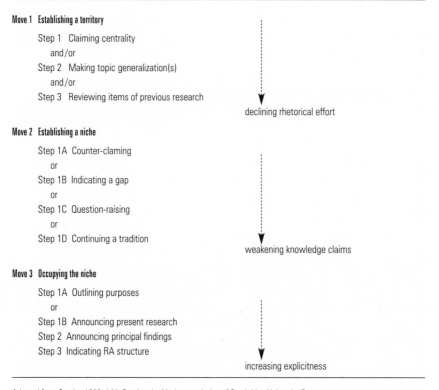

Move 1 Establishing a territory

    Step 1   Claiming centrality
        and/or
    Step 2   Making topic generalization(s)
        and/or
    Step 3   Reviewing items of previous research

                declining rhetorical effort

Move 2 Establishing a niche

    Step 1A Counter-claming
        or
    Step 1B Indicating a gap
        or
    Step 1C Question-raising
        or
    Step 1D Continuing a tradition

                weakening knowledge claims

Move 3 Occupying the niche

    Step 1A Outlining purposes
        or
    Step 1B Announcing present research
    Step 2 Announcing principal findings
    Step 3 Indicating RA structure

                increasing explicitness

Adapted from Swales 1990, 141. Reprinted with the permission of Cambridge University Press.

in genre analysis. Belanger (1982) has suggested that the following three moves occur in invariable order (though it is not necessary that each move appear in each article):

1. A summary of results and statement of conclusions with reference to previous research

2. An examination of what research suggests with reference to previous research and/or to the current work

3. A presentation of further questions, sometimes with possible explanations and sometimes with references

Though Swales and other genre analysts would accept that there is considerable variation in RAs across disciplines and communities in the center itself, the above genre conventions help explain the expectations of center-based reviewers and editors. In fact, a recent set of interviews with mainstream editors on their views of periphery submissions shows these editors using assumptions following these RA conventions to explain the limitations of periphery writers, although they don't explicitly use the labels formulated by Swales (see Flowerdew 2001). Furthermore, the descriptive/empirical research tradition that has generated the RA conventions described above confers an aura of finality and naturalness to this structure, so that its ideological underpinnings are not often understood. In discussing the conventions of the academic texts from the periphery in the following pages, I will not only attempt to understand the different logic motivating local writing practices but also deconstruct the RA structure as it is realized in the center.

Local Textual Conventions

Openings

A striking aspect of local RAs is the seeming lack of rhetorical effort and authorial investment in the introductory section. The opening of such articles appears cursory. What they do have in their brief introductions shows subtle rhetorical variations when we compare them with Swales's typology.[5] Many of the English and Tamil articles written for readership in local journals begin with broad statements of orientation typical of "funnel" openings. Though this could include a topic generalization or, more accurately, a topic announcement (as in Swales's model), the claim of centrality for the article is based more on general intellectual concerns and social relevance. There is little attempt to claim disciplinary centrality for the article.

Moreover, the process of reviewing previous research (move 1/step 3) is rarely undertaken at any depth or length. This of course means that a majority of the papers don't perform the second move of counter-claiming, gap-indicating, question-raising, or tradition-continuing statements in order to establish a disciplinary niche for the article. Swales would also find that the final move of occupying the niche (move 3) is not attempted or, in cases where it is found, is achieved only implicitly. Most papers indicate their purpose and/or announce the present research but rarely present their principal findings, thesis, or the structure of their reasoning. It is significant in this respect that most of the local journals, whether in English or Tamil, don't insist on articles beginning with an abstract (which would compel writers to summarize their findings or theses).

Consider a recent lead article in the locally published *Sri Lanka Journal of South Asian Studies (SLJSAS)* titled "Patterns of Basic Sentences in Tamil and Some Semantic Observations." This is written in English by A. Velupillai, who has doctorates in linguistics from both a local university and the University of Edinburgh and has previously published in international research journals. His first paragraph is set apart by white space from the next, which starts with a subtitle ("Assertive Sentence") to indicate that the writer is embarking on his analysis at this point. The unlabeled introduction is as follows.

> The sentence is a basic unit of language. Grammarians and linguists have defined the sentence in a great variety of ways, the criterion being that it must express a complete thought. There are some constructions, where some parts of [t]he sentence may be missing. They are called utterances. Sentences are of three kinds according to form: taṉi (simple), kuttu (compound) and kalappu (complex). The simple sentences are also called minimal sentences while the other two types are called non-minimal sentences because of their complex nature. Sentences may also be classified according to function as ceyti vakkiyam (affirmative or assertive sentences), eval vakkiyam (imperative sentences), vina vakkiyam (interrogative sentences), etirmarai vakkiyam (negative sentences) and unarcci vakkiyam (exclamatory sentences). The present study is confined to the sentence patterns according to function. Semantic observations here owe much to John Lyons." (Velupillai 1991/1992, 1)

The writer is providing here some basic information that needs to be shared by the readers before they can follow his semantic analysis. This is a classic "funnel" opening that defines the sentence and introduces the main classifications according to form and function, before announcing that the paper deals with functional sentence patterns. The first sentence is a claim of centrality—in other words, if we want to understand language, we have to understand the sentence. Thereafter, until the final two sentences, the paragraph may be considered to be dealing with topic generalizations (move 1/step 2 in the CARS typology). The penultimate sentence is an announcement of present research (move 3/step 1b). The final sentence is difficult to classify. It could be treated as a review of previous research (move 1/step 3)—but it is not done in the sustained manner typical of center articles, and there is only one scholar mentioned. It could be considered a statement of "continuing a tradition" (move 2/step 1d)—but the mention of a single scholar's name cannot be taken to represent a tradition. It is a rather unique move, which I will label a "statement of methodology" (whose functions I will demonstrate later). In fact there is no other statement of methodology, as the author embarks on his analysis in the section following the introduction.

How does this introduction relate to the assumptions of a good opening in the center RA tradition? In move 2 center writers would show the limitations of previous research, which their study attempts to fill. Since there is no literature review of previous relevant research (move 1/step 3) in this paper, the establishment of a niche (move 2) cannot be performed effectively. More significantly, the opening doesn't announce the principal findings (move 3/step 2) or indicate the organization of the paper (move 3/step 3). The missing moves are those that aggressively demonstrate the importance of the paper and assert its place in the disciplinary discourse. For center reviewers, then, the opening of this paper might appear vague, lacking a clear idea of its central argument or a commitment to its worthiness. Swales's model thus enables us to explain the possible dissatisfactions of mainstream reviewers (which I substantiate below with their comments from actual reviews).

We should take into consideration the local context of academic literacy to understand this strategy of the opening. *SLJSAS* caters to scholars from a variety of disciplines in the humanities and social sciences. In the local community, as in many periphery circles, it is difficult to find journals so specialized as to accommodate only scholars from a single discipline. In fact, lacking a publishing forum, scholars often resort to publishing their research in midbrow journals outside the academy. In this context, even an RA has to be oriented to the widest possible audience. The funnel opening works well to lead the general reader gradually into the area of specialization of the writer. We must also understand the "democratic ethos" prevailing in the local academic communities (to be discussed in chapter 6). There is less separation between the academic community and the wider society. Hence the writer attempts to include everyone as the audience for the paper.

In fact, through moves 2 and 3—which establish a niche for the paper by showing the limitations of previous studies and present the findings as filling a need in the disciplinary discourse—the CARS model reveals the extent to which center writers have to "sell" their papers. Not surprisingly, Anna Mauranen (1993b) states that American RAs are informed by a "marketing discourse" calculated to sell the findings to the readership for a variety of symbolic and material rewards. This attitude is no doubt informed also by the "publish or perish" culture in the American academy, where scholars have to compete vigorously to get their papers published in respectable journals. But such motivations do not come into play when local writers publish their work. Thanks to their unique academic culture, local scholars are as good as "tenured" when they are hired. Their promotions depend less on publishing, compared to norms in center academic communities. Furthermore, due to the shortage of outlets for academic publication in the periphery, local scholars don't have to compete for publication. In a sense, RAs don't have to clamor for attention among local readers, as these readers are not inundated with research literature. All this means that RAs can be more relaxed in their opening.

Introductions in center RAs are also informed by a hunger for new knowledge. Moves 2 and 3 insist on the need for each paper to present itself as constructing new knowledge in relation to what has come before. There is an agonistic positioning implied in the CARS model. Though authors show how their papers "continue a tradition," they still have to establish how they challenge/critique/transcend the findings of previous studies. Velupillai could easily make an argument for the originality of his ideas in this paper—it is easy to at least claim that no one has analyzed the semantic potential of the Tamil language in relation to the evolving scholarship in modern linguistics. But he chooses not to. Rather, Velupillai simply carries out his analysis in a matter-of-fact way, ignoring the many claims of originality he could make to "sell" his paper. This rhetorical preference could be explained by the more affirmative stance local scholars adopt toward their intellectual tradition. They would find ways of fitting their own research into the larger tradition, rather than positioning themselves as opposed to previous studies. Velupillai joins the flow of conversation that has been taking place for centuries in Tamil grammar as an equal, rather than claiming superiority or originality over previous scholars. We will discuss further reasons for this lack of polemic in the paper in a later section.

In the few cases where I detected any attempt to "sell" a paper to local readers, it was done in terms of its relevance to ongoing social concerns of the community. This move might even have a functional orientation, implying that the paper could be of practical use for solving problems. The choice between satisfying community concerns and filling a disciplinary niche is dramatized in K. Sivatamby's (1992) "Understanding Jaffna Society: A Preliminary Inquiry into its 'Formation' and 'Dynamics,'" written in Tamil for the local audience. (The English wording of the title is the author's own, published under the Tamil title in the article.) I will translate the introduction of the paper, which is made up of a series of short paragraphs, while annotating the moves and steps according to Swales's typology. (The paragraph endings in the author's text correspond to the division of moves I provide below).

(move 1/step 1) One of the features about Jaffna culture that is always visible but never discussed is a realistic depiction of the society. We don't speak or even attempt to speak about culture, which is always in front of our eyes regulating and controlling our social practices.

(move 1/step 2) Since this silence hampers the healthy development of this society, I am undertaking this analysis to overcome this limitation at least academically.

(move 1/step 2) At a period when our community is facing a serious crisis in its history, when it is undergoing radical changes, it is the duty of the social sciences to at least provide some preliminary thoughts and data on our community's fundamentals and assumptions.

(move 1/step 3) Research ventures relating to Jaffna society from anthropology and sociology are poor indeed. There are only a few foreign scholars working in this field (Bryan Pfaffenberger, Kenneth David, Skjonberg). Tamil scholars who have earned international prestige in these disciplines—like S. J. Tambiah—themselves do not give full attention to anthropological and social scientific research relating to the concerns of Tamil Eelam people.

(Move 1/step 1b) In a situation like this, doing research on the nature of the changes taking place in this society is the duty of academics at the University of Jaffna.

("Statement of methodology") I have been drawn to this subject from the experience of reviewing the tradition of Tamil literature from the disciplinary perspectives of social history, sociology, and anthropology. This article is being written from that academic background. (Sivatamby 1992, 2–3)

This introduction is a bit different from Velupillai's, as it cites certain previous studies relating to the writer's research. However, there is no sustained engagement with these studies to make a strong second move (i.e., establish a disciplinary niche for his work). The writer cites three scholars (two American and one Swedish) to make the point that the subject has not been adequately dealt with. He also a names a Tamil sociologist to argue that local scholars (now working abroad) have failed to discuss matters of concern to the community when they are preoccupied with issues relating to other communities. Though Sivatamby is establishing a niche that he then attempts to fill, he cites the scholars from the perspective of performing a civic service. He is not undertaking this study primarily to fill a disciplinary vacuum. It is in this sense that the other opening moves are significant for showing the centrality of the subject in terms of ongoing problems in the community. He bemoans the ironic silence of the community on its own caste-ridden social structure and ideology. He also points out the importance of this work in the current climate of ethnic conflict and political crises. In fact the author uses the word "duty" at least twice to show the motivations for the paper. The invocation of "Tamil Eelam" (the name for the de facto Tamil state) taps ethnic sentiments. Therefore, though the author can easily make an argument for disciplinary centrality and even show how his perspective as a local scholar can challenge the studies undertaken by foreign scholars, he chooses not to develop that orientation for the paper.

In a sense, then, it is the civic responsibility of dealing with this subject that functions as the rationale for Sivatamby's paper. Such introductions show the writers trying hard to situate their papers in the local social context. If scholars from the center do not prefer such claims of centrality for their papers, this is because the center-based academic communities have made a virtue of "pure" knowledge and social detachment (Geisler 1994). For local scholars, on the other hand, the frame of reference in intellectual activities is the contribution they can make to addressing the challenges facing their society. This integration with the community at large—outside the walls of the university—is a defining feature of local academic life that necessarily influences the rhetoric of RAs. It is not that there are no vested interests for local scholars, or no motivation for them to define themselves as separate from the wider society in order to limit admission into their elite circles. It is rather that the status of academics is defined by the extent to which they can be useful to their community. The explanation above also doesn't mean that local scholars don't have any interest in constructing new knowledge. It is simply that this is a more implicit and indirect by-product of their research—not something undertaken always for its own sake.[6]

Sivatamby's brief mention of previous studies ironically suggests other reasons why local scholars do not engage in a sustained literature review. Though they can mention the names of scholars, they do not always have the publications handy to cite and discuss them in depth. A check of Sivatamby's bibliography shows that he has failed to cite any publication information about Skjonberg. It is usually the case that local scholars have heard about the work of foreign scholars but have rarely had the chance to read their publications. You may recollect the struggle I myself faced (in the opening vignette) of wanting to cite new literature pertaining to my research but not having the access to do so with confidence or familiarity. This state of affairs also affects the extent to which local writers can see themselves as contributing to the ongoing disciplinary conversation. The information relating to what is new knowledge or what is fashionable is not readily available to them. They are usually following the conversation at a distance, if at all. From this position it is difficult for them to establish a disciplinary niche or even invoke the disciplinary discourse with confidence. This may explain the lack of the second move in the introductions of many local scholars. Some African scholars have also pointed out the disappearing literature-review section in their colleagues' RAs, attributing this to almost the same reasons pointed out above (Muchiri et al. 1995).

In English articles written for (and published in) center journals, local scholars cannot always adopt the same claims of centrality they make in the local context. At least, the concerns of the local community are not always relevant to an international readership. How then do local scholars write when they publish in mainstream journals? Here's how Suseendirarajah opens his "Caste and Language in Jaffna Society" in the much-respected journal *Anthropological Linguistics*. The first paragraph is distinctly titled "Introduction" and is set apart from the other sections of the paper.

> The purpose of this paper is to correlate caste and language in the Jaffna Hindu Tamil society. This study is mainly based on data collected from a few sample villages in the Jaffna peninsula where the political and economic ascendancy of the VeLLaaLas (landlords) was very dominant in the recent past. (1978, 312)

This introduction is extremely brief. The author jumps straight into move 3/step 1b (i.e., announcing the present research). The second sentence is the peculiarly local move of a statement of methodology (which I will analyze under the methods section, later in this chapter). This introduction then doesn't have some of the crucial moves expected in center RAs—such as the claim of centrality, topic generalization, establishment of a niche, or presentation of the thesis. Perhaps the second move, of establishing a niche, was not necessary in this case because the reviewers recognized the lack of linguistic studies from this remote society of Jaffna. It is also possible that the novelty of the topic generated sufficient linguistic interest that the reviewers didn't insist on such moves for publishing the paper. Another of the author's papers in a center journal (Suseendirarajah 1980) shows the same brevity and choice of moves. It must be noted, however, that the writer's papers for the local academic community (whether in Tamil or English) adopt a different introduction. In his "English in Our Tamil Society," which I will analyze elaborately below, Suseendirarajah makes a claim for centrality based on the contemporary political upheavals and the need to consider the changing facets of English in the community from this perspective. In the concluding sentences he announces his research problem.

The example above shows that the same writer could be switching rhetorical strategies quite consciously to suit different writing contexts. We have to consider the rationale and effectiveness of such switching. It is possible that such a writing strategy, which is also found in some local publications in English, results from a case of *hypercorrection*.[7] In an attempt to move away from the rhetoric that is inappropriate for the changed context, the writer may move too far in the opposite direction. Here, in a publication in English for a Western journal, the author is moving away from the social-claims of centrality so prevalent in the local context. It is also the case that many local scholars stereotype the supposed restraint and tautness of center-based rhetoric. In some texts, then, the restraint and brevity are consciously employed by the local writers, under the impression that this is what is appreciated in the center. In discussions with local scholars, I often found that they exaggerated the impersonality and detachment of center-based academic writing.

The brief opening could also be a coping strategy. Since local writers don't have the knowledge of center discourses and publications that would enable them to pitch their papers for this context, they simply refrain from saying too much about their research. They jump straight into their analysis after announcing their subject. You may recollect from the vignette above how I myself resorted to this strategy after debating whether I should try to open my paper with a clear location in the current disciplinary discourse. Since I didn't have access to the relevant publications or an insider's familiarity with the research conversation, I finally decided to open with a simple announcement of my purpose and intentions. In the few papers where I tried to establish a disciplinary niche for my work while writing from Sri Lanka, the reviewers commented that the lead-in was inappropriate, as the disciplinary conversation had changed somewhat from the one in which I was trying to take part. This is a frequent response by center reviewers to the openings of many local papers. In a paper comparing two ethnographies of literacy—of African American and Sri Lankan students—I chose to frame my discussion in terms of the deficit/difference debate (which now appears as Canagarajah 1995a). A reviewer felt that the debate had now been resolved in the center and urged me to use a different framework for the paper. Even though this paper was written only two years after my return to Sri Lanka, after I had participated in the disciplinary conversation relating to this debate, the frames of reference had changed somewhat. The delay in keeping up with the explosion of research and publication results in many local researchers not knowing how to establish a niche for their work. There are indeed many other areas of local research that are not timely in terms of center scholarship.

What we have to understand here is that even when local writers *know* how they should write the opening for center audiences, they cannot always realize it textually. Their conditions of work don't provide them with the type of resources to write in this manner. We should also take into account the epistemological constraints local writers face. In many cases, the subjects treated don't fall within any existing (center) disciplinary discourse; they are of mostly local relevance. For example, the papers on the intellectual contributions of the local savant Pandithamani were situated within the traditional discourses of learning, which don't fall easily into the categories defined by the Western academy. Rather, the papers by Suseendirarajah (1991) and Paranirupasingham (1993) cut across areas like philosophy, religion, literature, sociology, and anthropology. For many center scholars these papers may appear to be nothing more than glorified biographies.

What do local scholars feel about the typical openings in center RAs? Their impressions were brought out effectively in the responses to the very first paper I wrote in Tamil after returning from postgraduate studies abroad. In an essay on contemporary Tamil poetry, I adopted my newly learned writing skills from American graduate school. My introduction followed a move typical of Swales's CARS model. I outlined my purpose, defined my contribution to existing scholarship, indicated the structure of my argument, and spelled out my thesis (Canagarajah 1994b). My UJ colleagues, who rarely indulged in metatalk on writing styles, were suddenly quite vocal in expressing their disappointment. Even some of my students came up to me and said that the introductory paragraph sounded a bit too pompous and overconfident. They reminded me that in the vernacular tradition (especially in lectures, sermons, and oratory) one should open with an *avai aTakkam* (humbling oneself in the court). The speaker starts with a brief confession of his or her limitations, praises the knowledge of the audience, and attributes whatever knowledge he or she might develop in his or her talk to superiors (i.e., elders, teachers, God). As the term *avai* (court) reveals, this rhetorical practice must have developed in the feudal social formation of the past, perhaps in the king's court. Though these features aren't found explicitly in contemporary Tamil writing, the ethos of the scholar/rhetor is still influenced considerably by what I label a "humility ethos."

My cocksure way of beginning the essay—announcing my thesis, delineating the steps of my argument, promising to prove my points conclusively—left another bad taste in the mouths of the local readership. They said that this excessively planned and rigidly calculated move gave the impression of a formulaic, mechanical, matter-of-fact style of writing. I had put off my readers by sounding overly self-conscious and self-controlled. My opening was considered very awkward by almost everybody. Some even charged that I had treated the readers condescendingly. The circular structure of anticipating the conclusion at the beginning, and then reaching the same point in the conclusion, is rarely found in local RAs. Part of what motivates this distaste is what Hinds (1983) has insightfully discussed as the differing reader/writer responsibility in literacy in different communities. For local scholars, the reader should be treated as intelligent enough to understand the evolving argument without too much guidance from the writer and left independent to make his or her judgment on the acceptability of the argument without the "lobbying" of the writer on behalf of his or her position. The thesis therefore evolves in a linear fashion, in slow accretions, culminating in the final pages. As in the case of Hinds's Japanese scholars, for local scholars the responsibility for deciphering a text rests largely with the reader—which differs from the American attitude of blaming the writer.

These realizations help explain why local writers don't adopt move 1/step 3 and move 3, where they define the thesis explicitly and position themselves agonistically toward other scholars. The referee comments that some of my colleagues and I have received speak loudly of center attitudes toward this style of writing. These are some of the opinions expressed.

The opening sounds too tangential and broadly focused for the specific concerns of the paper.

The writer doesn't appear to have a clear plan or purpose.

The paper is not aggressive in showing that it merits a place in the disciplinary discourse or showing what it has to offer the reader.

The paper shows little awareness of the larger disciplinary context and the ways in which it relates to other studies and research.

The brevity and casualness of the opening show a lack of force and conviction in the writer.

The introduction misleads the reader by talking about matters that are not directly related to the research objectives of the paper (such as civic relevance).

It is easy to see how these attitudes can affect the chances of local scholars getting published in mainstream/center journals.

But we must qualify the generalizations above on local literacy practices with a consideration of the exceptions. A paper by Sitrampalam (1991/1992), "The Form Velu of Sri Lankan Brahmi Inscriptions: A Reappraisal," stands out for the way the introduction creates a niche for his study. The polemical manner in which the title is worded is itself indicative of the strong rhetorical positioning of the writer. The opening paragraph has all the traits of being a complex introduction in the CARS tradition.

> In recent times an active interest has been generated in the study and reinter-pretation of the early Brahmi inscriptions (Kanagaratnam 1978; Velupillai 1979, 1980, 1981; Sitrampalam 1980a, 1980b, 1986–87, 1988; Gunawardena 1983; Seneviratne 1985, 1988; Karunatilaka 1986). This study has helped us to understand more profitably the political, economic and the social fabric of early Sri Lanka and the process of state formation during this period. During this early phase of our history it was the group of clans which held sway in various parts of the country with the system of ranking as evident from the use of titles such as Rajas, Paramukas, Gamikas, Gahapatis and Kutumbikas, although many details of these clans are missing. Moreover the whole system went out vogue of [sic] by about the 1st or 2nd century A.D. Tantalisingly enough, many scholars who acknowledged the above process failed to take cognizance of a similar process which was in operation on [the] other side of the Palk Strait in the neighbouring Tamil Nadu whose culture too stemmed from a common Proto-historic megalithic cultural base as in the case of Sri Lanka (Sitrampalam 1980a, 1988a). Because of this, even some of the clan names have been interpreted as titles or personal names (Nicholas 1950; Perera 1951; Paranavitana, 1970; Hettiarachy, 1972; Karunatilaka, 1986). The purpose of the present paper is to study one of the clans mentioned in the early Brahmi inscriptions which has been interpreted as a personal name Velu (Ellawela, 1969; Paranavitana, 1970). This study becomes more feasible in the light of the earliest extant literature of Tamil Nadu, namely the Sangam literature which has preserved some details of their clan society. (1991/1992, 60)

This paragraph begins with a claim of centrality based on scholarly/disciplinary interest (move 1/step 1). Then the writer goes on to further establish the territory by providing general information on the background of the issue studied and the significance of the emerging findings (move 1/step 2). In the process, the writer also reviews the literature related to the study (move 1/step 3). Then he goes on to skillfully establish a niche (move 2) by indicating a gap in research (the failure to connect to parallel research in South India) and making a counterclaim (against interpreting clan names as personal names). He quickly moves to occupy the niche by announcing the present project (move 3/step 1b). Before considering the reasons why Sitrampalam is able to achieve this canonical form, we must also consider how this introduction still confirms many peculiarities of a periphery opening. Note that the introduction does not have move 3/step 2 or move 3/step 3, which are common in center RAs (announcing principal findings; indicating RA structure). Moreover, the final statement of the data source that informs the paper is very much like the "statement of methodology" structure, unique in local articles. Furthermore, the claim of civic-mindedness is evoked—though only mildly—as the study on state formation has relevance to the community's ongoing struggle for an autonomous state.

What this skillful introduction shows is that local scholars can employ the moves analogous to the CARS model if they choose to, provided certain crucial material requirements are met. Since Sitrampalam's research is closely related to local expertise, the relevant publications are accessible to the writer (note that all publications cited are by Sri Lankan authors in mostly local publications). The disciplinary community is located within his reach, and he occupies an insider status with the ability to participate in the ongoing conversation. All this is a source of confidence for the writer because he is able to claim a sound understanding of the relevant research tradition. On an ethnographic note, it is important to note that there had been a heated controversy in UJ between two camps of archeologists relating to the subject in the paper described above, with Sitrampalam leading one of the camps. The subject had also gained importance in the political context of having to define the nation's cultural history in relation to its neighbor South India. This charged atmosphere of ongoing debates influenced the writer to pitch his paper polemically. This writer, however, does not use this mode of introduction in other papers on different subjects. (He too is switching styles, like Suseendirarajah above, as he sees a specific structure suiting his purposes.) It is also of note, finally, that this paper gained from considerable assistance in writing by a senior instructor in English (which help the writer acknowledges at the end of his paper). Educated in the vernacular and conducting much of his writing in Tamil (in which he is more fluent), the writer indulges in the quite uncharacteristic practice (for the local community) of getting the paper revised/edited by a colleague. This turns out to shape his rhetoric in remarkable ways.

Citation Patterns

Though the authors considered above do not cite previous publications in the expected sections of their introductions in order to establish the territory (move 1/step 3) or indicate a niche that they will fill (move 2), they discuss relevant literature in other places. In this form, the literature review never appears as a distinct section *as* literature review. It is spread throughout the text as and when necessary to develop the writer's point of view. Swales (1990) argues that this is especially possible in cases where the discourse in the discipline/field has not been standardized to the point where there is a recognized canon of literature to cite. He especially sees this possibility in the cycling of move 1/step 3 and move 2 in the introduction. Others have observed that citations may be integrated into the discussion in cases where there is a highly developed sense of standardized disciplinary discourse (Bazerman 1988; Paul 1996). The way references are used by local scholars is different. In a majority of cases, the publications are referred to only in a confirmatory manner. The writers do not discuss previous research to raise questions, signal opposition, or indicate gaps (which are some additional functions performed by citations in center RAs). Local scholars mostly use these works for the following reasons: to provide definitions of key terms required for their study; to endorse their own positions; and to offer some facts or information necessary to build their perspective. Another feature of this use of literature is that there is rarely any extensive discussion of the publications referred to or close reading of the texts—a matter also observed by Mauranen (1993b) and Silva (1993) in texts by ESL writers. Usually the references remain at the level of a "mention." The writers are satisfied with signaling an awareness of the publications.

In examining the use of citations in local RAs we must keep in mind the modes of reading that are common in periphery communities. Geisler (1994) distinguishes between a *rhetorical reading,* which situates the text in its widest possible context to interpret it as a socially constructed document, and the *autonomous-text* approach, which simply focuses on drawing out the main concepts and information within a narrower frame of textual context. In the former there is a dynamic and critical engagement of the reader with the text for meaning; in the latter the reader stands detached and treats the text as an objective document loaded with an authorially intended "correct" interpretation. Geisler argues that much of the power of center scholars derives from their confident rhetorical reading that opens up the text to its contextuality, enabling it to be easily critiqued. They are able to do this because they have with them the information required to deconstruct the text in light of the wider disciplinary discourses, other texts, and the institutions/agents of production. Local scholars, on the other hand, tend to treat mainstream scholarly publications as autonomous texts, partly because they don't have adequate contextual information to place the text in its contexts of construction. It is a fact of their working conditions that they are distanced from the disciplinary communities, institutions, and discourses that produce these texts. So they cannot help but read the text in a much narrower context, isolated from its larger frames of reference.

Such styles of citation may also derive from a cultural background that respects the authority of printed media. In the local Hindu tradition, sacred texts and their interpretation were assigned to priests, who alone had the training, knowledge, and status to offer authoritative readings. The messages from the texts are treated as sacrosanct, prohibited from being freely interpreted outside the accepted ways (Viswanathan 1989). The practice of close reading is also not widely shared in the vernacular tradition, and local readers have questions about unpacking the text to conduct a critical and analytical reading (as I demonstrate in Canagarajah 1994b). The local attitudes toward close reading were dramatically conveyed to me in one of my few addresses to the scholarly community in Jaffna. I was asked to review a book of poems written by a colleague at UJ when he formally released this publication. While the other two main speakers from the faculty touched on the messages and styles of many poems, I performed a close analysis of a single poem. Since the reaction to my presentation turned out to be very critical, I made it a point to note down my colleagues' attitudes. These were their impressions:

- that my reading focused on hair-splitting differences that were tedious and unnecessary;

- that the dissection of the text destroyed the message and the experience communicated;
- that my analysis may be acceptable in other fields (such as natural or mathematical sciences) but was misdirected for literary texts;
- and that this was plainly an eccentric approach that was difficult, if not unpleasant, to follow.

Perhaps for these reasons, local writers prefer to keep the referenced text whole and not take interpretive privileges for their own rhetorical purposes.

While the authors choose not to use citations of publications in the introductory section to create a disciplinary niche for their studies, there is no shortage of citations in general. The limitation, however, tends to be related to the recency of the works cited. Following the practice in citation analysis (Swales 1990), I offer in table 4.2 a catalogue of the citation dates that appear in an issue of *SLJSAS* (published at UJ in 1993).[8]

We must be wary of making judgments on the quality of the paper based merely on the date of citations. It must also be mentioned that the papers that have the least amount of citations belong to specific disciplines that may not require much library research. Elankumaran's study in econometrics and Kailainathan's in descriptive linguistics deal with analyses of empirical data and cannot be expected to engage in textual discussions. Some papers—like Sivasamy's on temple architecture and Sitrampalam's

Table 4.2

Author's name	n.d	pre-1940	1950	1960	1970	1980	1990	total
Velupillai		1		5	5	5		16
Nadarajasundaram	1	2		3	1	4	1	12
Elankumaran						4		4
Manivasakar			2	6	6	10	1	25
Sitrampalam		1	2	10	4	15		32
Gnanakumaran				2			1	3
Kailainathan					4			4
Sivasamy		1	2	6	1	2	1	13

on epigraphy—may in fact require considerable reliance on earlier-dated texts. Gnanakumaran's paper on Saiva Siddhantha includes undated quotations from ancient scriptures, which happen to be the primary texts for the writer's analysis.

In general, local scholars accommodate a greater spread of publications across time partly because they do not have complete access to the most recent literature. The lack of publications in the 1990s is noticeable. Only four scholars show an awareness of the publications that have come out in the 1990s by citing at least a single recent work. Some of the more recent works cited in the papers actually include self-citations of publications by the authors themselves. Much of the diffidence the writers display in not employing a separate literature review section to establish the territory or create a disciplinary niche may result from not having a good understanding of the expanding horizons of their disciplinary discourse. Lacking access to the most recent literature, it is foolhardy for anyone to claim originality in contributing to research advances. I have been through the embarrassing predicament of making claims of originality, only to be told by referees that these advances had already been made in the field in the center. In a paper on sociolinguistics, for example, where I coined the term *politicist approach* for a more ideologically sensitive reading of code-switching, the referees pointed out that such a reading was already well underway (although it was represented by very recent journal publications that hadn't reached Sri Lanka). Many of my colleagues at UJ frequently complained about their cluelessness regarding the state of the art in their fields.

While the type of literature familiar to scholars constrains their rhetoric, the ways they use citations also show differences. A paper by Nadarajasundaram, comparing the cultural influences on management practices in Japan and Sri Lanka, is a case in point. The writer cites scholarly authorities for the basic concepts he defines as relevant to his argument (such as the definition of culture) and in discussing the practices related to his local culture. But there are few or no citations when he refers to practices of Japanese culture. It would appear that more support is needed for assertions about the latter, as the writer is neither Japanese nor an expert in Japanese culture. Furthermore, some of the texts listed in the bibliography at the end of the paper are not integrated into the discussion in the body of the text. That is, these texts do not inform the discussion actively but appear to be listed in the bibliography for their own sakes. The pattern of citations is therefore uneven. It appears that the author is citing publications only in places where they are available to him. We must recognize that for many local writers there is no free choice on the type of publications they can cite in their papers. With the library at UJ cutting down on the number of journals and books it can acquire, and the technological facilities for calling up references and information remaining in an underdeveloped state, local writers make do with the material available. For the rest, they would build their discussions around information they have acquired from many undocumented everyday means. Related to this is of course the strategy I touched on in the vignette—getting to know about recent studies through other texts. Writers may cite texts that they learned about from book reviews, publication announcements, and citations in other RAs. Though it is unconventional to cite these modes of reference, at a time when there is greater appreciation of intertextuality, journals should accommodate the various nondirect ways in which scholars get their information. After all, postmodern scholarship is now ready to recognize the many subtle ways in which texts embed other texts and written documents even without the agency of writers.

Sometimes local scholars may not get the most suitable citation for their purposes. In a section entitled, "Culture and Social Organization," Nadarajasundaram (1991/1992, 16) defines culture as follows:

> Culture provides an unquestioned context within which individual action and response take place. But there is a strain towards consistency in culture consisting of perception and style as well as of values. As Benedict (1946, 42) concludes:
>
> > A culture like an individual is a more or less consistent pattern of thought and action, [*sic*] within each culture there come into being characteristic purposes not necessarily shared by other types of society. . . .

This quotation runs for five lines. At the end of the quotation, the writer begins a new section titled "The Social Cultural Environment in Sri Lanka." What may sound curious to center reviewers is that the writer fails to comment on the quotation or integrate it critically and insightfully in the text. Perhaps the quotation merely plays the symbolic role of signaling the writer's learning and authority. In fact, the writer would say that the quotation is not strictly required to build his argument in the paper. He has already said more about culture than the quotation says. He still chooses to quote Benedict, presumably because he would like to signal to the audience that he is keeping up with the academic conventions of citation and that he has done some research for writing this paper. (That the writer should quote Benedict and not a more contemporary anthropologist like Geertz is of course an indication of the dated material available locally.) Some writers have told me that they could not comment extensively on a publication because they had the opportunity of reading it only once—when they copied down some important points or quotations—and didn't have the possibility of getting the book again at the time of writing the paper. While local scholars realize the need to provide citations, then, they can do this only according to the access they have to sources.

Given the difficulties with getting relevant publications, many local scholars develop certain coping strategies for using research literature in their RAs. As in the case of Nadarajasundaram above, they cite the few publications they are aware of, however distantly connected to their study, for the symbolic purpose of establishing their authority and scholarly status. In many cases, this is what local readers are themselves looking for in a paper. They do not scrutinize the recency of the publication or their specific connections to the study. They find any reference informative and useful. More important for them is the ethos of the writer created through such citations. In a paper entitled "English in Our Tamil Society," Suseendirarajah (1992) displays this coping strategy. Of the thirteen references in the paper, only two comment directly on the subject. These are local materials—one is an unpublished dissertation by a fellow faculty member on educational policies in Sri Lanka; the other is the handbook of the university on admission policies. Among the rest, four are by Indian authors on language policies and the nativization of English. The others are works by center scholars on general linguistics (such as Hudon's *Sociolinguistics,* Hockett's *A Course in Modern Linguistics,* and Trudgill's *Dialects in Contact*). None of the latter is employed in depth to comment specifically on the subject of the paper. They receive only cursory mention. The bulk of the paper, on the history and social functions of English in Sri Lanka, is narrated without much documentation. The citations therefore serve a rhetorical purpose even if they are not functional in the text. It is easy to understand the name-recognition value of these texts. Those outside the field of linguistics too may have heard of these classic texts and their well-known authors. These references may boost the image of the author as a learned and widely read scholar who has the credentials to comment on the subject. The citations also show that the paper is indeed a learned treatise informed by major publications. The references thus sanction anything that the author may state in the work.[9]

But this strategy of quoting and citing papers without critical engagement may give center readers an impression of plagiarism. In some cases writers appear to be so heavily dependent on their sources that the voice of the writer may appear to find little scope for expression. In some cases, the quotations and paraphrases are not appropriately attributed, possibly because (as many writers have confessed) the publication details are not available from a text that is now beyond their reach. This cavalier attitude to texts derives from many influences. As I will proceed to show in detail in chapter 6, the idea of intellectual property is less clear-cut in the local community. Borrowing from other texts, like borrowing freely from others' words in the communal stock of oral knowledge, is unrestricted. The ownership of knowledge is fluid, just as copyright laws are hardly in operation. Local scholars see themselves as freely borrowing from and contributing to the pool of available knowledge.

There are other ways of looking at this practice of unattributed textual borrowing. As center scholars themselves will now acknowledge in the context of postmodern knowledge construction, knowledge is communally constructed through fluid texts. Local scholars are simply being up front about this reality rather than going through the charade of distinguishing their words from those of other writers. It has also been pointed out in many cases of recent research that members of oral communities have more fluid practices of borrowing and employing other people's words. (See Howard 1995 for a discussion of how this practice emerges in the African American community.) Pennycook (1996) argues that Chinese students borrow other people's words as a shortcut and as an efficient means of tapping notions already well expressed. They also do this in appropriating words that are published by center scholars for their own purposes. After all, these words could have easily been their own—if they had only the material resources and academic connections to engage in publication.[10]

However, local scholars may encounter ideological problems when they use center-produced texts. A paper entitled "Intellectual Colonialism vis-a-vis Pseudo Developmentalism: Irony and Agony of the Third World," by Manivasakar (1991/1992), is an example of this problem. His very argument, that models of development are exported from the center to the local community, is paradoxically dependent on center publications themselves. Since there is little empirical data from local contexts employed, Manivasakar's paper is developed with the help of radical center scholars as his authorities. In many senses, the paper is itself an example of intellectual dependence on the West. To understand the predicament of the writer, we must realize that it is hard to find published sources from the periphery that will support Manivasakar's critical perspective on center intellectual hegemony. It is certainly difficult for local scholars to get such a perspective published in a mainstream journal (although they may discuss such concerns all the time in their face-to-face oral interactions). If Manivasakar is then to cite relevant publications to situate the paper in the scholarly conversation, he is left only with center publications. This may explain the half-hearted and hesitant manner in which local scholars use published sources. (This conflict is at the heart of this book too: in order to make my argument on behalf of periphery scholars to the mainstream scholarly community, I have to employ center-based publications, leading to certain embarrassing forms of self-contradiction. As I argued in the introduction, the best we can do is to critically appropriate center-based texts for our local purposes.)

Methods

In many of the papers analyzed above, we find the curious phenomenon of some comments on methodology in the final lines of the introductory paragraph. I labeled this section the "statement of methodology" earlier. Sivatamby (1992), Suseendirarajah (1978), Sitrampalam (1991/1992), and Velupillai (1991/1992), discussed above, display this textual feature. This move involves the mention of a label for the methodology, the source of the data, or the analytical paradigm employed. There is little else by way of describing or justifying the methodology in the rest of the paper.

Some papers add a few lines on data collection, location, subjects, and duration in their appendices. Suseendirarajah's (1980) paper in *Anthropological Linguistics* titled "Religion and Language in Jaffna Society" is an example of this strategy. He inserts an asterisk in the title of the paper. He then glosses it as follows: "I am grateful to ————, ————, ———— and ———— for their help in my fieldwork." A person who knows the ethnicity markers in the four names mentioned will identify that there are two Hindus, a Christian, and a Muslim who have helped with the data collection (or functioned as informants). This is important in a paper that purports to discuss the influence of religion on the Tamil language. Apparently, the three main religions that could influence language in Jaffna are represented by the informants. The other paper by this author discussed earlier—on the influence of caste on the Tamil language (Suseendirarajah 1978)—also has an asterisk in the introduction. This one is glossed as follows: "Sample villages selected for study are Myliddy, Puttur and Kaitady." Though this statement is somewhat more informative than the one in the article about religion, center readers will demand more information: How/why were these villages selected? How long was fieldwork carried out? How was the data collected? What methodology was employed to collect data? Such are the many questions that are assumed to be answered by the single statement writers make on methodology. Footnotes like this appear to be purely a rhetorical device to indicate that fieldwork has been done and that empirical data informs the paper.[11]

Why do local scholars give such brief mention to methodology? The experience I had when I undertook the research reported in the opening vignette will help explain the paucity of reference to methods in local RAs. Discovering that the local fishermen were using English in rhetorically significant ways, I took notes on the contexts and features of their codeswitching. The data on codeswitching was recorded in a notebook as the interactions occurred. I couldn't audiotape their speech for several reasons. First, due to the civil war and the economic blockade in the region, I couldn't purchase batteries to use in my tape recorder, and the fuel ban and power stoppage made running recording equipment on electricity impossible. Second, in the politically sensitive situation that obtained, anyone walking around taping other people's talk would have been suspected of being a spy or informant and could have been summarily executed by the militants. Third, due to the crowded and noisy nature of the marketplace where I encountered the fishermen I couldn't have audiotaped their speech with clarity, or done so without affecting the natural nature of the communicative interactions. When I then sat down to write the paper I debated whether I should frankly explain why I believed that my disci-

plined observations would be no less insightful—even though I wasn't
blessed with impressive equipment or favorable conditions for recording
the conversations. But this was another paper in itself. This discussion
would have taken me too far afield from presenting my main findings and
results. I also feared raising a hornet's nest of other questions that would
distract readers from my report. I eventually included a brief discussion of
the final methodology—only slightly longer than the ones seen in the papers discussed above—giving the contexts and modes of data collection.

When I submitted the paper to *Language in Society,* the reviewers ques-
tioned the methodology, even though they indicated that they found the
findings insightful. Rejecting the paper for publication, one reviewer
wrote: "The main problem I have at this point is with the methodology. I
can't believe that people would address an issue like code-switching in the
1990's without recording actual speech. . . . Ideally the author should go
back and find a way to record some interactions." It should be mentioned
that this paper was written just two years after I had returned to Sri Lanka,
having conducted a sophisticated sociolinguistic study for my doctorate in
the United States in which I conducted audiotaped interviews, recorded
in-group conversational interactions, obtained data from online discussions, and collected multiple drafts of writing from my subjects. The problem for me was not ignorance about conventions of research processes and
reporting but simply the lack of resources and the unsettled conditions of
work in Sri Lanka.

By the time the paper was eventually published in another journal, I
had made some cursory tape recordings of conversations and written an
expanded methodology section (Canagarajah 1995d). In order to do so, I
had managed to purchase a few batteries in the black market (smuggled il-
legally into the region) at an exorbitant price for a pocket tape recorder.
Though the interactions I recorded didn't radically change the claims I
had previously made in the paper, my statement that data was audiotaped
undoubtedly helped win the paper's acceptance. What was fascinating to
me in this experience was the extent to which technology was fetishized
in research activity. Similarly, the sophistication of the methodology—at
least the extent to which it involved instruments—was being given undue
importance. Needless to say, relying on the intuition, experience, and disciplined reflection of the researcher—or other unconventional procedures
for constructing knowledge as befitting the situation—tends to be deval-

ued by reviewers. In fact, Swales (1990) mentions that many fields in the humanities and social sciences are giving increased prominence to their methodology sections, possibly with the intent of matching the scientistic/empirical approach in other disciplines.

However, local scholars don't enjoy the facilities, time, technology, research assistance, or funds to make the type of claims made in methodology sections by center researchers. Their research procedures will often still look clumsy and rudimentary to scholars in the center who enjoy superior facilities. It is easy to see, therefore, why local writers will be tongue-tied when they come to the methodology section. Perhaps they think the less said, the better. For example, a colleague mentioned to me that it is far better not to talk about methodology, as it will only unnecessarily expose our technological and material limitations. This then is a coping strategy to deal with the unfavorable research conditions faced. Furthermore, local scholars don't necessarily display high regard for a study simply because it used expensive or sophisticated instruments.[12]

There are other things about research methods that are more important for local scholars. Adopting practices involving situated thinking and embodied knowing, their inquiry accommodates relatively more personal/subjective approaches. They seem to give more credibility to studies that derive from the sustained, lengthy, disciplined contemplation of the writer on the subject. The mere fact that somebody employed superior instruments doesn't mean that all their claims have to be taken seriously or their findings treated as valid. Suseendirarajah's (1991) paper on Panditamani shows the wide range of data sources that have influenced his claims—conversations with laypeople, correspondence with knowledgeable sources, the stock of community knowledge on the subject, and the writings of others and the *pundit* himself. But it is a reflection of the conflict facing local scholars that he glosses over these types of data and highlights empirical approaches. It is also significant that after all these claims of scientificity, Suseendirarajah doesn't show whether he adopted a controlled, detached method for studying his subject. What is more important for him about the empirical approach is the attitude with which the study was undertaken—in other words, with an open mind, rigor, discipline, balance, sincerity. These, after all, are more valuable considerations compared to the use of standardized instruments and controls. Yet it is difficult for many local scholars to be frank about the wide-ranging data sources they use for their studies. They are usually under pressure to show themselves to be adopting center-approved scientific methods.

In light of these problems, some of us have adopted another interesting coping strategy to get through the methods section with dignity and integrity: resorting to low-cost, nontechnological methods like ethnography and participant observation. While impressing center scholars with a method that is receiving much prominence lately, the method also satisfies the more relaxed and personalized forms of knowing we prefer in the local context. Ironically, though I had obtained audio and digitized forms of data for my doctoral research in the United States, I had to retrain myself to conduct research according to the material realities in the periphery when I returned to Sri Lanka. Sivatamby (1990), in his paper in the Swedish-based journal *Lanka,* mentions ethnography as having provided the methodological basis of his work on the ideological formation of Jaffna society. Curiously, in a paper on a similar subject in Tamil for the local audience, he mentions that he had happened on the subject as he was researching the social context of Tamil literature (Sivatamby 1992). Sivatamby is in fact a professor of Tamil language and literature. Although he is very interested and well read in the social sciences, his primary area of expertise and teaching is in literature and drama. His claim of ethnography in the paper therefore appears to be a rhetorical switch, calculated to assuage the concerns of a center-based reading audience. But this strategic mention of ethnography is not altogether untrue. As an informed member of the Jaffna community who has a keen understanding of the everyday life there, and as a disciplined researcher who has read theoretical and empirical studies on culture in other societies, it is not wrong for the author to claim that he is an ethnographer of sorts. After all, Sivatamby has a better claim to the label than do foreign anthropologists who spend a summer or two in Jaffna and then go on to make less insightful claims regarding the local culture. Such methodological claims could also be considered an oppositional strategy of local scholars to appropriate the labels of the center and deploy them for credentializing purposes in their papers. Similarly, mentioning the method vaguely, and leaving it to the readers to decide how the label influences the paper, is also a coping strategy some local writers adopt—with varying levels of success—to deal with center conventions.

Discussion

Having seen the introduction treated in a generalized and relaxed manner, methodology given short shrift, and data rarely cited in a decontextualized fashion, we move on to peculiarities of the discussion section of local RAs. What is simply the fourth section in the IMRD structure of center RAs dominates local papers in the humanities and social sciences. Most discussions are a linear exposition or narration of the key issues surrounding the subject in a very personal voice by the author—as in the *author-centered rhetoric* of seventeenth-century RAs in the center (Atkinson 1999). The discussion is rarely oriented as an analysis (as is the case with the *object-centered rhetoric* of center writing today).[13] Also, the authors rarely adopt a *dialogic orientation* by positioning themselves agonistically toward other researchers or studies in the discipline. The writer focuses directly on the subject and articulates his or her view on it for what can be added to existing knowledge. This effect is especially dominant in Tamil and English papers written for the local audience, though, as I will show later, writers may adopt a dialogic and object-centered rhetoric when they submit papers to center RAs.

Consider Suseendirarajah's "English in Our Tamil Society: A Sociolinguistic Appraisal" (1992). The paper was written in English and distributed to the faculty of UJ for study and discussion. Though the subtitle might lead one to expect an analytical treatment of the subject, the paper is a straightforward narrative. After a two-paragraph introductory section, where he delineates the scope of the discussion and invokes civic significance, the author begins narrating the changing status of English from the earliest days of colonialism to the present. It is a complex story that embodies mixed feelings and attitudes: anger against the colonial activity of promoting English to the exclusion of the vernacular; sarcasm toward locals who absorbed colonial linguistic values; the sadness of a bilingual professional at the educated populace's declining proficiency in English; and sober reflection on realistic alternatives for policy planning in the future. The structure of the paper is largely episodic as each section takes the story from one period to the next. The sections are loosely connected, set apart by numerals rather than titles. There are also some interesting anecdotes and digressions that offer a thick description of details here, ground the discussion in everyday life there, and increase one's understanding and enjoyment of the paper. It is clear that what influences the conclusions of the writer are his personal observations, his disciplined reflection, and information informally gathered from others.

The following description of the place of English in Sri Lankan society during the colonial period suggests the characteristic discourse style of this paper.

> Bilingualism in English helped speakers earn some kind of esteem in the society particularly among monolinguals. In certain social situations people spoke English in common or public places intentionally to assert superiority over monolinguals. People especially those who were in the lower hierarchy in the society, took pride and pleasure in exhibiting their fluency in English in contexts where they felt that others thought them to be totally ignorant of English. That was a time when it was considered shame not to know English! Even a beggar who spoke English got more than one who spoke Tamil. People thus used English because it gave a more educated impression of the speaker.
>
> There were also some bilinguals who felt shy to speak Tamil in public. A small section in the society neglected their mother tongue and when situations demanded them to speak in Tamil either declined to speak pleading ignorance or spoke Tamil with an alien accent and strange sentence constructions. In a way they took pride in doing so. (Suseendirarajah 1992, 4)

The writing adopts a relaxed narrative flow with the use of the past tense. Note also the exclamation point (one of many in the paper), which strives for an effect. The language also communicates the feelings of the writer in no uncertain terms. The sarcasm of the writer regarding the attitudes of the "bilinguals" is conveyed clearly at the beginning and end of the above section. The reference to the beggar is typical of the anecdotes that function as evidence for the writer's statements. Though the writer is discussing a historical period in which he didn't live, or was perhaps very young if he did, his interpretations are very strident, bold, and unqualified. He reveals no pressure to document these impressions with empirical rigor.

The concluding section of the paper broaches the issue of ESL teaching at the university level. The writer thus preserves the linear structure of the essay, moving from the past and present to the future—progressing from historical description to pedagogical applications and policy implications. After considering how the sociolinguistic realities of bilingualism in Sri Lanka affect tertiary-level education, the writer concludes with a brief final paragraph.

A separate detailed study of the status and functions of English in our universities both in academic as well as administrative sections will be a desidera-
tum. A comparison of language use among universities may be useful to understand language trends and problems in our universities. (1992, 20)

Note also that even in the conclusion the writer doesn't provide a summa-
tive statement on the thesis of his paper. In most papers, the discussion
ends with the implications of the study for practical application or future
research. This kind of conclusion is therefore different from the conventions for conclusions typical of center publications. Belanger (1982) claims
that RAs end with a summary of results, statement of thesis, and answers
for gaps in existing research. The lack of a summary or thesis statement is
in line with the local rhetorical preference for embedded discourse, different from the overtly object-centered and polemical rhetoric of the center.
What is preferred, then, is an implicit embodiment of findings/conclu-
sions, to be decontextualized and formulated by the readers. The structure
of the paper therefore differs from the hourglass model of center RAs (as
typified by Swales's IMRD structure). Suseendirarajah's paper in fact displays a "reverse funnel" structure that opens up gradually throughout the
paper to proceed toward larger generalities and implications.

The sentiments expressed in the conclusion should also be noted. What
is being signaled here is what I call a humility ethos. In most local RAs, the
writers confess the additional work that has to be done for a fuller treatment of the subject or to understand the implications deriving from this
particular paper.[14] This humility in local publications derives from Hindu
religious thinking, which cultivates one's insignificance in relation to the
vastness of knowledge. The oft-repeated proverb in local scholarly circles,
"kaRRaTu kaimaNNaLavu kallaaTaTu ulakaLavu" (What we know is a
fistful; what we don't know is a world full), summarizes the attitude behind
this conclusion. What is asserted here in words is embodied more subtly in
the tone and structuring of the whole text. In many papers this can give
the impression of diffidence in making claims or of a lack of originality,
conviction, and force in relation to the disciplinary discourse. The attitude
will serve to explain why local papers don't reflect the aggressive tone and
polemical structuring of center papers.

There are many things in Suseendirarajah's paper that would be unsatisfactory to center scholars: the lack of solid integration into the disciplinary discourses of the relevant field; insufficient engagement with the lit-

erature and ongoing studies in the research tradition; the paucity of objective, "hard" sociolinguistic data; limited evidence of systematic data collection or research methodology; and the want of an analytical stance. Ironically, such were some of my own criticisms of this paper when it was first distributed at UJ. In a written rejoinder to Suseendirarajah's paper, which I presented to the Academic Forum, I pointed out that the writing was anecdotal and impressionistic, generally lacking in rigor, objectivity, balance, and current research knowledge—all of which prevented it from qualifying as a serious research paper (Canagarajah 1992). Fresh from my doctoral research in the United States, I was obviously using center-based assumptions in my evaluation of this paper.

Inspired by Suseendirarajah's paper—and identifying the research potential of this subject—I undertook to gather data through empirical work (to document contemporary linguistic practices) and from archives (in order to document bilingualism during the colonial period). The paper was accepted three years later in the sociolinguistics journal *Language in Society,* my first choice for submission (Canagarajah 1995c). I find it interesting to compare my paper with Suseendirarajah's in order to bring out the differences in discourse that have to be adopted to satisfy center-based editors and reviewers. Not able to make assertions regarding linguistic practices of the past in author-centered rhetoric, I document my claims with the writings of colonial bureaucrats, missionaries, and local literati. I cast the analysis in a current theoretical framework—namely, that of Bourdieu's notion of linguistic capital. I adopt multiple layers of polemical positioning—against dominant schools of bilingualism for ignoring the ideological and material implications of code choice; against Bourdieu himself for being too deterministic and failing to bring out the subtle forms of resistance in everyday linguistic practice; and against Suseendirarajah for overstating the demise of English in the local community. To buttress these hair-splitting arguments, I perform a close analysis of recorded conversations. The paper is also peppered with the specialized terminology that reflects the state of the art in bilingual studies and Bourdieu's sociology, in addition to numerous citations that document my scholarship. What my paper shows is the distance that needed to be traveled textually in making Suseendirarajah's paper suitable for center journals.

But Suseendirarajah had the last laugh in a sense: while his paper was widely read and discussed, my paper didn't strike a resonant chord among

local readers. To account for this difference, we have to understand the attitudes of my colleagues to the center-based structuring of my paper.[15]
The polemical stance, the aggressive lobbying on behalf of my thesis and
findings, and the explicit presentation of data created the following impressions in my colleagues (as I noted down from my discussions with
them):

- that the paper lacked the aesthetic and emotional appeal that comes
  from a more relaxed development of the thesis;
- that the paper was unnecessarily and unproductively contentious;
- that simply annihilating the views of others doesn't necessarily mean
  that my view is superior;
- that the paper displayed an aggressive individualism that bordered on
  unseemly pride, attention-grabbing, and self-congratulation;
- that this need to pit one's own research against that of others leads
  to unnecessary, hair-splitting arguments that end up confusing and
  baffling the audience;
- that too many new theories, schools, and technical jargon are
  proliferating in the name of originality, clouding the broader
  connections and similarities between studies.

It was frequently discussed among local scholars that the need for an agonistic stance—with the accompanying emotional aggression and unbri-
dled individualism—was motivated by the working conditions of center
academic communities. The importance of tenure, the need to show productivity for annual evaluations, the requirement to win grants and professional awards, and competition between educational/research institutions
for economic viability (all of which placed considerable pressure for academic survival on the individual writer) were perceived to feed this high-
pressured style of writing. Since these were not issues in the more relaxed
local academic culture, local scholars also faced no need to aggressively
prove themselves (not to deny the usual competition between personalities
and cliques, which is always there as an undercurrent).

In my four years of successful academic publishing in the center while
at UJ, only one paper was complimented unconditionally by my closest
colleagues. After reading my paper on Sri Lankan English poetry for *World
Englishes* (Canagarajah 1994a), my mentor, A. J., raised his head from the
script and said, "This is the best you have written—since your article on

——————— in *Saturday Review.*" (He was referring to an essay I had written in a local newspaper before going abroad for my graduate studies.) What is common about both articles is that they employ a more personal voice, more evocative prose, and a relaxed approach to thesis development. Ironically, my mentor's comments reduced to insignificance my prized empirical publications in such journals as *Language in Society* and the *TESOL Quarterly*. My more impressionistic papers grounded in local contexts and texts were better evaluated compared to the more explicitly analytic linguistic papers.

What accounts for this stylistic preference for nonadversarial modes of structuring in the local community? The preference for narrative and grounded forms of writing has implications for alternate forms of knowledge making practiced by local scholars. For local communities, knowledge is a collaborative enterprise that develops in line with tradition and community (Li 1999; Scollon 1991; Shen 1989). (In the center, however, individuals have to position themselves agonistically even as they work collaboratively in the context of tradition.) Furthermore, knowledge is more effectively processed, comprehended, and constructed locally when it comes embodied with its full richness of context, rather than in decontextualized form. Situated thinking is considered a valid form of knowing. Therefore narrative (which includes a richer context and thick description) is as suitable a vehicle for knowledge as argumentation or analysis. This epistemological background could also indicate the influence of oral forms of communicating and thinking. There is a greater tendency to approach knowledge as contextualized, personal, intuitive, tradition-confirming, and collective in orality-dominant communities (Heath 1983).

The advantages of these alternative forms of knowledge making are clear in Suseendirarajah's paper. The direction of his main argument is very straightforward. In situating the "data" in the relevant historical, social, and personal (i.e., concerning the author's own life) contexts, the argument gains force. The attitudes of the writer toward the subject are unequivocally presented, as his feelings accompany his data. Making the point with force is valued more in the local community, when it is supported by concrete examples, rather than speaking with a heavy use of citations. The thesis of the author is better accepted because he develops his argument in relation to alternate perspectives on the subject, not rival scholars. It is possible to say that the paper is indeed original and contributes to new knowledge in the field. Though the author doesn't claim originality aggressively, there is an implicit contribution to the knowledge on local bilingualism. There is also an implicit argument—against teachers of English who fail to take into account the changing status of English and against popular attitudes about the health of bilingualism in the community. On the other hand, the narrative and personal discourse shouldn't be taken to mean that the research was not done in a disciplined way. The author—having been trained in linguistics—is employing analytical tools from his discipline when he accesses relevant "data" and interprets them. As an insider to the community, having observed it for many years, the writer offers valid data, even though they do not derive from controlled procedures. In fact, the richness of the data comes from their more holistic context. His considerations are, furthermore, disciplined and rigorous, as he writes with years of reflection on the subject. Therefore, the type of contribution such local papers can make should not be ignored simply because their arguments are presented in more implicit and contextually embedded forms.

We cannot, however, draw the reductive conclusion that this descriptive/narrative mode of writing is the only structure local scholars are capable of practicing. We should examine an RA constructed by the same writer for the center audience and published in a mainstream journal to examine the shifts in style and discourse. While the discourse in Tamil and English for the local audience may reflect some of the writing practices appropriate for the local community, the strategies adopted by local writers to address an out-group audience will show the levels to which they can "codeswitch."[16] Suseendirarajah's paper "Caste and Language in Jaffna Society" (Suseendirarajah 1978), which appeared in the University of Indiana–based *Anthropological Linguistics,* shows the adjustments he has made for the center audience. What we see in this paper is a restriction of the more contextually embedded and narrative modes of structuring. There is also a hesitation in making bold moves of interpretation. What we get is the raw citation of relevant data with minimum commentary. Considering that caste is a controversial subject in the South Asian context, one would have expected a more engaged authorial discussion. The extremely brief paper (running to only seven pages) is structured through subheadings and numbers in the following manner (after the introduction):

2. Caste names and substitutes
3. Uses of caste names
4. New names for traditional caste names
5. Caste and personal names, kinship terms, etc.
6. Caste and language structure
7. Conclusions

There is little authorial attempt at building smooth transitions between sections. There is also no sustained argument developed in the text. The following passage shows the dominant style of discourse.

> Across the castes only one caste, namely the Kooviyar uses fictive kinship terms to address VeLLaaLLaas. Kooviyaas use the terms aNNai <u>elderly brother</u> and tankacci <u>younger sister</u> if the addressees are younger than they.
>
> Until recently some of the main streets in the Jaffna town had names based on castes that were dominant either along the streets or in their vicinity. Recently caste complexes have sought replacement of these names. But the older generation still continue to use the old names based on caste. Examples are taTTaa teru <u>goldsmith street,</u> ceeNiya teru <u>weavers street.</u> (Suseendirarajah 1978, 317)

The largely simple present-tense exposition and the detached point of view build the effect of an object-centered rhetoric. The purely descriptive presentation also hides the attitude of the writer toward this controversial subject.

It is perhaps in the brief concluding paragraph that the writer gains some space for a more personal voice.

> In concluding it may be said that the man has awakened. He has a sense of human equality and humanity. He is for better change. Sooner or later we may miss most if not all of the sociolinguistic correlates recorded herein. They are on the verge of dying out. (318)

The writer thus strikes a philosophical note and a moralizing attitude that we miss in the impersonal prose in the rest of the paper. We wonder whether this paragraph has been transposed here, perhaps demoted, from a more significant earlier position in the paper. That some radical revision has taken place before acceptance by the journal is evident from the endnotes, where the author says, "I am grateful to James W. Gair for his encouragement. A brief discussion with him helped me to rearrange and restate some of the ideas" (318). The allusion is to an American scholar who was visiting Sri Lanka on an academic furlough at the time of the writing. Suseendirarajah had collaborated with him on a few other projects published locally.

What we find then is a form of *hypercorrection*. The writer has rid his text of interpretation and narration in deference to the supposed scientific ethos of center-based academic writing. He simply moves to the diametrical opposite of the discourse adopted for the local audience. There are many reasons for this strategy of switching discourses. Lacking the opportunity to interact intimately with center-based disciplinary communities, local scholars are left with stereotypes of what their discourse sounds like. They are also unaware of the subtler changes taking place in the discourse, holding on to more rigid forms of scientific discourses and the object-centered rhetoric of earlier periods. Moreover, as discussed earlier, this could also be a coping strategy of saying the least amount possible because periphery scholars don't enjoy the resources to engage more fully with the ongoing conversation in the center. Whatever the mix of reasons on each specific occasion, it is clear that there is little engagement or investment in this kind of writing. In fact, the jarring discourses—in other words, the disinterested first part and the personalized conclusion—could be negotiated better to develop a multivocal/hybrid discourse with interesting oppositional possibilities (as I will demonstrate in the concluding chapter).

Note once again the conclusion of the paper, where the writer doesn't summarize the findings or the thesis even for the center audience. This is in keeping with the implicit and open-ended reverse-funnel structure typical of local papers. But RAs in the social sciences may display variation from this mode of development. They display a funnel-like structure and move to a position where they conclude with a more explicit statement about findings, purposes, or themes—even though they begin at a broad point of generality. Both modes, however, contrast with the hourglass model that Swales describes as typical of center-based writing. In that model, the paper begins by positing the general significance of the study in the disciplinary discourse, narrows down in scope to present the specific research procedures and data of the study, and finally broadens again in significance to discuss the implications of the findings.

We may consider "The Cultural Differences and Their Impact on Management Decision Making: An Overview of Japan and Sri Lanka," written by M. Nadarajasundaram—a faculty member in business management—to understand the strategies of development in the funnel-like structure. This paper is written in English and appears in *SLJSAS,* intended to be read primarily by local scholars. This is how the paper begins:

> The term culture refers to social heritage, that is, all the knowledge beliefs, customs and skills that are available to the members of the society. In other words, it is the product of a specific and unique history. It is the distinctive way of life of a group of people and their complete design for living. Culture is an emotive issue which will have a significant impact on economy, society and polity. Along with ethnicity and religion it has become one of the key issues in the world today. Culture can be defined in many ways. . . [the author provides a few more general statements on culture]. The importance of cultural issues generally enhances at a time the society faces crises or in times of deep structural change. In Sri Lanka, culture became a controversial issue with the escalation of the ethnic conflict and crises after July 1981. The structural changes that are going on in the Soviet Union also are faced with problems with traditional cultures. Their value groups (pamyt movement) and other groups are of, more on the western orientation [*sic*]. (Nadarajasundaram 1991/1992, 15)

Much of this appears to fall into topic-generalizing comments (move 1/step 2). The author orientates readers to the notion of culture. The final four sentences perform the function of claiming centrality (move 1/step 1). But this is done by showing the local relevance of the notion of culture. The writer shows the way culture underlies contemporary sources of conflict (in Sri Lanka and Russia). He doesn't claim centrality in terms of disciplinary discourse or include any statement of purpose (or thesis) in this opening. The paper thus starts at the broadest point of generality, introducing some of the fundamental concepts required for the appreciation of the discussion.

The paper goes on to provide some illuminating comparisons on the ways the Japanese and Sri Lankan cultures influence their management practices. Though the discussion may appear disjointed, digressive, and nonexplicit, all the threads are drawn together in the final section, entitled "Evaluation." The six paragraphs (numbered explicitly) summarize cogently the main points of comparison emerging from the paper. Consider the level of specificity in one of the paragraphs here.

> The general Management information techniques adopted by Japanese are quite different from that which Sri Lankans adopt in their organization. In

Japan, information techniques play a more influencing role than an information role, whereas in Sri Lanka, the information techniques play an informative role for the top Management to take decisions. The standard costing systems are more prevalent in Sri Lanka and the variances arising out of the actual and standard are studied carefully and necessary steps are taken to rectify the unfavorable variances. On the contrary in Japan decision makers rarely look into details of the cost system operations. In advance before the production starts, they look into these aspects and as soon as the production starts they will be more worried about the output and the production process. Further, the standard costs cannot be revised quickly enough for many products in the changing environment. Therefore, the usefulness of variance is increasingly open to question in Japan. As a result, many companies in Japan now rely more heavily on departmental budgets than product by product variances from standard costs. (31–32)

It is important to observe the many logical connectives the writer employs in this section (e.g., "therefore," "as a result," "on the contrary," "whereas"). Certainly, greater rhetorical effort and explicit reasoning processes are evident here. It is not as if the writer cannot write a thesis statement. It is simply that the structure desired by the writer is different—one that progresses in a linear manner to develop the thesis gradually. Anna Mauranen (1993a) calls this "end-weighting"—a rhetorical strategy of reserving the main point for last—which she illustrates with the writing of Scandinavian scholars.

There are many reasons why local writers employ this structure. The center-based rhetoric of defining the thesis and purposes explicitly in the beginning of the paper is considered a way of unfairly stacking the deck in favor of one's own position. It represents a circular—tightly knit—process of demonstrating how the preannounced thesis of the writer can be proven, with the reader brought back to the starting point at the end of the paper. While this follows a somewhat deductive reasoning process (however inductive the writers may have been in their inquiry), the persuasive strategy of local writers is different. They follow a more inductive process of providing the necessary warrants and "data" for the reader to make the necessary inferences. While the center writer orientates to the reader as a teacher and leads the audience carefully to the desired conclusion, local scholars treat the reader as a fellow traveler. Colleagues at UJ have told me that they consider front-weighted papers from the center as somewhat heavy-handed in persuasive strategies. (Recall their response to my own paper that adopted the canonical CARS structure.) They rather prefer a softer, more relaxed attitude to winning the reader's confidence. Still others have expressed the view that front-weighting is too rigidly rationalistic and, therefore, esthetically distasteful. They haven't been able to explain why they consider end-weighting more pleasurable. Perhaps it is the feeling of being surprised into knowledge after a journey through many digressions and nonexplicit references. Perhaps it is the feeling of discovering all the blocks neatly falling into place at the end of the paper.

Another striking feature in Nadarajasundaram's paper is the shortage of *metatext comments.* In using this term, Mauranen (1993a) refers to reflexive comments writers make about the structuration and progression of their text in order to "sign post" their evolving reasoning process to the reader. Through text-linguistic research, Mauranen finds center scholars using a profusion of such language—perhaps in keeping with (what she considers) their didactic rhetorical strategies. Though Nadarajasundaram's concluding paragraph above encodes at least certain logical connectives (which fall into metatext comments in a broad sense), even these are rare in the rest of the paper. As in Suseendirarajah's second paper above, Nadarajasundaram's paper is structured according to numbered subtitles, with what may appear to center readers as little effort at building cohesion and coherence. Such rhetorical devices as paragraph and section transitions, section summaries, cross references to other parts of the paper, and self-reflexive comments on the purposes and intentions of the writer are hardly used. In a paper running to eighteen pages, there are only ten places where we find such references (in a very charitable estimate):

- "For my purpose I shall confine myself to the following aspects" (16)
- "It is relevant to mention that" (16)
- "I can refer back to the cultural variables listed earlier and relate them conceptionally [*sic*] to" (18)
- "We can analyse the role of values in four key areas of" (20)
- "As a prelude to go deep into . . . it is necessary to discuss briefly" (21)
- "To analyse the comparative decision making process in both Sri Lanka and Japan, it is better, as a prelude, to look back at some important characteristics of the Japanese Management model" (24)
- "Under this system which will be discussed in detail" (24)
- "We go a little deeper and analyse further about" (25)

• "As discussed earlier" (30)
• "As I have already discussed under decision making" (31)

The relative paucity of metatext comments contributes to the implicit style of writing we found also in Suseendirarajah's paper above. The style invites readers to take responsibility for processing the text and reconstructing its coherence and logic. Local scholars consider this a way of respecting the reader's intelligence and autonomy. They consider the excessively sign-posted text of the center communities as condescending to the reader. The preference for less sign posting is connected to Hinds's (1983) notion of the differing reader/writer responsibility in writing. Local writers assume that the readers gain more pleasure by processing the text in their own terms, rather than by being led by their noses to the thesis. We can understand this preference also in terms of *positive or negative face*—as defined by conversation analysts (Brown and Levinson 1987).[17] In this sense, center-based writers are seen as being officious in their concern for the reader and in trying to maintain a positive relationship (i.e., positive face); for local writers it is more important not to intrude too much into the reader's way and to maintain the minimum contact necessary so as to respect the individuality of the reader (i.e., negative face). This writing practice might also come from the audience orientation of scholars from more homogeneous communities. In communities like UJ (and the Scandinavian communities documented in Ventola and Mauranen 1996) writers do less sign posting, as they consider their implicit rhetoric clear to their audience. But center scholars (especially those coming from more urban, multicultural, pluralistic communities, in both academic and cultural terms) have to assume a heterogeneous audience for whom all aspects of the text have to be made explicit. Needless to say, unable to decipher the logic behind our end-weighted, implicit RAs, center scholars blame us for not being sufficiently reader-friendly. They find our papers rambling, unfocused, and incoherent as they reject them for publication. When a reviewer judged the first draft of my paper in *Language in Society* as lacking coherence, this is how I angrily responded to the editor: "It appears that all I am being asked to do in my revision is to provide more sign posting to indicate explicitly the stages of my argument. But sign posting is for lazy readers." Eventually, I ended up providing more metatext comments anyway—not to mention those added by the editor himself—in order to see the paper into print.

Voice

To some extent, the management of authorial voice gets manifested through the structural and linguistic issues we have discussed in the previous sections. Many of the papers cited above employ digressions, anecdotes, analogies, and narration that frankly express the feelings and attitudes of the writers toward their subjects. In fact, local authors appear to be too personal in places that require detachment and not aggressive enough in places where they need to be. Some of the mainstream editors interviewed by Flowerdew (2001) criticize periphery authors for the inept and inconsistent management of voice in their submissions. We will reconsider here from a periphery-based perspective how voice relates to the place given to feelings and involvement in local writing.

Consider again the paper by political scientist Manivasakar (1991/ 1992) in *SLJSAS,* which we analyzed earlier for its citation patterns. In a passionate critique of only seven pages, the writer argues that Western-biased models of development enact a form of intellectual hegemony over local scholars. The very title draws attention to the gravity of the crisis: "Intellectual Colonialism vis-a-vis Pseudo Developmentalism: Irony and Agony of the Third World." The meaning of the word "agony" is not explicated in the text. It could have been used because it rhymes with "irony" and perhaps as a desired hyperbole for negative consequences. Thus the opening of the paper itself draws the reader into an emotionally charged critique of intellectual colonialism.

The body of the article involves other rhetorical devices of impassioned writing, reflected by statements like the one below. In many cases the author himself has highlighted certain phrases through the use of quotation marks. In other cases, I have highlighted the phrases and words that seem to form certain patterns of parallelism and rhyme that add to the effect desired by the author:

"Speaking with ontolog<u>ical,</u> epistemolog<u>ical</u> and teleolog<u>ical</u> implications, intellectual colonialism is not a mere manifestation of colonialism; it is the <u>s</u>ubtle, <u>s</u>inister and <u>s</u>ophisticated instrument of (neo)colonialism to control and dominate the non-western world politi<u>cally,</u> economi<u>cally,</u> soci<u>ally,</u> cultur<u>ally</u> and psychologi<u>cally</u> by producing and exporting pseudo developmentalism." (51)

"After the World War II, Americans have become self-appointed

preachers and promoters of democracy and development and global po-
licemen to protect the interest of the free society. Following the inception
of three major American Schools in the 50's and 60's—'Comparative Politics', 'Comparative administration' and 'Comparative Management'—
new theories, models, strategies and rubrics on development mush-
roomed in social science disciplines. These theories mainly based upon
'the experiences of administration and advisors attached to the new
American thrust in foreign policy,' and heavily loaded with American superiority complex and anti-socialist tendency view development as the
growth of a system closely resembling the American pattern." (52)

"We are living in an era of colonial <u>dissemination and indoctrination</u>
which entombs the <u>truth and justice</u> of development by <u>contradictions
and mystifications</u>." (53)

"The free market model development of the west has 'reduced justice
to a mechanical concept of maintaining the market equilibrium.' . . . As a
result, 'social welfare' is substituted for [by] 'capitalist welfare' and the concept of 'welfare state' tends to take the form of 'ill-fare state.' No doubt,
the alien models have provided the basis for <u>external</u> dominance and cor-
respondingly for <u>internal</u> dependence and <u>decay</u>." (54)

Note, for example, the piling up of rhymed technical terms and nominalizations in the first statement. The rhetorical effect is of a hard-hitting
prose calculated to make an impression on the reader—almost oratorical
in structure. This approach gives the impression of the inevitability and
magnitude of the hegemonic impact. It should be noted that in Tamil such
alliterative phrasing (termed *aTukku moLi,* or "patterned language") is appreciated for its beauty. These phrases may also function as rhetorical tools
to provide conviction and force for one's claims. In the second example
there are certain phrases that might be considered highly provocative by
American readers: "preachers and promoters of democracy," "global po-
licemen." and "American superiority complex." Note similarly the image
of entombment in the third statement cited above. There is no attempt
made to show any linguistic restraint here. To see that such effects are intentional, consider how the author himself draws attention to certain constructions in the fourth and final statement through the use of quotation
marks: "social welfare"/"capitalist welfare" and "welfare state"/"ill-fare
state." The pithy, epigrammatic phrases show a play with ironies and puns,

calculated to convey sarcasm. This kind of writing creates a hyperbolic and exaggerated effect that center-based readers may not commonly associate with academic rhetoric.

There are many factors that motivate this *high-involvement* style of writing. The distinction of high/low involvement in discourse was originally formulated by sociolinguists to capture the differences in the styles of different contexts and communities (Tannen 1982). In face-to-face communication the message and the medium are relatively closely intertwined, whereas in written communication the message can be objectified in the text and separated from the speaker/writer. While restraint is valued in literate contexts, where the text can be read repeatedly, rhetorical force is necessary to make an impression in oral contexts, since the spoken word is evanescent. Ethnographers of communication point out that in many oral communities strong expression of feelings is an indication of sincerity and credibility (see, e.g., Kochman 1981). A person who directly displays such affect shows that he or she cares very personally for the argument made. Kochman (1981) applies these differences to explain why Anglo-American subjects prefer arguments based on decontextualized logic, while the African American community focuses more on the ethos of the speaker in an argument. Though these levels of involvement are rarely exclusive in actual texts, it is possible to understand that some communities may prefer the high-involvement style of communication. Local scholars often strive for an effect in their argument and writing. I have seen local audiences praise speakers of emotionally charged language for their conviction, sincerity, and truth on many occasions. The arguments of such speakers usually win in any public debate. I have sometimes felt frustrated in not being able to generate the same extent of rhetorical and emotional heightening to give force to my arguments in the local community (probably because my postgraduate training in the West influenced me to value low involvement in writing).

We mustn't fail to see that ultimately there is also an epistemological difference here. For many local communities—especially those influenced by oral communicative traditions—there is less of a rigid distinction between knowledge and feelings. The center practice of effacing the self and feelings (for fear of betraying personal bias) according to the positivistic and empirical tradition of knowledge, championed in academic circles since the Enlightenment (Atkinson 1999), fails to make sense in the local community. This is not to say that it is impossible for local writers to produce this form of writing. Sivatamby (whose writing is discussed above), for example, employs a style of writing that is quite detached and abstract even in such impressionistic subject areas as literature and drama (his field). He also uses technical jargon that befuddles local readers. His complex syntax and learned ethos sometimes lack the affect that local readers look for. His writing is of course influenced by his quite extensive reading in center publications and his research training in Britain. Even so, though many of my colleagues accept the scholarly superiority of Sivatamby at least in this sense, they have told me they are not always convinced by his arguments. They sometimes suspect him of making his writing deliberately difficult and cerebral.

We must recognize that there are profound ideological implications involved in adopting a rhetoric that is detached, neutral, and uninvolved. Consider the dilemma for Manivasakar, whose work was quoted at length above. Accommodating the detached/impersonal writing conventions of the center will only mute his critique of center academic hegemony. Also, the writer cannot adopt the very conventions and discourses associated with this intellectual colonialism. His hard-hitting, passionate writing displays a refreshingly polemical approach that conveys his position in no uncertain terms. (But note that the hostility he generates is against an abstract position, not against rival scholars.) This author-centered rhetoric in his writing differs from the adoption of the scientistic/positivist ethos that Bazerman (1988, chapter 10) finds political science to be using somewhat inconsistently and inappropriately for its disciplinary rhetoric. Manivasakar's rhetoric certainly sounds more appropriate to his subject and purpose. It is important that he resist the expected genre conventions in order to express a position that questions the dominant discourses associated with the discipline. More importantly, to suppress his feelings is to neutralize and muffle his critical position on the subject.

Consider the many ironies behind my own experience of writing a paper on the social and cultural conflicts for local students in using an American textbook in ESL classrooms. I sent the paper to an American journal after considerable revision, well aware of the need to restrain the expression of feelings in my writing. However, no amount of postgraduate training in the West and further efforts helped to efface all direct indexes of affect (some of which were necessary to carry out my purposes in that paper). The paper was subsequently rejected, primarily on the findings of the referees that a demonstration of excessive feelings betrayed my ideological biases. This is how one referee stated his or her judgment:

> Certainly, impassioned writing is to be admired, especially if it is grounded in theoretical writings, as much of this article is. . . . Despite these valid aspects of the article, the unnecessarily hostile tone of the writer towards the specific materials used and towards western society and values in general undermines the logic of this argument. . . . While I will always support provocative articles which enable readers to re-examine long-held beliefs, articles whose logic is obscured by hostility are counterproductive. Rather than open dialog, they preclude it. For this reason, I am not recommending publication.

It is interesting how in such an important gatekeeping context this reviewer adheres to the classic Western stereotype that feelings are automatically opposed to logic. Feelings are translated as "hostility," which is then ruled as "unnecessary" and turns out to be a reason to bar the paper from publication. It is significant how easily something "critical" becomes something that is "hostile." It is in this sense that writing conventions can become a weapon for suppressing positions oppositional to the dominant discourse. Style colonizes!

But the story doesn't end there. While the American reviewers (revealed by the spelling conventions in the quote above) rejected the paper, I next sent it to a British journal (whose editor was based in Ireland). Since I didn't fully agree with the views of the American reviewers, I submitted the paper without any substantive revisions. Surprisingly, the paper was accepted without a single alteration to the text. The manuscript was not sent back to me; the editor's letter simply stated that the referees had unanimously recommended publication and that the paper was being scheduled for printing. (The paper now appears as Canagarajah 1993a). This pronounced turn of events suggests that the reception of feelings is often subjective and relative. What is unreasonably passionate for one is consummately logical for another. It is possible that there were other reasons for the differences in the publishing decision: for example, the British reviewers were less piqued by the criticism of an American textbook; the British journal was less selective; the British journal was more comfortable with a more relaxed writing style, more typical of British academic writing compared to American RAs; there is a lack of widely shared criteria for evaluation in the review of manuscripts in the humanities and social sciences.

But such possibilities only point to the subjectivity still present in the review process of RAs. It is for this reason that center referees have to be more tolerant and flexible in their evaluation of periphery RAs. If not, they would impose their personal peculiarities in the name of a presumed rhetorical standard that doesn't exist.

Conclusion

The description of local textual conventions in the UJ community shouldn't be construed to mean that all periphery writing displays such rhetoric. We must conduct more research on variation in the RAs of non–Anglo-American communities. There are of course some interesting studies from other periphery communities that both confirm the above description and show additional variations.[18] As for explaining why local writers may adopt the styles and strategies discussed here, we have considered a range of factors: the cultural predisposition of the local community; its preferred linguistic/rhetorical practices; its level of integration into the respective mainstream disciplinary circles; and, finally—something that has a bearing on all the above factors—the material conditions of the local communities. The purpose here is not to demonstrate only the "problems" resulting for local writers. These texts display other writing conventions and knowledge-making practices that are at times refreshingly oppositional to the discourses in the center. I have tried to suggest that it is for this reason unfair, if not hegemonical, for center reviewers to judge periphery RAs according to conventions that apply mostly to their own cultural and material conditions.

It is also important to recognize that local writers are not passive in the face of conflicting discourses. If we consider what happens in the contact zones where these writers meet divergent conventions and conditions in writing for publication, we find that they develop creative alternatives for communication. For example, there are many coping strategies they practice to overcome the conflicts and limitations they face. New features in their RA structures—such as the brief statement of methodology (in order to cope with the lack of sophisticated research instruments and procedures); the introduction focusing on the general significance of the study (to make up for the lack of recent publications that would enable them to conduct a literature review); and the citation of references from book notices and reviews, with the impression of personal knowledge—all show the development of alternative textual conventions. The switching of discourses (analogous to codeswitching in bilingual communication) shows how these writers are adept at adjusting to changing contexts. More fascinating is the presence of divergent discursive traditions within the body of a single text (such as the detached analysis, the emotional appeal, and the frank personal voice in Suseendirarajah's and Sivatamby's papers). They exemplify the *literate arts of the contact zone,* which Mary Louise Pratt (1991) theorizes as the creative communicative strategies developed in situations of cultural contact. We will consider in the final chapter how these strategies can be developed more consciously among periphery scholars to create multivocal and hybrid text traditions that can resist the intellectual hegemony of the center.

5. Publishing Requirements and Material Constraints

I've heard all sorts of airy-fairy kinds of things about how we'll all be connected by technology and be able to call up anywhere in the world and find out about epidemics. But we still have to actually go there with gloves and masks, get samples and get them out to a lab, even in a country where there isn't one. During the Ebola outbreak in Zaire, we sent a satellite phone with our people so they could tell us what they needed most urgently. In Kikwit, a city of 250,000 people, there was no E-mail, fax or regular electricity. There was no radio station to deliver health messages. They had to be delivered, instead, by bicyclists with megaphones.—C. J. Peters, Center for Disease Control and Prevention.

Putting pen to paper and composing thoughts coherently doesn't complete the publishing process. There are many other requirements one has to meet in order to see the paper in print in an academic journal. These are the publishing practices and conventions, which are usually treated as having no implications for the language, content, or style of writing—requirements such as the format of the copy text; bibliographical and documentation conventions; the weight and quality of the paper; the copies and postage required; the procedures in negotiating revisions; and the styles of interaction with the editors and reviewers. Part of these requirements is effective communication in certain non-RA textual genres, such as the composition of a cover letter accompanying the paper, interpreting the editor's decision letter and reviewers' commentary following the refereeing process, and writing the "follow-up" cover letter after revising or proofreading the original manuscript. Swales (1996) mentions some of these texts as what he calls "occluded genres": "those which support the research publication process but are not themselves part of the research record" (45). My consideration of these practices in this chapter includes many other publishing requirements that can be added to those listed by Swales. While many of these para-textual conventions and requirements are taken for granted by center scholars as mundane details of publication, they create considerable problems for periphery scholars. Looking at these practices from the point of view of periphery scholars will serve to defamiliarize them, revealing their hidden assumptions and consequences for closer scrutiny.

Although certain publishers and editorial committees have started giving thought to the discursive aspects of writing and committed themselves to more democratic publication practices—as in the avoidance of sexist language; the use of a language accessible to classroom practitioners; and the accommodation of a wider range of research methodologies, styles of presentation, and modes of textualization (see, e.g., the guidelines for contributors in *College Composition and Communication* [*CCC*])—the publishing conventions mentioned above are not considered problematical. Perhaps this attitude exists because some of these formal and physical requirements are perceived as nonideological or nonpolitical and as not discriminating against anyone. My contention, however, is that these publishing practices can still hamper scholars who may successfully overcome the linguistic/discursive differences in writing for center journals. We will see in this chapter that even scholars who have effectively been inducted into center-based academic discourses and RA genres during their training/research in the West find these "nondiscursive" requirements too overwhelming to continue publishing on their return home.

Although these requirements may broadly be referred to as nondiscursive (see Canagarajah 1996b for previous usage of this term), it is important to assert that these publishing practices do have implications for discourse—whether in the sense of knowledge paradigms, ideological complexes, or communicative practices. Therefore these requirements are not extraneous to the construction and constitution of the text. Bazerman (1988, 257–77) has shown how some of these para-textual conventions have been growing in significance and sophistication as disciplinary communities have evolved across time. He traces how the style manual of the APA has grown in size from six and a half pages in 1923 to "approximately two hundred oversized pages of rules, ranging from such mechanics as spelling and punctuation through substantive issues of content and organization," in 1983 (259). For him, the tighter definition of publishing conventions in the APA appears to have kept step with the discourse of behaviorism as it progressively gained scientific respect during the years under consideration. For example, he observes that the APA citation system "is very convenient for listing and summarizing a series of related findings, but it is awkward for extensive quotation or discussion of another text, and even more awkward for contrasting several texts in detail" (274). What this means is that "individuals assumulate bits, follow rules, check each other out, and add their bits to an encyclopedia of behavior of subjects without subjectivity" (275). Thus the conventions rigidly provide roles for writers, readers, and research participants, evoking the highly positivistic orientation to human subjects adopted by behaviorism.

This example shows that requirements relating to bibliography and documentation have ideological implications. First, the close fit between a disciplinary community's beliefs and its para-textual conventions presents alarming implications for knowledge construction. Those from divergent knowledge paradigms, and presumably different communicative conventions, will be kept away from the dominant circle's publications. Asking periphery scholars to adopt these conventions without question, or penalizing them for not being able to practice them, will therefore lead to the center's continuing monopoly on scholarly knowledge. Second, since these publishing requirements are more directly implicated in the availability of material resources, they place a special burden on periphery scholars. Access to computers, fax machines, E-mail, and copiers, and funds for postage and durable stationery, are matters that have to do with economy. Third, the fact that these practices are often tacit or uncodified also means that scholars who are off-networked are denied an important means of learning these rules. How to interpret an editor's decision and how to frame a cover letter are skills acquired primarily through repeated engagement with publishing circles. Therefore these publishing practices cause special problems for periphery writers. They can disable even sound academics who are otherwise armed with valuable data and scholarship. We shouldn't underestimate the extent to which these seemingly innocent para-textual conventions may be implicated in the intellectual hegemony of the center.

I can give a better understanding of the ways these publishing practices affect local writers by narrating my own experiences in attempting to publish from the periphery. The experiences of my colleagues regarding how they too struggled with these conventions are also reproduced here from my notes. This narration will help us understand the ways in which the para-textual and publishing requirements of periphery circles differ from those of the center.

From Draft to Manuscript

It was after I had finished composing my paper (referred to in the last chapter) on fish-vendor codeswitching that I wondered which journal I should send it to. I am now aware that many center scholars have a good idea of their target journal early on so that they can tailor their text to suit its dominant discursive and scholarly characteristics. And I have wondered why my colleagues and I at UJ virtually always tried to finish a paper before thinking of the most appropriate journal to send it to. One reason may be that we didn't have too much choice. In the local library, there was sometimes only a single journal related to the field whose editorial address and requirements we could obtain for our purposes. In other cases it might take a few months to inquire from knowledgeable colleagues about the best journal for the paper. In my case, I was lucky to find the journal *Anthropological Linguistics (AL)* in the library. Although I had a nagging suspicion that *AL* might not value very highly sociolinguistic studies on contemporary communicative events, I didn't have a better alternative. This was the only journal locally available for fields broadly related to sociolingusitics. It is well known that even if one has an excellently composed paper with sound data, the paper may not get published if it is not sent to the appropriate journal. The areas of specialty, preferred writing styles, and typical ideological stances of the journal can make a big difference in the prospects of the paper getting published.

Many periphery scholars are denied the ability to screen journals in order to choose those that are appropriate venues for their submission. Interviewing forty scientists from eighteen periphery countries, Gibbs (1995) found that their foremost complaint was the dwindling number of journals available in local libraries. While unfavorable exchange rates often prevent periphery institutions from subscribing to more than a few journals, even foreign funding agencies are gradually cutting down on the journals they send local libraries. At UJ, for example, the Asia Foundation, which had been sending a complementary copy of the *TESOL Quarterly* for many years, curtailed this practice in 1990 due to their own budgetary constraints. Given these conditions, the journals usually available in periphery institutions are, at best, only the major publications in the field. More specialized ones are normally inaccessible. At UJ, for the field of ESL, the *TESOL Quarterly* and the *ELT Journal* would be available (somewhat belatedly and intermittently), but not the *Journal of Second Language Writing, English for Specific Purposes (ESP),* or even the *RELC Journal* (which is published closer to home in Singapore). A related problem is that most periphery scholars don't know the pecking order of journals. Senior scholars in linguistics at UJ who had done research work in the 1960s were familiar with *Anthropological Linguistics* but didn't understand the significance of more recently established (but highly rated) journals like *Language in Society* and *Multilingua*. The proliferation of journals in the West is often confusing to local scholars, especially when most of them cannot be seen/read there.

Apart from the fact that we do not always make the appropriate choice in sending a paper for publication, the target of most scholars is usually quite high. We unwittingly attempt to get published in the leading journals of our field because they are the only journals we know of. But facing such stiff competition, most periphery scholars tend to give up after the initial submission. However, scholars in the center have a variety of other options for getting their papers published in middle- or lower-rung journals. It has been shown that their papers usually get published one way or another—through redrafting or serial submission down a pecking order of journals (Relman 1978). In my own experience, however, I found that most local scholars don't enjoy those possibilities. For example, a colleague in philosophy abandoned a manuscript after attempting to publish it in the only journal available in the university library. Although he was aware of a few other journals, he didn't know their bibliographical conventions or mailing addresses, as the library didn't subscribe to these journals. My now-abandoned discourse analysis of American media reports on Sri Lankan violence would have faced a better chance of getting published if I had known of less specialized but ideologically informed journals like *Text,* rather than relentlessly resubmitting it to the somewhat technical *Language and Communication*.

There are additional problems for scholars who might focus on areas of specialization whose journals may not be available in periphery libraries. Thus, having done research work on composition instruction in the United States, I could not consider publishing my work on returning to my home institution. Composition remains a very North American enterprise (Muchiri et al. 1995), and most periphery universities don't subscribe to journals in this field. Though I had fascinating data from the dissertation I had just completed, I couldn't disseminate my findings from Jaffna, as I was cut off from composition journals. Similarly, while I was studying issues relating to the interface of sociolinguistics and pedagogy in ELT, it was after relocating to the United States that I came to know of journals like the *Journal of Multilingual and Multicultural Development* and *Language and Education*. Not knowing that these specialized and focused journals existed, I was trying hard to publish my research in the general ELT journals that were available in my library. There is a different problem confronting the dissemination of studies like that of Panditamani (discussed in chapters 3 and 4) that are of largely local relevance. As it doesn't fall into any of the recognized disciplines as defined by center communities, this knowledge has to be shaped to suit the journals of a specific field. In the process of doing so, the subject is likely to lose the type of significance it has for the local community.

As for my paper on codeswitching, having decided on *AL,* I obtained a recent issue of that journal from the library to adopt their bibliographical conventions for my manuscript. To my chagrin, I found that their style sheet had to be obtained by writing to the editors. Knowing that this would take at least six months, given the breakdown of our postal system, I resorted to getting some clues about their conventions from the papers they had published in their pages in previous issues. In fact, many journals do not carry their style sheet in every issue. Even in cases where the style sheet appears in a single issue each year (like *CCC*), this practice poses difficulties for periphery scholars whose libraries do not hold all issues of the journal. In the case of a paper I submitted to *World Englishes (WE),* matters were even worse: I didn't have a single copy of their journal in the library to check their conventions. Therefore I mentioned in my cover letter that I would change the format if they sent their style sheet after reviewing my paper. It is also the case that many periphery libraries do not have the standard style manuals, or have only earlier editions of them. Thus I couldn't obtain the APA or Modern Language Association (MLA) handbooks at UJ. In fact, the different conventions of documenting and formatting the manuscript that we find in academic publishing can cause considerable confusion. Leaving aside the successive revised editions of better-known style manuals like the APA and MLA, different journals sometimes adopt their own in-house conventions. In cases where local scholars attempt to resubmit a paper, the manuscript therefore has to be completely retyped according to the new conventions (when most center scholars can make the changes conveniently on their soft copy). Perhaps because of these practical problems, many local disciplinary communities have adopted a lackadaisical attitude toward bibliographical conventions. As a result, my colleagues have often been chastised by center editors for failing to closely follow the expected conventions. Their papers are treated as if they were shoddily or unprofessionally prepared. Many journals, in fact, threaten to mail back the papers if their conventions are not followed closely. My colleagues, on the other hand, ask me whether all these different styles and conventions—often within the same field—are indeed necessary.

As I prepared to get my manuscript on codeswitching typed, I was surprised to discover another occluded requirement—the quality of the stationery. The dirt-colored, lightweight recycled paper that was available locally looked unimpressive. In fact, the stationery I had was quite special by local standards, as I had managed to get a friend to bring it from the capital. Because of the ongoing fighting, the government had banned stationery in my region, fearing that it could be used for propaganda purposes by the nationalist militants. The only paper allowed was that in ruled notebooks for school purposes. Interestingly, the local newspapers were printed on this ruled paper. I had typed some of the submissions for local journals on this paper. But I knew I had to do better for center journals. Some journals specifically request paper of a particular weight and color (e.g., *Language*). At any rate, reviewers and editors can be biased against manuscripts that are produced in an unimpressive fashion. I had to eventually type my manuscript on this recycled paper, as I didn't have any alternative.

Consider also the technical difficulties in composing the written product for submission. As computers are hard to come by, one normally has to manually type the manuscript. Leaving aside the difficulties of finding computers freely or obtaining support services for them, the shortage of power in the region makes them inoperable. For that matter, we couldn't even use a much-coveted electronic typewriter, one of which happened to be available in my department (having been a gift from the Asia Foundation for the purpose of preparing teaching material). Even if one does get access to one of these machines, and the necessary electricity, there are several problems to be faced in manually typing a script. The ribbons are usually worn out since they are not easy to obtain. As they are also expensive, we have to use our ribbons to the maximum extent possible. Such conditions having existed for a long time, local readers have probably gotten used to light print and thin paper, whereas readers in the West (used to the sharpness of laser-printed texts) tend to find such typing all but indecipherable. There have been many instances where center reviewers have complained of my typed manuscripts from Jaffna being illegible. Some have advised me with good-natured helpfulness that the text should be neatly word-processed and laser-printed when I submitted the next draft (as happened with a manuscript I sent to *Language in Society*). There can also be cases (although they are difficult to substantiate) where the print distracts reviewers from the argument and makes them reject the paper. Swales (1990) quotes an editor "of an international journal" whom he interviewed as saying, "We get single copies of these papers from India. They are manually typed with an old ribbon on that grey recycled paper. As they won't photocopy there is I'm afraid little that we can do with them" (103). Similarly, it is reported that Chinua Achebe's manuscript of the now-famous *Things Fall Apart* lay unread in a dusty corner of the publishing house it was sent to for many months, as it was written by hand, till a friend in England got it typed for Achebe there (Currey et al. 1990, 149). Likewise, an editor of *ESP* recently shared with me the fact that they get many handwritten submissions from China and are unsure as to how to deal with them (D. Belcher, personal communication, 12 March 1999). I have myself wondered many times whether it would be better to just send a handwritten script, as they are generally clearer than our typed manuscripts. But then I realize that editors might just as easily reject such a paper out of hand, as they clearly state that only typed papers are accepted.

It took about three weeks to type my twenty-odd pages for *AL*. This was partly because there was only one typewriter in the department, and its use had to be negotiated in light of other departmental demands, such as routine correspondence and official business. It was rare at that time for anyone to have a typewriter at home in Jaffna. When our department stenographer finally finished typing the paper, I was excited. The time had come to mail the paper off and see what the referees had to say about my research. But one look at the first page showed that it would not be so easy. There were so many typographical and spelling errors that it was necessary to spend several days correcting them. Our mostly monolingual stenographers, lacking a knowledge of English, usually make many mistakes in their typing. Given the above-mentioned constraints, retyping the corrected manuscript would have caused further delays and additional work amidst other departmental needs for the typewriter. Therefore it is common to find local manuscripts that have editorial marks and correction fluid all over them. In many cases, there is not even an attempt to correct at all. On some occasions I have been so exhausted by the typing process that I have rushed the paper to the mailbox without proofreading it carefully.

There are other cultural reasons why we in the periphery don't mind submitting a clumsily typed or edited paper. The print culture creates a unique orientation to the language and presentation of the text that is absent in nonprint or oral cultures. While the practices of printing develop a sharp sensitivity to the materiality of the text among center scholars, the local culture encourages looking at the printed message and ignoring the imperfections of the medium. In the academic culture of the center the perfection of the textual product appears to be valorized for its own sake. Leaving aside the communicability of the content, the text must be meticulously printed to be acceptable. Whereas an occasional failure to "dot the I's and cross the T's" doesn't cause much trouble for local scholars, for Western reviewers these are spelling problems. They treat such an incidence so even in cases where the same word is correctly typed in another context in the same paper. Peer reviewers at UJ who commented on my papers always ruled out the imperfections of the copy as of no consequence. They rarely noticed these. For center referees, however, the appearance of our texts typically indicates sloppy writing, linguistic incompetence, or a shabby lack of professionalism, damaging the prospects of the paper getting published. Reading the life of a famous Tamil poet/scholar who prospered as a publisher in England (M. J. Tambimuttu), I was amused to find that he had refused to redo an early collection of e. e. cummings when the poet objected to some typesetting problems (Williams 1989, 290). When Tambimuttu argued that the mistakes were inconsequential, cummings offered the manuscript to another publisher, denying him the honor of publishing a famous poet. Habits die hard, however closely we are involved with the print culture of the West!

On the Way to the Editor

There was more work left to do before the manuscript could be sent to the journal. The cover letter had always been a confusing thing for me to write. I debated whether I should compose a short matter-of-fact letter that wouldn't influence the professional judgment of the editor or a more aggressive one suitable for "selling" my product in the intellectual market-place. The latter is the stereotype held by my colleagues and myself as typical of the tone adopted by center scholars who present a more confident and elevated image of their "self," contrasting with our preferred self-effacement.

Eventually, my letter to *AL* had the following features: I gave the title of the paper at the top and started by saying, "I am sending herewith the original typescript and a copy of my manuscript for publication in your journal." In the next paragraph, I said, "To briefly introduce myself," and went on to mention the institute I obtained my doctorate from, the name of my well-known thesis advisor, the topic of my dissertation, and my present position in the local institution. In the following paragraph, I highlighted the significant features of my manuscript. I insisted on its originality and its appeal to the academic community. In the next paragraph, I talked about the difficulties in receiving mail in Sri Lanka and gave a second address in the capital city for a copy of all future correspondence. I even nominated my brother who was a student at Cambridge to read the proofs on my behalf! I concluded by "hoping that you will receive the manuscript safely and we can manage to communicate uninterrupted by the fighting here" and gave the editor permission to make necessary changes in the manuscript before printing the paper. I have found that many of my colleagues employ such features: the long personal introduction, the insistence on the originality and value of the paper, and the assumption that the paper will appear in print shortly.

John Swales's (1996) study of submission letters reveals that my letters from UJ contain all the ingredients of a bad submission letter. Comparing a corpus of submission letters by both native speakers and non-native speakers of English (NNS), he says, "NNS were more likely to press for an early response, to express hope for success, or to make *credentialist* claims about their qualifications and experience" (1996, 46; emphasis in original). Here is how Swales lists the components of the letter and advises on the content:

1. *Submission.* He recommends a "neutral submission statement" and advises against being too "pushy" about the worth of the paper.

2. *Commentary.* He recommends only a few statements about the content of the manuscript but suggests stating the previous forms of the paper, such as conference presentations. He advises against including a summary of the paper.

3. *Advocacy for the paper.* He says that this is "usually unnecessary" unless the paper may at first sight appear unsuitable for a particular journal.

4. *Bio-data.* He feels that "none of [this] is relevant to the quality of the paper" and that it is unnecessary, as most journals request a short bio-data to accompany the paper anyway.

5. *Publication plans.* He advises that the writer should declare that the paper is not being considered elsewhere for publication.

6. *Offers and invitations to revise.* He advises against this. That the writer agrees to revise is usually taken for granted, and asking editors to revise (which Swales finds many NNS doing) is treated as somewhat peculiar.

7. *Request for response.* He permits a formal expression of hope of hearing from the editors soon but advises against expressing even "justifiable anxieties" about delays. (Swales 1996, 55–56)

Swales finds other components of NNS submission letters peculiar to these scholars' concerns, such as information about scholarly networks (mutual friends, thesis advisors, or other well-known scholars who have read and approved the manuscript) and reference to mail/address contingencies, and leaves them out of his recommended components.

There are many reasons why we periphery scholars include some of the peculiar features ruled out by Swales in submission letters. Coming from off-networked academic circles and institutions that have no prestige or name recognition, there is a need for us to make credentializing statements. (There is also a peculiarly South Asian convention of overly relying on one's certificates to prove one's worth—as Gumperz [1982b] brings out from an analysis of a failed communicative encounter in a British workplace.) In our submission letters, therefore, we indulge in providing lengthy biographical comments to show that we have undergone training in respectable Western universities or that we hold very high administrative positions in our local institutions. We also feel the need to indulge in some "name-dropping"—mentioning our better-known supervisors, colleagues, and research associates—to assert our "insider status" in center academic circles. This networking information is expected to make up for our relative obscurity in the academic landscape. Note that the mere letterhead, or even the logo on the envelope, is sufficient to indicate the respectable academic pedigree of center scholars. Similarly, the detailed discussions on ways of receiving mail and communicating must be understood from our geographical location and availability of resources. The problems we face with our mail systems—which I will elaborate below—make it important that we forewarn editors about the possible delays and difficulties in corresponding with us. Although such details may bore center editors, and even seem redundant, they are of real and necessary importance to us.

Some of the other peculiarities in our submission letters may result from the lack of insider awareness of center publishing processes and practices. The aggressive lobbying for the paper and the assumption that the paper will go straight through to print result often from ignorance of the protracted refereeing process. Failing to mention that the paper is not being considered elsewhere again results from an estrangement from the culture of serial submissions. Ceding control over the revising process to the editor can be attributed to our lack of experience in the collective negotiation practices of the West. Our limited involvement in the publishing practices of the center also contributes to our inability to strike the right balance between formality and involvement in our letters. We tend to adopt one extreme or the other in our tone. In fact, not all my colleagues write such chatty letters as I did. Some of them sound very professional as they simply write a couple of lines, thinking that they should let the research paper speak for itself. A colleague from linguistics wrote this after the salutation: "I am enclosing a paper analyzing some of the differences in the patterns of sentence structure in Tamil and Sinhala. I hope you will find the paper suitable for publication in your esteemed journal." This was all that her submission letter amounted to. Such a letter could create an image of someone lacking involvement and confidence in his or her work. All this leads to periphery scholars cutting a peculiar image in submission letters. If, as Swales (1996) observes, "the arts and skills of professional self-presentation are not restricted to the main text" (56), then the image we convey of ourselves through our fumbling attempts at striking the right tone in our submission letters can damage our chances of getting our papers published. ·

After composing the submission letter mentioned here, I discovered the need to get multiple copies of my manuscript for the referees of the journal. The few Xeroxing machines available in Jaffna are so overused that the copies are often too light or too dark to be easily legible. In fact, for long stretches of time the whole town may not have photocopying facilities if the shipment of Xerox paper doesn't arrive. The incessant power cuts also limit Xeroxing services to a few hours in a day. After making some inquiries, I cycled to the only store in the town center that still had a functioning Xerox machine at that time. I was relieved to find that they did have some copying paper, even though they charged an exorbitant rate. Copying is not cheap in most periphery communities, and Xeroxing machines are not ubiquitous as they are in the West—as also attested by scholars from Kenya and Tanzania (Muchiri et al. 1995, 187). But, in spite of the effort and expense, the results did not meet my expectations in this case. The irregular shading on the pages made the script difficult to read. I even considered sending carbon copies of the typed original instead— these were surprisingly clearer than the original and the Xeroxes. But I wasn't sure if the editors would accept the carbon copies in place of the Xerox copies. In fact, the requirement for additional copies is taking many sophisticated new forms these days. There are more and more journals that require a soft copy to be sent with manuscripts. Some journals even state that it is not advisable to submit a manuscript if a soft copy is not available (e.g., *Georgetown University Journal of Languages and Literature*). There are also editors who have begun requesting manuscripts to be transferred electronically. Since many journals are published in both soft- and hard-copy versions these days, the submission of a diskette becomes important. Scholars who do not have access to computers or word-processing facilities cannot consider publishing in many of these journals. Such requirements convey the impression that only the technologically well disposed can engage in academic publishing.

When I then went to the post office to mail my bulky package to the editor, I realized that one also has to be rich to publish academically. It is not often realized that submitting a manuscript for consideration is an expensive affair for periphery scholars. Mailing multiple copies of a paper (sometimes with envelopes for each referee) is very costly, as the package will be heavy. Furthermore, many journals request that stamps be sent for the manuscript to be mailed to referees and/or for it to be returned to the writer.[1] Since foreign stamps are not available locally, periphery authors are requested to enclose a money order for that amount. Foreign postage is expensive in the local currency due to the often unfavorable exchange rates. Added to all this are many other expenses, such as for the Xerox copies of the manuscript. In cases where journals charge page fees from authors for publishing their work—as high as $150 per page for some, like *Physics Essays* (Gibbs 1995, 12)—additional financial burdens are incurred. One can imagine how costly would be the repeated process of revising and resubmitting papers from the periphery.

After all this, one must still contend with the fact that the safe delivery of the manuscript is not under one's control. Manuscripts from the periphery often get lost in the mail. In other cases, the receipt of manuscripts is acknowledged, but the decision of the referees fails to arrive. In still other cases, there is no acknowledgment of receipt at all. My colleagues advised me that since mail could get lost either going out or coming in, it was often difficult to know at what point communication had broken. Furthermore, all mail coming into the region is screened by the local political authorities for seditious matter. Apart from the delays this creates in receiving the mail, the letters are often torn or tattered beyond recognition. Sometimes the local post office calls people to come and identify the mail that may belong to them from among the many tattered envelopes in their mailbags. Keeping in touch with publishers is therefore not an easy matter. While sending my own manuscript through multiple channels, I resorted to asking editors to send an additional copy of their correspondence to the second address, in the capital city, in order to ensure receipt of at least one copy. Many editors didn't have the patience to accede to this unusual request. The editors of the *TESOL Quarterly* and *Language in Society* were the most obliging, as they had been made aware of periphery academic conditions during their own fieldwork in such regions. One can imagine how problems with the mail can severely constrain the ability of periphery scholars to engage in the interactive process of revising papers in collaboration with editors and referees in the center.

After all the trouble I took in composing and mailing the paper on codeswitching for *AL,* the story had a premature ending. Though I received an initial postcard acknowledging receipt of the paper, I failed to receive the decision letter from the editors following the review process. After sending repeated letters inquiring about the fate of my paper and getting no reply, I assumed that contact had broken down at some point. Having waited for more than a year, I took a chance by sending the manuscript to another journal—well aware that this represented the academic sin of simultaneous multiple submissions. Finding an advertisement for *Language in Society* by chance in the pages of a book I was reading, I retyped the paper and sent it to the editorial address given there. This was a "blind" submission, as I didn't have access to any copies of that journal to understand their discourse, areas of special interest, or ideological leanings. But my colleagues and I have often submitted manuscripts to a journal's address we had obtained from somewhere, even though we didn't know much about the previous studies that had appeared in that journal or its publishing conventions. This practice has become part of our publishing culture.

From the Editor with Love

The grueling process of negotiating with editors and referees calls up other conventions one has to master. Understanding the editor's letter of decision can be tricky. The euphemistic modes of expression and politeness strategies create considerable problems of interpretation. Discerning the final decision of the editors, and understanding the revisions they would prefer, may take much effort. There is at present a confusing variability in how decisions are coded and conveyed—creating misunderstandings among even center professionals. Some scholars have just begun studying the genre conventions of editorial decision letters (Flowerdew and Dudley-Evans 1999). This difficulty in understanding and interpreting the decisions from the refereeing process perhaps accounts for the fact that very few periphery scholars resubmit their papers for consideration. An editor of *ESP* recently mentioned that the primary reason that his journal doesn't feature too many papers from the periphery is because contributors from there rarely resubmit their papers after the initial review (T. Dudley-Evans, personal communication, 7 March 1999). There are many cases where my colleagues have abandoned as hopeless manuscripts that received a guardedly enthusiastic "revise and resubmit" decision. The fact is that unless periphery scholars receive a clear and unambiguous signal of the potential in their papers, they won't expend the effort to revise them. Given all the insurmountable material problems described above, we can imagine why they would lack the energy to revise a paper with uncertain publishing prospects.

In my files I have different kinds of editorial correspondence I have received. Some letters are very detached, ambiguous, and vague, letting me read the referee comments and use them any way I like for my revisions—if I care to resubmit the paper. Some editors have summarized and interpreted the comments from the multiple referees to support the editorial decision—in what has sometimes appeared a partisan interpretation! In other cases, the reviewer commentary was not enclosed, as the editor presented the final decision on behalf of the referees and either rejected or accepted the paper outright. Typical of the latter is a letter I once received from the editor of *System:* "Your article ————— has now been considered by our referees and I regret that we have decided that we cannot publish it in *System,* at least in its present form. . . . You also draw some conclusions that are flimsily based. . . . Thank you for contacting us; perhaps we may hear from you again." There is a very sparse use of politeness strategies here. Perhaps as a result of this, the decision of the editors is conveyed in no uncertain terms. Though the news may be bad, one is sometimes thankful to receive a clearly conveyed decision. (That this paper was accepted soon after by *Language, Culture, and Curriculum* without any need for revision is a comment on the subjectivity in the refereeing process. The acceptance, too, was outright—conveyed solely by the editor's letter, unaccompanied by reviewer comments!)

In many letters, however, it appears as if the editor was unsure of the right tone to strike, vacillating between criticism, encouragement, and formality. In such letters there seems to be a tussle between being polite and being useful. While some lean on the side of offering constructive criticism to improve the quality of the paper (however unflattering the comments may sound), others are preoccupied with showing consideration for the feelings of the writer. Politeness is itself a cultural construct: ways of being polite by center editors sometimes sound condescending and equivocating to local scholars. For example, in the case of a paper I mailed to *Language Awareness,* I gave up after the first attempt, thinking that the editor was not interested in publishing the paper. The letter said: "The paper is of interest to the journal, but the editorial board feels that there is clearly more work to be done on it before it can be accepted for publication. If you feel able to address the points raised in the referee's report, they would be pleased to have another look at the paper at that stage." Though the last line ended on a positive note—"We look forward to receiving the revised version in due course"—I ignored it as mere formality. Phrases like "*clearly* more work to be done," "if you *feel able* to address the points," and "*another look* at the paper at that stage" sounded too off-putting to me. I was surprised, however, to get a letter a few months later from the journal's editorial assistant, inquiring if I had completed the revisions for the journal: "Mr. ———— has asked me to write and ask you whether your paper entitled ———— which he had suggested you revise for *Language Awareness,* is anywhere near completion. He is at present looking for possible papers for inclusion in this year's issues and would be very happy to receive your revised version." I had earlier failed to detect this enthusiasm toward publishing my paper. Such misinterpretations may be influenced by the stereotype we in the periphery hold of center communication as more formal and matter-of-fact than is warranted. When even scholars in the center have to interact over long periods of time very intensely with editorial boards and editors to develop the intuition to read their minds, periphery scholars lack the level of engagement to develop such an understanding.

A different kind of problem is interpreting the stance of the referees in their commentary. Referees themselves don't always declare their decision on publishability very clearly. In fact, their comments can range anywhere from four lines to four pages. Furthermore, journals don't always inform the contributors of what criteria were used to evaluate the paper. To complicate matters, negotiating the differences in the judgments of multiple referees can be a problem. Similarly, negotiating the tensions between the editor's decision letter and referee comments can require a lot of work at times. In the case of a paper I sent to *WE*, the editor's response sounded somewhat positive (it sounds more encouraging through the years whenever I reread it, having read many more negative decision letters in the interval!). This is how the editor's brief letter is worded: "We have now received evaluations on your above paper from the reviewers. I herewith enclose a copy of one of the evaluations which is very detailed and should be helpful to you in revising your paper. We would be very happy to consider your paper for publication in *WE* after we receive the revised version." But I decided not to resubmit the paper because the referee sounded too negative. The referee's comments began: "In its current form, this paper is not suitable for publication. However, it could be made publishable if certain revisions were made. Currently, however, this paper is really two papers in one and as a result attempts to cover too much ground." I failed to note at that time that only one reviewer's comments were sent to me—perhaps because the comments were detailed enough to help prepare the final form of the manuscript. It is possible that the other referees commented even more positively.[2] (This selective mailing of reviewer comments can also be disconcerting.)

Lacking an efficient peer-reviewing circle in the periphery to help revise papers, we often treat the referees' comments from the center as the sole means of obtaining feedback on our writing. But we are not always assured of getting in-depth comments from referees that will be of help to us. The lack of adequate comments to help revise the text constructively can also hamper many periphery scholars' decisions to resubmit. Perhaps there should be more commitment from the referees to the review process. In some cases, they may have to adopt a mentoring role to shepherd quality periphery papers into print. Though some kind of standardization in the format, scope, and language of referee comments is also desirable, it is idealistic to expect that to happen any time soon.

Another genre of writing that many of my colleagues have had problems with is the "follow-up submission letter," by which I mean the cover letter we enclose with the revised manuscript. I have not always been sure how detailed the letter should be. Especially after the rigorous process of revising and retyping the paper, I have felt too exhausted to compose a long cover letter. Some of my early resubmissions were accompanied by a brief letter that reminded the editors of the previous correspondence and simply assured them that I had addressed the reviewers' suggestions as best as I could. But this often led to misunderstandings. In the case of the submission for *Language Awareness* (whose editor had taken the initiative to seek my revision), when the paper was sent to the original referee for a second review he or she was not satisfied with the changes made. The referee felt that I had not addressed all the criticisms. Even more surprising, the referee made additional suggestions, claiming to have forgotten to mention them in the first letter:"There are two related points here which I should perhaps have spelt out in more detail in the original report." I might have written a more detailed letter (recounting both the suggestions made by the different reviewers and articulating the rationale for my own changes) if I had known that my cover letter would be sent to the referees. In a few other cases I have found referees commenting on my position as it was spelled out in my cover letter, in addition to scrutinizing my revisions. But in many instances (it appeared to me) only the manuscript had been sent to the referees by the editor. If there were clearer conventions relating to the follow-up submission letter, periphery writers could use them to their advantage and help avoid any misunderstandings.

The revising and editing stages of accepted papers can pose problems of their own. Most journals, functioning with quick deadlines, warn contributors that any delay will involve postponement in printing the paper. The time given for returning the proof is as little as three to four days sometimes. Few editors realize that for the proof to reach periphery scholars may take three to four months by the local mail system. The inability to return proofs in time usually involves confusion at both ends—and sometimes a mistaken bad impression of the diligence and professionalism of the scholar. There are often penalties for not sending corrected proofs quickly: the *Journal of Multilingual and Multicultural Development*, for example, warns that the publication of the paper can be indefinitely postponed. And imagine the request by some editors that I "fax" my agreement to some suggested changes or "call" them with additional questions about their comments. While some of the minor editorial changes in a text could usually be negotiated in a telephone call in the West (especially when time is of the essence), such advantages are usually not available to periphery scholars. To compound matters, referees may ask the writer to consult a particular publication to amplify a point during the revision—a paper appearing in a specialized journal unavailable in local libraries. *Language Awareness*, for example, charged me with revising my paper based on mimeographs and monographs available only in the British institutes where the referees were teaching. It is not surprising that my revision didn't satisfy the referees completely. An important reason why I decided not to revise my first submission for *WE* (as narrated above) was that the referee wanted me to use Phillipson's *Linguistic Imperialism* (1992) as my theoretical framework, just a few months after the book had been published in the United Kingdom. Since I had no prospects of getting the book soon, I gave up revising the paper for that journal. It is important for editors and referees to take the time to orientate to periphery scholars differently from their center colleagues when they engage in revising or editing a paper for publication.

The conditions of work characterizing the academic life of periphery scholars may also hamper the single-minded concentration and commitment required for the arduous process of negotiating a manuscript into print. Since the income of academics is relatively low, many have to do a second or third job to support their families. The political instability in many periphery communities also results in the frequent closing down of campuses for indefinite periods of time. Strikes, protest demonstrations, ethnic tensions, and intensification of fighting can result in the disruption of teaching. At certain times, the government itself announces an indefinite closing of schools to facilitate security operations in a particular region. (For testimonies of similar working conditions for academics, see Reutten 1998, regarding Ivory Coast, and Muchiri et al. 1995, regarding Kenya, Zaire, and Tanzania.) These problems prevent scholars from putting forth the sustained efforts that the repeated process of revision and resubmission requires. I have seen many of my colleagues abandon work on their manuscripts in deference to other pressing everyday concerns.

Since the RA is a "shaped and negotiated" product, as Swales (1990, 93) has reminded us, the limited opportunities periphery scholars get for shaping the manuscript in collaboration with the editorial board significantly affect their ability to get published. It is precisely for this reason that the technological and other material limitations periphery scholars experience matter. The geographical distance, compounded by problems in mail and by limited access to fax, E-mail, or telephone, hampers the level of interaction necessary for collaboration. As the RA is a socially constructed product (in a much more direct and physical sense than we have been trained to understand this clichéd concept in the West), the material disadvantages of periphery scholars affect their writing. Channels for greater interaction and acquaintance with editorial circles are necessary for periphery scholars to negotiate the shape of the written product.

To make matters worse, the shaping process cannot be done with the help of one's periphery colleagues. Depending on fellow periphery scholars is bound to be self-defeating. Being off-networked, they are limited by the same problems that confront the writer. Although they have mature academic sensibilities, they are unaware of the recent scholarship on the subject and the peculiar conventions of each journal. I found that colleagues rarely commented on the subtle preferences of different journals on style, language, or ideological perspective. Similarly, while center colleagues have shared with me that they have been able to get advice from senior scholars when dealing with the occluded genres of academic literacy (such as interpreting the editor's letter or writing a submission letter), periphery scholars lack this form of mentorship from within their circles.

Finally, it is important in this section to explore the extent to which the identity of periphery scholars may damage their chances of getting published. That there is already a bias in the center against submissions from "obscure places" was proven in an experiment by Peters and Ceci (1982). Sending a set of published papers with fictional authorial identities for review from institutions of differing prestige, they proved how the papers with less prestigious identities were not rated positively in the refereeing process. This may suggest how the cards are even more heavily stacked against periphery scholars. It is for this reason that the quality of the stationery and letterhead and the resolution of the print matter. Going through some of my reviewer comments, I find that some referees address me (the author) by name, indicating that they were aware of my identity when reviewing my paper. (My first submissions to *Language in Society* and *WE* had undergone an open review—and in both cases the submission was unsuccessful!) Not always is the review process anonymous, as it is claimed to be.[3] I have also had suspicious instances where the editor rejected publication even though the reviewers had warmly recommended my paper after their anonymous review. The reason given once by the editor was that my subject was not of central concern for that journal. But sometimes I wonder!

Local Publishing Practices

It is interesting to consider here the para-textual conventions periphery editors and reviewers themselves adopt in their local publications. It is reasonable to expect that periphery academic/scholarly journals will take into account the limitations in material resources and other peculiar sociocultural conditions local scholars confront. The publishing practices are therefore less formal or elaborate. I narrate below my experiences in publishing with four local journals: the *Sri Lanka Journal of South Asian Studies (SLJSAS), Navasilu: The Journal of the English Association of Sri Lanka, Thatched Patio,* and *Panpaadu.*[4] The first three are published in English, while the last is published in Tamil. While the first two are clearly academic (always edited by university lecturers and professors), the latter are published by scholars outside the university. However, these journals too are scholarly and serious, often publishing the work of university teachers. As typical of the academic culture in the local community, all four journals are multidisciplinary, publishing work broadly related to the humanities and social sciences.

It is significant that local journals don't publish a style sheet or a policy statement. The inside flap of *SLJSAS,* for example, has information on where the journal is published, subscription information, and the names of the editorial board members. The only statement that has relevance for its publishing practices is the following: "The Journal is intended to cover subjects of relevance to South Asia that are of both contemporary and historical interest." Nearly all journals also have a statement of disavowal, as the one here from *SLJSAS:* "The views expressed in the articles of this Journal are those of the Contributors only and not of the Editor or the Faculty of Arts." Both these statements prepare the ground for a broadened publishing context where writers can feel free to make their submissions with remarkable flexibility—whether in style or content.

Not surprisingly, manuscripts here can be handwritten. I typed mine only on occasions where I had an opportunity to use the department typewriter. In the case of papers in the vernacular, I always submitted them in handwritten form, as I am not used to typing in Tamil. Furthermore, in many cases, editing and some revision could be done on the master copy itself (with the relevant sections crossed out by pen). Usually, editors would get a manuscript typed in their offices, on typewriters specially dedicated for such a purpose, before sending the article to the press. Moreover, there was no requirement for multiple copies in submission. There was also no policy relating to the quality of the stationery. Some authors in fact wrote their papers on pages of composition books.

In the submission, review, and acceptance policies there are again interesting differences from the publishing practices in the center. The cover letter and the whole submission process are very informal. In cases where the journal is an in-house publication of the university the paper can be hand-delivered without a cover letter. In other cases, the cover letters of my colleagues were very brief and cursory. They have a couple of sentences mentioning that the author is submitting the enclosed paper and that it is hoped it will be of value to the readers. Where the editor is acquainted (even vaguely) with the author, it is customary to indulge in a "chat" about matters of mutual interest, before casually mentioning the enclosure of the manuscript. In fact, due to the dearth of research journals and formal research papers, in many cases the editors themselves will write to scholars inquiring if they have any publishable essays. My paper in *Panpaadu* was published after a colleague in my university got me to type out a presentation I had made in a local seminar and sent it to the editor himself with a recommendation. Thus the submission process for the paper is not always as impersonal or guarded as it is in the center.

The review process is again informal. In most cases it is the editor who peruses all the papers and makes decisions. Sometimes the editors confirm their reading with some colleagues before going ahead with the publication. In the case of a paper I published in *Navasilu,* the editor mentioned that he had asked two "anonymous" reviewers to read the paper. He conveyed to me a couple of concerns they had but didn't send me their commentary. It is possible that the comments were made in conversation, and not in writing. At any rate, I rarely heard of papers being rejected outright. When scholars write these papers, as perhaps their only paper for the year, the quality is often good. There is also less competition to get published. But this informal review process denies local scholars training in the rigors of negotiating and shaping the product for publication—which in the center is a much-needed practice for succeeding in the competition to get published.

In an act that was quite untypical of local publishing practices, my papers were rejected on two occasions. When my first contribution to *SLJSAS* was rejected, I learned about it only at a late stage, when the journal was already in press and I accidentally met the editor on the road. He mentioned that the reason my paper was not published was because it was too directly political. The editor felt that the discourse analysis I was conducting of the news reports that had appeared in Western mass media on the ethnic fighting in Sri Lanka was ideologically uncomfortable for the university administration. (UJ is a public institution funded by the Sri Lankan government, and the paper was perceived as being critical of the government.) It is significant that it was inappropriateness of content that influenced the decision to reject the paper. However, there was no letter to inform me of this decision. I had nearly the identical experience with *Thatched Patio*. Many months after submission, I had to drop into the editorial office during a visit to the capital city to find out what had come of my manuscript. The editor only said, "Some people thought it was too biased." In both cases, the editors implied that they had obtained some feedback from referees, but they didn't provide me with any written comments or specific details about the review process.

The interaction between authors and editorial personnel is therefore considerably limited in the local publishing process. I have rarely heard of editors/reviewers and authors negotiating changes in the text to make it suitable for publication. If changes are made at all, they are made by the editor singlehandedly before publication. In fact, a cavalier attitude was displayed in editing my papers that were printed in *Panpaadu*. For example, there were changes made in the title, subtitles, division of subsections, and length of the paper without consulting me in any way. Also, the paper was divided into two parts and serialized without my consent. The trail of paper that accompanies the published product is very thin or nonexistent in the local community. There are many reasons why the revision process is minimal and the author/editor relationship is flimsy. The different orientation to intellectual property rights in Jaffna should be taken into account. The written product is considered communal property, which editors can use almost at their own discretion without consulting the writer. The fact that communication is delayed, expensive, and difficult may be another reason why interactions are limited.

To consider issues of style and bibliographical conventions, finally, local journals show considerable variety. A look at a recent issue of *SLJSAS* (1991/1992) shows the nine papers published there all adopting different bibliographical conventions. Some have endnotes only (with bibliographical information), without a separate section for works cited. Some have both endnotes and a separate bibliography. Others have parenthetical documentation, followed by works cited. Again, in the parenthetical documentation, different styles are adopted. Thus, for citing books, one author adopts the convention *last name; initials; year of publication; page number*. Another adopts *last name; year of publication; page number*. In the works cited section, there are also different formats. One author adopts *last name; first name / initial; title; publisher; place; year.* Another adopts different conventions within the same paper (depending perhaps on availability of information): in some cases he uses *last name; first initial; title; place; year.* In others he uses *last name; first initial; title; publisher; place; year.* If the documentation of books is thus different, the citations for journals are even more diverse. The organization of the papers also reveals different styles. Some papers have numbered subsections, some titled subsections, and many no sections at all. But hardly anyone complains about these differences. Apparently, these stylistic matters don't affect their reading pleasure or estimation of the paper.

In fact, this chaotic diversity in publishing conventions is taken for granted by local scholars. All that matters for most readers is that they can retrieve the necessary bibliographical information (if they want it) from the article and follow the thinking of the writer. In dissertations I cosupervised at UJ, I found that faculty members were prepared to accommodate much flexibility in style conventions. A very revealing episode during my tenure at UJ relates to an attempt by a young lecturer (who had just obtained his doctorate in Canada) and me to establish uniform style conventions for the journals and dissertations produced in the university. Our enterprise was abruptly halted by the senior faculty members, who insisted that the policy they had been practicing was to let scholars consistently maintain whatever convention they would like to use—even if it was a system personally devised by the writer. In fact, many felt that this flexibility in matters of para-textual conventions reduced unnecessary formalities and allowed writers to concentrate on their ideas and content. It was widely felt that these formalities were a waste of time and were of superficial significance, failing to add much to the value of the papers. The dominant opinion was that center journals and scholarly communities were nitpicking and excessively formal in their attention to publishing conventions, distracting one from the message of research/writing.

Conclusion

We find above that, due to a combination of factors, local scholars relate unconventionally to the publishing requirements of center journals. We have seen many constraints deriving from their geographical location (e.g., difficulties in corresponding with editors/reviewers); lack of material resources (e.g., limited access to quality paper, typewriter ribbons, printing, and Xeroxing); cultural practices (e.g., different orientation to textuality and print); and social conditions (e.g., political instability, lack of institutional support and funding, and general poverty). Partly as a response to these realities, local writers adopt minimal or less formal para-textual conventions in their own publishing practices in local journals. Being separated from the publishing practices of the center increases this tendency for local scholarly communities to develop their own para-textual conventions. But this could become a vicious circle. Getting alienated even more from mainstream publications, local scholars may lack the opportunities to develop the practices necessary to compete for publication within international scholarly communities. This is typical of many other aspects of periphery literate practices. Cut off from the publishing networks of the center, periphery scholars develop an academic culture that differs markedly from the mainstream. This is not to deny that both in the center and periphery there are cultural and social conditions indigenous to those communities that influence their members to relate differently to publishing. Therefore, I turn now to characterize the everyday academic culture in the local community in order to perceive its literate practices and communicative conventions through a broader lens.

6. Literacy Practices and Academic Culture

The notion of literacy practices offers a powerful way of conceptualising the link between the activities of reading and writing and the social structures in which they are embedded and which they help create. . . . Literacy practices are the general cultural ways of utilizing written language which people draw upon in their lives. In the simplest sense literacy practices are what people do with literacy. However, practices are not observable units of behaviour since they also involve values, attitudes, feelings and social relationships.—David Barton and Mary Hamilton, *Local Literacies*

This time the Academic Forum at UJ gathered to listen to a scholar from outside the university.[1] The presenter—Mr. S. Paranirupasingham, a retired secondary school teacher—was not university trained. He spoke on the same figure whom a senior professor in the university had previously discussed in the Academic Forum (see chapters 2 and 3). The paper was titled "Mr. P. Kailasapathy and His Search for Truth." This was yet another contribution to the ongoing conversation on the life and work of the local savant Panditamani, who was posthumously awarded an honorary doctorate by the university. The speaker's intention was to present Panditamani (which was the reverential title used for Mr. Kailasapathy by the locals) as having had near-mystical insights into the progressive cognitive stages involved in the attainment of Truth.

What was interesting about the presentation was the way in which the speaker attempted to win authority for himself. His thesis had already been announced to the audience through the printed paper that had been distributed ahead of time. Since his expertise was in the indigenous learning traditions, his treatment of the subject followed the framework of traditional scholarship. It was reasonable to expect the academic community to adopt a skeptical attitude toward this subject and methodology and challenge the credentials of the nonacademic scholar. The speaker's rhetorical strategies were therefore calculated to negotiate these tensions in his favor.

The paper was prefaced on the title page with a verse from a religious hymn, praising God for his providence to frail/errant human beings. Inside, the text was preceded by an inscription from a sacred verse, which conveyed that it is only those who are humble before God who can perceive his mysteries. The meeting began with a moving rendition of the hymn on the title page by an instructor in traditional music. The ensuing religious atmosphere and meditative attitude had a telling effect in the auditorium. The audience was thus strategically converted to a religious frame of mind, suitable for understanding the mysteries of Truth articulated by the savant.

The speaker's oral presentation similarly started with some interesting rhetorical moves. Just as academic papers begin by recounting relevant previous literature in order to create the proper context to appreciate the scholar's findings, the speaker narrated a few stories suitable for his purpose. Some initial stories were about the gurus of our guru—in other words, the mentors and acquaintances of Panditamani. These stories had the effect of impressing the audience with the respectable background of the savant. The audience was also told of the testimonies by Panditamani's mentors and associates about the value of his insight into Truth. Boosting the spiritual and intellectual credentials of Panditamani may have been intended to convince the audience of the significance of his thinking. The next set of stories (whose significance the audience would realize only later) recounted how Panditamani had routed Western-educated scholars in his debates. Finally, there were stories about the speaker's own access to the thinking of Panditamani through informants who had been close to the savant. We got the impression that the speaker had enjoyed reliable insight into Panditamani's thinking. The ethos the speaker thus acquired helped develop a respect for him as a competent interpreter of Panditamani's message.

Before going into the subject of the paper (the cognitive stages in attaining Truth), the speaker made some enigmatic remarks against Marx and Marxism. The limitations of Marxist thinking (specifically, its reductive materialism) and the brutalities of Stalin in Russia were alluded to. Since

Marxism was the currently popular ideology among local academics, these comments may have been aimed at displaying to the largely academic audience that its preferred forms of knowledge could not match the Truth discovered by Panditamani. This message, together with the earlier stories of how Panditamani routed Western/Christian thinkers, also conveyed to the audience that such philosophical approaches would not help them understand the presentation to follow. In fact, behind the presentation was the conflict between different approaches to Truth. The speaker was attempting to discredit scientific and Marxist approaches to knowledge so that the audience would be prepared to give Panditamani's findings a better hearing. If the earlier moves were calculated to boost the credentials of the speaker and the subject, then this final set of moves was an attack on the competitors.

With the academic audience effectively disarmed of their skeptical outlook, and presumably influenced into lending an ear of faith (more than reason), the speaker proceeded to outline the cognitive stages in the progression toward Truth. Interestingly, there was a change of discourse at this point. A leisurely narrative in the past tense gave way to language that was abstract and marked by diagrams, prose in the simple present tense of universal truths, and a proliferation of Sanskrit terminology (which is the local equivalent of Latin for learned discourse). But the exposition of the savant's theory was not presented in a polemical or analytical manner. If this constituted philosophical discourse, it didn't follow the more dialectical *faulty path/correct path* structure adopted by Western scholars (Geisler 1994).[2] This approach was unnecessary, as, for the speaker, understanding was intuited rather than argued. Unlike other colloquia in the Academic Forum, the bulk of the present session was taken up by the speaker's discourse. It is a tribute to the success of the speaker's rhetorical strategies that the audience suppressed its questions and arguments. At the end of the presentation, the discussion time generated more stories about Panditamani's life and times. A few members requested help in the exegesis of the spiritual steps. I must confess that after repeated readings of this paper I haven't understood the cognitive stages fully enough to be able to summarize them here. But that, after all, is its message: a rationalistic detached reading will not help us understand the Truth articulated by Panditamani.

While the forum ended with the usual platitudes on the learning of the scholar, things were not calm in the academic community. The speaker's presentation implicitly contested the representation of the savant by the senior professor from UJ who had promoted scientific objectivity as his analytical approach earlier. It was not surprising then that in the next faculty meeting the said professor moved that future presentations in the Academic Forum should be screened before acceptance. He emphasized the importance of permitting only presentations that are "academic." Presumably the tradition of learning represented by the speaker—the indigenous religious tradition—was not considered by the professor to be worthy of a place in the academy. But this resolution was defeated as others argued that establishing screening practices would be undemocratic. The professor who presided over the presentation, the chair of the Department of Education, argued that this would lead to other scholarly approaches being denied a fair hearing.

This literacy event and its aftermath reveal many features characteristic of the local academic culture (which we will explore in detail in this chapter). Though there is internal conflict within the community on the legitimate mode of knowledge construction and communication, it is resolved in favor of providing a democratic forum for all parties. This suggests that the local community prefers to be hybrid in its orientation, accommodating even indigenous/religious traditions of knowledge. It prefers to be civic-minded in pursuing issues of local relevance, such as the contributions of the savant. It moves away from tendencies of uniformity and specialization in knowledge creation in favor of being more pluralistic in its interests and activities. In engaging in these academic practices, local scholars are required to display diverse rhetorical competencies, switching between multiple codes and conventions in their professional life. They need the resources of both narrative oral discourse and learned Sanskrit discourse, in addition to restrained/detached forms of literate academic argumentation.

But more important to note here is the priority given to oral forms of knowledge construction. The speaker deviated significantly from the written version of his presentation. In fact, the more significant moves were made in the oral version. The anthropologist Roberto Kant de Lima (1992), who has compared academic conferences of Brazilian and American scholars in his research, identifies features in the Brazilian presentations that are similar to those in the academic fora of UJ. Brazilians treat "papers" more often as occasions for oral presentations or talk. They prefer this mode to the (more typical) American style of carefully planned and impersonally read papers, as the oral presentations are more flexible, enabling a contribution that is more personalized and relevant to the local audience.[3] De Lima also finds that the discussion time following the talk can involve expanded conversations and rambling monologues, which require personal and contextual background information to fully understand their import. This is again different from the American practice of a brief, pointed, question-and-answer session oriented strictly toward the content of the paper. In Brazil, as in Jaffna, the overriding concern is with a process of knowledge construction that is not detached but embedded in the interests and concerns of the local community. We have to understand other locally preferred forms of academic communication and literacy practices and assess the implications they have for global knowledge production.

Being off-networked from the academic mainstream and cut off from the publishing networks and written products of the center enables the periphery academy to develop in a different cultural direction. In one sense, this is a blessing in disguise, as it enables the local community to sustain its culture of relatively more egalitarian, civic-minded, pluralistic practices in knowledge construction and communication. However, in another sense, it is such an academic environment that also influences the literate products and practices in the periphery to be different from those of the center. Becoming a liability in the periphery's struggle against center communities for written knowledge construction, this culture can lead to the marginalization of its knowledge.

In the ethnography of academic communication that follows I am moving from the *product-oriented* and text-based approach toward literacy featured in the preceding chapters to a *process-oriented* approach. That is, I am situating the textual and publishing conventions presented in the previous two chapters in the broader cultural and communicative practices of the local community. What is manifested in their RAs is shaped by the practices of reading, writing, speaking, and interacting in the everyday lives of periphery scholars. Therefore it is important to characterize the local academic community in regard to its assumptions, practices, and rationale in knowledge creation.

Institutional Culture

The academic culture at UJ revolves around community concerns. At the cost of disciplinary specialization and research publishing, the university is interested in performing its civic responsibilities effectively. The overriding concern is therefore how the institution can help the community through its service. This goes beyond exploring subjects of local significance in the Academic Forum. The university is always open to social needs and cultural events outside. Classes may be canceled so that students can go outside and collect food, clothing, and cash for refugees or the homeless at times of ethnic violence. University classrooms and auditoriums may be offered for cultural events or community group meetings. University lecturers are themselves often featured speakers at these meetings. Students and lecturers are often asked to head community groups and cultural associations. In a community where university education is available for only a select few, those who go through this system are looked upon to provide leadership to the community. Since higher education is free (which means that it is funded by the state), those who benefit from it are expected to contribute in turn to the community's good.

A particularly important (and recent) dimension of this civic consciousness is the involvement of the university in the ongoing military struggle for autonomy. The university has been engaged in such subversive political activities for a long time. Since around the early 1980s, the university has been at the center of the militarization of the local community. Political groups drew their cadres from among the students. They held consciousness-raising sessions for youth in the university classrooms (after lectures). Resistance leaders met at the university to plan out their strategies. Presently, at a time when the resistance movement has become more established, research is carried out in collaboration with the local de facto military regime to serve the community in many areas: purifying the Tamil language; rewriting school textbooks to provide greater awareness of community history and its resistance leaders; developing industries to tap indigenous natural resources; planning economic development; and organizing rehabilitation efforts. Thus, when I was the head of the English Language Teaching Center I was called one day by a senior administrator of the university and asked to set up a separate wing of the unit for translating and writing publicity material for the rebel regime. This had to be done somewhat surreptitiously, as the university was funded and run by the Sri Lankan state.

That the periphery university is a center of community life is now well noted by many other scholars (Muchiri et al. 1995; Reutten 1998). UJ, for example, is a hub of all community and political activities in the region. This may be partly due to the immunity universities enjoy from the operations of the security forces and the government. Therefore they have become safe havens for radical causes. Also, educated people in the periphery are presumed to be politically radical, typically Marxist. The expectation is that modern learning brings enlightenment and free thinking that would influence one to question the status quo. It is not unusual to find local academics under peer pressure to profess commitment to Marxism and other radical ideologies. A group of African graduate students and teachers (Muchiri et al. 1995) has recently recounted how such an image of the university community is prevalent in African countries as well. Students and teachers would be ready to drop their education at any time their assistance was required for social and political causes. Mary Reutten (1998), working as a Fulbright scholar in Ivory Coast, found it difficult to coax her local colleagues to stay away from the protest activity outside that threatened to shut down the university. She tried to convince them that teaching should not be sacrificed for "external" political causes. But the easy distinction that can be drawn between politics and education in the center doesn't hold for periphery scholars. They perceive these two domains as fundamentally interconnected.

This civic consciousness has powerful implications for the intellectual life of the community. First, the university's knowledge-creating and -disseminating functions revolve around concerns important for the community. As a result, among the different seminars and projects organized during my tenure at UJ, many focused on understanding and formulating the principles of Saiva Siddhantha. This is the religious code of ethics of the Hindu denomination most Sri Lankan Tamils follow. Research activities involved exegesis of canonical texts, interpreting the doctrine in the light of modern discourses, and generating greater understanding of its historical development. Faculty from different disciplines joined traditional scholars from outside the academy to engage in this work in seminars and workshops. (That this religious preoccupation sits uncomfortably with Marxism only testifies to the hybridity of academic culture in Jaffna, which I will discuss later.)

Such a variety of activity calls for scholars who are multidisciplinary in perspective. To function in the local academy, scholars have to be conversant in both traditional and modern scholarship and in the different disciplines of colleagues with whom they must closely interact in such projects. It is expected that they be able to go beyond their disciplinary confines and discourse on a wide variety of subjects as and when needed. It is much more important to display a wide knowledge of traditional and modern scholarly authorities and disciplines and make an impressive presentation accessible to a lay audience than to indulge in reporting obscure/specialized research with detachment. Thus the local professor of traditional drama is also a highly acclaimed literary theorist, social scientist, and cultural commentator (notwithstanding some criticism from scholars belonging to those specializations). Such requirements influence local academics to move in a different trajectory of scholarly expertise from their center colleagues. Once scholars have obtained the doctorate by displaying proficiency in a narrowly focused area of research, then they quickly move on to become generalists. The authority deriving from the doctorate thereafter qualifies scholars to discourse on any field desired. The lack of pressure for specialization in the local community, however, may work against these scholars when they attempt to publish in specialized center journals.

In keeping with the local academic culture, the status of faculty members is also defined differently. Faced with the immense difficulties in getting published in mainstream journals, local scholarly communities have developed a culture that devalues the place of publications in assessing scholarly standing. Academic performance (and promotions) at UJ are not judged primarily on the basis of research publications. The publish or perish rule is nonexistent here. Increasingly more emphasis is given to community/institutional service and teaching. Gauging intellect or scholarship by number of publications, a major practice in the West, is not one shared by many local academic communities. While teaching and service earn considerable points, even these are not rigidly evaluated or assessed. So, for example, there is no practice of student and peer evaluation of teaching. Unless an individual is so outrageously lethargic that his or her teaching performance becomes a public issue, no one comes under the purview of superiors. The annual promotions and salary increases are almost automatic, based on the required years of service and not strictly dependent on the number of publications or merit points earned. An individual's track record is taken into consideration simply to confirm the new designation achieved primarily through the required years of service. There is more scrutiny of the merit points earned when promotion is made to the status of professor—the highest designation—after the preceding stages of assistant lecturer, lecturer, senior lecturer, and associate professor. Tenure is already achieved in the entry-level position, after evidence is provided that the individual is engaged in research leading to a postgraduate degree. In general, there is immense job security in the local academic system. Once an individual is hired at the rank of assistant lecturer, there is no reason why he or she shouldn't move up the academic ladder smoothly. While this situation would take away any motivation to engage in active publishing, this doesn't mean that scholars are deadwood, uninvolved in diverse forms of knowledge production. My own experience has been that I was relatively more productive (even in terms of academic publishing) in the secure work environment in Sri Lanka than I am in the West.

That teaching is the primary responsibility of the faculty is stressed by the compulsory hours of instruction for each member. Instructors are expected to teach a minimum of twenty-one hours each week per semester, while lecturers are expected to teach twelve hours. Supervising postgraduate research is in addition to the usual teaching load. Interaction with students in individual conferences or counseling is expected of each faculty member and not granted credit. Similarly, there is no course-release time for research or publishing. Those who are motivated have to find time for this outside their regular teaching schedule and institutional service.

The service orientation of the academic community is reflected in the fact that considerable credit may be earned toward promotion this way. With faculty members giving a lot of time for planning and policy meetings, bureaucratic functions gain an exaggerated importance in local institutions. Members get grouped into different statutory bodies. Some of these meetings are many hours in duration. In fact, faculty members derive great pleasure in meeting and interacting with their colleagues in these meetings. Tea and snacks are served, and members savor these as they continue discussing serious matters. Sometimes, for example, policy statements and regulations will be collectively revised and edited in the course of a meeting by the heads of departments. Many aspects are added under "new business" from the floor. There are times when the agenda is not fully covered and meetings have to be adjourned, to be continued another day. The digressions, personal reflections, and ego massaging that may take place in these (from some points of view) long-winded meetings contrast with the strictly functional, well-focused, impersonal meetings of academic bodies in the center. But the meetings in Jaffna display the genuine pleasure faculty members get in talking and socializing. This institutional culture contrasts sharply with that of center institutions where faculty members rush back to their own work after a brief/disciplined meeting. Such activities may take away the time and energy that local scholars might otherwise devote to research and academic publication.

As faculty members find it difficult to earn the credit assigned for publications, many try to make up for this loss by scoring points for institutional service. Since the evidence of institutional service is membership on committees and appointment for offices, there is a scramble for these positions. The competition for offices can lead to rivals visiting the homes of members at all times of the day to lobby for votes. Much time was taken in this enterprise during my tenure at UJ. The election of editorial committee members for *SLJSAS*, of faculty representatives for the university senate, and of the dean of the Faculty of Arts saw colleagues visiting me at home or meeting me personally in my office to canvass for support. I found it peculiar that the position of chair of a department (which could be tossed around to different faculty members in the center) could generate keen competition locally. Since appointment is based on seniority, faculty members would insist on their status to lay claim to the office. In the case of the geography department, the competition had to be resolved on the basis that one faculty member was more senior than another by a single day (based on their dates of first appointment at the university). On another occasion, when the chair of the Tamil department went abroad on a furlough, three others rushed to the university from their own leaves of absence to claim this position. Since on each occasion only the junior person came first, each appointment was canceled in favor of the more senior member who arrived later. This desire for office is also motivated by the fact that power in the academic community and one's general reputation are largely defined by the office one holds.

There are, however, certain ways of earning credit for publications (by those who are motivated to do so). Given the dearth of academic publications in the local community, publishing in "popular journals" (which can often deal with intellectually challenging subjects—as I will define later) also earns points for scholarly contribution. These journals could cover or focus on literature, politics, and current affairs. Although there was a minor crisis in the faculty in the early 1980s, when even senior professors began citing popular journals for their annual record of work, the matter has gradually been resolved in favor of accommodating such publications. Presently, one also finds scholars citing articles published in local newspapers for their scholarly credentials. Faculty members are frequent contributors to these publications, writing on a range of serious cultural and scientific issues, in addition to creative writing and literary appreciation. These articles are largely essayistic and highly readable, falling into the belletristic tradition (as I will illustrate in the next section). Many of them are short pieces, of one or two pages.

The hierarchy in rank is hawkishly guarded in the local academic community. This is largely because younger faculty who gain access to current center-based knowledge tend to be perceived as a threat to the status of senior faculty. The difficulty of gaining access to new publications and contributing to written knowledge production is disconcerting to members who have done their postgraduate training in the past. Younger faculty who have returned after research abroad—presumably with a knowledge of the latest developments in the field and all the trappings of the state of the art—are armed with information largely inaccessible to the older faculty. In such situations, the older faculty use their institutional seniority to suppress the activity and initiative of the younger faculty. The latter's perspectives are often dismissed as immature or half-baked, notwithstanding the published authorities they may muster on their behalf. There is, for example, the baffling case of a young faculty member in physics at UJ who was fired for "insubordination" to a senior professor, at a time when the university was short of faculty and was in the throes of being temporarily shut down by the government. The young lecturer had recently returned from MIT after postgraduate work, was actively publishing in international journals during the height of the fighting, and was popular among the students. The ouster by senior faculty was widely interpreted as resulting from scholarly rivalry. Such are the lengths to which senior faculty members will apparently go to assert their power.

There is another level of tension among the faculty members—between locally (vernacular) trained and foreign-trained scholars. It can be said that the monolingual vernacular-trained scholars are gaining ascendancy in some limited but significant ways, although previously a doctorate from the West was considered the sine qua non of academic respect. To some extent, it is those who are foreign-trained who hold more power and status among the older faculty members. But among the junior faculty, the chances for going abroad are dwindling. This is partly exacerbated by the fact that many in the latter group cannot cope with research work in English in the West, having received their basic education in the vernacular locally. Since they are in the majority among junior faculty, the locally trained scholars dominate the offices and positions. We therefore have a two-tiered hierarchy of the following nature.

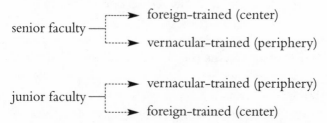

What this hierarchy suggests is the changing ideological character of the local academy. Since there was greater recognition for foreign training in the past (during and soon after British colonial rule), the senior members who earned foreign degrees still enjoy a measure of power. But in the nationalistic ideological context of the present, with chances of foreign studies dwindling and a majority of lecturers being trained locally, foreign-trained scholars don't enjoy as much power in the junior ranks. Standards for promotion are also changing to give credit to the strengths of locally trained faculty, although there are still traces of center-based standards in policy decisions.

To turn to departmental relationships, although local scholars are multidisciplinary in orientation, departmental identities are rigidly maintained. Perhaps it is because of the fluidity in disciplinary concerns among individuals that departments are strict about their identities. This compartmentalization is especially manifested in the recruitment policies of the university. A faculty member's suitability for a position is defined according to his or her initial degree (the bachelor's). Receiving additional/related degrees (outside the first area of specialization) may disqualify an individual for the position. A scholar who first received a degree in math and then earned a master's in physics (both at Oxford) was not recruited for a position in physics because his first degree was not in that discipline. (That this happened at a time when many lecturers were deserting the country at the height of the separatist war, leaving many positions vacant, shows how strictly the rule is adhered to.) Another scholar who received a bachelor's degree in Tamil and later received his Ph.D. in linguistics (in Edinburgh) was not permitted to lecture in the department of linguistics (but had to remain in the Tamil department). This partly has to do with the constitution of departments as "minifiefdoms," run by senior professors with their own students and associates (as I will illustrate below).

In fact, discipline/department formation and maintenance take a bureaucratic shape here. The strength and growth of a specific discipline are defined by lobbying, "politicking," and the display of power. In the center, disciplinary identity is tied more closely to knowledge-formation processes (though it is not totally devoid of some political maneuvering). Theories or paradigms that demonstrate adequate vitality through research and publication will qualify for new disciplinary status. Since local scholars are cut off from scholarly publishing, maintaining departmental status or expanding its boundaries becomes a largely political process of lobbying, gaining peer support, and petitioning diverse committees. For example, at UJ, certain closely related fields are divided into two units—the "Department of English Literature and Linguistics" and the "English Language Teaching Center." The latter, which is only a service "unit" and doesn't enjoy departmental status, mostly houses "instructors," all of whom hold a first degree in English and literature. But the instructors (defined as nonacademic staff) are strictly prohibited from teaching in the former department. Many simplistic reasons are provided to keep English literature yoked to linguistics and separated from the ELT unit. But the real reason, according to many, is different: Since linguistics has an imbalanced student/staff ratio—in some semesters, as many as five lecturers for one student—it faces the danger of cutbacks in staff and funds. Keeping English literature linked gives linguistics more clout. The English literature students make up for the lack of linguistics students and justify the department's inordinate resources. The departmental status quo is jealously guarded by other disciplines too. Lacking discipline-specific research and publishing, sustaining the vitality of the disciplinary communities becomes an end in itself. The very survival of the department becomes the main activity of the faculty. Considerable time is spent in committees for proposing and resisting the formation of new departments or programs. Much of the energy required for research and publication thus gets channeled into these bureaucratic and political processes.

David Hess's (1995) observation about the patterns of governance in some European academic communities helps us consider a similarity in the structure of local academic communities. He states that the practice of a full professor controlling a department or circle with a number of junior faculty members (in something resembling a minifiefdom) is attributable to patriarchal family structures and aristocratic influences. At UJ, again, certain senior professors lead cliques composed of less powerful colleagues. Patterns of voting on crucial issues can follow the lines of clique allegiance. I found it hard to stand clear of any clique identity in many cases as a junior faculty member at UJ. This practice is so rampant that one may be assigned a group identity by default. The mere fact that you fail to support an issue sponsored by one clique is enough to make everyone treat you as belonging to a rival clique. This practice possibly shows influences from feudal and patriarchal social values that still prevail in Sri Lankan society. Sharon Traweek (1988) finds similar forms of feudal structuring in Japanese universities. Hess (1995) furthermore finds such factionalism and patron-client relationships in Brazilian and Mexican academic communities.

However, this notion of hierarchy at UJ has to be qualified a bit. It is possible for faculty members marginalized in the institution because of their designation or disciplinary identity to use "influence" and manipulate some of the inherent inconsistencies/gaps in the system to get special favors accomplished (such as instituting a new department or an endowed chair). One can sometimes lobby a senior professor or maneuver group rivalries and get some matters achieved. Hess (1995) finds such a "mediated hierarchy" also in Latin American academic communities and compares this to the function of intermediaries (such as saints in the religious domain or rich patrons in the art world) who may intervene and bend the rules of the status quo to accomplish something for someone lower in the hierarchy.

The anthropologist Sharon Traweek (1988) brings out some points about the hierarchical structure of a Japanese community of physicists that confirm the pattern of ascribed status in other Asian communities such as UJ. She points out that while the American system highlights the individual position in an *achieved* hierarchy, the Japanese system highlights the institutional and age hierarchy. As at UJ, the latter pattern often translates into a question of "seniority" based on age and date of academic appointment. While the achieved hierarchy of the center is based on principles of equality and competition, the *ascribed* hierarchy of the local community is based on social and institutional status. This pattern of hierarchy lessens the motivation one may have for academic publishing, as status is predefined irrespective of the amount of papers one may publish.

Furthermore, the types of mobility found for professionals in the East and West also help explain other characteristics of UJ. Traweek (1988) points out that there is less *horizontal mobility* in the Japanese academy, unlike in the United States, where scholars move from one institution to the other seeking professional advancement. She finds this limited geographical mobility based on the desire of Japanese to stay close to their families and hometowns. This situation also accounts for a certain amount of job security for Japanese academics, as there is less competition for their positions from rival scholars from other institutions. There is, on the other hand, some amount of *vertical mobility* based on systems of patronage: a senior professor would promote one of his or her faithful students to step into his or her shoes in due course. Traweek therefore shows that there is more security but less mobility in the Japanese system, compared to the Western system. Such a pattern is also found in Brazil (Hess 1995, 156). As at UJ, Brazilian scholars are hired with "tenure" and given six years to better establish themselves and move to higher positions. They have less mobility, as they generally work in the same institution for a lifetime (Hess 1995, 156). This institutional culture seems characteristic of traditional/feudal communities in Asia and Latin America. At least in the case of UJ, this arrangement functions to dampen enthusiasm for publishing success, as scholars may not move across institutions competitively or cut across status hierarchy radically.

While there are some characteristics that UJ shares with other non-Western academic cultures, to some extent it is torn between two or more strands of conflicting academic cultures. It is perhaps a testament to the hegemony of Western academic culture that local universities still look upon center scholarly practices as the norm. They fail to fully acknowledge the differences in their own academic practices and develop their institutional infrastructure accordingly. For example, though academic publishing in mainstream journals is difficult (and a majority of the scholars don't indulge in this activity), a relatively large proportion of points for merit is assigned to such publishing activity anyway. Though faculty members are committed to the needs of the larger community and expend a lot of time on community service, institutional policy is still tilted toward giving considerable credit for publications. In terms of political work, though much help is provided to the local regime's development and military efforts, much of this takes place unacknowledged, at a personal level, while the institution outwardly maintains the image of being detached and disinterested, typical of Western academic communities.

The tensions in the two cultural poles here—broadly, those of the center and the periphery—are evident to the members of the faculty themselves and cause considerable internal conflict. These cultural differences sometimes contribute to a lot of misunderstanding in academic communication and institutional procedures. For example, during my stay at UJ, I counted that in a particular year there were seven out of fifteen meetings where certain members walked out in desperation at the misunderstanding and hostility caused during formal interactions. Such a "walk out" would bring the meeting to an immediate halt. The following is a transcription of one such dysfunctional argument leading to a walk out, involving two senior members during a faculty meeting. Through a microanalysis of talk we can discern the academic cultures in tension here. This is a meeting of the heads of departments to finalize the rules and regulations of a new program that the dean is interested in starting soon—an external degree in the arts for students who fail to enter the university in the competitive selection procedure.[4]

Dean: We will have to rush through the revisions in the syllabus because I want to start the external degree in the coming academic year. So we have to work fast.

Professor S.: There are a lot of mistakes here in this document. Why should we rush? This is a document that goes out to the public. We have to be careful with a document like this.

Dean: No, now we can't take too much time. Earlier you wanted two weeks to read this. I gave you that much time. Now we can't delay this process.

Professor S.: We can't hurry in a matter like this.

Dean: I know you, no? We can't go on like this all the time=

Professor S.: =What do you MEAN by I know you? (Visibly agitated.) *itenna cantayilai kataikkira maatiri kataikiratu. Enna?* "I know you" *enRaal enna?* <u>What is this talk? You are talking like those who talk in the village market. What? What does "I know you" mean?</u>

Professor V.: (softly) Cut it off now.

Dean: We know you, no? You are not a progressive=

Professor S.: =If this talk continues I'll ask you to shut up. I am not ASKing you to shut up. But I'll be forced to ask you to shut up.

Dean: [Please cooperate with me.]

Professor S.: [Members of the house!] Have I offended anybody by thought, word, or gesture? Have I insulted anyone by my behavior? (Hands tremble as he appeals to everyone.)

Dean: Earlier you wanted two weeks. I gave in, no?

Professor S.: I can't cooperate with you. I am leaving. I can't be part of this meeting. Damn it! (Walks out. Meeting ends.)

At the heart of this argument is a difference of opinion about the mission of the university. While the dean is interested in starting new programs that democratize university education by offering it to many, Professor S. is interested in maintaining the elite status of the institution. In comments in other places he has frequently mentioned how the university degree will be made "cheap" if degrees are granted hastily without clear criteria and stringent assessment procedures. He is also concerned about the image the university may project outside through an ill-written handbook. He refers to the bad editing in the document and specifically notes the impression that may be conveyed about the professionalism of academics. But for the dean (who happens to have done his basic education in the vernacular, although he went to England for his doctorate) the message in the document appears to be more important than the packaging. It is safe to say however that the type of faculty member represented by Professor S. (who was educated in the English medium in a missionary school and then in universities abroad) is growing less in number.

Behind the differences of opinion in this exchange are two different conventions of talk. The metadiscursive comments of Professor S. ("What is this talk?" and "If this talk continues") show that the members are themselves conscious that their mode of talk is at the center of this conflict. It appears that the dean resorts to a nonformal and nonparliamentary mode of talk. His personal references to the background of Professor S. ("I know you, no?") are objected to by the latter. Professor S. uses parliamentary modes of expression in addressing the "members of the house" and also shows care in his use of language as he warns that he will be forced "to ask you to shut up" although "I am not ASKing you to shut up." The subtle distinction he makes here also shows his detachment, poise, and tact. However, what is interesting is the manner in which Professor S. straddles both discourses, contrary to his posture of being more detached and formal. His talk shows influences of both a detached, literate, argumentative discourse and a more personal, emotional, argumentative discourse (reflecting dichotomies such as formal/personal, urbane/local, etc.). Though he waits on decorum, appeals to the rest of the faculty, and insists that he hasn't insulted anybody, soon he utters "Damn it," which is insulting to the dean. His threat that he is not asking the dean to shut up but will be forced to do so also straddles, comically, both forms of discourse. He wants to be careful and decorous, but the utterance he threatens to employ is indecorous. Furthermore, the codeswitch to Tamil is not only to gain rhetorical force or reflect his spontaneous anger but may also be intended as an insult to the addressee (implying that the addressee is not educated enough to understand English). It is useful to know that much of the force in the argument derives from the personal animosity between both figures, which is then translated into an institutional/bureaucratic issue. The interaction shows the community straddling a detached, rule-governed discourse and a more orality-based, personal, high-involvement discourse.

In general, we find a mixture of cultural elements—belonging both to the center and the periphery traditions—characterizing the local academy. Though this situation contributes to healthy pluralism, democratic spirit, and independent knowledge-construction activity, it can also cause certain limitations. Some of the unreconciled tensions can be debilitating to the strength, autonomy, and progress of the local academy. Since it still has one eye on earning respect from the center academy according to its values and practices, the UJ community is unable to define its own unique mission with greater openness. Faculty members too are confused between the competing academic cultures, unable to make their scholarly contribution fully according to the local needs and aspirations.

Other Genres of Local Writing

While the local academic culture explains to some extent the lack of pressure to engage in research publications and the motivations behind the divergent discourses found in the RAs of local scholars (such as civic consciousness in the RA introductions), we must note that local scholars are always engaged in many forms of writing. In this section we will move from RAs to the other genres of texts they construct in their professional life. These other texts are perhaps more in tune with the constraints and values shaping local academic life.

A curious phenomenon among local scholars is the amount of time and energy intellectuals devote to literary writing. Many of the well-known literary writers in Tamil are by training academics in the hard sciences. A popular novelist who writes under the pen name "Nandi" is a professor of community medicine. The poet Sivasekaram is a professor of engineering. The sociology lecturer N. Shanmugalingam is a poet, song-writer, and performance artist. These scholars are publishing more in literature than in their own areas of academic specialization. Many other academics are actively involved in writing criticism or reviewing current literature and the arts. There are many explanations for this practice. Being off-networked in their own areas of specialization, and marginalized professionally by the unfair domination of center academics, local scholars find outlet for creative expression in literature. Literary publishing is not constrained by the requirements of competitive speed, expensive research instruments, and rapidly changing disciplinary constructs. Observing a similar preference for literary writing among the Latin American intelligentsia, Jean Franco (1988) explains this as follows: "Because it was blocked from making contributions to the development of scientific thought, the intelligentsia was forced into the one area that did not require professional training and the institutionalization of knowledge—that is, into literature" (504). Literature has therefore become elevated to the position of a knowledge-producing activity and is not simply a medium of pleasure/entertainment. It is interesting to note also that this genre of writing accords well with the preference for culturally embedded knowledge in the local community.[5] Through creative writing, academics and lay readers can participate in knowledge creation/sharing without being put off by the specialized language, abstract constructs, or obscure paradigms typical of RAs.

Among the nonliterary genres, the belletristic articles for popular magazines and newspapers are significant. These publishing fora can include serious essays on intellectual concerns. But they tend to be represented in a mixture of styles and genres, in a range of authorial voices. Consider the biweekly *Lanka Guardian,* for example, which features contributions from many university lecturers. There are essays on current social and economic developments, on cultural trends, and on the social implications of scientific activity, along with political commentary and reviews of art and literature. In many cases, a single author can indulge in all the range of genres listed above. Consider the weekly regional newspaper *Saturday Review,* which differs from the *Lanka Guardian* in adopting a tabloid format. The articles I wrote for this newspaper include the following: a review of a one-man theater staged in the town by the British Council; a review of a collection of short stories in Tamil; a report of a visit to a "lower-caste" community that was being harassed by an "upper-caste" group; an analysis of the emergent separatist militancy and mass uprising; and informal "research" on a unique breed of horses (shaped by the local geographical conditions) in our region. Though I never cite these essays for my academic record, they are among the most challenging I have ever written. While both the *Lanka Guardian* and the *Saturday Review* are in English, there are many others published in Tamil, featuring a similar range of essays. These journals are widely read by an informed audience, comprising both intellectuals and laypeople. One is therefore ensured an eager audience with insightful feedback—something that's not always guaranteed for RAs.

A less frequent source of semischolarly writing is the commemorative volume. These include publications put out by temples to coincide with their annual feasts, by cultural organizations to mark their anniversaries, by schools to celebrate their prize days or special occasions, and by followers of famous personalities (e.g., religious or political leaders) to commemorate their achievement. Articles are invited from academics and respected elders in the community. Not all the articles are about the person or event commemorated. Others may include creative writing, research observations, and scholarly reflections. The commemorative souvenir issued to mark the opening of the rehabilitated Jaffna Public Library (which was earlier burned down, allegedly by government security forces) contains some of the most informative articles on Jaffna's social and cultural life I have ever come across. The publication has articles in both languages (English and Tamil) and includes felicitation messages (from political officials and civic leaders) apart from scholarly articles. I have cited the essays on the Jaffna Tamil dialect, the Jaffna community's ideological makeup, and regional folk dramatic traditions from this volume in many of my RAs published in mainstream scholarly journals. The scholarly contribution of these articles is invaluable. Other such publications also come to mind. The felicitation volumes for Kailasapathy (the first president of UJ), Arumuga Navalar (who resisted missionary activity during British colonialism), and Ludowyk (the first local professor of English in Sri Lanka) also feature a useful collection of academic articles. Putting out such publications is perhaps driven by the desire to leave a long-standing memorial for a particular person or institution in writing. (Though there is usually a meeting to coincide with the event, the oral proceedings are considered insufficient for the historical record.) But in terms of knowledge construction/dissemination, this genre solves many problems that arise in periphery publishing. Since the organizing committee raises funds from the community, the problem of financing the publication is taken care of. Since these are mostly "one-time-only" (or sometimes annual) publications, there is no need to think of continuity (saving local publishers from the anxiety of getting material and money for successive issues). The readership is also well defined, as the members of the association or those involved in the organization of the event are a ready audience. In a sense, this writing satisfies the civic consciousness of many academics by enabling them to engage in knowledge construction that is relevant and useful to the community. It must be acknowledged, however, that the articles in these publications generally receive only local circulation and currency.

While some amount of new knowledge production takes place in the pages of newspapers, magazines, and souvenirs (as is evident in the examples above), a related purpose of these publications is disseminating already-known knowledge in the respective fields of the different contributors. The primary contribution of such articles is to popularize the empirical findings and theoretical developments in center scholarly communities. There is a tremendous need for disseminating international scholarly developments for the local readership. Academics are able to function as intermediaries between the outside world and the local community. Given the interdisciplinary bent of the local academics, readers appreciate learning from their colleagues about whatever material has reached their hands. Furthermore, since not everyone can manage to get the latest books even in their own fields, the few publications that one manages to read are still useful for dissemination among peers in one's own discipline. Thus these publications serve to widen local communication on scholarly matters and help keep communal literacy alive.

Given the difficulties in getting access to recent publications, whatever literature is received then becomes a communally owned property as it is passed around among interested readers—or reviewed in popular media for wider dissemination. In fact, local scholars are expected to perform the function of disseminating knowledge through popular journals. Furthermore, the fact that the local academic community is primarily a reading (as opposed to a writing) community creates a demand for this genre of writing. The popular media thus serve the communal sharing of knowledge quite effectively.

Textbook writing is another activity many local academics are involved in. This is again a knowledge-disseminating activity for which there is a lot of demand. Since it takes much time for recent knowledge from the center to become available locally, academics who have had the opportunity to get this information in their studies abroad or from their postgraduate research feel motivated to pass along their knowledge to students and other scholars. Furthermore, since knowledge of English—the language in which most recent publications are available—is not widespread, there is a demand for textbooks in Tamil. Even university students find it difficult to do reference reading in the scholarly books available in English in the library. Some therefore indulge in fairly direct translations of books from English and publish these as textbooks. There is a market for translated books in the local community. (Sometimes, a compendium of statements by other scholars and passages from foreign books is published in Tamil as a book in its own right, without sufficient attribution. I have encountered a few cases where some of my university lecturers read out as their own notes in Tamil what later transpired to be their personal translations of books in English.) Even scholarly books deriving from the research of local academics are pitched as textbooks in order to appeal to a wider reading audience (which includes students). The writers don't engage in polemical writing, challenging rival literature and studies, but adopt a popularized form of writing with a simple narrative and a catchy title and cover.

Bureaucratic writing—involving genres like memos, proposals, and syllabi—takes an incredible amount of time and energy for many members of the faculty. Since one earns credit for engaging in institutional service, there is some motivation for doing this writing. In committee meetings, these documents generate considerable debate and discussion. Often there is collective editing/revising of these texts in department meetings. It was the proper construction of the handbook for a new external-studies program that occasioned the dysfunctional argument analyzed earlier, after which the text was carefully revised and edited by the committee of the heads of the departments. I have never seen that level of engagement in the construction of texts in the research writing of UJ faculty members. We must understand this preoccupation in light of the fact that there is a strong tradition of bureaucratic writing from colonial times in the local community. Clerical jobs were the highest positions locals were recruited into. An important goal of English education was to develop literacy in bureaucratic texts. Therefore those proficient in the legalistic and bureaucratic discourse are still highly respected in the community.

It is interesting to compare Latour and Woolgar's (1979) description of the types of writing done by their scientist subjects with the range of writing described above. We can use this as an example of the repertoire of center scholars:

a. Texts written for a select band of insiders (55 percent of publications)

b. Texts written to the membership of the specialty as a whole (13 percent)

c. Texts written for specialists in other fields (27 percent)

d. Texts written for lay audiences, including those generally interested in popular accounts of scientific research and practitioners looking for useful information (5 percent)

The first two (a and b) contain new information and contribute to fresh scientific knowledge, while the second two (c and d) are written to disseminate and popularize information well known to specialists. It is important to note that the writing practice of local researchers shows a reverse ratio of publications. There is very little writing done for insiders in their discipline. Into this category will fall the occasional writing a minority of scholars do when they make submissions to center journals. In fact, there is no local journal that caters solely to specialty groups. Local communities don't enjoy the funds or resources to publish a journal for a select band of disciplinary insiders. It would also be difficult to get publishable material continuously from the few actively writing scholars. Journals like *SLJSAS* and *Navasilu,* discussed in the previous chapter, are multidisciplinary in orientation and cater to a general academic audience. They fall into the "category c" genre of Latour and Woolgar. Much of the writing done by UJ faculty—in magazines, newspapers, souvenirs, and commemorative publications—falls into "category d." However, a minority of UJ scholars stubbornly insist that they solely do writing of the first and second varieties. One senior professor, in conversation with me, dismissed the idea of writing for temple or school souvenirs and insisted that he always avoids such fora. The implication was of course that scholars who write for these publications are cheapening their academic status. (Still, a paper by this professor does appear in the commemorative souvenir of the rehabilitated Jaffna Public Library.) At any rate, such scholars who present an elite image of their professional writing are dwindling in number.

Consider also the different discourses encouraged by these sources of publication. Latour and Woolgar (1979) describe the gradations of statements possible in various kinds of texts:

Type 1 statements: Speculations or conjectures, usually found at the end of an article or in private discussions

Type 2 statements: Claims that call attention to the circumstances affecting their status, usually found in research papers

Type 3 statements: Statements with attribution or modality that links the basic claim to the source of the claim, often found in review articles

Type 4 statements: Claims about things in the universal present tense, found in textbooks

Type 5 statements: The taken-for-granted facts that rarely get mentioned except to outsiders

Texts in categories "c" and "d" (written for the popularization of knowledge for lay readers or scholars in other fields) would have type 4 and 5 statements, while texts in categories "a" and "b" (written for specialists within the disciplinary community) would cluster around type 1, 2, and 3 statements. Since local scholars mostly practice knowledge-disseminating articles, they adopt discourse constituting statements of types 4 and 5. Thus the discourse they mostly practice is not the one preferred by the center academic journals in RAs. It is possible that even in the rare cases when they send a category "a" or "b" text to a center journal, their writing would show traces of such popular discourse. The greater volume of writing they do—creative writing done in the personal voice and narrative discourse; bureaucratic writing in a formal voice and legalese—doesn't get mentioned in the repertoire of writing done by center academics.

In terms of the potential for publishing RAs in center journals, the lo-

cal culture of writing may present certain disadvantages. The lack of outlets for writing discipline-specific papers dampens enthusiasm for new research. In fact, the academic culture itself recognizes this predicament and
has started acknowledging popular writing as worthy of academic credit.
Even the few who would have considered doing discipline-specific writing (for at least earning professional credit) may now turn away to other
genres. Furthermore, some of the writing local academics do—for knowledge dissemination in popular publications—encourages a culture dependent on center knowledge. Time that could be devoted to actively
constructing new knowledge through original research and RA publications of their own is now wasted on translating and disseminating center
knowledge through these genres. However, there are other benefits of
such a state of affairs: scholars are able to construct grounded/local knowledge by contributing to publications of significance for the community;
they bridge the gap between academics and lay scholars by writing in
popular publications; they nurture community literacy by contributing to
nonacademic publications read by an eager local audience.

Practices of Reading

The writing practices described above suggest how social and material
realities shape literacy in the local community. For example, the lack of
specialized journals, largely due to the limited funds, audience, and suitable
publishing infrastructure, influences local academics to move into non-RA
genres of writing. Material constraints similarly shape the reading practices
of these scholars. After all, one can only read the publications one gets.
Since chances of getting discipline-specific research journals are remote,
academics engage in alternate genres of reading. In fact, around 1992 the
head librarian at UJ sent around a letter asking each department to mark
the journals that were most important for its work in order of priority, as
he had to stop subscribing to some. This was a difficult task for faculty
members, as they were already getting only a handful of journals in each
discipline. Thus even the meager amount of journals we were getting in
the library had to be cut down for lack of funds. Reading RAs for up-to-
date research is therefore an elite preoccupation of a minority of local
scholars. They usually spend their own money or get help from their foreign contacts to keep up with publications. Apart from not actively engaging in research reading, many of my colleagues disliked the RA genre

(considering it boring and esoteric), preferring other genres of reading material.

Since obtaining book-length publications is more convenient (as they are independent bodies of work and don't depend on the timeliness and continuity of serial publications), scholarly books are the main genre of academic reading for the faculty. Such non-RA genres (with mostly type 4 and 5 statements, which reflect a nonspecialized discourse) also lend themselves to the interdisciplinary bent of most local scholars, who find reading across the disciplines pleasurable. The university library also finds it cheaper to buy books rather than subscribe to expensive serial publications. Most of the classics in the humanities and social sciences are available in the local library—such as all of Marx, Freud, Descartes, and Durkheim. Some of these had been donated from the private libraries of older scholars who had studied abroad. Books discarded from center libraries would also find their way to UJ through generous foreign donor agencies. I found that some of these books still display on their inside covers the names and borrowing regulations of libraries in American universities and British community associations.

Books published in the late 1980s on poststructuralism and postmodernism constituted some of the recent acquisitions in the university library. I read Hutcheon's books on postmodernism, Norris's and Culler's introductory books on Derrida, and Rabinow's work on Foucault there. For some strange reason, getting the original books by the scholars themselves was difficult, compared to getting commentaries about them by others. Sometimes, we got a scholar's work out of sequence (i.e., a more recent work was accessible first, before the scholar's earlier publications). Therefore, we were left to piece together Foucault's thoughts from commentaries, expositions, and critiques, leaving us confused about what really constituted his thinking. This situation always gave me the sense of being kept dependent once again on Western scholars, as we couldn't consider ourselves proficient in these schools of thought without reading the original works themselves. We were always left with a tremendous sense of diffidence and incompetence when discussing contemporary scholars or areas of developing scholarship. Whether it was codeswitching, critical linguistics, or cultural studies, we knew only bits and pieces of this scholarship, which prevented us from engaging authoritatively with these fields in our publications.

Another interesting source of reading in Jaffna is college- and high school–level textbooks donated by the Asia Foundation, the British Council, and other cultural agencies. These are usually books discarded because of their datedness. Many of these books still have the names of the students who used them and that unmistakable mark of student use—highlighting with yellow markers. Since faculty members lack enough books for reading in/about their disciplines, it is not uncommon for them to take a look at these books for summary statements of the established knowledge in their fields. Some of them initially use these books with the intention of preparing lectures for students but end up finding them informative in themselves. Furthermore, since students may not be expected to read books in English, they are eventually of more use to lecturers. I myself found college-level introductory books on sociology, anthropology, and psychology informative, not withstanding a colleague's warning that these books were too dated and simplified for serious scholarly purposes. There was no better alternative for me to get a perspective on the established knowledge in disciplines outside my specialization.

As in the case of writing, literary texts constitute an important body of reading material. It is typical for many faculty members to be reading a novel or a collection of short stories in their spare time between classes. Some carry around a literary journal or other collection of fictional writing in their hands as they come to campus. Unlike the publications mentioned earlier, much of this reading material is in the vernacular. Many subscribe regularly to periodicals that feature literary writing.

Popular magazines, newspapers, and news periodicals form another source of reading in Jaffna. The faculty common room will have all the local Tamil newspapers in addition to many of the national tabloids. Periodicals on current affairs, such as *Lanka Guardian,* and other international ones, like *Time* and *Newsweek,* are also regularly received. The university library also has many international journals published in India, Singapore, Hong Kong, Britain, and the United States, in addition to a range of newspapers. The fact that these magazines are considerably cheaper than research journals is an important reason why they are subscribed to. Besides, they cater to a wider range of readers, justifying the funding. Much of the talk between faculty members in the common room focuses on news reports and features. In a society where news is censored, and often biased against the minority Tamils, there is considerable interpretive work involved in reading between the lines and discerning the hidden agenda of news reports. Often editors and writers from outside the academy come to the common room to discuss current affairs over a cup of tea. Faculty members are found mostly in the common room, reading and discussing local and international news, rather than working alone in their offices.

It must be pointed out that, despite the limitations in obtaining publications, local scholars are avid readers. Lacking the pressure to churn out RAs according to the "publish or perish" culture of the center, local scholars have more time for leisurely reading. It is also possible that material constraints affect reading much less than writing. While text production requires a lot of facilities and resources, reading a text that has already been produced elsewhere is less costly. In fact, many read voraciously in diverse disciplines outside their specialization. This helps them develop as synthetic theoreticians and interdisciplinary scholars, as noted earlier. It might even be fair to say that in sheer volume and range of reading material, local scholars are ahead of most center scholars. It is a paradox, then, that despite the availability of copious amounts of literature, center scholars read piecemeal, in fits and starts, functionally, for limited purposes, within their specialized domains (Bazerman 1988). Local scholars, who don't enjoy the same access to publications, read more widely and holistically (even though the literature is not always the most recent or the most respected in their field). My mentor, A. J., who is one of the most widely read scholars I have met, has an enviably rich personal library with many of the classics in fields like sociology, literature, and philosophy. Despite all this, he has himself contributed minimally to new knowledge construction through writing. Another junior colleague at UJ told me that he is so addicted to reading that when he doesn't get any serious literature he has to at least read a popular magazine like *Sports Illustrated* to satisfy his craving for reading. These facts give further proof to my earlier observation that the local academic culture is one based more on reading than writing.

In fact, local scholars don't fail to invoke recently published authorities from the West in their popular writing, teaching, and public-speaking assignments. If they read but don't write as much, then this is a recipe for intellectual dependence. This furthermore encourages a one-way traffic in publications between the center and periphery. Local scholars give currency to center publications but don't themselves infiltrate the West with their thinking through self-authored literature. Furthermore, since the reading is not always systematic, based only on the availability of literature, local scholars don't always make the best use of their reading material for new knowledge creation. The political economy of literacy is such that the disadvantaged are not totally excluded from literate activity altogether. They are allowed to participate selectively. This way the center maintains a market for its literate products but does not let its monopoly get challenged by new written products from the periphery.

Apart from the differences in the types of texts read, there are also differences in reading processes between center and local scholars. Bazerman (1988) makes some perceptive comments on the practices of physicists in the center. He finds that center scholars rarely read an RA holistically from beginning to end. They employ modes of skimming and scanning to ferret out information on the main findings, the methodology used, or the theoretical constructs employed to see the relevance to their own work. In interpreting/assessing the paper, they attempt to quickly fit the content into the preestablished paradigms of their discipline. The schema they bring with them (shaped by the current disciplinary discourses) enables them to perform a quick, functional reading. My observation of the reading practices of local scholars, on the other hand, showed that their approach was holistic. They mostly read in a linear fashion, from the beginning of the text to the end. Their reading is therefore quite slow and patient. A tremendous investment of time and energy is made in the reading process. Hurrying through a text is considered to produce an incomplete and superficial reading. A colleague of mine would always read the text a second time, more slowly, to jot down notes and quotes because he had no prospects of seeing the book again. Taking notes also helped him understand the text better. Once, when I skimmed through a theoretical work by Barthes and returned the book in two days to this colleague, he was puzzled by this and discouraged this fast reading, as it would fail to yield a reflective and critical perspective on the book.

Since local scholars do not have an active or focused schema based on the recent discourse of their discipline, they don't have convenient ways of absorbing a new text. Local scholars are therefore performing the dual function of constructing a schema suitable for processing the text, while at the same time trying to interpret it. It is perhaps because local scholars are still developing a schema of their disciplinary discourse—and constantly updating it, one step behind the progress taking place more rapidly in the center—that they adopt the above reading strategy. I could always detect a diffidence among my colleagues, as they were unsure if their existing schemas were too dated to interpret a current text. Therefore each new text is carefully read, sometimes behind and between the lines, to ferret out maximum information about the evolving disciplinary discourse.

Local scholars display a care, seriousness, and reverence toward the text that borders on conformity to the myth of *autonomous textuality*—in other words, an orientation to the text as a self-constituted entity that sets the terms in which it should be read and understood (Geisler 1994). This attitude can of course have various explanations. Printed literature has always held a privileged place in knowledge preservation in the Hindu religious tradition. Not everybody is free to read or interpret the scriptures. The often-Sanskrit-based scriptures can only be understood by the priests. Interpretation is controlled by those given the authority to interpret. It is perhaps under this influence that readers stick reverently close to the text and show a lot of care in making sense of the writing, assuming that there is an "objective" meaning that must be extracted carefully. As in the case of the colleague mentioned above, many readers take down quotations, main points, and important data or findings from the texts. Summary and paraphrase have been popular pedagogical exercises in schools for students of both English and Tamil for a long time. Practices like summarizing and note-taking are also encouraged by material conditions. Since Xeroxing or buying a book is costly, and there is little prospect of having the book for a second reading, readers are forced to keep a written record for their purposes. Through these practices readers turn the published material into an autonomous text to filter out the abstract information/thinking/facts, devoid of contingent information. The writer and context are forgotten as the text takes an all-powerful role in the representation of knowledge.

One implication deriving from Bazerman's study of center scholars is that it is only those who are actively publishing (and therefore researching) who will have the resources to undertake a critical processing of the text. But local scholars are not engaged in the feverish process of publishing competitively. Therefore they don't have the pressure to fit each new publication into an actively constructed schema of their field and their own place in it. They are not thinking primarily of absorbing the new text to build an evolving argument. This lack of a utilitarian or functional orientation may lessen the urgency for processing the new information analytically. There is lacking, therefore, a conscious critical engagement with the writer or the text in terms of local scholars' own writing projects (although I will demonstrate later that they employ many unconscious appropriations of the text, influenced by local discourses and cultural frames). In fact, the reading/writing relationship is reversed in the local community. While center scholars typically tend to read in order to write, local scholars write down in order to comprehend and remember the reading. This is one form, among many, in which writing is servant to reading in the periphery.

Confirming Bazerman's perspective, Cheryl Geisler (1994) finds similar motivations for why center academics practice resisting reading. They break free from the influences of the writer and the careful scripting and structuring of the textual world to freely move through the text at their will. They resist treating the text as autonomous and give attention to its *rhetorical process*—the contexts of production, the background information on the writers/researchers, and the contingent forces that shape the research findings. She also finds that center readers adopt this reading practice to attack the findings of other scholars and thus make a space for their own work. However, they insist on treating their own writing as autonomous when they fight to win acceptance for their own knowledge. When center scholars write, they attempt to erase the steps leading to the discovery of knowledge, aiming toward autonomous textuality. Therefore details about contingent features—such as the context-bound aspects of the knowledge, the material processes of lab work, and scholarly interaction—are suppressed in their RAs. The written academic text thus strives toward the status of a self-standing objective document. The modifiers, passivizations, and nominalizations are taken by Geisler to be rhetorical devices that shape the reader's understanding according to the intentions of the writer while giving the impression of knowledge free of influence from the scholar. As she puts it: "Research scientists seem to use these two repertoires in different circumstances. . . . Thus, language about contextually-dependent variables is almost always used to attribute error to others whereas language without reference to context is generally used to attribute scientific validity to the work one accepts" (1994, 17). Geisler states that it is this disjunctive practice in their reading and writing that is at the heart of center scholars' ability to produce new knowledge. Through rhetorical process reading they find gaps/problems in other people's research;

through autonomous textuality they seek acceptance for their own findings.

If local scholars don't develop a rhetorical orientation to texts in their reading as their center counterparts do, there are many reasons for this phenomenon. Geisler notes that in order to know the contingent forces behind the knowledge recorded in academic texts one has to be well networked inside the relevant disciplinary communities. Information on aspects such as the scholar's personal background, the research contexts, the political and cultural influences on the findings, and the scholar's institutional and professional circles of connection is passed along by word of mouth through personal contacts. This is insider information not easily accessible to everybody. There is then a real problem for off-networked local scholars attempting to develop a rhetorical knowledge about scholarly publications. They find it difficult to effectively negotiate the contexts of production and contexts of interpretation with adequate rhetorical resources. Needless to say, the critical perspectives generated by such contextual information also take time to develop.

This mode of reading/writing connection may have adverse effects on local scholars' publishability. The types of texts they read encourage written discourses that are discouraged in center RAs. For example, the scholarly books that are most available to these scholars employ a different discourse from that of journal articles (Myers 1990). Mostly, they adopt a more deductive structure and synthesize existing research in a seamless narrative. Textbooks employ an even more definitive discourse, as they tend to reduce the hedges, passives, tentativeness, and modifications of the prose, offering decontextualized facts and theories. The other source of information for local scholars, popular scholarly writing in semischolarly journals, also employs a more conclusive prose. Myers (1990) has stated that such journals construct a *narrative of nature* (unmediated by the contingencies of the researcher and research context), whereas RAs offer a *narrative of science,* which attends to the processes and complexities of arriving at the facts/ theories through research and debate among scholars. We can guess the challenges for local scholars influenced by these discourses when they write for refereed journals. They may adopt a similarly unqualified, definitive, generalized discourse that is inappropriate for research journals.

Furthermore, since publications arrive belatedly from the center, local scholars cannot always keep pace with the knowledge construction in the

West. The dominant intellectual currents and fashions are followed several steps behind. The advent of "new knowledge" is determined by many factors in the local community: the sporadic shipment of books; the return of local scholars recently trained in the center; the occasional visits of scholars from the West; and colleagues who obtain publications in their trips to the capital city or foreign institutions for conferences. A scholar who charts the history of ideas in the local academic community will find that paradigms discarded in the center enjoy prestige in the local community. For example, Enlightenment science arrived late and is presently experiencing its zenith in local disciplinary communities. As we saw in previous chapters, the paper on Panditamani, delivered in Tamil by a senior professor at UJ, is prefaced by the principles of personal detachment, inductive reasoning, and empirical objectivity (in an unqualified sense) to validate the professor's findings and authority (Suseendirarajah 1991). Other competing streams of thinking, like Marxism, have had to make a compromise with scientific positivism in order to survive. Some of the leading academic Marxists writing in Tamil have adopted a progressivist, impersonal, and economistic attitude to social change (Kailasapathy 1981). It will no doubt take more than a decade for any of the trickling publications on post-Enlightenment critique to make a dent in the positivism of our science or the determinism of our Marxism. This pace of development is again a form of hegemony, as it endows center scholars with the ability to define what is trendy in the different disciplines. Before local scholars have had the time to understand the dominant paradigms and develop their critiques, they will find that center scholars have changed the terms of the game with a new paradigm.

The recent international thinking that seeps into the local community through reading is absorbed in diverse ways by local scholars, as they are detached from direct interaction with the Western communities that produce these publications. For example, while there has been a spurt of vernacular publications introducing/interpreting postmodernist thinking to the local audience in the last couple of years, these theories take a different shape in periphery soil (as I have pointed out in a critical review of hermeneutical publications in the vernacular—see Canagarajah 1994b). Reception of center scholarship can range from innocent misinterpretation to casual appropriation. It is inevitable that these publications have to be interpreted according to the divergent schema brought to play by local scholars in terms of their own cultures and traditions. Though it is not possible to say that they simply reject all center publications and thinking, even when they are excited about center developments it may be for different reasons or with a different understanding of the nature of the theoretical developments. Consider the reception of structuralism. Tamil scholars in South India have praised it for being closer to the hermeneutical tradition of ancient Tamil scholars or (conversely) for heightening Marxist paradigms. However, Sri Lankan Tamil scholars have been suspicious of these developments, taking them to be a meaningless play with words and an exaggerated textual orientation to life. Thus the slightly different social contexts of these two Tamil communities make them understand structuralist developments in different ways. That *traveling theories* go through these processes of sociocultural adoption and adaptation is understandable (Said 1983). It is perhaps a blessing in disguise that, lacking strong ties to the Western academy, local scholars are able to adopt a measure of critical detachment from the thinking of the center. It is this detachment that also contributes to their intellectual hybridity—letting them hold different paradigms without being pressured into conforming to a particularly fashionable theoretical discourse. While there is little systematic/sustained development of new knowledge in terms of center research interests, periphery scholars still generate thinking related to local traditions by absorbing center scholarly constructs on their own terms. As we can see, such reading strategies have oppositional possibilities, but at present they are not practiced in a conscious, sustained, or programmatic manner.

The Culture of Talk

If writing takes on less importance as compared to reading in the UJ academic community, both take on less significance as compared to talk for purposes of knowledge construction. In Jaffna, much of the scholarly activity occurs orally in seminars, public gatherings, and informal interactions. As we have seen in the depiction of everyday life in Jaffna, things revolve around talk. In the proceedings of the Academic Forum, knowledge production takes place primarily in the oral presentation of the author and the subsequent lively argument with the members. We have seen the amount of involved talk that goes on in the interminable committee meetings. Oral knowledge construction takes place when academics are featured as speakers in religious, cultural, and social gatherings in the community. The university itself hosts a variety of public meetings and seminars on various subjects where academics are given leading roles. There is a lot of talk in the faculty common room as staff members negotiate the hidden messages of journals and newspapers. In offices, corridors, and streets faculty members are busy talking. In sheer volume, time given, and energy expended, the primary activity that goes on in the academy every day is talk—not reading or writing. While lively oral interactions between faculty members are not unusual in center academic communities, the importance given to talk relative to other modes of scholarly interaction at UJ is quite striking.

In fact, this culture of talk can get in the way of academic writing. Not being able to make much progress writing a paper for a journal in my office, I had to partition my desk from the rest of the office space in order to escape from the waves of people who walked in and out of the room to initiate a conversation. The academic culture in Jaffna differs from that of the center, where faculty members are busy working in their own offices (which practice had perhaps influenced my own attitude after my stay there). Faculty members in the center enter a colleague's office/cubicle for mostly functional purposes. There is a grave seriousness in the corridors and departments of center institutions, creating an eerie silence sometimes that contrasts with the pleasant human voice of talk in local institutions. Apart from the cultural influence of a semirural and homogeneous community that values talk, there are material conditions influencing this state of affairs. In wartime Jaffna, where the already limited electronic mass media is defunct, people lack other forms of entertainment or relaxation. Talk is the only available pastime. Also, since not all faculty members are given cubicles or offices, they naturally congregate in the common room and corridors after classes to talk.

Furthermore, in these informal speech events local scholars are under no compulsion to avoid scholarly topics. There have been many occasions when I have tried to escape scholarly discussions in the faculty common room, where I went to relax from some intensive writing I was doing at that time. But my colleagues from other disciplines prodded me into talk about academic developments of mutual concern. Once, a couple of colleagues wanted to further explore a reference I had made in one of my Tamil articles on different styles of communication in orality- and literate-dominant communities. Providing additional examples, they made the dichotomy more complex in a very engaging discussion. It appears to me that there is a careful boundary between personal and scholarly concerns in interpersonal interactions in the center academy. Informal interactions are strictly defined as personal—and, therefore, professional talk is kept out. Conferences and seminars are reserved for the discussion of professional matters. In the local community, this distinction is not strictly maintained. This is so for many reasons. I gradually realized that for many of my colleagues who lacked opportunities to attend scholarly conferences (both because there were very few of those in the national scene and because they didn't enjoy the institutional funding to make such trips), these informal conversations were their only opportunities to exchange information. In the midst of their responsibilities for their families and extra activities for earning money, they got few opportunities to share disciplinary developments with their colleagues. Furthermore, since different people read different material according to availability, sharing of information becomes functional and meaningful.

Though professional conferences for specialized disciplinary communities are rare, other fora of formal oral interactions are important sites of knowledge construction/dissemination at UJ. Despite the curfews and lack of transport in Jaffna, there were always some meetings or colloquia held at UJ. Institutions outside the university would attempt to hold their meetings on the campus, featuring one or more academics as speakers. Religious bodies, cultural organizations, political organizations (including the military regime), nongovernmental social-service organizations, student associations, and a range of university organizations (e.g., the workers union, the English Forum) would organize public meetings. There would sometimes be more than a couple of meetings on the same day on the campus. These meetings would muster large audiences from both outside and inside the university community. Similarly the speakers in these meetings would include scholars from outside the academy as well as faculty members. Although seminars and talks receive considerable intellectual importance in center communities—as in New York, which features many talks in YMCAs, large bookstores, and community libraries every week— they don't hold the same importance for knowledge-construction purposes as in the local community.

There is a lot of motivation for local academics to participate in these speech events. Performance in these events gains recognition for academic promotion and is accepted as a contribution to scholarly discourse. I have seen colleagues citing their talks in these meetings as part of their credentials. More importantly, performance in these oral speech events becomes the primary criterion for one's scholarly ethos and authority. A professor who publishes in professional journals, but doesn't participate in these public speech events, will not be held in high esteem in the community. On the other hand, scholars who obtained their graduate degrees locally hold a high status as intellectuals, as they are featured often as speakers in these meetings. Of course scholars trained abroad, or those who received their basic education in the English medium, are at a disadvantage in these events held in the vernacular—the language of everyday public interaction. Senior scholars who received their complete education primarily in the English medium during the colonial period have to develop their fluency in Tamil in order to participate in the vibrant everyday intellectual life of the community. It would appear that the scholarly persona is locally associated with the role of a rhetorically effective speaker on any given subject.

But, however, we mustn't exaggerate the oral character of these speech events. In many of these interactions talk revolves around texts. Sometimes written texts are the focus of the talk, as in the Academic Forum or the interactions in the common room over journal articles. The practice in the Academic Forum and some of the other scholarly fora at UJ, where a pre-distributed written text is always followed by an oral presentation and face-to-face debate on the day of presentation, suggests that the written text cannot stand by itself in knowledge construction. The written text is often only a starting point for the more important oral construction of knowledge. In other events, texts are the end product of talk—as in the case of the committee meeting that discussed the appropriate way of structuring and editing the handbook for the external-studies program. In certain interactions, writing serves to record/store knowledge that was primarily constructed in oral interactions. Examples of this are reports in magazines and newspapers of meetings that have already taken place. Even everyday conversations in domestic and interpersonal domains can involve the discussion of texts. Therefore, texts are often the focus and sometimes the background of talk.

Texts thus receive a lot of attention in this orality-dominant community, as they are pondered, interpreted, and mulled over. However, knowledge production is more significantly taking place in face-to-face oral interactions, rather than in print. Although this is a community proficient in literacy, orality is the valorized mode of knowledge construction and interaction in local academic circles. The many examples provided above suggest that contemporary disciplinary communities are continuing the traditional practice of using literacy as an auxiliary for oral interactions and knowledge production (as described earlier—see Narasimhan 1991). It is interesting in this connection that ethnographers of center academic communities (Bazerman 1988; Latour and Woolgar 1986; Knorr-Cetina 1981) find center-based scientists subordinating talk to writing. While they are interacting with their colleagues in both formal and informal oral interactions, these scholars are gathering information and approaches for their writing projects. The ideas shared in face-to-face conversations later find their way in diverse forms into their RAs. But this relationship is reversed for local scholars. They interact orally in order to talk about the texts they have read and in order to engage in active interpretation and application. They enjoy the talk for its own sake, rather than using it as a vehicle to generate ideas and information for writing projects.

It is important to observe closely an oral interaction where the meaning of a text is negotiated to find out the implications for knowledge production. The informal literacy event presented below contrasts with the formal speech event reported at the opening of this chapter. We have to also consider how the ways of "communal reading" presented here modify the individual reading practices discussed in the preceding section.

It was A. J. who had first spotted this brief article titled "Life in the Postmodern World" in an old issue of the American journal *Dialogue* in one of his weekly visits to the university library. After reading it, he passed it on to me and recommended it as an article that attempts to define the movement in relatively simple terms. He also requested that before we returned the journal to the library we should get our stenographer to type out the article in full so that we could pass it around among our colleagues. (Typing was necessary because we didn't have Xeroxing facilities.)[6] After explicating the connections between premodernism, modernism, and postmodernism, and illustrating the different manifestations of postmodernism in fields like philosophy, literature, architecture, and the social sciences, the article concludes with an explanation of the popularity of this movement in the late capitalist period. When I cycled the next evening after classes to A. J.'s house to return the journal and have one of our usual chats over tea (a popular form of relaxation in war-torn Jaffna), Sankar was already there. Sankar was a final-year student in theater who read voraciously, keen about developments in a variety of other disciplines. Krishna, who was an assistant in the local public library, and with whom A. J. shared a house at that time, had already returned home from work. His wife, Soma, a lecturer in history at UJ, walked in with mugs of tea for us. But she was too busy feeding her twin infants to join us in the conversation—although she was listening to what was going on and would interject at critical points.

Soon our talk turned to the article. Krishna had skimmed through it when A. J. brought it home. Sankar had become sufficiently interested in the article that he asked A. J. to lend the journal to him that night. He began browsing through it as we talked. Each of us possessed different forms of background information, none complete enough to authoritatively interpret the article. Krishna had seen modernist and postmodern art while living as a "refugee" in France for a couple of years. I had read some theoretical writing on the movement while I was completing my doctorate in the United States. But as the philosophical discourse had reached an advanced stage during my stay in the West, I hadn't mastered it adequately to be able to explain things coherently to my colleagues (or to myself). A. J., though widely read in other intellectual movements, was still trying to come to terms with this newfangled thinking. Sankar had read some South Indian books in Tamil that offered their own jargon-ridden interpretations of the movement. Therefore, we had to pool together our resources and information to make sense of the article.

While A. J., Krishna, and I mentioned the different aspects of the article that had attracted our attention, Sankar read aloud some statements that he found puzzling: "In the postmodernist sensibility, the search for unity has apparently been abandoned altogether. Instead, we have textuality, a cultivation of surfaces endlessly referring to, ricocheting from, reverberating onto other surfaces." Krishna gave some interesting examples from his visits to museums in France, where collages made of jostling disparate images challenged the viewer into sense-making. Sankar went on: "The implied subject is fragmented, unstable, even decomposed; it is finally nothing more than a crosshatch of discourses. . . . Dance can be built on Beach Boys songs; circus can include cabaret jokes; avant-garde music can include radio gospel." The ease with which the writer referred to Western popular culture angered the others. I had to then explain the references to the Beach Boys and the gospel-music tradition from my limited acquaintance with them. But A. J. quickly steered the conversation to the feeling of entrapment of the Western intelligentsia. Their failure to achieve social change, their own vested interests in the system, and the general apathy of the people had made them find radicalism and meaning in the textualized world of things. Sankar related at this point a Tamil article he had read, which described postmodernism as a cultural reflection of the social degeneration of the West. The failure of the workers' "revolution"; the bourgeoisification of the working class; and the welfare cushioning in capitalist states, which muffled the disillusion of the exploited—all these were blamed for the tendency to play with images/surfaces and enjoy the shreds of the postcapitalist social fabric. We thus constructed a different schema for the interpretation of the article—one that diverged from that of the writer.

At this point there was a noise of machine-gun fire far away, which made A. J. sit up and ask us to stop talking. As the noise came closer, it was clear that it was one of the nightly helicopter patrols to enforce the government's six o'clock curfew from the air. A. J. rushed into the makeshift underground bunker outside the house and motioned everyone to follow. As we all went inside the bunker (including Soma and the four children) I commented on the carving on the mud walls inside. There was a small niche where they had placed clay figurines of Hindu deities. Krishna pointed out that the bunker was a good place for meditation. While staying inside the bunker, his son had dug a small hole in the mud wall and used the clay to sculpt the figure of a god. Krishna said that he had seen such carvings in other bunkers too—perhaps everyone found that doing such work kept them preoccupied and creative while nerve-wracking bombardment was going on outside. This led us to talk about the functional nature of art under these circumstances, which differed from the attitude toward art as an apathetic play of "surfaces" or ironies. Although we didn't refer to anything specific in the article, we were all aware of the implications of this discussion for its message. Perhaps Sankar was reading the statements close to the end of the article in front of him at that very moment: "There is a deliberate self-consciousness, a skating on the edge, dividing irony from dismay or endorsement . . . the quality of deliberateness and the sense of exhaustion in the postmodern are what set it apart."

As we emerged from the bunker, sensing that the strafing had ended,

A. J. half-ironically pondered what prospects there were for changes in the militarized nature of our social environment in the scholarly activity of deconstructing news reports and state proclamations. There was no consolation we could draw from the splintered reality and shredded social fabric, as the postmodernists could do. They wouldn't help us withstand brute force inflicted on us by a military regime. Sankar was gradually coming to the end of the article and read with some sarcasm: "Postmodernism rejects historical continuity and takes up residence somewhere beyond it because history was ruptured: by the bomb-fueled vision of a possible material end of history, by Vietnam, by drugs, by youth revolts, by women's and gay rights movements." We all realized at this time that it was getting dark and we should be getting home if we didn't want another confrontation with the soon-to-return helicopter. People were already gathering outside their huts in the narrow alley to inquire about the casualties from the helicopter strafing and to seek the location of the attack.

What is interesting about this literacy event is the manner in which talk embeds, reconstructs, and interprets written texts. The text gets situated in a clear social context, as we wrestle with linguistic signs and produce meanings that were perhaps unanticipated by the original writer. In this collective and collaborative reading we pool together our resources insightfully to interpret the text. If individual/formal readings take an abstract orientation toward knowledge content (in the autonomous-text tradition), these communal literacy events take a different approach. They adopt a contextualized, rhetorical-process approach. Through personal experiences and stories we construct a suitable schema for our purposes. The resulting interpretation has a clear local relevance and oppositional implication. This is a more critical reading, as it adopts a skeptical attitude toward the writer and the text. Though we start with the intention of arriving at a straightforward definition of postmodernism, we end up adopting a critical orientation that is loaded with value judgments.

As I cycled back home, I thought to myself that I should note down the points we had discussed and write a paper on that subject, developing a periphery view of postmodernism. But soon I gave up that thought when I realized the practical obstacles in getting the project accomplished in Jaffna. I realized, however, that what had passed through my mind is the typical attitude of center scholars after an interaction of such a nature. They would have their eyes set on producing a paper out of an enlightening conversation. I had naturally been influenced by this attitude during my studies in the West. As for the other three participants, writing a paper was far from their minds. For them, it was a rich moment of discovering new things in interaction with others and in engagement with the text. The collective experience of passing the evening together in talk was what mattered. The talk did make each of us richer in thought and feeling. But that was it. We didn't do anything with those insights to record them, pass them to others, spread them through publications, or gain credit for ourselves by claiming ownership over them. Perhaps, if we chanced to have another encounter on such a topic in another gathering, we might share some of the insights we had produced earlier and build on them unconsciously. But such interactions were rare—we had many other topics to discuss in other gatherings, and we had many other insights to share in those speech events. As I reached home, I bemoaned the waste of intellectual resources in this momentary, fluid, random sharing of ideas—even though it had something romantic, radical, and idealistic about it. But perhaps this attitude is again colored by my center-based postgraduate learning experience!

Comparing Academic Cultures

It is important now to consider how we may characterize academic cultures in the periphery. I have to quickly acknowledge that there are variations *within* the center and the periphery. For example, in the United States, there are colleges and universities, teaching institutions and research institutions—with the former often displaying an academic culture similar to that of the periphery. (Note, however, that it is the latter that always enjoy power in society and knowledge production.) We can of course finesse and relativize the description to such an extent that academic cultures of the center and periphery begin to lack differentiation. It is also not difficult to point out how a feature of the local community described above can be found in certain atypical or isolated center contexts. But this is a pointless academic exercise. It won't help us understand the real inequalities existing between communities in literacy and knowledge production. Therefore I am going to amplify some of the peculiarities of the UJ community to bring into relief the distinctive ethos that I believe characterizes many periphery communities and accounts for their differences in publishing prospects from the center.

At least the following significant features emerge through the depiction of the UJ community.

It is more a reading community than a writing community in its literate practices.

It is more an oral community than a literate community in its dominant modes of knowledge construction and communicative conventions.

It is more a teaching community than a research community.

It is a hybrid community that accommodates influences from both the center and the local community in its scholarly activity, institutional policies, and literacy practices.

It is a civic-minded community that earns its status and sustenance by serving the society (rather than leaning toward detachment and autonomy motivated by a preoccupation with disciplinary specialization).

It is a loosely constituted community that accommodates members and institutions of the wider society in its scholarly activities (moving away from elitist and exclusionary practices).

The extent to which the cultural differences and institutional structure of the local academic community are influenced by its off-networked publishing status is important to understand. Its separation from academic publishing has implications not only for its status in knowledge-construction processes but also for its identity and relationships. It is possible to imagine how the sense of community built around publishing networks will be different from that of circles that construct knowledge primarily through face-to-face oral interactions. For example, communication through print reduces the need to always interact in spatially and chronologically proximate domains (Eisenstein 1979). Printed texts permit the community to be displaced in time and space and still feel connected. Besides the fact that the printed text can be passed around or distributed along different generations or different localities, it also makes possible "imagined communities" (Anderson 1984). The free access to knowledge and information among distant groups creates a mental/attitudinal connection among people to constitute themselves into an invisible community. The publishing process thus enables members of disciplinary groups to network with scholars of similar fields or persuasions living in different geographical and historical zones and develop a sense of community even if they have never met face to face. This way they are able to engage with research and information encompassing a wide domain. But communities that are excluded from publishing are more localized in their knowledge-construction processes. Apart from their knowledge having limited influence outside, they are also not able to interact widely in regard to transregional developments. Their sense of community is thus localized according to the time and space constraints of face-to-face interaction.

Bazerman (1988) details the extent to which the academic roles and relationships of center scholars are built around practices of academic writing. Personal conflicts and power struggles are played out in journals in the clash of opinions, perspectives, and research findings. Through the activity of writing scholars gain or lose power/authority because publishing is the accepted way of claiming a place in the academic community. Reputations are made and destroyed in the pages of the academic journal. It is the extent to which one has published that helps decide many of the other rewards of the academic career—fame, recognition, tenure, promotion, professional awards, and research grants. Print media also constitute the community differently, providing a unique sense of ethos, identity, and relationships for members. Basically, identities and relationships are "textualized" in literate communities. The image one acquires in the community is the one developed largely through print. Since all members in a discipline don't necessarily meet one another face to face, it is the textualized ethos that often represents the scholar. Similarly, one's roles in the production of knowledge—as journal editor, referee, proponent of a theory, et cetera—are those that define one's academic status. Roles and relationships are functional—based on the production of knowledge in texts. Therefore the identities and roles constructed in texts take precedence over those displayed in face-to-face interactions. Removed from possibilities of direct (face-to-face) interaction, roles and relationships are built on detached values of expertise and contribution to knowledge construction rather than traditional sources of status (e.g., birth, family, caste, breeding, wealth). But in orality-dominant communities, the roles and identities could be based on a traditional understanding of social hierarchy and not based functionally on one's ability to produce new knowledge. Another way to put this is to say that whereas status is largely *earned* in the center, it is mostly *ascribed* in the periphery (Hess 1995).

Bazerman (1988) points out that the overlapping roles in the publishing enterprise provide firsthand experience for center academics with processes of writing and knowledge construction. This makes them effective writers/researchers who develop important skills in the ways of negotiating the processes of publication and knowledge construction. For example, the roles center faculty members play as writers, reviewers, critics, referees, and editors generate conflicts similar to those in knowledge-construction activity. Just as conflicts are played out in texts, they are also resolved in texts. The editor, who is somewhat detached from the reviewers, tries to resolve the difference of opinion between author and referees on the status of the new knowledge proposed through the RA. These activities develop important skills of negotiating knowledge and texts. To take another example, a person who works as a reviewer for a journal learns many things about the inside workings of the refereeing process and the ways in which editorial judgments are made. After later graduating to the position of a member of an editorial committee, the person gains even more insights into the processes of new knowledge construction through journals. Through these processes the scholar also gets inducted into the inner circles of the disciplinary community—getting to know the established scholars and forming working relationships with them. Managing the different roles played—as a supportive peer reviewer, a detached referee, a diplomatic editor—requires considerable mediating and negotiating capabilities. Thus scholars in the center gain considerable expertise useful for their professional careers. The conventions and practices that matter for the workings of the academic institution are often carried over from the negotiation of articles in research journals. It is as if the academic community is built bottom-up from the pages of research journals. Bazerman takes this further: the very point of academic writing is the construction and constitution of the disciplinary community.

What implication do these differing senses of community spell out for academic literacy? Since the roles and relationships in the center disciplinary communities are developed textually there is greater motivation for literate activity in knowledge production. Furthermore, since the rationale for these disciplinary communities is the production of new knowledge, their interactions are focused on this functional goal. Besides, the possibility of increased competition as geographically different disciplinary communities engage in knowledge construction results in richer intellectual paradigms. This knowledge can be disseminated again to communities separated by time and space through the medium of print, which is the central form of interaction here. The printed word also encourages relatively more detached processes of knowledge construction, granting certain forms of efficiency. The objective record of knowledge in texts enables a systematic and focused creation of new knowledge. There is also a better track of the progress made in thinking and findings through the print record. Knowledge making is, furthermore, centralized through print. Greg Myers (1990) has pointed out how textual practices in the academy serve to work toward uniformity in the disciplines, keeping in check the scholarly eccentricities of members as they negotiate the elaborate screening/refereeing processes involved in getting into print. The process of competing in and negotiating the publishing process makes knowledge production more disciplined and focused.

On the other hand, a community that is cut off from journals will not only develop a different institutional culture but also have different placement in knowledge construction. Periphery scholars are cut off from the print-based roles and relationships available in the center. The alternate roles they gain through extratextual means (i.e., bureaucratic, community-wide) don't dispose them well toward writing and knowledge production. There is also less motivation to discover sources of status and power that come through academic publishing.

To compare the structural dynamics of both types of communities we can borrow the remarkably insightful constructs proposed by sociolinguists James Milroy and Leslie Milroy (1992) to describe speech communities in terms of network ties. It would appear that members of periphery academic communities would display *strong* network ties—that is, there is a greater level of interaction and investment in the interpersonal relationships between the frequently interacting members. Located in a clearly defined geographical space, constituted as a homogeneous community with a shared history, periphery communities display all the ingredients for strong interpersonal ties. Furthermore, the ties would be *multiplex*. That is, the community would interact on many different goals and concerns—not just academic. As depicted above, faculty from UJ meet each other at various political, cultural, and social gatherings, in addition to enjoying relationships even at a personal/family level. As a result, relationships would be *dense,* as scholars would interact with many others within the community, at different levels and at great frequency, with the academic community beginning to overlap in its concerns with those of other discourse communities.

The center academic communities, organized around print, are geographically and historically dispersed. They are functional communities that interact for limited/specific goals (namely, disciplinary concerns). Therefore they are *monoplex* in their ties. Furthermore, they are somewhat impersonal, as members lack deep investment in relationships among themselves. The network ties are therefore *loose*. Furthermore, not everyone in the community knows everyone else or interacts closely with everyone in these "virtual communities." Interactions are thus less frequent, and connections are less numerous. In this sense, the relationships are *sparse*. These are of course changing communities: members come and go. They always splinter into smaller groups in addition to reformulating their own composition. More importantly, members have relationships outside the disciplinary circle and introduce new ideas and perspectives from other communities—which would lead to rethinking the goals and rationale of the disciplinary community. Center academic relationships are, therefore, more fluid, as they are formed and abandoned based on the functional concerns that bring them together. But for the same reason, they are also more dynamic. Relationships and ideas are always changing, as members are more open to new ideas. In contrast, Milroy and Milroy propose, communities with multiplex, dense, strong ties (like the one at UJ) are more conservative and less engaged with novel ideas and perspectives. Such a community is largely self-contained and stable.

The lack of strong integration with other communities based on print culture provides periphery communities a sense of autonomy in their knowledge production (which can be both enabling and limiting). Orally interacting communities are more homogeneous, as they are stipulated on the ability of individuals to be located in a specific geographical and historical space. The lack of systematization of activity enables the possibility of heterogeneous/hybrid intellectual traditions and epistemologies that can be inconsistent with each other. The nontextualized, embedded nature of knowledge in oral construction provides other differences in the nature of knowledge. There is little urgency for new knowledge construction. The point of scholarly interactions is to "experience" the knowledge through collaborative exploration of the ramifications and implications of the findings/publications rather than acontextually analyzing these. Since there is no written objective text that regulates the proceedings and activities, the knowledge construction of periphery members is relatively more spontaneous and relaxed. Scholars aren't obsessed with utilitarian motivations of earning credit through publications. Such communities may also begin their theorization from their personal location/experience rather than abstractly from previously published theses and paradigms. The heterogeneous concerns discussed in multiple small circles momentarily, without a systematic record of the intellectual work accomplished, not only cause slower, less cumulative progression but are also less focused or systematic. However, since written products have the relative advantage of permanency and displacement, published texts (especially in a lingua franca) hold power in the international marketplace of knowledge transaction. The oral production of knowledge in the vernacular is too ephemeral to have transregional or global influence. The domain of such knowledge is local, as it is largely represented orally. It is less systematized or institutionalized and displays less focused continuity of activity.

It is important to point out that the inequalities in knowledge construction don't derive purely from the periphery's dominant orality.[7] Both center and periphery communities need (and do use) oral and literate modes of communication to accomplish their scholarly activity. Geisler (1994) confirms that while abstract *content knowledge* may be developed purely through the medium of texts and literacy, the more productive/constructive (and developmentally advanced) phase of *domain-specific knowledge* is developed largely through oral interaction in face-to-face communication. It is through their oral interactions that center communities develop the ability to apply abstract disciplinary constructs to different situations to explain practical problems. However, if, in the dominant geopolitical reality, writing is the primary means of constructing new knowledge, periphery scholars (who for complex cultural and material reasons are excluded from academic publishing) are missing key experiences in the knowledge-construction business. In fact, writing turns out to be a key medium for exploring, discovering, and formulating knowledge in the contemporary world. The more actively one is involved in writing, the more critical a reader and researcher one becomes. Excluded from writing, periphery scholars miss the urgency, momentum, and focus that encourage knowledge production. In effect, while center scholars negotiate the literate/oral strategies of communication to their advantage (helped no doubt by the facilities they have for doing so), periphery scholars do not seem to negotiate this tension effectively. This is not because periphery scholars intrinsically cannot engage in these literate practices—those who join center academic communities prove that they can play the same games their center colleagues do—but because their material conditions and academic cultures are not always congenial to doing so.

Of course, it is the particular makeup of the periphery community that accounts for its desirable features. Members are able to nurture a healthy pluralism of paradigms, democratically accommodate diverse scholarly orientations, and practice scholarship that has civic relevance. These communities lack motivation for specialization and therefore accommodate wider participation in scholarly activities. This in fact enables members of these scholarly communities to adopt more holistic approaches toward knowledge and life (accommodating teaching/students, local relevance, and civic responsibility in their work). It is interesting, in light of the relaxed/holistic scholarly culture of the periphery, that Hess (1995, 153) relates a comparison Latin American scholars make with their North American counterparts: while U.S. academics live to work, they work to live. This reversed set of priorities is shared by UJ scholars also, who despise what they see as mindless, mechanical orientations toward research and disciplinary specialization.[8] Perhaps we have to say that periphery scholars play a different game from that of the center—and they are successful in the game they have defined for themselves.

Hess (1995, 118) compares periphery scientific communities to *diaspora communities* (such as those of Jewish or African people), which consider an originary homeland as the point of reference, even if they also share the cultural features of the new communities in which they are located. For Hess it is Western Europe and North America that are the "originary homelands" of periphery scientific communities, while they borrow cultural features from their own "national cultures in which they are embedded." If we apply this perspective to the UJ community we will realize that though its members are culturally quite different in showing influences from native traditions, they are also influenced by center academic norms. They are somewhat compelled to borrow the points of reference in their work from center communities, who enjoy hegemony through their superior material resources and political history. Periphery communities are inextricably tied to the center in their knowledge-production activities, partly because the global academic enterprise is structured as it is. From these orientations we have to think of periphery academic communities as dependent communities. They are integrated structurally as a satellite that "consumes" center products and also provides intellectual and human resources for the hegemony of the center.

I recognize that the above characterization of academic relationships goes against the more fashionable theorization of multidirectional cultural flows in globalization studies by those like Appadurai (1996), featuring more autonomy for the periphery and characterized by local divergences. My characterization posits a more one-sided relationship not because I like to theorize things according to unilateral and deterministic models but because I see geopolitical realities working out that way at the macrosocial level in the communities I observed. However, this relationship doesn't *have* to be one-sided. There are different outcomes possible in the *microsocial* domains of writing and publishing. It is here that the more dynamic contact zones perspective (introduced earlier) becomes useful. Though center and periphery communities are characterized by different academic cultures and are structured unequally, they may negotiate their statuses differently in the specific contact zones of knowledge construction. But resistance doesn't come naturally or simply reside in the cultural logic of globalization (as theorized by Appadurai). Resistance has to be *achieved* with ideological sensitivity to one's interests and contexts. We will discuss in chapter 8 how the differences and strengths of periphery communities can be tapped to further develop the discursive strategies of resistance we saw in the writing of local scholars in chapters 4 and 5 in order to reconfigure geopolitical relationships.

7. Poverty and Power in Knowledge Production

> Poor countries—and poor people—differ from rich ones not only because they have less capital but because they have less knowledge. Knowledge is often costly to create and that is why much of it is created in industrial countries.—World Bank, *World Development Report, 1998/1999*

We have already encountered A. J. in the previous pages as a man of prodigious reading and radical perspectives, a thinker who had a tremendous influence on young academics in Jaffna through his mere friendship and conversation. As for making his own contribution to knowledge, A. J. was surprisingly hesitant. To begin with, his academic position was marginalized even locally. Although he held a special degree (i.e., had "majored") in English literature for his bachelor's degree, he had never proceeded to do graduate studies. He often bemoaned the lack of opportunities that made him indefinitely postpone traveling abroad for higher education. After a restless tenure in unsatisfactory job situations—assistant teacher in secondary schools, assistant editor at a nonprofit weekly—he became an instructor in the English Language Teaching Center when UJ was established in our hometown in 1974. This post didn't require any advanced degrees, as it was designated a nonfaculty position. However, A. J. was always very active in the informal oral circles of knowledge production, featuring scholars and writers outside the academic context. He also did some writing (often under pseudonyms) in local literary and political journals. Still, whenever he was invited to do a more prominent piece of writing or a lecture, he would shrug his shoulders nonchalantly. His oft-repeated excuse was: "I am out of touch." Perhaps he felt a tremendous sense of inadequacy about addressing subjects on which it was difficult to catch up with the relevant scholarly developments abroad. Perhaps it was simply the cares of everyday life that were sapping his energy and enthusiasm for serious work. Living alone in a ramshackle room, he periodically went on drinking binges from which nothing or nobody could extricate him. All that people around him could do was bemoan the appalling waste of potential.

What some colleagues succeeded in doing on a hot July afternoon in 1981 provides an excellent example of what A. J. could contribute—if only he had the resources and the peace of mind to do so. A faculty couple invited him home, served him his meals and his usual intake of alcohol, seated him at a comfortable desk, and encouraged him to compose his thoughts on a matter they had been discussing for some time. The subject was the way in which the American textbook used for ELT in the university (published by Longman and donated by the Asia Foundation) presented values that were influenced by what they perceived to be a WASP ideology. The short essay—just two printed pages long—is very insightful. A. J. conducts a discourse analysis of sorts, semiotically interpreting the visuals and text to bring out the hidden curriculum. (Needless to say, none of the trendy jargon I am using here is used in his paper.) The article appears in the *Lanka Guardian,* the semischolarly journal published from the capital city. This article also appears under a pseudonym (Raj 1982). The essay was an eye-opener for many of us ELT practitioners on the reproductive effects of schooling/education. It oriented me to issues of critical pedagogy far more effectively than any publication by Henry Giroux or Paul Willis could do. The paper turned out to have considerable influence on my future scholarly work in developing ideologically sensitive approaches to language and literacy (Canagarajah 1993b).

The issues A. J. addressed have become fashionable concerns now in the field, although the American ELT consultant from the Asia Foundation brushed aside the essay as a distortion of the textbook and as irrelevant to our pedagogical mission in a conversation with me at that time. About ten years after A. J.'s paper was published, the field of ELT awoke to the politics of pedagogy with a bang (Peirce 1989; Pennycook 1989). Ironically, critical pedagogy has become the orthodoxy now. Awards and accolades—including those by the prestigious American and British Associations of Applied Linguists (the AAAL and BAAL, respectively)—have been showered on those center scholars who have published on this subject (Phillipson 1992; Holliday 1994; Pennycook 1994). I have often wondered what would have happened if A. J. had attempted to publish his paper in a center journal—especially a prestigious research journal respected in the field. There are many reasons why it would have been rejected. The paper is a straightforward account that follows some of the key narratives in the textbook chronologically; there is no literature review and, thus, no attempt to situate the argument in the disciplinary discourse; there is no mention of a conscious methodology employed; there are no bibliographical citations, endnotes, or section divisions (as in the IMRD structure). In short, while the essay is intellectually challenging, it is not "academic." Furthermore, it is largely framed within a Marxist theoretical discourse popular in the wider scholarly community in the periphery. It shows no awareness of the dominant disciplinary discourses on linguistics or education in the Western academy. Moreover, for the times, it was too early to broach topics on multiculturalism, postcolonialism, and cultural politics. The point then is that the paper is inappropriately framed for the academic conversation in the center. Even if A. J. had managed to overcome the nontextual publishing requirements (which I catalogued in chapter 5), the discursive differences would have influenced mainstream reviewers to reject the paper.

There are many things that are tragic about examples like this. That there are formidable scholars like A. J. in the periphery, with powerful insights, whose thinking doesn't inform knowledge construction at a wider level because of their alienation from mainstream discourses and publishing networks is indeed sad. More unfortunate is the fact that even when these scholars publish something, their work is marginalized in the field. (Of course, A. J.'s paper has some functionality in the local community. But, even in Jaffna, the paper has to contend with the dominant discourses emanating from the center.) When we contextualize A. J.'s paper in the history of critical pedagogical discourse in the ELT profession, we realize many ironies relating to the geopolitics of knowledge construction.

The relative obscurity of periphery scholars enables center academics to take credit for everything—including the types of scholarship that already have a vibrant tradition in the periphery. While the politics of ELT has just become a fad in the West in the last few years, this issue has been an ongoing subject of concern among periphery scholars and teachers for a long time now. However, since much of their knowledge on this subject has been formulated orally and/or in the vernacular, there is no objective record of this development for the international scholarly community.

Even the meager written work on this subject in English by periphery scholars in local journals goes unnoticed. This state of affairs enables center scholars to take credit for theorizing or popularizing this subject. In fact, they win recognition for having broached the subject for the first time and having made an original discovery. (This smacks of Columbus's claim to have discovered the New World!)

This example also reveals certain inconsistencies in disciplinary discourse formation. The academic communities in the center and periphery seem to conduct different discourses at different times even within the same discipline. Therefore a subject that is being discussed in the periphery won't receive attention if the center is not ready for it. Given the Western monopoly on academic journals, these periphery discourses won't have any chance of getting a hearing or influencing mainstream thinking. When the center does promote this discourse at a later time, motivated by its own social conditions, it may not be able to tap the contributions already made in periphery circles. (The periphery itself may be preoccupied with other discourses at this time.) Eventually, the body of work in the center gets canonized and mainstreamed, while the work from the periphery passes into oblivion.[1] Apart from the unfairness of this situation, we have to consider how these disjunctures in time and space affect (indeed impoverish) the formation of discourses in the different disciplines.

Consider also the irony behind the fact that the knowledge of periphery scholars *on their own communities* is marginalized, while that of center scholars enjoys repute. While the work of scholars like Phillipson, Holliday, and Pennycook on linguistic imperialism in the periphery earns universal recognition, the work of periphery scholars like A. J. on a similar subject is unknown. Implicit in this situation is the irony that while those who may have never lived extensively in the periphery become authorities on our affairs, the knowledge of local people who live this reality intimately is untapped, unknown, and disregarded.[2] This makes it appear as if foreigners know more about the local reality than the local people do. Moreover, it appears that whatever realities periphery subjects may live, center scholars are needed to theorize them and give them a perspective in order for work to achieve the status of established knowledge. (Though there is a case to be made for the "experience far" perspective, which provides an advantage for the outsider—as explained by Geertz 1983—this doesn't mean that local scholars cannot demystify their everyday reality as center scholars do when they study their own communities.)

Furthermore, the monopoly on academic publications creates a self-constricted space within which academic discourses are constructed. Even though radical scholars from the center always acknowledge the lack of adequate data on local manifestations of linguistic imperialism in the periphery, they still discuss this subject with whatever information is available to them. Someone has to. Many of those scholars have limited experience in periphery classrooms and communities themselves (granting even the brief research trips or teaching stints they may undertake). Eventually, those with limited knowledge on the periphery become authorities on this subject. That mainstream disciplinary discourses have to be formed with inadequate local knowledge (even when papers of those like A. J. are available in the periphery) shows the narrow scope of knowledge formation.

A logical extension of this situation is that periphery communities turn out to be consumers of center knowledge about themselves. Due to the one-sided nature of publishing, we are forced into a position of understanding ourselves through center eyes. How else can we explain the current situation at UJ? After considering the writing of A. J. as being of only marginal relevance for our work at a time when psycholinguistic/structuralist models were considered the acceptable orientation, local teachers are currently finding that critical pedagogy is becoming "mainstream." But the texts to understand this stream of work come from Phillipson, Holliday, and Pennycook. A. J. himself is trying to read these scholars to understand the definitive work on this subject (although with considerable reservations). Local teachers are attempting to practice critical pedagogy for periphery classrooms by reading center scholars. The superior status of Western publishing networks and the professional recognition granted to work emanating from center academy and publishing institutions influence local teachers to treat this body of work as more authoritative (even on matters about themselves).

Even resistance to the West, or a critique of the center's linguistic imperialism, has to be first articulated in the West before it can become an acceptable project in periphery communities. It was after the aforementioned center publications that this mission won approval in periphery (and center) educational circles. In fact, in the periphery, there is a tradition of discourse on this subject from during colonial times—four hundred years back—which has unfortunately been relegated to "folk" or "unscientific" thinking and is not being taken seriously by even the local ELT practitioners.[3] Such concerns were considered tangential to the ELT pedagogical mission, defined in structuralist and positivistic terms as the teaching of value-free grammatical units to students.

There are some serious concerns regarding the center's attempt to represent the periphery, even on subjects where the center scholars appear to be sympathetic to periphery interests. The differences in the publications by A. J. and the center scholars show considerable variations in the "linguistic imperialism" discourse as it relates to the influence of center ELT projects, textbooks, and constructs in periphery classrooms. Phillipson (1992) adopts an orientation of linguistic and ideological reproduction, suggesting that English has been imposed by Anglo-American communities as a vehicle for their cultural and political control. But an awareness of publications by those like A. J. would have shown that there is resistance from within the periphery to these reproductive tendencies. Phillipson would have also realized the complexity of periphery communities where English is considerably nativized and has been appropriated to represent periphery interests. A. J., furthermore, articulates a vision for pedagogical resistance. At least in this case, the center scholar adopts an overzealous and deterministic perspective on the issue. (It is periphery perspectives and discourses that are stereotypically considered politically extremist; in this case, however, it is the center scholar who represents periphery realities in this fashion.) This example also shows the dangers behind the center's ability to represent periphery realities and perspectives on behalf of local scholars who are alienated from the publishing world.

As we can see, there are multiple levels of irony in this state of affairs. It will become evident below that this situation is true of many other fields in the academy today. There are certain typical tendencies involved in the mainstream academy's relation to periphery knowledge, by virtue of its control over the publishing media. Periphery knowledge is marginalized in favor of center thinking. Periphery experiences and resources are exploited or appropriated for purposes of knowledge construction in the center. Center versions of phenomena (even on matters closely connected to the periphery) enjoy global respect. These forms of domination in the realm of ideas have implications for the material inequalities and power differences in geopolitical relationships. After all, knowledge is power. Having shown in the previous chapters the unfair relationships in the publishing domain and the corresponding inequalities between center and periphery academic communities, I wish to now elaborate on the stakes involved in reforming publishing practices by considering the geopolitical impact of this inequality on the wider ideological and material life. This chapter deals with the macrosocial implications for knowledge construction and material development deriving from the center domination of the academic publishing industry, before we go on to consider how periphery scholars may complicate this geopolitical inequality in certain specific sites of intervention.

Processes of Intellectual Hegemony

Inequality

To begin with, although knowledge production is going on freely in the everyday life of many communities, by virtue of its monopoly of the publishing industry the Western academy is able to establish its own scholarship as authoritative. Since it is through publishing that new knowledge gets accepted and legitimized, center disciplinary circles are able to win recognition for their own research work and epistemological traditions. Dominating the publishing industry also enables the center to function as the clearinghouse for research work globally, enjoying the privilege of defining intellectual trends and practices. The scholarly publications present the distorted picture that any intellectual work worthy of note is going on only in the center communities, whose writers publish in these journals. Excluded from the publishing networks, the scholarship of periphery academics is relegated to the status of "local knowledge" or "folk wisdom," secondary to the intellectual currents of the center-based "mainstream." The life of their discourses will be restricted to the local context—always facing the threat that the mainstream discourses (via the powerful global reach of print) may smother them into oblivion.

There are many reasons why academic publishing gives the impression that any valuable work even on periphery concerns is being undertaken by center scholars and academic institutions. First, although both center and periphery scholars may study similar issues in the periphery, it is the research of center scholars that has greater chances of appearing in print in mainstream journals. While periphery scholars already face material limitations in their communities that prevent them from meeting the publishing requirements of journals (as has already been made clear in previous chapters), there are other factors that compound this inequality. Being armed with the latest theoretical/methodological constructs valorized by center academic institutions and having access to publishing/scholarly circles are factors that provide a lot of advantages for center scholars. We also mustn't ignore the fact that those who publish a piece of research first are credited with the intellectual property rights for that knowledge construct. Speed, too, helps in such matters: before periphery scholars can write, mail, and negotiate their papers for publication, center scholars can get into print because of their geographical proximity and technological efficiency. With a brief trip for fieldwork on a prestigious grant, center scholars are able to get their work published quickly and prominently, while the periphery scholars who live these realities daily are marginalized. Consider the example of Brian Pfaffenberger, who visited Jaffna a few times. As an American graduate student newly entering discourses on caste and South Asian studies, he had to depend on senior scholars at UJ for data and information. These respected local scholars, who had been interested in these subjects for almost their whole scholarly careers, shared their knowledge freely with the foreign scholar. Pfaffenberger returned home to the United States and was able to produce a stream of publications on caste in no time (Pfaffenberger 1982). Local scholars Shanmugalingam and Manivasakar are still struggling to get their voices heard—not because they don't have knowledge about these realities or haven't done painstaking research but because they don't enjoy the connections and resources to publish.

Besides deprivation, we should also consider the impact of outdated research instruments on the reproduction of intellectual dependency. Since the periphery lags behind in technological development, its backwardness turns out to disqualify papers emerging from local institutions. Referees are often biased against authors who do not appear to employ sophisticated current technology for their research. Therefore periphery scholars often spend their time mastering technology at one remove from the West, while center scholars move on with producing new knowledge using the latest instruments. By the time periphery scholars finally manage to master the technology, the state of the art has moved ahead far enough for them not to be able to use these instruments for acceptable research purposes. An Indian colleague in immunology relates the following as an example of the handicap scholars in his field face.

> Much of their [his colleagues'] time is wasted in learning the technologies only, and by the time they try to use this technology for solutions of some of

their indigenous problems, the West declares that these instruments are obsolete and unreliable. The ten year lag in integration of technology makes the work of these scientists redundant. If any scientist sends some research reports pertaining to the diseases of their areas of habitation or present[s] some report pertaining to some likely scientific breakthrough, it would be summarily rejected without giving a chance of proper scrutiny as their instruments are inferior. (Jagveer Rawat, E-mail communication, 7 January 1997)

While periphery scholars continue in their fumbling attempts to master technology, they are sidetracked from constructive intellectual work. This process then becomes a tale of the tiger catching its tail: while periphery scholars keep trying to catch up with technological developments, knowledge production proceeds in the center without their participation.

Even in the case that periphery scholars manage to publish in regional or local journals, their knowledge is devalued in mainstream circles. The greater status enjoyed by center journals props up the knowledge represented in their pages as more prestigious and valid. Center publications enjoy many forms of advantage over journals published in the periphery. Their superior technological resources enable center journals to put forward a sophisticated and impressive appearance. Because of the marketing infrastructure already in place in the center (i.e., through advertising networks, online marketing, efficient transportation facilities, etc.) these journals receive a wider circulation. These factors also assure the center a head start in competition for contributors and readership. There is thus a hierarchy in the publishing world. Whatever is published in the center is treated as the mainstream; the journals that come out of the periphery are treated as fringe. The knowledge represented in the pages of the respective journals also gets treated with a similar bias. For example, while the studies on my own Tamil culture by center-based scholars David (1974), McGilvray (1982), and Pfaffenberger (1982) are widely cited, those of local academics Sanmugadas (1984), Sivatamby (1984), and Vithiananthan (1984) in periphery journals are relatively unknown.

This difference also affects the scope of knowledge dissemination. The scholarship presented in periphery journals circulates in the local academic circles. The readers of these journals, similar to their contributors, are local (usually from the same community the journal is published in). This also means that center knowledge receives transregional reception through its complex marketing channels. Even abstracting and indexing systems focus on center scholars and center-based publications, providing greater access to these works (Swales 1990). Lacking the means to disseminate their own knowledge widely through print, periphery communities have to be satisfied with having their research and scholarship receive limited hearing. Given this knowledge vacuum, center scholars can assume that no knowledge exists on certain periphery realities and go on publishing work based on limited data.

Furthermore, the publishing domain establishes a one-way traffic in knowledge between center and periphery. While periphery scholars don't have a suitable vehicle to convey their work to the center, scholars from the latter region enjoy powerful resources to spread their knowledge globally. This of course contributes to a lot of imbalance in intellectual work. Knowledge creation becomes one-sided. Center communities—and in fact the global community—are denied the constructive process of debate, negotiation, and consensus-building that derives from the clash of divergent perspectives. We have to also fear the one-sided spread of values from the center to the periphery, which can lead to ideological domination. Furthermore, without the opportunity for center communities to understand the social and economic tendencies in the periphery, the publishing industry exacerbates the misinformed and underinformed condition that characterizes center/periphery relations. As we will see in the next section, unaware of the ground realities in the periphery, many well-meaning center organizations involved in economic and educational development apply models of thinking that turn out to be counterproductive (if not self-serving).

A particularly damaging source of inequality derives from the fact that, given the practices of modern education, periphery institutions have to depend on publications from the center for many purposes. For example, for teaching purposes local scholars find center-published textbooks indispensable. Though textbooks in the vernacular for secondary education are published locally, those needed for college and more advanced levels are from the center (in English). To ask students to read further about matters discussed in class, one has no alternative but to send them to the library to read a publication by a center scholar. Periphery scholars have to depend on center publications for reference and citation even on knowledge pertaining to local realities. Given the predominantly oral production of knowledge locally (which leads to few of their own findings being recorded in writing), local knowledge is not available as a textual product. Also, the resulting slow, implicit, disparate development in oral knowledge construction means that such knowledge is not always clearly formulated or centrally codified. Teachers and students therefore find local knowledge inconvenient to use. When published texts are indispensable for many purposes in modern education, it is inevitable that those without a highly developed print culture reproduce published knowledge from the center.

The fact that periphery academics constitute primarily a reading, rather than a writing, community also plays into the center's thrust for intellectual hegemony. As we found in the previous chapter, the reading culture of periphery scholars creates a demand for published products— which cannot be fulfilled by the local community. As a reading community, local academics have little reading material from their own communities. Even in informal conversations, periphery subjects who are given to frequently citing authorities to back up their claims find it easier to quote center scholars who are readily available in books. While sometimes periphery authorities may be quoted, this has to be done through personal knowledge and memory—and therefore their currency is relatively limited. We have then a consumer group among periphery scholars who don't produce scholarly publications themselves but voraciously read center publications for their intellectual activity at home. All this is to the advantage of the center publishing industry, as it has a ready market in the periphery communities (even for books and journals that are outdated in the West). In purchasing these books and treating the published scholars of the West as authorities, periphery scholars provide currency to center materials in their own communities. In terms of intellectual products, then, the periphery academic culture is largely consumerist.

But even in the case that periphery scholars manage to get something published in center circles, it is still the center scholars who are recognized. Consider Kailasapathy (1968), who published on classical Tamil poetry with the Oxford University Press soon after his doctoral research in Birmingham. After returning to Sri Lanka he was not able to publish a book with an international press again. Meanwhile, his scholarship has been overshadowed by many center scholars who have become authorities on classical Tamil poetry. The fact that center scholars are able to churn out more publications on a subject, compared to the rare publication by a periphery scholar, gives greater prominence to the work of the former. In many other cases, while the single publication of the periphery scholar gets old, center scholars are able to reinterpret and republish matters according to current paradigms and fresh findings. Center scholars are also able to publicize their work in conferences, seminars, the mentoring of younger scholars, and their wide scholarly travel. Thus the isolated work of a remote scholar passes into oblivion.

We must also realize that publishing generates other resources required for knowledge construction, which in turn exacerbate the inequalities in publishing. The more center scholars publish, the more resources they get for studying and researching other matters. The less periphery subjects publish, the less resources they can claim for their intellectual work. We must remember that in the competition for grants and fellowships, having a good record of publishing is treated as proof of one's intellectual caliber. In cases where a person has won a grant but not produced notable publications deriving from it, this fact can become a damaging testimonial to that person's credentials. When the quantity and quality of publications help give an edge in the competition for awards, periphery scholars will not only have less publications on their CVs, but they will also have less respected regional and second-level journals. In a sense, publishing reproduces the dominance of the center in knowledge production—more publications, more resources for research, more publications from research, and so on. It is a case of the rich getting richer, the poor getting poorer.

Exploitation

Having seen how the inequalities in publishing enable the center to claim greater prestige and validity for its knowledge constructs, we will now turn to ask how publishing enables the center to exploit periphery intellectual resources for its purposes. The unequal access to the publishing infrastructure enables Western scholars to borrow less known periphery knowledge and use it as their own. They borrow the data/findings of periphery scholars from unpublished manuscripts, from less known publications in the periphery, or from dissertations submitted to Western universities. Using this information, they are able to build their own knowledge in mainstream journals and take credit for intellectual contribution. Capitalizing on their networking and access to major journals, center scholars are often able to present hidden periphery knowledge with a claim of originality. Holliday (1994), for example, uses eight citations of periphery scholars labeled "unpublished" or "in process" (apart from some more citations from less known regional publications) to develop his thoughts on the differences between center and periphery ELT "cultures." In one sense, it is good that scholars from the center are giving wider publicity to some hidden works of periphery scholars. But this cannot ever substitute for letting periphery scholars speak for themselves in their own voices in more widely recognized international fora. The use of these texts is therefore a form of exploitation—an exploitation of the intellectual products of periphery scholars.

We must also consider here the periphery knowledge in unwritten form that is exploited for constructing written knowledge in the center. Traveling researchers borrow from local informants their knowledge stored in oral memory. They observe and theorize periphery everyday experiences through their fieldwork. They profit from conversations with periphery scholars who have observed and reflected on the realities of their communities for a long time. They borrow indigenous practices of healing and living based on local biological resources to form useful knowledge. It is also possible that if and when research is encouraged on periphery realities, this is done with the motive of benefiting center communities themselves. My Indian colleague from immunology, for example, writes to me of ways in which the scholarly circles collaborate to shape research agendas to suit their own needs and purposes.

> Millions of dollars are poured into the research of the diseases like cystic fibrosis which kill very few people. Western scientists on the other hand ignore the study of the diseases solely affecting the developing nations. Relative importance accorded to diseases like leprosy and malaria by the Western scientists is guided solely by the fact that organisms of the diseases are good models for the study of the biology of the related parasites prevalent in West. In addition to this, the pharmaceuticals put their R&D resources in very few diseases of the concern of the third world. (Jagveer Rawat, E-mail communication, 7 January 1997)

The point made is that the periphery diseases on which research money is spent and knowledge is created are chosen according to the needs of the center. The mainstream journals and research centers encourage this tendency by their publishing priorities and biases. This situation results in occasional imperviousness to the plight of millions of Third Worlders who die of diseases that are neglected by the academic and professional community.

In addition to producing knowledge useful for center scholars, publishing enables them to gain other incidental profits by using periphery data. They may earn a postgraduate degree; obtain a grant for their living, and get expenses met during study in the periphery; land a job and professionalize themselves through this research; and gain recognition and fame as a scholar. Moreover, this exploitation of marginalized knowledge enables them to fulfill the "publish or perish" axiom of the Western academy and assures them of much-needed publications at a time when faculty positions are becoming difficult to get or maintain in the center. Their ability to publish also gives center scholars an upper hand in competitions for research grants and other academic resources. Furthermore, this state of affairs often assures them lucrative employment as international consultants and experts. In general, through dominating the publishing industry center scholars are able to ensure their professional survival and well-being.

It is interesting, in some of the examples cited earlier, how the political economy of knowledge production resembles the industrial processes of exploitation. Just as raw material is taken from the periphery to be manufactured into synthetic products by Western entrepreneurs and sold back to the periphery for a profit, data from the periphery is used by Western scholars to produce academic papers and knowledge. So, for example, center scholars (like Pfaffenberger [1984]) visit Jaffna for a few months on a grant and gather data for theorizing caste. They return to their institutions and, using their academic networks and access to publishing circles, construct models to explain caste (a social phenomenon that is not found in Western societies). Then their intellectual products are sold everywhere as the dominant/established perspective on caste. Ironically, even periphery scholars have to depend on these journals and books to profess the authoritative knowledge on these subjects. They have to study these publications to justify their own work and guide their future research on their own societies. Eventually they may have to apply these so-called dominant or established paradigms to explain caste in their own theorization and social planning. If the reason why periphery communities cannot turn their raw material into synthetic products is lack of technology, the same explanation applies in this case—lack of material resources prevents them from transforming their experiences and observations into established knowledge paradigms through academic publications. As we have seen above, this mode of academic activity only helps center communities.

Jean Franco (1988) observes that there are certain common attitudes toward the periphery among center scholars that enable them to take responsibility for producing knowledge about/for the periphery. Considering the dominant ways of orientating to Latin America by the Western intelligentsia, Franco sums up their recurrent attitudes in the following ways.

1. *"Exclusion."* The Third World is irrelevant to theory. This means that center scholars can theorize matters based on center realities and experiences and then universalize them as applicable to all communities.

2. *"Discrimination."* Knowledge from the Third World is subordinate to the rational knowledge produced by the metropolis. This means that if the knowledge from the Third World has to be fitted into theory at all, it can be accounted for as exceptional or regional. Treating periphery knowledge as of local currency, the center can again universalize its own knowledge as holding global significance.

3. *"Recognition."* The Third World is only seen as the place of the instinctual. This means that the knowledge from the periphery is given significance for the wrong reasons—in other words, for representing nonrational forms of thinking and behaving. Perceiving the periphery through condescending stereotypes, the center can still claim superiority for its knowledge. In whatever case, the center intelligentsia take the responsibility for theorizing the experiences of the periphery, as it is not capable of doing so. Raw bodily experiences, cultural artifacts, and natural objects of the periphery communities have to go through the higher-order "brains" of the center (as if through a technically more sophisticated factory) to produce valid theory.

Control

Another important process in the intellectual hegemony of center communities is that through the publishing industry the center can keep a tight hold on the production of knowledge, policing the ideas that can claim legitimacy. It is not that center journals do not publish a range of alternative opinions on a given subject or do not permit periphery scholars to occasionally use their pages. It is simply that the diversity of opinions published will be within a *range* tolerable to center interests. The views won't be so divergent as to challenge radically the bases of Western discourses. Deepika Bahri (1997) analyzes how the supposedly radical paradigm of postcolonial discourse is shaped by Western publishing networks.

She begins by asking which postcolonial texts enjoy scholarly recognition and thus feature heavily in curricula, research, and publishing. Her finding is that it is those texts that make opposition manageable that enjoy popularity. Even though this literature is ideally resistant to the interests and ideologies of the center, it cannot escape being manufactured according to the logic of the market, eventually resulting in selective publications that tame or distort the power of this discourse. The fact that only literature written in English is published (and canonized in English departments) may be based on ensuring a wider international readership. But this also functions to keep hidden more radical vernacular writers. Other market considerations that determine publishability and account for the popularity of certain postcolonial writers are the following: "intelligibility" of subject matter and experience (by which is meant experiences that are similar to those of readers in the West); a general preference for the novel over poetry or drama (as the former is considered less personal/local); a restricted use of vernacular and local images; writing that engages with the West (as opposed to writing that addresses local people in terms of their everyday struggles, according to their own points of reference); "universality" (which usually means relevance to the interests of the Western reader); and, generally, differences that can be accommodated within the existing paradigms and schema of the center. Market forces thus ensure that cultural and intellectual products of the periphery will continue to be produced with the center as the reference point. It is such literature that is canonized by critical and scholarly opinion. Bahri catalogues the many periphery writers and texts that have failed to reach the Western audience because of these publishing considerations. Not surprisingly, such silenced texts have more disturbing implications for the status quo.

By selectively publishing periphery writers and writing, the center has also formed a postcolonial discourse that is tamed of its radicalism, even while it is promoted as oppositional. Thus the theoretical constructs produced by the publishing world favor the interests of center communities. Take, for example, the celebrated postcolonial notion of *hybridity*. The fact that postcolonial subjects and communities draw values from Western culture and other plural cultures to form the mix that constitutes their cultural hybridity provides a point of connection to the center. The construct of hybridity draws attention away from the recalcitrant elements of periphery difference. The construct is somewhat complimentary to the center communities, as it shows that their values still continue to play a role in the cultural and ideological life of periphery subjects. Furthermore, hybridity focuses attention more on the transplanted periphery subject in the center, at the cost of the poor and underprivileged who remain in the periphery. The latter are subjects with limited contact with cosmopolitan cultures and values. The construct also draws attention away from the historic evils of the past, focusing on the transformed/reconstituted present. Bahri (1997) argues: "The bases for celebrating texts for their transnational and transportable content lie in the privileging of hybridity as produced within global movements *of the present,* with the emphasis on movements *away* from originary postcolonial locations rather than also toward and inside them. These selective emphases allow the postcolonial thus dislocated in the West to be mobilized as the desirable other in a largely dehistoricized context" (290; emphasis added).

While in some cases mainstream publications impose an interpretation on periphery realities that suits center interests, the other side of this coin is that periphery knowledge that is too oppositional and recalcitrant can be downright suppressed. Although it sounds conspiratorial, this mode of control too can occur unconsciously by virtue of the unequal academic publishing system. Bahri provides examples of sociological scholarship and creative writing from India (both works that have been translated and works originally written in English) that are unknown in the West because they employ a discourse and perspective that do not fall within the existing paradigms in the center (Bahri 1997, 288). Not finding outlets for publication in the center, these scholars are relegated to little-known presses in the periphery. Thus the writings of these local scholars and activists don't find a place in what is defined as *postcolonial discourse* by the Western academy. In Bahri's perspective, these scholars are not only too radical for center interests but may question many of the fundamentals taken for granted in the West.

David Hess (1995) raises the possibility that even though laypeople in the center have understood the benefit of certain non-Western health practices, professional publishing circles still resist publicizing evidence of success. He points out that despite promising signs of success from acupuncture and uses of meditation in the treatment of cancer, "the results remain in the category of anecdotal research" (201). He goes on to say: "Although non-Western therapies may be flourishing in Western societies, they have not had much impact on bio-medical research. When non-Western therapies do make their way into biomedical research projects, they are usually shorn of their non-Western theoretical framework and reinterpreted in terms of current biomedical and psychological knowledge" (1995, 201). Hess pointedly remarks that although the medical system as a whole may be becoming increasingly pluralistic and multicultural, the theorizing of the universities and large research organizations remains largely impervious. It is clear that publishing has a role to play in this suppression of indigenous medicine. As evidence of success fails to reach the mainstream research community, the knowledge from these periphery medical traditions is relegated to the level of folk practices.

Sometimes publishing conventions like recency and relevance may serve to suppress periphery concerns. In many cases, the issues we want to talk about are outdated concerns (or old news) in terms of center scholarship. Since it is not topical in terms of center interests, our subject may not get a forum. Consider the sad story of one of my ethnographic papers, where I critiqued the use of a popular textbook in local classrooms. The paper featured an ESL book published in 1977 by Longman (mentioned earlier in this chapter) and donated by the Asia Foundation for local use. The view of the referees was that the book was too old to interest them or their readers. They also felt that my argument was not relevant, as recent books are published according to slightly different paradigms and newer principles. Therefore the discussion of these books wouldn't serve much purpose in enhancing the newer paradigms. The problem, however, is that it is such old books that are used in periphery classrooms. As periphery communities lack publishing facilities and funds to obtain newer books, they receive from foreign funding agencies English language books that are out of date for the center's purposes. Like unsafe medicine that is being dumped, books that are discarded in the center often arrive in the periphery as generous donations (Phillipson 1992 for examples from other periphery communities). There are therefore important pedagogical and ideological points to be made in analyzing the effects of these books on local education. No less is it important to educate center funding agencies and textbook writers on the damages implicit in donating irrelevant and outdated books. But if center journals reject the papers that discuss these problems in the name of topicality, the evils of these pedagogical practices are allowed to continue. Thus oppositional perspectives from periphery communities (on issues that are definitely topical for *them*!) are suppressed in mainstream circles.

A far greater problem for periphery scholars in the grip of center publishing conventions is the inability to talk about many subjects of importance, as they don't find relevant paradigms existing in center disciplinary circles. Consider the dilemma for A. J. How could he talk of ideological issues in ESL curriculum and pedagogy in the early 1980s, at a time when the dominant paradigms were psycholinguistic and structuralist? At most, he could have developed a critique of the one-sided emphasis on the psychological processes of learning and argued for a social perspective on education. But this line of argument would have appeared to him tame and innocuous. The paper that he did write is very radical in exposing the reproductive effects of curricula as the classroom is turned into a veritable ideological site. Perhaps A. J. could have taken a cue from movements of critical pedagogy, initiated in education by those like Giroux and Aronowitz around the late 1970s—in works published just about three years before A. J.'s paper was written (see, e.g., Giroux 1979). Even if he could have surmounted the problem of getting his hands on this literature, the movement itself was so marginalized in education at that time in the center that to use it as a lead-in for a journal in ESL would not have proven advantageous for achieving publication. To make a space for his thesis by critiquing the existing paradigms would have taken insider knowledge of these discourses—something difficult to achieve for periphery scholars, given the problems in getting all the relevant literature pertaining to that paradigm.

Assimilation

While there is one set of problems facing periphery knowledge that is marginalized, exploited, or suppressed, there is another set of problems facing local knowledge that periphery scholars do manage to present in mainstream journals. There are many publishing conventions and rules by which the center can assimilate such knowledge. For example, one's research contribution has to be presented in an appropriate way to enter the ongoing scholarly conversation. One needs to profess/cite the dominant discourses in order to get published—or speak "within the true" as Foucault (1972, 224) puts it. Scholars therefore have to present their work in relation to the work that has already appeared in print. This means that periphery scholars have to frame their contribution in relation to the scholarship of center researchers (which is usually what is available in print). This practice not only justifies the centrality/dominance of center publications and scholars but also imposes an ideological straitjacketing on periphery scholarship. Even work related to periphery social and cultural realities has to be certified by quoting the prior work of center scholars in those sites. So, in order to present my data on culture in rural Tamil Saiva communities, I have to frame my paper in relation to the work previously published by David (1974), McGilvray (1982), and Pfaffenberger (1982). Similarly, in order to discuss the hegemonic thrusts of the ELT enterprise on periphery communities in my papers in leading pedagogical journals (Canagarajah 1993b) I had to cite center scholars like Pennycook (1989) and Phillipson (1992), whose publications were the only ones available in the field at that time. Would the referees of any sensible journal be satisfied if I cited as my authorities colleagues from UJ who have made these points (and more) in everyday conversations or taught them in local classrooms? Would a paper that cites "personal communication" as its primary form of documentation (containing a cacophony of unknown names) pass muster?

Furthermore, bibliographical conventions can function as a filter on the thought of periphery scholars. Consider the need to provide relevant citations in the paper. In order to document previous studies and the significant constructs employed in the paper, periphery scholars have to use center publications. Although it is possible to use related or similar ideas/constructs from the periphery, they are rarely available in published form. This practice then results in the overbearing presence of center publications in a periphery article. This is what explains the ironies in the paper (discussed in chapter 4) by my colleague Manivasakar (1991/1992). In order to argue against the intellectual hegemony in models of political science, he has to cite center scholars to define basic constructs necessary for his argument. He has to also marshal scholarly authority from the center to bolster his case. Eventually, this bibliographical usage contradicts (and compromises) his argument against center hegemony.

In fact, the bibliographical conventions of different disciplinary groups can transform the representation of periphery experience in surprising ways. Recollect Bazerman's analysis of how the style manual of the APA has become progressively more rigid and comprehensive, achieving a synchrony between the governing ideologies and the publishing conventions of behaviorist psychology (mentioned earlier, in chapter 3). Bazerman (1987) shows how writers have to adapt their findings and reasoning to fit a behaviorist view of human beings. Apart from the representation of research subjects and experiences in mechanistic terms, the writers themselves get transformed into automatons who follow predesigned conventions and rules of writing in formulaic ways. Bazerman points out the serious problems facing postbehaviorist paradigms as scholars of these persuasions contend with the dominant conventions for a fair representation of their perspectives. If such tensions can exist within center discourse communities, we can imagine the far more serious problems facing periphery scholars who approach the psychological and social functioning of human beings from nonbehaviorist perspectives. Periphery scholars (like Mr. Paranirupasingham, discussed in chapter 6) who perceive human beings, actions, and motivations as holistically in harmony with the environment, community, and the gods have to fit their understanding into the positivistic tradition that looks at outward behavior as indicating patterns of general psychological rules. The disturbing consequence of trying to fit periphery realities into center academic conventions is the reproductive effect these textual requirements have. Periphery experiences and perspectives, filtered through these conventions, will take a shape that is consonant with the governing ideologies of the center.

It is important to consider how the contemporary dominance over periphery knowledge capitalizes on the steps taken in this direction by colonial regimes. There is a strong opinion among periphery scholars that the publishing domain seems to continue the intellectual hegemony begun by the West in the past. My colleague from immunology in India sees the history relating to the suppression of local medical practices this way:

> All the scientific and research set-up in these countries have not evolved on the foundations of their cultural systems of scientific enquiry. The original systems of many of the civilizations like Ayurveda from India and [the] Chinese system and many aboriginal systems of medicine were effectively subjugated and strangled during the colonial rule of the Westerners and the western system of medicine was universally imposed. This system had been actively sponsored and nurtured beginning from the Renaissance to the end of colonial rule. By that time it had established its sound rules and regulations. These rules and regulations control the nature of enquiry in the various scientific disciplines. Failure of the Third World scientists in Medicine and al-

lied discipline[s] has been, therefore, dictated by political subjugation of their scientific enterprise. . . . They have to depend [for] guidance, evaluation and validation of their knowledge production processes on the Western academic media. (Jagveer Rawat, E-mail communication, 7 January 1997)

From this scholar's perspective, since Western medicine is treated as the norm by mainstream academic circles and journals, periphery scholars have to relate their local medical knowledge to these norms and standards in their research and publishing. In doing so, local knowledge gets muted, transformed, and sometimes suppressed. In this sense, the journals are reproducing the hierarchy in knowledge that was begun much earlier in history. We shouldn't consider periphery scholars paranoid when they assume that colonizing nations are using research journals now for what was accomplished in the past by guns.

Academic Implications for the Center

As I have pointed out above, there are many benefits for center scholars deriving from this control over academic publishing. Apart from incidental professional and economic benefits, this monopoly also provides power for center academic circles in the disciplinary politics of knowledge construction. But there are even more limitations. Without the publishing industry opening up to off-networked scholars, the production of knowledge in the center will be narcissistic. The activity of center scholars will take place within narrow thought paradigms, nurturing discourses that are self-confirming and self-congratulatory. At least according to the Kuhnian perspective on the history of knowledge, it is the tension and struggle between conflicting discourses that functions as the mechanism of scholarly development. The more democratic the process of knowledge production, the more significant the progress. Paradoxically, therefore, center academic institutions are themselves impoverished by their hegemony. It is important to realize that the damages in knowledge production are not limited to periphery communities.

In fact, if all knowledge is situated/personal (Harding 1991), then periphery perspectives on different disciplines may provide unique insights not only into certain specialized fields of regional relevance where local knowledge is valuable—such as the behavioral and environmental sciences, language and communication, or social/cultural studies—but in fields like the physical, biological, and mathematical sciences, which are often considered simply "universal" in import. Hess (1995, 207–10) offers many examples of how so-called *culture-bound syndromes*—which are folk illnesses treated as located only within a specific culture—can help center communities themselves expand their definitions and classifications in medical knowledge. Consider, for instance, *koro*, which refers to the sudden fear of East and Southeast Asian men that their penis is going to retract up into the body and kill them. It is now widely documented that this is not a superstition but a syndrome that leads men in these regions to engage in self-destructive behavior. More surprising is the growing evidence that men in other cultures (including the West) experience symptoms that resemble *koro* (Hess 1995, 210; Osborne 2001). It is possible, then, that what is marginalized as a folk illness in remote or underdeveloped regions is in fact a widely experienced condition. It is furthermore possible that what is recognized, named, and theorized as an illness in certain specific cultures (because of the heightened sensitivity to particular conditions among local people) may not cause the same level of concern in other cultures. Or, perhaps, such illnesses are named and classified differently in different cultures, thus failing to receive the concerted attention they deserve. The syndrome could also get distorted as the different sources of local knowledge fail to get integrated. Giving voice to folk knowledge on *koro* has thus drawn attention to affected people in other communities. This move has also helped mainstream psychiatrists and physicians reexamine their classification of illnesses. Though *koro* is still not featured in the DSM-IV (the *Diagnostic and Statistical Manual of Mental Disorders*), a similar culture-bound syndrome, *latah*—the propensity to be startled among Malay village women—has found inclusion from 1994.

A similar breakthrough may be occurring in the understanding of what is called "alien abduction" in the West (Kristof 1999, F1). In Japan and other Asian cultures this syndrome is associated with abduction by spirits. What is locally understood in different ways is now emerging to be a specific type of sleep disorder. Scientists are now studying the different cultural interpretations of the condition in order to better understand the syndrome. Slowly but steadily, there are more efforts being made in the center to consider how illnesses and "folk cures" from other cultures may help advance the medical field in the West (Osborne 2001). In addition, respectable research agencies like the National Institutes of Health (Stolberg 2001), the Center for Disease Control (Hitt 2001), and the Memorial

Sloan-Kettering Cancer Center (Rosenthal 2001) are now undertaking the testing of herbal medicine and folk medical practices from other cultures to develop them for diseases affecting people in the West. In some of these cases, it was concerned individuals who obtained information on their own initiative and then pressured mainstream institutions to adopt non-Western medical practices.

A particularly ironic way in which the control of publishing conventions may be self-defeating for the center is that much knowledge that is oppositional to its paradigms and practices is prevented from reaching the intended audience—the center. These articles that present alternate knowledge will be excluded, to begin with, because they do not fall into the established disciplinary paradigms and discourses of the center. This is like a self-fulfilling prophecy: what is not defined as acceptable knowledge is always going to be kept out and thus be prevented from becoming accepted knowledge. This situation denies the chance for center scholars to conduct thoroughgoing critiques or reconsiderations of their dominant assumptions and practices. Perhaps such a paper/book will get published in the periphery—and there are many publications in the periphery that conduct powerful critiques of center practices and knowledge (which Bahri [1997] lists in her paper). But this defeats the purpose. If these publications are not accessible to the center audience the force and point of their critique will be blunted. And what point is served by preaching to the converted—in other words, presenting these critiques for the periphery audience—anyway?

It must be acknowledged that the center sometimes does take considerable initiative in trying to understand periphery realities. However, this research activity can be motivated by selfish reasons. Periphery social and environmental conditions have to be understood, for example, for the industrial motivation of using periphery resources, the economic and business motivation of marketing center products, and the political/ideological motivation of controlling these communities. But it is doubtful whether this knowledge created by center scholars, without attempting to understand periphery scholars and discourses, is reliable. There are serious questions of representation affecting such activity. To what extent is this work a construction of the West, in terms of its own discourses and predisposition? Whose interests does such representation serve? Certainly, we cannot treat this intellectual activity as a fair-minded and sincere attempt to understand periphery realities. We will see examples in the section below on how the distorted knowledge produced by this activity becomes counter-productive, defeating even well-meaning attempts at funding/develop-ment sponsored by international organizations in the periphery.

Finally, the development of a critical consciousness among center scholars can be limited by the control on thought enforced by the publish-ing industry. Considering the field of applied linguistics, Pennycook (1994, 321–26) argues that periphery knowledge can help reform, enrich, and ex-pand the narrow knowledge base of center disciplinary communities. Marshaling evidence from experiences of periphery students and scholars, he goes on develop a critique of the positivistic and mentalistic paradigms in the discipline, which had previously ignored (and sometimes indirectly endorsed) the linguistic imperialism of the English language. Ironically, then, periphery knowledge can have a healthy subversive effect on center academia and society. Other postcolonial theorists like Edward Said (1993) and bell hooks (1990) have considered the ways in which knowledge from the margins can complicate the self-assurance and complacency of the center. In fact, the Third World intellectuals who came for education to the West and articulated their oppositional thinking during the decolo-nization period contributed immensely to the current academic culture that questions Enlightenment and humanistic ideals (Said 1993). The pe-riphery had a role to play in constructing the current climate of diversity, pluralism, civil rights, and tolerance in the West (however imperfect and tenuous the change may be). These examples show that journals can play a similar constructive function today in the West if they can be democra-tized to accommodate a greater range of periphery scholars and dis-courses.

Material Implications of Knowledge Control

The control of knowledge through academic publications not only impoverishes disciplinary discourse. It also has implications for the politico-economic relations between center and periphery communities.

How seemingly innocent disciplinary constructs can lead to the mate-rial and ideological domination of periphery communities can be illus-trated with a construct central to linguists and applied linguists: that of the "native speaker." The idea that a speaker is native to one language and, by extension, the possessor of a "mother tongue" has recently begun to be deconstructed by periphery scholars (see the collection of articles in Singh 1998 and Braine 1998). This construct has meaning only in the center communities, which traditionally have been relatively homogenous in linguistic terms. But in the pervasively multilingual periphery communities, each speaker is born into multiple languages. Sometimes the father is from one tribe, the mother from another, and they communicate in a third common language. The children inherit all three languages. Consider the confusion for such subjects when the "native speaker" construct is reproduced in censuses and other official documents, making people identify with one language as native to them. This construct thus shows the limitations of knowledge produced according to the conditions true to a specific community. The construct attains more damaging implications when it helps scholars coin terms like "native English speaker," "native English speech community," and the concomitant "non-native English speaker" and "non-native English speech community." Many periphery speakers find that English is part of their expanded linguistic repertoire—acquired from birth, parallel with certain other local languages. Moreover, the indigenous variants of English (such as Indian English, Nigerian English, and Singaporean English) cannot be classified as non-native (Kachru 1986). They are acquired as a first language and used as such in many periphery communities. They display the same processes of adaptation found in other transplanted varieties such as American English, Australian English, or New Zealand English (which are treated as "native" in the discipline). Though speakers in the latter speech communities can become bilingual (i.e., hold English in parallel with other languages) and not lose their "native" status, periphery speakers are denied native speaker status because they speak English with other languages. It emerges from this perspective that the native speaker construct is being applied in racially biased terms—those with European-based ancestry are native; colored people are non-native.[4]

Now consider the implications of treating the construct as legitimate and applying it to make professional and public policies. The center varieties of English are treated as superior and established as the norm for pedagogical purposes. This means that often periphery varieties cannot be taught in schools even in the periphery. These varieties are denied the possibility of developing and expanding further. They are used, if at all, in a surreptitious or unacknowledged manner (Canagarajah 1995b). Moreover, this bias influences the notion that it is "native speakers" who are the legitimate teachers of the language. This bias enables a cadre of center-based English speakers to travel all over the world as teachers of their variety of English. Even if they don't have professional credentials, their mere linguistic status qualifies them to be teachers. Ironically, the bias is most rigid in periphery communities, as their institutions strictly adopt the policy that "non-native speakers" (their own people) will not be hired for teaching positions.[5] This policy functions in effect as an informal system of job protectionism in favor of center-based speakers. (Even in other kinds of employment or educational opportunities, this linguistic bias would affect periphery speakers of English when they faced center gatekeepers.) Furthermore, "native" professionals also become the authorities on questions of appropriate usage and grammatical rules. Such assumptions and practices ensure that they become the knowledge producers on the language, publishing textbooks, research papers, and theoretical statements that are exported to periphery teachers as authoritative. (This leads to many related pedagogical and communicative paradigms being constructed according to the conditions true of center communities, irrelevant to periphery realities. But a consideration of these will take us too far afield.) Furthermore, the standardization of a specific dialect for teaching purposes means that textbooks can be produced in a uniform manner for communities all over the world. Textbook publishers don't have to worry about the diverse periphery varieties of English—many of which first need to be adequately described with additional investment in research and personnel. In another form of protectionism, that of the market, a privileged position is reserved for center textbooks. Finally, there are ideological implications. With the power deriving from being the "standard," center varieties of English convey the values and discourses of center communities to the periphery. The traveling teachers, research literature, and textbooks also perform ideological functions by purveying center values and thinking. This ideological hegemony is all the more effective as the periphery varieties are prevented from developing in terms of their local needs, social relations, and cultural values. Knowledge paradigms from other disciplines should be deconstructed to understand their limited context of construction and partisan implementation.

To consider the field of pharmaceuticals, the Indian physicist (better known as a feminist and environmentalist) Vandana Shiva (1990, 250–55), provides an illuminating example of the damaging effects of suppressing periphery knowledge. Digestive problems have always been managed in South Asian communities through everyday foodstuffs such as rice water, rice porridge *(kanji),* curd, and coconut water. These non-allopathic means are known to preserve the balance of the biological system, while controlling the malady. But center-based pharmaceutical companies that market "medicine" for these purposes assume an alien cultural construction of sickness. They convert digestive dysfunction into a sickness that requires therapeutic cure. Apart from making money on what is a "natural" process for periphery communities, Western medicine actually makes the situation worse through drugs that cause serious side effects (which may require additional costly medical intervention!). Shiva narrates how clioquinol was introduced in 1934 as a drug for all kinds of diarrhea by the company Ciba-Geigy, after establishing its effectiveness for amoebiasis in lab and clinical trials. This drug went on to become a commonly dispensed medicine for digestive disorders. But from as early as 1935, and extending up to 1970, many examples of patients suffering from toxic effects were documented in periphery communities (Shiva 1990, 251). What is noteworthy is that this knowledge didn't reach the medical literature, partly because "attempts to hide facts, deny facts and attempts to convince doctors not to publish their negative experimental findings have been made throughout by Ciba-Geigy" (Hanson, quoted in Shiva 1990, 251). As sales continued, with countervailing evidence safely hidden away, the situation worsened to an epidemic of the disease SMON (Subacute Muylo Optic Neuropathy, which leads to loss of sight, bladder control, and leg functions). Some of its 10,000 to 30,000 victims were introduced in a press conference by a neurologist (Dr. Beppu). When about 5,000 victims from Japan sought legal recourse with the help of Japanese doctors, and the Tokyo district court in fact decided that clioquinol was the cause of SMON, the drug company resorted to a racist explanation. It argued that Japanese were genetically prone to SMON—while, presumably, all other communities were free of this syndrome. As more cases of the disease were found in Sweden and other countries in the West (debunking the racist explanation) and the Japanese victims began raising funds to inform the international community about the dangerous effects of the drug, Ciba eventually withdrew its product in 1978.

We therefore see how the control of information in the publishing domain (leading to the suppression of contrary evidence and the imposition of culturally partisan definitions of sickness) can result in serious human consequences of epidemic proportions. The irony here is that the consequences of this knowledge suppression are harmful to center communities as well (resulting in the suffering of people in countries like Sweden), as the side effects of this drug experienced in the periphery are swept under the carpet. It is of note that much of the information dissemination in this case had to be done by concerned civilians through grassroots-level community and legal agencies. This manifests the desperation of communities that find no outlet for their grievances, especially when the scholarly media are controlled by powerful interest groups. Since the scope of the grassroots-level dissemination was understandably limited, many periphery communities were not aware of the dangers of clioquinol. Shiva notes that doctors in India strongly objected to the withdrawal of this drug later. The stories from other periphery communities hadn't reached them, perhaps because the mainstream professional literature failed to adequately publicize the effects of these drugs. In this sense, even communities within the periphery lacked efficient means of information, leading to their isolation and exploitation, when contrary findings were not well publicized. Shiva's example is significant because it shows the complicity of market forces, industries, research institutes, and publishing networks in the control of knowledge and the victimization of local communities.

Even well-intentioned development work undertaken by the center has ended up with counterproductive results, aggravating poverty and damaging ecological and social balances in the periphery. This is so because projects have been informed by the center's own paradigms, with little input from periphery subjects. Consider the much-touted Green Revolution of the 1960s. There are mixed views about its success. Critics point out that local farmers and scholars were not adequately consulted or permitted to participate as equals so that local knowledge could be incorporated. The path taken to improve production was biotechnological aid for farmers. This approach advocated fertilizers, pesticides, and the so-called high-yielding varieties (HYVs) of rice (Anderson 1991; Anderson and Morrison 1982). The HYV seeds were developed in international research institutes in primarily laboratory settings. They therefore didn't relate well to the local needs and conditions. Neither was adequate attention given to many nonstandard seeds that better suited local ecology. The research institutes hadn't gone out of their way to study them. Eventually, as the standardized HYVs replaced the indigenous variants, the diversity of the agricultural gene pool was reduced. The nondiversified crops became more vulnerable to pestilence. This resulted in damage to the local ecology, in addition to reduced productivity. Even the meager benefits that accrued through the project rarely reached the hands of poor farmers. Hess (1995) describes the beneficiaries with mild sarcasm.

> The state bureaucrats benefited, because they controlled the distribution of the new HYV's. The elites of the Western countries benefited, because they entered into a partnership with third world countries that became partially dependent on Western funding, research, and technology to support the Green Revolution. In the case of rice, the international rice companies also benefited, because the standardization of rice varieties simplified their work of storing, milling, and shipping. Petroleum-producing companies and countries also benefited, because the fertilizers and pesticides that accompany the HYV crops are made from petroleum products. (236)

Shouldn't we conclude then that the agrarian development work in the periphery eventually benefits mostly the center communities?

On the economic front, the World Bank has recently been alerted to the possibility that their development efforts and poverty-reduction projects do not relate well to the everyday experience and lived reality of poverty in periphery communities (World Bank 1996). Though these activities are motivated by a considerable amount of fieldwork and research information in periphery sites, that there are negative consequences is not surprising. Given the fact that the views and knowledge of members of these communities have no prospects of appearing in print and are not solicited by researchers studying periphery realities, the knowledge that informs these activities has been one-sided. Much of the World Bank's work on poverty reduction hitherto has been influenced by econometric models that perceive the problem in terms of capital and that propose solutions based on accelerating economic growth. But this approach has not done much to alleviate poverty in all sectors of the community; in addition, there is the threat that the patterns of growth achieved are not enough to reduce poverty significantly. A key problem is that poverty reduction will have to involve multifaceted environmental, cultural, and social considerations (which other disciplinary perspectives have to offer). On these sources of knowledge it is the local people who possess important information. But lack of participation from the local people in the activities of the World Bank has prevented it from developing more effective approaches. As a result, not only are well-meant funds going to waste, but the periphery communities are becoming even more indebted to international organizations in a spiral of poverty. (Cynics would treat such detrimental processes as perhaps already *intended* by these agencies of development work for self-serving reasons!)

A team that studied poverty in sub-Saharan Africa finds that while the World Bank spends 58 percent of its funds for creating the conditions necessary for growth through policy change and large-scale investments, the problem lies elsewhere (World Bank 1996). The real reasons for poverty are the lack of adequate educated/skilled people; the destruction of natural resources, leading to environmental degradation and reduced productivity; inadequate access to the means of supporting rural development in poor regions; inadequate access to assistance for those victimized by transitory poverty; discrimination that favors boys' enrollment over girls' in schooling; inequities between urban and rural areas in educational opportunities; higher population growth among poorer people than among the non-poor; inequities among countries, among different cultures and ethnic groups, and among women in regard to access to resources; and, finally, political instability in budding democracies, compounded by ethnic tensions. It is clear that an external intervention motivated toward raising economic growth indices is the wrong solution. The ground realities militate against economic growth. Furthermore, foreign investment will do little to reduce the complex syndrome of poverty in Africa. In belated wisdom, a World Bank research team now recommends that "Africans must take the lead in reducing poverty, and donors must accept and facilitate that leadership" (World Bank 1996, 16).[6]

The *World Development Report* of 1999, sponsored by the World Bank, finds that a crucial limitation of many of the development projects studied is the dissemination of knowledge and sharing of information. It argues that information flow may mean the critical difference between being a developed or underdeveloped community. While encouraging the sharing of information generated in diverse communities, it envisions a need for every local community to produce its own local knowledge, and negotiate global information, to sustain its development activity. The report goes on to argue: "International research may produce knowledge useful for development, but the most important knowledge for development comes from developing countries themselves. . . . Amassing this knowledge, assessing it, and making it available to others is a task beyond the capacity (and self-interest) of any single country. So the task falls to international institutions" (World Bank 1999, 7). The World Bank has itself planned to develop a knowledge-management system that will disseminate its own information and also provide access to the new knowledge being created by local communities. But the report doesn't provide enough evidence about how this system is going to be set up. It is important to see that adequate participation from periphery nationals is ensured if this activity is not to end up exploiting local knowledge all over again.

More promising are informal fora created by concerned scholars from different regions through the Internet and other new media. Such recent creations as the African Poverty Reduction Network attempt to address the imbalance in knowledge creation that causes lopsided development work, in part by promoting the reduction of poverty through participation of the poor in the design and implementation of poverty-reduction programs for the reduction of poverty. Its objectives are to encourage the exchange of information; improve information, education, training, and communication among all parties involved in poverty-reduction programs; and facilitate the knowledge of effective activities and encourage their implementation.[7] Activities of such a nature show the emerging consensus that the development and dissemination of local knowledge can spell the critical difference for creating social and economic equity.

Conclusion

In many of the cases of material exploitation and social domination discussed above it is not possible to pin blame solely on the exclusionary knowledge-producing practices of academic journals. Apart from mainstream journals, there are other center-based publishing institutions and information systems that have to share blame for the one-sided flow of knowledge. My purpose here, however, is to show that there are important motivations for reforming academic publishing. The possibilities inherent in scholarly journals and academic writing have to be considered in the light of the damages created for the human community in general by unequal processes of knowledge formation. Academic journals should play a role in facilitating a greater exchange of information so that more democratic geopolitical relations are created. Engaging in one-sided knowledge production is not only unethical, but it is impoverishing for all of us.

8. Reform, Resistance, Reconstruction

We need to grant the lay perspective respect, to say: "I know that you have something I do not have. I need you to understand what I am saying, but I need to know what you think as well. My profession depends on it." Indeed, the academy depends on it. Only through this reconceptualized general education can we change the social facts behind academic literacy, build into our disciplinary knowledge the need to listen to those not so "disciplined," and thereby remake the nature of expertise.—Cheryl Geisler, *Academic Literacy and the Nature of Expertise*

In a narrow corridor on the second floor of an aging building, flanked by a collection of small offices including one for himself, sits busily typing Prof. Dr. Peter Schalk—the chair of the Department of the History of Religions at Uppsala University (Sweden). He is putting the finishing touches on the next issue of the journal *Lanka*. As soon as some of the minor editorial changes are made, the journal will be ready to mail all over the world. Professor Schalk has been publishing this journal for the past five years. His laptop and the laser printer (which sits on the next table) put the publication of this journal fully within his control, enabling him to realize one of his long-held dreams. The journal has provided a place for scholarship on the multiethnic Sri Lankan community by local scholars as well as researchers from all over the world. This is one rare journal where teachers from UJ can be certain of getting a paper published—in fact, of seeing their paper appear next to those of center-based scholars like A. J. Wilson, F. Richter, and S. Lindberg. The journal thus motivates them to put their pens to paper and make forays into the publishing world. It also provides them access to the recent international developments in a range of disciplines in the humanities and social sciences. Above all, the journal inspires them with the possibility that the culture and society of their own remote Jaffna are worth making knowledge about.

How did Peter Schalk achieve this publishing miracle? How does he cope with the discursive and publishing constraints discussed in the previous chapters? Schalk's area of specialization was initially Buddhism. Later he became interested in Tamil culture and Saivism, intrigued by the Tamil community's struggle for autonomy. A maverick scholar, he has made many dangerous trips into the battle zone in Jaffna to study the emergence of Tamil militancy and the implications for Saivite religious discourse. He has gradually become an activist, making several representations to the Sri Lankan government on ways of solving the political crisis in the country. Having thus displayed his commitment to the concerns of the local community—showing a more than academic interest in the affairs of the country—he enjoys the respect of all parties in the conflict. Thus he can come and go into the war zone with confidence. He has also initiated a "link program" between Uppsala and UJ for the exchange of faculty and students for research purposes. Having achieved the status of a relative insider in the local community, he understands the social changes in this region that are worthy of interest for knowledge brokers outside. His understanding of the local culture and the difficulties scholars face in writing has enabled him to adopt publishing practices that are more flexible and supportive.

Lanka is published from Uppsala University, with the resources available in Schalk's department and an editorial board comprising Lankan and Western scholars.[1] Though the members of the editorial board referee the submissions carefully, they are flexible in applying some of the other publishing conventions. With the advantage of fluid deadlines, the editor in Uppsala is able to wait patiently for manuscripts and revisions to arrive from Jaffna. Often papers arrive handwritten. Sometimes, they arrive with inconsistent bibliographical conventions or gaps in documentation. Some papers arrive in Tamil and are then translated in Schalk's office and printed multilingually—in other words, in English, Tamil, and Swedish. Papers written in English may have to be edited to suit appropriate usage and style. The Tamil graduate students presently residing in Uppsala help translate, type, edit, and proofread Tamil manuscripts. After performing much of this work, the editorial assistants in Sweden word-process the papers on their office Macintoshes for desktop publishing (of course making sure to print impressively on quality paper with a professional layout!). There are times when the editor waits frantically for the one final paper that has not arrived from Jaffna after being sent back for additional work. There are times when he has to contact colleagues in London or New York (including me) to get some crucial information relating to a paper before publication, as he cannot call the writer in Jaffna.

There are both benefits and limitations in publishing a journal this way. The flexible policies and deadlines may give the impression of a lack of rigor and professionalism. These practices may be detrimental to *Lanka* in the competition for prestige and profit. The journal may not be treated as "mainstream" and may not attract contributions from celebrity scholars. It cannot be profitable, as copies have sometimes to be sent free of charge to interested scholars in the periphery. However, the journal has been immensely useful for providing access to the work of periphery scholars. It has helped in democratizing the production of knowledge and widening its dissemination. The lack of stringent publishing policies should not be taken to mean that the papers are not intellectually sound or rigorously constructed. Actually, this is a rare source for periphery scholars themselves to find a record of knowledge relevant to their work (as oral knowledge is not easily accessible outside its local site of production). There have been many times when, lacking a source crucial to my paper in a center journal, I was able to document my work with a paper published in *Lanka*. I find it useful to read the journal for the views and observations of respected periphery scholars on matters pertaining to local life. Unfortunately, market forces are now proving to have their effect on the journal. Since the fifth issue, *Lanka* has been facing problems in publication. The institutional funding obtained from Uppsala University seems to be drying up—especially when it is hard to convince the administration that the knowledge produced on periphery communities in a low-profile publication with flexible editorial policies is worth the expense. Such are the perils *and* blessings of publishing an alternative academic journal!

As we consider how both center and periphery communities can adopt creative measures to improve the global traffic in knowledge, it is important to note that there is some value in periphery scholars maintaining a certain amount of independence and detachment from center publications. They should not abandon their local literacy events or publications for knowledge construction. As we have noted earlier, there are many advantages for periphery communities in practicing scholarship in their own terms in their own contexts. To list some: they are able to enjoy the strengths of an alternate academic culture; their detachment from center scholarship enables critical perspectives; they can afford to be less specialized (and, therefore, less elitist and narrowly circumscribed) in their preoccupations and interactions; and they are able to orientate better to local needs and traditions. In fact, they should retain the power of the restless/vibrant "margin" to offer a critical and constructive contribution to the often conservative/stable "center." It is possible to argue that while there is a tendency for the mainstream/center to consolidate knowledge, the margin/periphery plays an oppositional function by developing constructs that are not canonized. But this is precisely the reason why periphery scholars have to also take measures to interact with/through center publications. They have a part to play in the constant reexamination and reformulation of established knowledge. Furthermore, isolationism is debilitating for its own sake. It is important for periphery scholars to negotiate knowledge with center intellectual currents in order to maintain their own dynamism and growth. Moreover, they cannot abdicate their responsibility to interrogate knowledge related to periphery concerns in international academic fora. Ghettoizing periphery scholars will only prove advantageous for the mainstream in making its own knowledge about the periphery suit its own interests. We will therefore have to consider how periphery scholars can maintain their critical detachment from the mainstream, while productively interacting with center scholars through their publications.

In relation to this standpoint, it is important to consider here a criticism directed at me by a center-based reviewer of my paper on this subject (Canagarajah 1996b). The reviewer's question raises a valid concern that many will have at this point in this book: "The academic culture in the periphery—where scholars are not governed by the publish or perish rule, where there is greater interaction with the community, where there is a sense of civic responsibility—appeals to me. Why is it necessary for periphery professionals to get integrated into center academic communities? If things are so idyllically good about their academic culture, what should they gripe about?" We should note here that the pleasant, relaxed nature of periphery academic culture can itself become a source of marginalization for local scholars. Not exposing themselves to the challenges of divergent discourses from other academic communities may lead to a state resembling one of happy idiocy. While periphery scholars blithely conduct their scholarly lives according to their local norms and restrict their domain of influence to the periphery, center scholars continue to dominate the global scene of knowledge construction. This domination will be especially successful if no challenges are faced from periphery scholars. While periphery academics remain content with their condition, like ostriches with heads buried in the sand, center scholars will construct knowledge about the periphery and encourage the intellectual dependency of local communities. Therefore, center scholars who make this seemingly sympathetic argument may be perceived as being somewhat opportunistic. The position I am articulating, however, is not for periphery scholars to abandon their uniqueness and strengths to get totally submerged into center academic culture. What I am suggesting is that they need to *interact* with the literate forms of knowledge production in center-based journals if they are to play a critical role in mainstream knowledge production. I will show below that the center too stands to benefit by the increased participation of a wider range of scholars in knowledge production. So it is an attitude of detached involvement or attached detachment (to use a Buddhist metaphor) that periphery scholars should adopt toward center publishing networks.

To create changes in the status quo of academic publishing and knowledge production we need a multifaceted approach. Both center and periphery academic communities have to take initiatives in redressing the existing disparities. Apart from changes in institutional policies toward research and higher education, we also need a reconsideration of the current publishing practices of academic journals. At a more microsocial level we should consider the changes in style and written discourse that may be accommodated in academic communication. Furthermore, different attitudes may be adopted toward change. In some cases, both center and periphery professionals may collaborate in minor acts of institutional reform; in other cases, periphery professionals may have to actively resist the hegemony of center discourses in order to reconfigure power relations.

Changing Publishing Practices

Realizing the limitations in getting certain marginalized forms of knowledge published, even center scholars are having to discover nontraditional fora for publishing their research these days. Some of these initiatives will be of use in enabling periphery scholars too to participate in knowledge construction. Since academic publishers tend to reject narrowly focused areas of research, such as in doctoral dissertations, scholars are exploring the possibilities afforded by new media and new forms of literacy. The use of the Internet is one promising avenue. The New York–based Andrew W. Mellon Foundation has spent about $20 million teaming up with university presses, colleges, and professional associations to publish monographs on the Internet for disseminating research, especially that of young scholars (Smith 1999, B7). The project, named Gutenberg-e, may expand the definition of scholarly publishing in interesting ways. For example, pages of data and transcription that book/journal publishers would refuse to publish, or video- or audiorecordings that they cannot make available, will now be accessible for readers. Since academic publishers work within a constricted space motivated by marketing and profit considerations, they usually excise such valuable supplementary information. Gutenberg-e will also be more widely accessible, as it will be available free of charge. The research of periphery scholars, which is sometimes treated as equally narrow and uninteresting for the center readership, will now have greater prospects of getting published and read in such new publishing fora. Steps are being taken to earn academic recognition for such publications and make them count toward a faculty member's tenure and credentials.

Alternatives for traditional academic journals are also being sought so that the papers of a wider range of scholars can find publication. The director of the National Institutes of Health (NIH) has recently proposed an electronic publishing forum on the Internet, called *E-biomed* (Pear 1999). Scientists could not only access all the research information available there free of charge but could also post their own findings for others. While one set of papers would be published with the typical processes of refereeing, a second tier of publications would be posted with less rigid modes of screening. The director has proposed a wide set of referees, amounting to a thousand scientists, two of whom have to approve any paper that is to be posted on *E-biomed*. This arrangement would enable a larger range of scholars from the periphery to publish their research work. Despite the mistaken assumption that everyone in the periphery has a computer or has access to the Internet, this project does hold possibilities for expanding academic communication.

However, these creative proposals have come under attack from other center-based scholars who are bent on maintaining the status quo. Their opposition exposes the economic and ideological interests motivating academic publishing. The editors of many of the existing medical journals have been the first to voice their opposition to *E-biomed*. The prestigious *New England Journal of Medicine* has stated, "*E-biomed* could have a disastrous effect on clinical journals. . . . subscribers would have no reason for subscribing" (Pear 1999, F1). The American Society for Microbiology, which publishes ten scholarly journals, and the American Physiological Society, which publishes fourteen, have expressed similar opposition based on marketing considerations. It is sad that such economic motivations should stand in the way of democratizing knowledge production. Others express fears that publishing without rigid screening procedures would lead to the dissemination of "junk science." But these critics are ignoring the ideological implications of denying access to perspectives that don't meet the approval of a narrow band of referees. Research that doesn't meet the approval of a closed circle of like-minded scholars doesn't have to be junk science. It may simply constitute oppositional knowledge emerging from alternate perspectives. It is clear therefore that there are vested economic and ideological interests that militate against the establishment of alternative journals.

Some Web-based sites have gradually developed to the position of encouraging international collaboration, though this was not the original intention and these sites were not aimed to supplant the status of elite disciplinary journals. The physics archive centered at Los Alamos National Laboratory in New Mexico has been lauded by scholars everywhere as leveling some of the inequalities in this field (Glanz 2001). It now attracts about two million visits a week, with two-thirds from institutions outside the United States. Scholars can post their papers at any stage of the work, even before they are reviewed. They also have the option of posting a revised version at a later stage. About 35,000 new paper submissions were expected for 2001 alone. Predictably, many are the testimonies of U.S.-based academics who are finding that their research findings have been already scooped by unknown scholars from remote regions of the world.

In addition to such projects, which attempt to tap the new possibilities afforded by electronic communication and postmodern media, other activities focus on expanding the content covered. Ethnobiology can lay a claim to being the best-developed field in creating new fora for accommodating non-Western scholarship. The field now has a professional society and many journals like the *Journal of Ethnobiology*, the *Journal of Ethnopharmocology*, and *Ethnobotany*, which provide a forum for the publication of local knowledge. An important area of discussion in these circles at present is non-Western classification systems for plants and animals. These journals are serving to reexamine the dominant biological constructs taken for granted in the center academy. More fields have to open up their journals to the alternate paradigms and knowledge that exist in the periphery. While it is necessary for new journals to be established in order to represent areas of knowledge that have been previously suppressed or ignored, existing journals also have to expand their coverage.

We have to consider eventually the ways in which the current publishing conventions of mainstream journals can be reformed to provide greater access to periphery scholars. If center scholars are convinced that there is value in interacting with periphery scholarship, they cannot let incidental publishing requirements exclude contributions by their periphery colleagues. It might even be argued that journals that call themselves "international" and carry banners that prominently read, for example, "contributions are welcomed from all countries" *(Language in Society)* have greater responsibility to live up to their claims. It is important to make minor sacrifices and adopt some amount of flexibility in nontextual requirements while maintaining standards of excellence in other matters of content/research. For example, international journals should not insist that "if your article is not submitted according to the recommendations in the Guide, it may not be possible to consider it for inclusion" *(ELT Journal)*. While some of my manuscripts have been returned right away for not following the in-house style sheet, I have been fortunate in other cases to receive the style sheet for revision after the referees had reviewed the submission and recommended publication. This was once done by *World Englishes* when I mentioned in my cover letter that the journal was not available anywhere in my region. (I had mailed my manuscript after seeing their advertisement in another journal.) Similarly, the deadlines for proofs and revisions must be made more flexible for periphery scholars. We must also reconsider other petty requirements. Can the demand for stamps and envelopes for referees be waived? Would it be too much to ask that the requirement of multiple copies of the manuscript be dropped? Could Xeroxed copies be made in center editorial offices for submissions from the periphery? Can publication charges in scientific and technical journals be adjusted to fit the financial circumstances in the country of the potential author? Though it is true that center academic institutions are under increasing budgetary pressures, these concessions might be a small price to pay for enhancing global knowledge transaction.

Some would say that it is not sufficient to accommodate flexibility but that we must actively seek periphery contributions on certain subjects. In fact it is possible for center journals, if necessary, to sidestep bureaucratic editorial processes in order to accommodate well-deserving papers in their pages. Even the most prestigious journals, with reputations for tough refereeing processes, sometimes *invite* center scholars (not always the experts in their fields) to contribute to their special issues. There are times when a "buddy system" operates in center journals—when friends of editors and guest editors are given soft treatment. I have heard from a couple of center colleagues how an "anonymous" referee in fact got in touch with them regarding a paper they had submitted and helped revise it subsequently for publication. We also know how the editorial decision can tilt toward publishing a paper that received mixed reviews because the author is well known or he or she represents a position that requires publicity. If the refereeing process can be sidestepped this way (granted, in exceptional cases) it is difficult to understand why this cannot be done in the case of more worthy instances involving senior periphery contributors who may not be materially disposed to go through multiple resubmissions and reviews.

Among the more substantial changes that journals can make is to truly widen the composition of editorial boards. There are too many journals that claim to be international in scope and yet comprise editorial members from a narrow range of nationalities (largely North American and West European). At the most, some journals may include scholars from other developed countries (Australia, New Zealand, South African, and Japan) to prove their international stature. But this is insufficient. While it is granted that establishing a working relationship with scholars from technologically underdeveloped communities in Africa, South Asia, and Latin America can be difficult, not to make the extra effort to include them in the editorial process is inexcusable. Inclusion of periphery scholars can help a journal in many ways: they will use their contacts to solicit more periphery contributions; they will act as mediators who can translate center requirements and practices to their colleagues and demystify the publishing process; they will critique and help broaden the publishing conventions of the journal; and they will help maintain some sense of balance in the decision-making process while refereeing papers and establishing policies for the journal. To exclude minority scholars from editorial affairs is to reproduce the structure of intellectual inequality that already exists in global knowledge construction.

Certain other reforms may be more controversial. Is it possible for all journals (at least within a specific discipline) to adopt fairly uniform bibliographical and documenting conventions? Are there compelling reasons why the *TESOL Quarterly* should follow the fourth edition of the APA style manual, the *Modern Language Journal* the MLA style manual (1985), and the *ELT Journal* and *World Englishes* their own in-house style sheets? While changing the bibliographical conventions in a soft copy takes only a few minutes for center scholars who word-process their papers, many periphery scholars have to painstakingly retype a whole manuscript before sending it to each new journal. Such reform would also save writers from the worry of obtaining and studying the peculiar conventions adopted by each editorial committee in style sheets that are not always accessible to them. Reform in this respect would help encourage periphery scholars to attempt more resubmissions to journals—which shortcoming happens to be one of the biggest drawbacks at present in finding publication.

Furthermore, it would help if editors could use less euphemistic language to communicate their decisions to periphery scholars. Unused to the publishing culture in the center, many periphery writers find it difficult to interpret what changes the referees desire in the manuscript. In fact, some center editors have recently awoken to the fact that there is little uniformity in the communication of editorial decisions to contributors (Flowerdew and Dudley-Evans 1999). Editorial correspondence can be confusing to even seasoned center scholars. Recent attempts to describe the conventions governing editorial communication may help periphery scholars construct better-informed revisions and negotiate publication more confidently. It would also help if referees offered more constructive suggestions in their reviews. The comments of reviewers should be more lengthy and informative. Some referees simply write a brief paragraph, which may not be of much use to periphery writers who don't enjoy a good support group for peer review. Often, for me, the reviewer comments were the first and only feedback on which my revision could be based. In general, referees should think that they are not just judges (making pronouncements on the publishability of the submission) but collaborators in the construction of the paper for publication. They should use the refereeing process as an opportunity to guide a periphery writer in revising a paper in relation to center discursive conventions. They should also try to mail with their comments the recent articles from specialized journals that they recommend the writer consulting. Assuming that periphery scholars have the facilities to trace the publications themselves, referees sometimes don't bother to give complete bibliographical citations in their commentary. The *TESOL Journal* has recently started a practice of having promising new scholars work with a mentor (suggested by the journal) to revise a manuscript for resubmission. Mainstream journals should be able to go this extra mile if they understand the value of opening their pages for more participatory knowledge construction.

We must not fail to explore what periphery communities may do on their part to rectify the unequal relationship in academic publishing. A good strategy is to pool their limited resources to set up alternate publishing fora that are more accessible to periphery and center scholars. Indeed, such centers of alternate research encourage scholarship and publishing that are relevant to the periphery and influenced by its needs, traditions, and values. Regional institutions like the Third World Academy of Sciences, the Caribbean Academy of Sciences, the Regional English Language Center, and the Indian Council of Medical Research function as "centers within the periphery" and serve as significant fora for the collection, storage, and dissemination of periphery knowledge. Scholars who may not have the resources to get their papers published in center journals may still enjoy ways of getting their research introduced to the wider academic community through these institutions. These regional publications can also help in networking among periphery institutions and academic communities—which are at present fragmented and isolated, as they lack the means of collectivization or centralization that technologically developed and literacy-dominant communities enjoy. Such periphery "centers" can thereby function as nuclei of ideological resistance to center modes of research and scholarship.

Although there are some prominent journals already published in the periphery, they suffer from an inferiority complex in relation to the center. They usually attempt to compete with center journals on their terms and, thus, model themselves on the policies and requirements of those journals. Sometimes even the special considerations that need to be given to the practical disadvantages faced by periphery scholars are not given. Many of these journals attempt to attract well-known center scholars to their pages (in order to boost their status) rather than give importance to periphery voices and traditions of research. This practice turns out to be redundant, as they give their valuable space to scholars and perspectives that are already widely available through other professional circles. It is important to consider whether ELT publications like the *RELC Journal* (published in Singapore) and the *Asian Journal of ELT* (published in Hong Kong) can adopt a more geopolitically conscious mission of sponsoring scholarship relevant to periphery realities and traditions, apart from giving greater opportunities for local scholarly voices. This will involve changes both in publishing requirements and in the content published. Journals should be prepared to accept submissions that are handwritten, clumsily edited, unaccompanied by Xerox copies, deviating from the in-house style sheet, and failing to keep to the schedule of revisions and editing. Journals should also actively seek manuscripts on areas of scholarship and themes that are of interest to local communities. There are of course a few exceptional local journals that are developing a formidable academic stature for the work they publish—often to explore theoretical alternatives to the currents in the West. The South Indian journal *Nirapirikai* (Prism)—published in Tamil—is one example of a journal that consciously defines its role as developing scholarship oppositional to the center in literary theory and cultural studies.

Finally, a word of clarification. My argument that mainstream journals should democratize participation should not be taken to mean that journals of national or regional significance should not exist. *College ESL* and *Texas Papers in Foreign Language Education* have every reason to cater to a local audience in the center, just as *Nirapirikai* and *Lanka* will function relatively exclusively for periphery concerns. What is important is that the journal clearly define its policy. If the journal is of local or regional relevance, it should stick to its policy. But if the journal claims to be of international scope, then it should attempt to widen its coverage. Publishing the papers of in-group members under the flag of international scholarship is what smacks of hegemony.

Institutional Support

It is important to keep in mind that academic communication cannot be democratized without related changes in practices of research, funding, fellowships, exchange visits, and higher education. Both center and periphery communities should take necessary action to facilitate greater sharing of intellectual, economic, and technical resources. Academic institutions, state agencies, and nongovernmental (international) organizations will have a role to play in eliminating the barriers that prevent periphery scholars from engaging in publishing and knowledge production. Assistance should also be provided to develop and disseminate locally relevant knowledge.

Center agencies should first consider how some of the existing channels of academic contact can be democratized. The postgraduate training provided to periphery professionals in Western higher-educational institutions is an important avenue by which changes can be made. Universities in the United States and some of the Western European countries continue to function as the institutions of choice for periphery academics.[2] A furlough in a center institution is a sine qua non for academic status. Sometimes this is a mindless activity in response to the claims of scholarly superiority by the center and the vast resources available for advanced research. Center institutions encourage this contact by providing scholarships to periphery scholars. But what usually happens is that scholarships expire at the point the scholar finishes his or her degree. Even the visa cannot be extended after that point. Usually the responsibility of the university is considered fulfilled once the degree is granted. Eventually, scholars have enough time to undergo training but not to publish or undertake work of their own. Publication is left to the individual's initiative. But the funding and mentoring provided by center advisers should continue to seeing a piece of research enter print. Perhaps center institutions should also continue to support the scholar once he or she returns home and attempts to write and publish from there.[3]

Consider the implications of sending periphery scholars back to conditions where they cannot continue doing their research or participate in knowledge construction. The lack of technical facilities and access to information would quickly make their expertise out of date. Even center scholars have begun to question the wisdom of providing training for periphery professionals in the center when they are quickly sent to conditions that would make their training and knowledge irrelevant (Swales 1990, 106). If periphery scholars are inducted into center forms of scholarly discourse and academic culture, but not offered opportunities to participate equally in knowledge production by contributing to research publications, they are trained (in effect) to be appreciative consumers of the work of center scholars. This is a cultivation of intellectual dependence, not unlike the politico-economic dependence of periphery communities on the center. The consequences for extrascholarly forms of domination should also not be forgotten. There is a possibility that the foreign-trained scholars may function as ideological representatives of the center in their own communities.

Enabling the scholar to have access to ongoing research and providing the means to conduct independent scholarship are ways in which center institutions can help periphery scholars bring local knowledge to the mainstream. (At present, the only link many foreign-trained scholars at UJ have is the periodic appeal for financial contributions from their center alumni associations!) The alma mater should consider sponsoring follow-up visits for students who return to their home institutions and help them devote time for publishing. Already, this is the only means available for many periphery scholars to engage in continued research and writing (see Muchiri et al. 1995 for a similar case made by African scholars). At home they are so bogged down with heavy teaching loads and insufficient remuneration that they are unable to indulge in reading and writing. Though these are certainly idealistic expectations at a time of widespread economic difficulties, center institutions cannot indulge in one-sided intellectual development. They should take steps to ensure that the scholars they have trained have the means to continue participating in knowledge production and developing their expertise with relevance to their own communities.

Center institutions should also consider ways of disseminating research information with fairness to off-networked periphery communities. The Harvard Project aims to provide medical information almost instantly to any physician in the world through an electronic pay-per-paper system (Salager-Meyer n.d.). The policy of Peter Sprague, chairman of Wave Systems, the information-technology firm participating in this project, is very constructive. Although many projects make idealistic claims, Sprague is aware of the difficulties in providing electronic information to marginal-ized communities. Not all periphery scholars can afford the price, and many of them are not connected electronically. Though this is a big prob-lem that cannot be solved in its entirety, the system proposed by Sprague sets an interesting trend that is worthy of emulation. Believing that "a great medical library should not be available to only 20% of the world popula-tion," Sprague proposes that the charges will be based on a country's wealth (quoted in Salager-Meyer n.d., 5). Therefore countries in the pe-riphery will pay much less than those in the center for accessing scholarly information.

Institutional collaboration and link programs with periphery scholarly circles are other ways by which research and communication can be widened. What is called the "academic exchange" program between Upp-sala and UJ is an example of the benefits deriving from such collaboration. Under this project, many periphery professionals have been able to visit Uppsala and conduct seminars and lectures on their areas of specialty. Doctoral research opportunities were provided in Uppsala for junior fac-ulty at UJ. A special research project on a classical Tamil text was carried out collaboratively by center and periphery professionals. This research ac-tivity spawned many journal and monograph publications producing new knowledge on Tamil society and culture. Knowledge that had previously existed orally was now recorded in print, enabling everyone to access this conveniently. Even those scholars who couldn't travel to Sweden had the opportunity to interact with foreign scholars who visited UJ for research purposes. Visits by Swedish students to Jaffna for research on Tamil culture were also planned (but could not be carried out due to the worsening se-curity situation in Sri Lanka).

All this was possible because the agreement was drawn in a realistic way, taking into account the available resources at UJ while supplementing its limitations (*Academic exchange* 1996). The agreement shows the special responsibilities facing center institutions in promoting collaborative initia-tives with periphery institutions. For example, the agreement states, "Both universities can send senior scholars for periods of up to six months. Ex-penses incurred in connection with the visiting scholar's stay and accom-modation will be covered by the host university. Travel expenses will be covered by the department concerned of the university sending out its member(s). The Swedish host department will, however, make efforts to apply for funds which shall completely or partly cover the traveling for the scholar from Yalppanam [Jaffna] University" (*Academic exchange* 1996, 15).[4] Note the one-sided commitment by Uppsala to generate funds for the traveling expenses of UJ scholars. What is recognized here is the unfavorable exchange rate in the currency. Even if UJ scholars are eligible to obtain state support for traveling and their living during the furlough, their stipend is inadequate to cover such costs abroad. Note also the seemingly balanced agreement to support the accommodation of the visiting scholar by the host community. As it owns a guesthouse for visiting scholars (from local and foreign universities), this condition is not difficult for UJ to meet. What UJ cannot provide is the cost of traveling for either its own or the visiting scholars. So Uppsala takes responsibility for travel. Furthermore, the implementation of some of these commitments can be realized differently, according to the available resources. For example, a Swedish visiting scholar always stayed in the houses of Tamil friends in Jaffna, enjoying local hospitality. UJ scholars, in turn, never stayed in expensive hotels in Uppsala. During the conference on Jaffna religions, for example, hordes of Tamil delegates simply stayed at a Swedish professor's house and cooked their meals at home collectively to reduce expenses. Such sacrifices have to be made if the exchange of knowledge is to take place freely under the bleak economic realities many are caught in.

Another form of scholarly sponsorship that may help periphery communities develop their local knowledge is research funding and materials donation. Phillipson (1992, 223–38), considering funding practices in ELT, charges that while center-based cultural agencies spend lavishly on sending experts and policy makers to the periphery to provide professional advice/training, they do not spend as much on research oriented toward the development of indigenous languages and discourses (whether by center or periphery professionals). Similarly, while they donate an ample supply of textbooks, they do not provide adequate scholarly books for professional development or encourage periphery scholars to write their own books. Such funding practices do not support endeavors that empower periphery scholars to contribute independently to knowledge construction. They promote intellectual dependency and are unethical.

The American physicist Michael Moravcsik (1985)—who has made a singlehanded lifelong mission of redressing the inequalities in center/periphery academic relations—proposes a multifaceted and wide-ranging approach to enable more periphery scholars to participate in knowledge construction. He has argued that the role of the center in sponsoring science development in the periphery should be sustained, holistic, and participatory. What is fascinating is that among his very comprehensive proposals (including changes in providing scholarships for periphery scholars, reforming educational policies in the periphery, creating a scientific awareness among the public, and advising governmental policy makers on educational priorities), a special place is given for democratizing scholarly communication. Though he has made proposals to bodies like the United Nations Conference on Science and Technology for Development (UNCSTD) for a "New Structure for World Science and Technology" as far back as 1979, not much headway has been made in implementing his suggestions. I restrict myself here to considering his recommendations relating to academic communication.

To begin with, Moravcsik provides an important place for enabling periphery scholars to have access to mainstream journals. He goes to the extent of proposing that "unused back issues of scientific and technological journals should be channeled to libraries in the developing countries" unilaterally by center libraries (1985, 376). It will help if at least the leading journals in certain fields can be sent to periphery libraries and institutions as a service to local scholars. Cultural and educational agencies like the British Council and the United States Information Agency (USIA) are well positioned to facilitate this transfer of excess unused back issues. Perhaps center libraries can build meaningful links with periphery libraries this way for the exchange of material.

Moravcsik then goes on to ask publishers to keep sending current journals to the periphery as they are published. Explaining the latter plan, he says, "The transaction of journals should be in exchange for 1/4 of the regular individual subscription rate of the journal and the payment should be made in the currency of country B [i.e., the periphery country]" (1985, 379). Knowing that there is an increasing monopoly in the publishing industry on academic journals, it is becoming hard to expect publishers to perform such charity. Reed Elsevier has presently grown to be the largest journal publisher, with 1,200 titles and $1.1 billion in annual revenue from science publishing (Kirkpatrick 2000). With its recent efforts to acquire other publishers, including Harcourt Brace, there is fear among center librarians that prices of journals are going to increase further. There has been an 11 percent average annual increase in journal prices in the past ten years. Already, U.S. libraries have cut their serial subscriptions by 6 percent to keep up with the price increases. Some journals, such as Elsevier's *Brain Research,* cost as much as $16,000 a year! Periphery institutions cannot cope with these expenses by any stretch of imagination. Moravcsik is right in proposing that unless center libraries and publishers make some unilateral effort, periphery scholars can never read these journals. It is important to consider also whether private endowments and international organizations belonging to the UN can help put Moravcsik's recommendations into practice.

In other essays, Moravcsik recommends that lighter publications such as preprints and letter-journals should be mailed to periphery scholars. He shows how center scholars already have networks of scholars who automatically mail each other their preprints and offprints. Moravcsik argues: "Compared to salaries of scientific personnel, to the cost of equipment, and to development and production expenses, the cost of communication among scientists is small. It would therefore be foolish penny pinching and administrative shortsightedness to be damagingly stingy with money destined to develop these communication channels" (1985, 237). Considering the lengths to which periphery scholars have to go in order to get even brief glimpses into ongoing research, such documents as preprints and offprints would be immensely useful to them. In this regard, Morvacsik is also perceptive in articulating the need for personal communication and interpersonal contacts. He argues that even in the center, "the most effective and frequently used method of communication between scientists and technologists is through personal contacts" (1985, 368). Though characteristically Moravcsik expects center scholars to take the initiative to maintain links with their former periphery colleagues or make new acquaintances in conferences and seminars, it should go both ways.

Moravcsik also outlines ways in which center scholars and institutions should sponsor publications and scholarly fora to enhance interactions among periphery scholars. In relation to this, he suggests assisting scientific and technological journals published in developing countries by refereeing of submitted articles; finding means of enhancing the internal communication between scientists and technologists in a given developing country; and strengthening regional interaction among scientists and technologists in developing countries (1985, 376–77). While these suggestions are well motivated, Moravcsik is not sufficiently alert to the danger that such sponsorship can lead to subtle forms of center appropriation of periphery knowledge. After providing the relevant resources to enable such regional communication, center scholars and agencies should see to it that periphery scholars run these publications and fora befitting their own needs and aspirations.

What can periphery governments and academic institutions do to help their scholars negotiate the challenges they face in developing, disseminating, and protecting local knowledge? It is important to first consider what can be done to resist the types of intellectual and educational dependence displayed by local communities. Often this attitude of dependence develops very early in a periphery subject's educational life. There are many practices in modern schooling that nurture this attitude. Periphery students are taught to be consumers of center knowledge, rather than producers of knowledge. Such practices as importing textbooks from the center and treating them as authoritative reference material (even at the college level) play a role in creating a culture of dependency. While this may be necessitated by the lack of published material in the periphery, it can cultivate the feeling that center-generated material and knowledge are superior and, in fact, more legitimate.

Furthermore, Western-based (nonindigenous) literacy practices exacerbate this intellectual dependency. Cheryl Geisler (1994) theorizes that modern schooling inculcates a mythology of autonomous texts that encourages novices to attend to the message of the text in an abstract manner, ignoring the contextual and rhetorical bases of production. Internalizing this mythology, novices abandon their everyday contextual modes of literacy and knowledge construction. The knowledge and facts of each discipline are provided to them in decontextualized, product-oriented terms, through textbooks and instruction. Textbooks often adopt a discourse that nurtures the autonomous-text myth. The objective/universal/factual "truths" that are conveyed in textbooks elide the uncertain and messy process that characterizes knowledge production. Even classroom discourse (characterized by the Initiation-Response-Feedback structure documented by sociolinguists—see Mehan 1985) works to suppress everyday knowledge and promote abstract knowledge as the norm. Transcripts of classroom interactions show how this discourse enables teachers to nudge students toward decontextualizing information for academic success. Similarly, the ubiquitous "display question" is also aimed at training students to extricate the abstract facts and information from the contextualized flow of spoken or written texts. Dependency can, furthermore, be reproduced through popular magazines/literature that disseminate scholarly information (e.g., *Scientific American*). These publications are more freely available in the periphery than are specialized journals. Greg Myers (1990) shows how the discourse in such writing also promotes the myth of foregone conclusions and agent-free discoveries about natural phenomena. These discourses train students to be satisfied with extricating and displaying disembodied facts as proper scholarly endeavor. Geisler (1994) theorizes that the literacy practices of novices are calculated to differ from those of scholars, as they provide an advantage to the latter in the game of knowledge construction: "The literacy practices of experts in the academy are organized around the creation and transformation of academic knowledge; the literacy practices of novices, on the other hand, are organized around the getting and displaying of that knowledge" (81). While such schooling practices do keep center students and laypeople dependent on the power of academics as well, it is more damaging to periphery students/scholars. The latter are even more removed from the networks of text production in the center and are, therefore, prone to hold on to decontextualized knowledge to a greater extent.

From the above perspective it is easy to understand the feeling of many that the democratization of academic literacy should start in schools (Geisler 1994). Preuniversity education is an important site in the preparation of future scholars for critical reading and writing practice. Local teachers should develop pedagogies that create a rhetorical self-consciousness among their students, an appreciation of local knowledge, and an attitude of critical interrogation of all (especially center) knowledge. Hess (1995), after discussing the marginalization of the knowledge of indigenous peoples, discusses the importance of controlling the domain of higher education if these communities are to empower themselves. He concludes his book with the following appeal: "Only through control over higher education and high technology can indigenous peoples and other rural communities have a chance at access to the intellectual and financial resources they need to control, protect, and preserve their lands and cultures and to resist the ethnocidal and ecocidal forces that surround them" (249).

Periphery institutions should take steps to develop greater awareness of rhetorical processes and written discourses among local scholars at school and university levels. While American institutions treat writing skills as mandatory for many levels of education and provide an important place for the teaching of writing, periphery institutions do not provide a significant role for composition courses in their curriculum. Western universities conduct writing courses and workshops even at the postdoctoral level to help professionals in their writing activity.[5] There are many reasons why composition instruction is devalued in many periphery educational traditions. The dominant role given to oral traditions of communication, the importance given to grammar instruction in largely product-oriented language-instruction traditions, and the understanding of writing as a spontaneous activity or a craft that evolves through time have led to the near nonexistence of writing instruction. At present there are many publishing conventions that my colleagues at UJ have to learn informally through their peers and mentors—for example, documenting conventions, copyright regulations, refereeing processes, and styles of interaction with the editorship of a journal. The purpose of initiating writing/publishing instruction is not to make local scholars model their writing on the conventions of academic writing as interpreted in the West. More important is the task of helping periphery scholars develop a rhetorical self-awareness that will provide them the confidence to negotiate the competing discourses from the indigenous and center communities more effectively. This orientation will help periphery scholars to develop a critical consciousness about their academic culture and knowledge-making practices. They may also form an understanding of the socially constructed nature of rhetorical and scholarly processes (Bizzell 1992; Brodkey 1987; Brufee 1983).

Since it is clear that writing is important for the construction and dissemination of knowledge in contemporary society, periphery institutions must provide adequate institutional support for their scholars to engage in publishing. The teaching load of faculty can be reduced to make time for the rigorous process of multiple drafting and revising of papers. Funding can be provided to defray the expenses incurred in manuscript production, copying, and mailing. Other infrastructure needs for writing/publishing should also be looked into. Free Xeroxing facilities and typing/word-processing facilities would help scholars tremendously in getting their manuscripts prepared more professionally. The mere donation of typewriters discarded in the West (perhaps through the good offices of an international organization) would mean a lot for encouraging more writing among local scholars. The provision of stationery is another simple step that would help prospective authors. Furthermore, better avenues for publishing are required in periphery institutions. Monographs and journals are needed not only to provide a forum for local scholars but to disseminate information to outsiders. Even Xeroxed or cyclostyled publications would provide a meaningful forum for scholarly interaction and knowledge dissemination among local scholars.

At a more philosophical level, periphery academic communities have to be strengthened if they are to develop their alternative academic culture and produce oppositional knowledge against the hegemony of the center. For a variety of reasons, the periphery academic communities presently lack sufficient autonomy, organization, and integration. To begin with, there is considerable institutional tension within the community. We must note the hierarchies within the periphery academic communities that can prove debilitating—between the bilinguals and monolinguals; the foreign-trained and the locally educated; the academically certified professors and the traditionally respected *pundits.* There are also cultural and ideological tensions within the community. As we found in the previous chapters, the community accommodates within itself both orality-based indigenous-knowledge traditions and literacy-based scientific traditions. These tensions can be healthy, fostering a hybrid intellectual tradition that helps local scholars negotiate center-based traditions critically. However, since the tensions are not mediated effectively, the sources of strength that could be developed for the definition of an autonomous periphery academic culture turn out to be elements that weaken its vibrancy. The failure to find their unique sense of mission and philosophy has partly to do with the fact that the periphery academic institutions still draw their frames of reference from the center. Caught between center and periphery academic traditions, lacking a clear sense of independence, periphery academic institutions don't find the strength and resources to stand up as an alternative force in knowledge construction. The hegemony of the center goes unchallenged.

Similarly, as we found in chapter 6, the literacy practices in the periphery academic culture serve no small role in reproducing such dependency.

Both in reading and writing, periphery scholars display a disjuncture between formal and informal literate practices. In writing, they practice decontextualized forms of knowledge representation, or they may practice indigenous forms of context-bound presentation as in literary/creative expression—without strategically negotiating either discourse in their favor. In reading, since periphery scholars depend mostly on theoretical books, semischolarly journals, and textbooks for their academic knowledge, the discourses in these texts promote the autonomous-text assumption. RAs that are more detached, tentative, and qualified may orientate scholars to a more critical discourse—but research journals are hard to come by. Ironically, though periphery scholars have a vibrant oral interactional culture and embedded epistemologies from indigenous traditions (which can serve them well on their path to expertise), they are often so inducted into center academic discourses that they don't gain practice in using these strengths to negotiate diverse forms of knowledge. While their own strengths are devalued, they begin valuing Western modes of knowledge making. Thus they end up playing second fiddle to center knowledge, rather than developing the practice of constructing new knowledge.

Among the institutional changes required to deal with this problem, foremost is the construction of new yardsticks for assessing the academic status of local scholars. As I have argued, at present there is a debilitating ambiguity in the policies and practices of periphery academic institutions. There is an attempt to use the yardsticks of the center (based on publishing in mainstream refereed journals), while also indirectly reinterpreting things to suit periphery realities. Since local scholars have access only to newspapers and popular journals, there is a need to recognize publication in these for academic credentials. If periphery institutions were more frank about the different material conditions and cultural practices shaping their intellectual context, they would develop frameworks that are more congenial for their scholars. Rather than half-heartedly accommodating the preoccupation of their scholars with community service, political activism, and oral speech events, periphery institutions have to recognize these activities as valid intellectual pursuits that deserve professional credit. Here again, what is needed is a better self-awareness among periphery academics about their own intellectual practices and academic traditions. The universities have to develop a mission for themselves that takes into account their historic strengths, critically develops their knowledge-making traditions, and furthers inquiry into the concerns affecting local communities. Rather than being torn within itself according to conflicting traditions of academic life, it is more productive to fashion a mission that is consonant with the periphery academic community's interests, values, and needs (though this doesn't mean cutting itself off fully from the mainstream).

To develop this sense of autonomy and independent consciousness, there is a need for greater networking, communication, and interaction among periphery scholars. Ironically, depending on and revolving around center-based channels of communication, periphery scholars are cut off from each other. While failing to develop regional cooperation, this also limits their ability to develop oppositional knowledge (given the fact that mainstream journals will tend to filter such knowledge). There are other benefits to improving periphery-based channels of academic communication: local scholars can pool their collective indigenous knowledge for further development; they can disseminate locally relevant knowledge for the communities that will find it of most use; and they can share common strategies of scholarly resistance and alternative knowledge creation.

Presently there are some useful ventures of alternative knowledge developed in the periphery that lack wider recognition due to limited channels for dissemination. In India, the Madras-based Shri AMM Murugappa Chettiar Research Center has adopted a strategy known as bio-dynamic gardening, in the process developing alternative seeds suitable for local conditions (Seshagri and Chitra 1983). Researchers from this center have worked with local farming women to help set up high-yield gardening that combines organic fertilizer and organic pesticides. The practice of growing multiple crops in a single bed limits pest infections and complements nutrient needs. These researchers prove that it is possible to produce seeds that outperform standard varieties even when traditional agricultural methods are used. Given the fiasco of the much-touted Green Revolution (described in the last chapter), it is important for other Third World communities to pay attention to this kind of research to develop locally inspired alternatives. But the lack of publishing media and efficient channels of communication have turned out to marginalize this institute's knowledge and products.

Third World governments and ministries of education have an important role to play in funding and encouraging such research ventures. The *World Development Report* of the World Bank (1999) insists that periphery

governments should do a lot more to sponsor new knowledge by supporting their own public and private institutes in their research work. The
World Bank commends Brazil, China, India, South Korea, and Mexico for
reforming their public research by making it more responsive to the market. "Their measures include corporatizing research institutes, improving
the pay and recognition of researchers, and offering firms incentives to
contract directly with the public labs" (8), states the report. Of course, care
must be taken not to make intellectual compromises in order to satisfy
commercial interests. A good example of such efforts is the Brazilian con-
sortium Fapesp, engaged in decoding the genome of pests that affect local
plants critical for the country's fruit industry (Rohter 2001). Though it is
funded by tax dollars, it enjoys considerable independence from the government in its activities. Spending little on overhead, the foundation
brings together scientists from about fifty research institutions in the state
of Sao Paulo to work on projects that are important for the local economy.
Though these projects hold very low funding priority for American agencies, the science is outstanding, and the results have global implications.

To make periphery state agencies respect appropriate indigenous
technology and scholarship can turn out to be no easy task. It is nothing
new to point out that periphery politicians often display wrong priorities.
Despite their profession of nationalistic sentiments, they spend considerable sums of money on Western scholarship, technology, and industry. The
social status and financial remuneration for local scholars are often low.
Perhaps Moravcsik (1985) is correct to argue that to foster a culture of
independent knowledge creation one needs a well-informed and literate
citizenry that can propel these movements forward through their elected
officials. No doubt, the wider intellectual culture of dependence (in the
society in general) sometimes militates against moves toward development
of local knowledge in the local academy.

We mustn't fail to explore how center and periphery scholars can collaborate in some cases if meaningful changes are to be brought about in
the literate representation of local knowledge. The *World Development Report* of the World Bank (1999) provides interesting examples of how center-based research centers can help disseminate periphery-based research.
The International Forestry Resources and Institutions Research Program
in the United States brings together a network of collaborating research

centers throughout the world. The centers agree on a common research method; they support the collection of primary data on forest conditions, management, and uses; and they interpret and analyze information gathered in the field. Their report states, "In this bottom-up approach, a university-based project serves as a clearinghouse for locally provided information with global implications" (World Bank 1999, 11). While their service will definitely be appreciated by periphery scholars, center institutions should take care not to impose their own models and perspectives on periphery realities. They should respect the paradigms constructed by local communities in terms of their own life conditions. Collaboration shouldn't mean constructing knowledge according to the expectations and traditions of the center.

Another responsibility for center institutes that disseminate/facilitate native systems of knowledge is to see that other international organizations don't exploit this knowledge for their profit. In fields like ethnopharmocology there has been some recent interest in understanding non-Western knowledge. But this opening in knowledge flow has also given way to increased intrusion into native communities and exploitation of their resources. Jason Clay (1990) argues that multinational companies frequently draw on the medicinal values of local plants and animals to boost their own profit, while native communities get further impoverished. An example he provides shows the dangers of unguarded knowledge dissemination. Some missionaries in western Brazil passed on a sample of arrow poison to some botanists, presumably with the good intention of developing indigenous resources. The scholars passed this on to a U.S.-based chemical company that supported their research. The company took a patent on the poison's muscle-relaxant properties, and its own business thrived. Not only did the native community not receive any royalties, but it also lost half of its land to the government (which was perhaps alerted to the economic possibilities in the tribal resources through the foreign entrepreneurial interest!). So increasing avenues for disseminating native knowledge has to be done with sufficient safeguards to the indigenous ownership of that knowledge.

The unfortunate example above shows why it is important to take steps toward ensuring the intellectual property rights of marginalized communities. Here again periphery communities have many limitations: they don't fully understand the bureaucratic processes involved in patenting;

they don't have the funds to pay for the application fees; and they don't have access to information if/when center institutions infringe on their patent rights. It is important therefore for center agencies to help "police" the observance of these rights. If these rights are honored by multinational corporations, it is possible that ethnopharmocological knowledge may be transformed into an economic resource that empowers indigenous peoples and protects their lands. The Smithsonian Tropical Research Institute in Panama City has helped the Kuna of Panama develop a twenty-six-page manual of guidelines for scientific research in their region. The institute acts as a clearinghouse that also disciplines researchers who violate the guidelines. As researchers work in cooperation with the Kuna and the Smithsonian Institute, Hess argues that the "issue of intellectual property rights can mean the difference between extinction and survival for some Native peoples. The stakes are far from minuscule, for even royalties of a fraction of one percent can run into the millions of dollars in the large international pharmaceutical industry. With funding available at that level, many Native communities would be in a much better position to resist incursion from the outside" (1995, 191). In recommending such intellectual property rights, the *World Development Report* of the World Bank (1999) argues, "Many developing countries have found that by establishing and enforcing intellectual property rights standards that comply with international practice, they gain access to foreign markets and to foreign technology through direct investment and technology transfer" (8).

In addition to collaboration at an institutional level, scholars on both sides of the geopolitical spectrum can take steps to collaborate at a personal level. Some of us in the field of ELT have recently been exploring the notion of "conduit scholars" (Amarou et al. 1998). We use this term to refer to professionals from both the center and the periphery who can function as knowledge brokers between communities if/when their work involves shuttling between different geographical locations. Although this term is misleading, as it doesn't capture the multilevel and multidirectional ways in which knowledge should flow, we use it for want of a better term. To illustrate, center professionals can act as conduit scholars when they visit the periphery for specific professional purposes—as consultants, experts, teacher-trainers, researchers, visiting lecturers, and project developers. From the periphery there are similar opportunities for travel—for graduate studies, exchange visits, research, and professional development.

Usually, these visiting scholars complete their specific professional assignments and return without a significant impact at the widest levels of the guest community. Similarly, when they return home they don't consider sharing their knowledge and experiences with the larger community beyond their professional capacity. But if these traveling scholars can be made aware of their potential to act as culture and knowledge brokers, they may promote greater levels of sharing over and beyond the expectations of their original assignment. For example, periphery scholars who return home after obtaining their higher degrees or spending their furloughs abroad may have to consider the following additional responsibilities for the sake of their colleagues: bringing recent publications or Xeroxes of papers in their fields; establishing professional contacts with center professionals on behalf of their colleagues; initiating collaborative research projects with center institutes (on behalf of their colleagues outside their own field); obtaining information on scholarships, funds, and fellowships for their colleagues; and sharing information on recent scholarly developments in the center. Many consider such responsibilities as irrelevant to their work. Given the limited information flow between the center and the periphery, and the limited opportunities for travel, these visiting scholars have to consider themselves representatives of their community while they are abroad, imbued with a clear sense of accountability to the professional and intellectual advancement of their colleagues at home.

Similarly, visiting center professionals are often shocked to find that periphery scholars expect much more from them than they were originally assigned to do. A former officer from USIA, Tim Robinson, recently related how he was pressured by circumstances to act as a conduit scholar in Africa. Although he was conducting professional-development seminars for teachers in secondary schools (usually those without higher degrees), senior scholars with doctorates attended his seminars voluntarily. They shocked him further by asking questions related to recent developments in their own fields and requesting relevant published material from him (Tim Robinson, personal communication, 21 March 1998). This incident made the officer realize that not only practitioners with basic degrees but faculty with foreign Ph.D.s expected help from him, as they lacked the means for obtaining current knowledge and information from the outside world. Robinson thus realized that more was expected of him than simply conducting weeklong seminars on pedagogy during hurried visits. He had to develop personal relationships with local scholars, maintain contact with them over the long term, and facilitate the flow of information and knowledge continuously. He had to consider even advanced periphery scholars as his constituency and mail them relevant research literature and information on scholarly developments in the center, in addition to his teacher-training assignments. Such personal linkages go a long way in helping periphery scholars (and, at the opposite end, center scholars who are starved of information from periphery communities) share information that can make a critical difference in their work.

Textual Resistance

While such changes in institutional practices will help in some way to rectify the inequalities in scholarly communication and imbalances in knowledge production, more far-reaching (and subtle) changes are those involving discourse. Changes in writing styles and genre conventions promote resistance from within (as it were) and infuse oppositional values and thinking in RAs. There is already a rethinking about academic writing styles underway in the different disciplines in the center, which may encourage periphery scholars to imagine such resistance. This stylistic experimentation has been initiated by the epistemological changes in the postmodern cultural context. The demystification of the positivist/empiricist claims of traditional science has spawned a search for alternate strategies of textual representation of knowledge (Canagarajah 1996a). Some examples of multivocal writing and hybrid text construction are now increasingly found in certain disciplinary journals and, in fact, encouraged in the pages of composition journals like *CCC*. Though much of this textual experimentation is being carried out by center scholars (albeit including marginalized groups like women and ethnic scholars—see hooks 1989), periphery scholars have not participated much in this venture. This flexibility in writing styles may provide periphery scholars more scope for employing their desired discourses more frankly in the academy. However, these scholars may fear that any nonformal or experimental moves in their texts will be construed by center reviewers as simply deriving from bad writing skills or linguistic incompetence. It has also been observed that experimental writing in mainstream academic publications may be motivated too much by the culture of center communities themselves (Geisler 1994). Certain versions of introspective and reflexive writing seem to be motivated by contemporary Western preoccupations related to identity politics and voice. Encouraging only this form of alternate discourse can function as a new form of discrimination against non-Western writers. Consideration should be given to accommodating the narrative and orality-based conventions of other periphery communities in academic writing.

Geisler (1994) goes further to envision an academic discourse that would prove accessible for lay readers, bridging the gap between professionals and the wider public. Her proposals augur well for the inclusion of the strengths of periphery scholars into mainstream journals. She argues that the disjuncture between the oral and literate modalities should be better reconciled in the academy. The oral modes of knowledge construction and communicative conventions may themselves have a legitimate place in academic discourse. Academics, after all, gather crucial contextual and contingent information from interpersonal oral interactions—which information enables their critical reading and writing practices. Related to this issue is the need to reconcile the spatial and temporal dimensions of academic texts. Geisler (1994) finds that academic writing is conducted purely on the *spatial* dimension, based on the abstract relationships of ideas within the pages of the text. It is necessary also to appreciate the *temporal* processes of textuality and knowledge production. Ideas, after all, are produced in time—in historical context. In the academic text, however, the history (both the immediate history of text production and the larger history of disciplinary practices) is elided as the knowledge encoded is given a self-evident, atemporal status of "timeless" truth. Hence the move to accommodate chronologically structured narratives in academic discourse. All of this is good news for periphery scholars. Many of the texts analyzed in the previous chapters already embody a narrative dimension—sometimes coexisting uneasily with a spatial dimension of knowledge construction. We have also seen that some UJ scholars codeswitch between a temporally organized text for the local audience and a spatially/abstractly organized text for the center audience. Negotiating these conflicting discourses more consciously and effectively is a means for their successful entry into mainstream journals. In other words, periphery scholars need not abandon their oral traditions or indigenously developed strategies of communication. They have to negotiate their use with the literate modes of mainstream knowledge construction to develop a creative oppositional discourse.

The temptation for periphery scholars may be to use the current tendency for textual experimentation and discoursal flexibility as an excuse to employ their indigenous discourses one-sidedly. To use their own discourses without consideration for the established conventions in their disciplines is to ignore the context and audience they are addressing. One can easily alienate the reader by not taking into consideration the conventions and rules that define meaningful communication for different contexts. This naive approach can lead to the same forms of marginalization of their writing that periphery scholars have experienced under the positivistic culture in the academy. The challenge then is to engage critically with the dominant discourses of one's discipline in order to work out the terms under which writers can bring in alternate discourses. Periphery scholars have to consider how some of the indigenous discourses can modify, reframe, or infuse established disciplinary discourses. This is truly a process of *negotiation*. While showing that they are aware of established conventions and are taking them quite seriously, periphery scholars should attempt to reconstruct these conventions by bringing in their own discourses. This way they *appropriate* the established discourses for their purposes according to their own ideologies and interests.

Signs that these modes of writing are being developed are already found in plenty among periphery scholars. In the previous chapters we saw how UJ scholars have developed writing strategies that have the potential to construct hybrid textuality. The codeswitching that many writers perform as they communicate in different languages to different audiences shows that they have the rhetorical competence to negotiate the terms of communication in diverse contexts. Writers have to explore how they can codeswitch within the same text to construct a multivocal text. Furthermore, the coping strategies they develop to outwardly conform to the established conventions of the center, even as they make the best of their limitations and deprivation, are of oppositional significance. Such activity shows that they can critically and creatively modify the existing conventions to suit their purposes. What is needed is greater rhetorical self-consciousness among periphery scholars in order to engage in this textual reconstruction more consciously. This is an experimental process that would show relative success in different contexts and may take a long time to develop.

Other studies show how novice writers (including graduate students) construct such multivocal texts by their own initiative (without expert advice) when they wrestle honestly with the discursive challenges they face in their academic tasks. In an illuminating case study of a Chinese and a Japanese female graduate student, Diane Belcher (1997) shows how they produced embedded forms of argumentation in otherwise narrative texts in order to gently and tactfully challenge the biases of their faculty advisors (and, in effect, the dominant discourses in their field). This writing strategy derives from a community-based and gender-influenced desire to show respect, understanding, and cooperative engagement in dialogue and knowledge construction. Despite the risks involved in antagonizing their thesis committees and being denied their degrees, the students managed to evoke respect for their arguments. Belcher goes on to make a case for such nonadversarial forms of argumentation, in terms of the discourses preferred by certain feminist and minority scholars. After all, well-meaning faculty members (and journal referees) should look for creative, original, and challenging modes of textuality that *add* something to the discourse, rather than demanding texts that slavishly mimic the existing style in a formulaic manner. Center scholars who believe in creative, personalized, "original" realizations of texts (admittedly belonging to the romantic tradition of writing) should make a space for nonstandard modes of writing from periphery scholars. Belcher in fact goes a step further to argue that these alternate modes of argumentation and reasoning are a healthy corrective to the established academic discourse. She relates how center-based scholars are themselves reconsidering the place of adversarial modes of argumentation, which are not conducive to generating meaningful dialogue and cultivating ethical relations in intellectual engagement.

I have discussed elsewhere the case of a graduate student at UJ producing a hybrid text as her thesis (Canagarajah 1999, 153–68). As a committed Christian and a woman, Viji was dissatisfied with what she perceived as the rigidities and detachment of academic prose. To make matters more complicated, her argument that the pedagogies and curriculum of past missionary ESL teachers were quite successful is unpopular in the contemporary context of Hindu chauvinism and linguistic nationalism. Her resolution of her discursive problems was wise: she produced a text that follows the usual conventions of cause/effect organization, occupation of a niche, rigorous archival research, and meticulous documentation, while still employing a personal voice and narrative flow to subtly embed her argument. As she interjects her personal/religious ethos in a relevant way into the academic discourse, her text gains a creative and critical edge. Viji thus attempts to find a space and voice for herself in the range of available discourses (though these are conflicting discourses) to encode the messages she desires. Taking seriously the academic discourse, she yet brings into it her preferred values to construct an independent text. Thus the text takes a multivocal, hybrid shape.

Viji begins her thesis with the following acknowledgment: "I thank my Lord and Master Jesus Christ for enabling me to complete this study with very limited sources at my disposal." Though this language is permissible in this somewhat more personal section of the dissertation, it is eschewed in the body of the text. Thus there is a recognition of the appropriate genres of discourse to be employed in the different sections of the dissertation. She finds a permissible way of expressing her religious identity in the pages of an academic work. The next page, which presents her abstract, suggests a scholarly tone with more detached prose: "This is an attempt at tracing the approaches of the American Mission in teaching the English Language during the British period in Jaffna. From most of the findings the course has been a successful one. In fact it could be pointed out that at a certain period of time the cry for English and more English came from the natives themselves." The impersonal syntactic structures, the hedging devices, and the qualifications here suggest a switch to more research-oriented discourse in the body of the dissertation. Viji is also able to detach herself sufficiently from her religious biases to acknowledge how education was sometimes used for the utilitarian purpose of evangelization. This is a politically astute concession in recognition of the dominant nationalistic sentiments in the local community. Making concessions of this nature is a good rhetorical strategy in order to win audience acceptance for her thesis.

As she proceeds, she is able to fuse divergent discourses more fluidly in textually appropriate ways. In the following excerpt, from Viji's first chapter, where she establishes the background to missionary education, consider her use of the standard practices of quotation and citation.

> "Ye shall be witnesses unto me unto the utmost part of the earth" (Holy
> Bible Acts 1:8)—the final command of the Master to the disciples of Jesus
> Christ has been fulfilled through the centuries ultimately paving the way for
> a band of missionaries from the American Board to reach the shores of Jaffna

in 1813. Though the supreme goal of the missionaries was to evangelize, they found themselves being compelled "to seek the aids of learning" (Plan: 1823) in order to prepare the ground for sowing the seed of the Gospel. (1)

It is interesting that the quotation from the Bible that was cited in her initial drafts as a proud announcement of the educational endeavors of the missionaries is cited here dispassionately to indicate the rationale for their educational activities. The citation that follows is from the proposal by a school board for starting one of the first missionary educational institutions. This bureaucratic text is at tension with the previous Biblical quotation, suggesting the hybrid discourses embodied in the dissertation. As the first chapter continues, we find that Viji adopts both a narrative and a polemical structuring. After orientating readers to the colonial period, she introduces the main terms of the debate regarding the missionary educational enterprise in the introductory chapter. She uses this chapter effectively to create a niche for her work in the scholarly conversation: she cites a variety of local educationists, linguists, and social theorists of the postcolonial period who have criticized the missionary educational enterprise to show why a reexamination is necessary in order to arrive at a more balanced assessment. She also argues that since the missionaries didn't leave adequate records of their teaching mission (as they were preoccupied with evangelization), there is a need to reconstruct this dimension of their work. The political and academic significance of her thesis is made to stand out as the text is situated in the relevant discursive contexts.

Viji thus appropriates the dominant conventions for her own purposes. Viji's strategy has the potential to interrogate center/academic discourses, reconstruct their conventions, and infuse them with alternate discourses for critical expression. In comparison with some of her colleagues who either mechanically followed a stereotypical version of the established discourse (which I call one-sided *accommodation*) or totally opposed the academic conventions to use their preferred oral/vernacular modes of discourse (which I call mere *opposition*), her strategy of negotiating and appropriating the dominant discourses suits what critical pedagogues define as strategic forms of *resistance* (Giroux 1983, 109–10). Similarly, I am myself attempting to critically negotiate competing discourses (i.e., from center and periphery, from orality and literacy) in writing this book. In the prefatory section entitled "The Project" I discussed extensively how I have attempted to make a space for local knowledge in mainstream research publications by paradoxically working along with and against the dominant discourses—without either totally ignoring them or totally conforming to them.

There are many other subtle strategies periphery scholars have developed to counterbalance their disadvantages in meeting mainstream publishing requirements. We identified what I called *coping* strategies in chapter 4. Some scholars make up for the lack of recent scholarly publications by citing works and quotations from secondary sources (including book reviews, publication announcements, and book advertisements). They have to resort to this activity, as they cannot get access to the book itself. They present this information as if directly gathered from primary sources, thus giving the impression of firsthand reading knowledge. Through careful bibliographical detective work and "reading between the lines" they are able to get to know the recent research findings and constructs well enough to sprinkle their papers with relevant citations. In doing this, the main intention of some of us at UJ was to give the referees the impression that we were keeping abreast of the current knowledge in the field. Perhaps this is an oppositional strategy of taking Western publishing conventions to their reductio ad absurdum. If some center-based referees value the publishability of a paper based purely on the recency of its citations, then periphery writers may provide these from whatever source. Some of my center colleagues have confessed that they too borrow information from incidental/secondary sources and discuss it authoritatively without giving the impression of borrowing.

Other coping strategies show periphery scholars developing alternate avenues for contributing to mainstream knowledge. It is now well known among periphery scholars that there is greater scope for publishing on theoretical matters than on empirical research (see also Gibbs 1995 for a testimony to this effect from an Indian scholar in physics). Apart from the sophisticated equipment/facilities needed for empirical work, there is also greater need to know the related studies already conducted in that area. Since empirical research is being conducted in diverse locations, it is difficult for periphery scholars to obtain information relating to all this activity in a timely fashion. Theoretical contribution, on the other hand, can negotiate a handful of major texts in a convenient manner. Recency is also not always a pressing issue in theoretical work. But in the case of empirical research, similar studies may be conducted by different scholars at the same time with preference often shown for the study that is most "cutting edge."[6]

Furthermore, local scholars choose to publish in journals whose conventions/requirements they can meet. So, among the reasons why I chose to contribute to the *TESOL Quarterly* from UJ are the following: the journal was available in the university library due to a generous donation from the Asia Foundation; the in-house editorial staff proofread accepted manuscripts, rather than mailing them back to authors; and there was no requirement of stamps, envelopes, soft copy, or page costs.[7] Given the living conditions in Jaffna, these publishing requirements were suitable for my purposes. Such incidental reasons will certainly motivate periphery scholars as they make decisions to submit their papers to center journals. (Fortunately for me, the *TESOL Quarterly* was the leading journal in my field. Not all my UJ colleagues are as lucky.)

The monopoly of the English language on academic publishing is a more recalcitrant reality to resist. Non-native writers—including those from other language groups in Europe—find that while it is unattractive to publish their work in the vernacular, since such work won't receive the recognition it deserves, writing in English leads to papers being rejected for linguistic incompetence (Connor 1999; Jernudd and Baldauf 1987; Li 1999). To get out of this impasse, Salager-Meyer (n.d.), a French-born teacher of ESP from Venezuela, argues for nothing less than *scientific multilingualism*. She envisions a time when all—or at least many—languages can be simultaneously used in academic literature. For this purpose she calls on international organizations outside the academy (the UN, UNESCO, etc.) to pool their resources. Her proposals include getting scholars in industrialized communities to become proficient in periphery languages, persuading mainstream journals to publish a quota of periphery papers in their original languages, and defraying the costs for periphery scholars in submitting a paper for publication. Some might doubt the usefulness of accommodating papers in different languages within the covers of the same journal. This mode of academic literacy demands polyglossic feats from scientists already encumbered with time-consuming research work. But there are ways out. We have had for some time the practice of scientific papers published simultaneously in more than one language. On pages facing each other, a paper can appear simultaneously in two languages. This publication practice requires some time and money for translating periphery papers into English, not to mention the commitment for page space. Despite the costs, this is a way in which the knowledge of many non-English scholars can be made available to the wider English-speaking world (without already disqualifying their contributions simply because of their lack of proficiency in English). In its ideal form, this publishing practice would encourage a multilingual academic culture that could initiate radical ways in which scholars may negotiate different traditions of knowledge.

If scientific multilingualism is too much to ask for, mainstream journals should at least accept divergent English dialects as suitable for academic communication. The insistence on English is complicated for many periphery scholars not simply because English is a second or foreign language to them but because they widely use other (nativized) variants of English for their purposes. Scholars at UJ, for example, may display traces of the "old-fashioned" British English that was passed on to them through the colonial legacy. (My own language in this book is not free of such traces, tactfully suggest the American reviewers of this manuscript!) But center-based referees often dismiss such language as examples of infelicitous and incompetent non-native writing, as it is bound to appear quaint to them. Furthermore, there have also developed indigenized forms of English that are considered legitimate and acceptable for local academic communication. (In Sri Lanka, the variant known locally as "educated Sri Lankan English" is treated as the most prestigious and systematic in relation to the other local dialects and is used in academic writing.) But referees in the center usually make pejorative comments on manuscripts that employ such indigenized versions of English. My intention here is not to dismiss the possibility that the use of these dialects will sound awkward to a center reader. We see in the passages I have quoted from the periphery RAs in chapter 4 that there are syntactic and idiomatic differences. This is to be expected. But we should be able to tolerate certain peculiarities as long as the meaning is clear. Is it absolutely important that a specific dialect of English is treated as normative for all academic writing? To what point can we accommodate other variants of English?

There may be a double standard held in the mainstream publishing circles regarding the acceptable usage of English. While center scholars are increasingly being permitted to use colloquial and ethnic dialectal features for stylistic effect (Smitherman [1999], who uses African-Americanisms in a paper that reviews the treatment of Black students in composition studies), periphery usage is still considered bad English. But Smitherman's example shows that changes are possible—at least some mainstream journals are accommodating the African American dialect in their pages.[8] Periphery scholars should sometimes take the risk of pushing the limits. They must test the extent to which mainstream journals would accommodate their own variants of English.[9] Negotiating the use of vernaculars and indigenized variants of English is part of the discursive resistance leading to the democratization of academic communication.

Reconstructing Knowledge and Society

While mainstream academic circles are proving recalcitrant to reforming publishing and knowledge-making practices, efforts to protect and develop the intellectual resources of local communities are taking many nonacademic forms these days. It is indeed embarrassing to find that when academic publishing networks are still closed, elitist, and inflexible, activist groups, media personalities, and entrepreneurs have taken the lead in protecting indigenous intellectual resources (perhaps not always without self-interest). The aborigines of central Australia, for instance, have sponsored a television and radio broadcasting project to educate not only the wider community but their own people about their ways of life.[10] Likewise, the Body Shop has helped to create a demand for rainforest products and has helped educate center consumers about preserving the rainforests. In other cases, periphery communities have had to resort to violence in a desperate attempt to protect their interests. For example, the Kuna of Panama have burned down hotels built on their land without their permission (and over their protests). The Chipko of India have formed human rings (mainly made up of women) around trees to prevent logging. The Sami of Sweden have chained themselves to bulldozers to prevent the construction of a hydroelectric dam. In the context of such desperate resistance activities in the periphery, it is important that center academic media open themselves up to the preservation of local intellectual and material resources. If not, they face the danger of becoming irrelevant to the real concerns of the people—whether in the center or the periphery.

We should keep in mind that creating more democratic processes of knowledge construction isn't purely an intellectual exercise. Giving page space for periphery scholars in mainstream journals is also not for the sole purpose of boosting the ego of obscure scholars or simply fulfilling some quota of token representation in knowledge-production processes. There are ways in which this richer construction of knowledge can make a difference in local people's everyday lives. The anthropologist A. P. Elkin (1977) relates the case of an aborigine shaman trained in Western medicine and allowed to practice both forms of medicine with institutional recognition. The greater respect developed for the indigenous medical system has won him the institutional recognition and acceptance of mainstream scientific circles to practice both forms of medicine. He is therefore able to wear the dual hats of "Blackfellow Doctor" (as shaman) and "Whitefellow Doctor" (as physician) and negotiate both knowledge traditions as he serves the local people in the best manner possible to suit their needs and interests. This practice can also lead to greater understanding of indigenous knowledge and give birth to newer, more complex medical approaches that enable a fusion of native and mainstream traditions. The local people are empowered to develop their native practices even as they take cognizance of experimental scientific information.

Neither are the changes in publishing practices I suggest here for the sole purpose of developing periphery communities. It is worth repeating that the democratization of academic communication can make a critical contribution to center communities themselves. The examples provided in chapter 7 suggest how the presumed "folk knowledge" from local contexts can insightfully question mainstream ways of knowing. An engagement with local knowledge from periphery contexts can help enrich, expand, and reconstruct mainstream discourses and knowledge. In fact, the clash of diverse perspectives is valuable for its own sake: it affords an opportunity to reexamine the basic assumptions and beliefs of a community.

The periphery scholar's ability to shuttle between discourse communities and negotiate discourses provides just the right stance to make meaningful contributions to mainstream discourses. Edward Said (1993) celebrates the ideal form of academic freedom as embodied in the postcolonial scholar's position as a migrant or transient. The postcolonial scholar enjoys the right balance between participation and detachment—in other words, he or she is aware of mainstream/center discursive developments while adopting a critical attitude to all this in terms of his or her membership in a less integrated periphery disciplinary community with a different scholarly culture. In saying this, I am not dismissing the reality of two other kinds of periphery scholars: (1) those who have absolutely no

interest in mainstream discourses or the desire to engage with them, sometimes forced to stay rooted in the periphery (with little prospects of traveling abroad); (2) those who have become so totally absorbed into center
discourses (perhaps because they live in the West) that they are not interested in the alternate discourses that come from marginalized communities. However justified the position of these scholars according to their different interests, from the perspective adopted here both situations
represent different forms of intellectual restriction. They pose the limitation of getting silenced by a specific paradigm of discourse(s). Scholars
who are aware of their location and subject position even as they shuttle
between discourse communities fit the model of the postcolonial transient
who enjoys the ability to make socially relevant and paradigm-changing
knowledge (Canagarajah 2001).

To understand the benefits deriving from scholarly interaction across
geopolitical boundaries, it is useful to invoke one final time Pratt's (1991)
notion of contact zones. The publishing domain is a contact zone that
comprises scholars from diverse sociocultural backgrounds who must not
only negotiate their own differing knowledge systems but increasingly
deal with texts from different discursive traditions. Although the meeting
of cultures and discourses takes place under asymmetrical power relations
(as the discourses of the dominant groups are privileged and often institutionalized), the interaction in the contact zone gives birth to hybrid forms
of knowledge, texts, and discourses that may resist homogeneity and domination. We have seen from the examples of periphery scholars how their
texts and literacy practices display complex skills of mediating alien cultures, appropriating hegemonic discourses, and negotiating foreign languages for their communicative purposes. Despite the marginalization experienced by periphery scholars in academic literacy, we see creative
practices such as codeswitching, hybrid text construction, transculturation,
critique, collaboration, parody, denunciation, vernacular expression, and
other coping strategies that are signs of oppositional knowledge construction. For Pratt, these are the literate arts of the contact zone. The act of
seeing one's own culture through the eyes of another cultural group is itself a sobering experience, enabling one to detach oneself from one's own
discourses, gain reflexive understanding, and develop a more critical attitude toward things. The tension of intercultural clashes can thus bring
forth new knowledge—generating new paradigms for understanding na-

ture and society. While such positive consequences are developed even under the existing unequal conditions of academic contact, we can only guess at the greater benefits that may derive from relatively more democratic fora of scholarly interaction.

It is pleasant to think that reforming publishing conventions to accommodate the work of periphery academics might very well function as a humble beginning toward democratic processes in knowledge production and, by extension, geopolitical relations. Those who have developed the center/periphery relations model, like Immanuel Wallerstein (1991), have recently argued that countercultural movements at the microsocial level have the potential to reconfigure the center/periphery arrangement. The strength of such movements—like feminism, animal rights (e.g., People for the Ethical Treatment of Animals [PETA]), and environmental concern (e.g., Greenpeace)—is that they are relatively independent of state sponsorship and often transcend national borders. Academic communities across the different disciplines share such transnational affiliations and relative autonomy in their respective societies and in this respect can act as agents of change. If power is established and sustained by knowledge, the diversification, democratization, and deconstruction of knowledge should have implications for reconfiguring geopolitical relations.

This book is not one more complaint by the materially underprivileged, seeking set-asides. This is not a plea to overlook excellence in order to provide greater representation for periphery scholars in center publications. This is rather an attempt to deconstruct the bases of "excellence" in published scholarship and knowledge construction. This is an argument for changing the relationships in the publication networks so that we can reconstruct knowledge—and presumably conduct international relations—in more egalitarian and enriching terms.

Notes

The Project

1. The identity of these reviewers is not known. Though referees of some journals have begun identifying themselves, all the reviews cited in this book were anonymous. I therefore use gender-neutral pronouns to refer to the referees.

2. Vavuniya is under government control. Therefore this Tamil region enjoys more resources than Jaffna, including telecommunication services. The typographical mistakes and idiomatic peculiarities in the message are left unedited.

Chapter 1

1. However we may want to finesse the center/periphery inequality (to satisfy the academic fashion of relativism these days), the United Nation's latest Human Development Report, published in 2001, confirms the usual differences between the postcolonial world and the West in material terms. Though India has pockets of high technology, it ranks just above the marginalized in terms of national comparison. Similarly, of the thirty-six nations considered lowest in human development, twenty-nine are African (Crossette 2001, 4).

Chapter 2

1. The forum was held on 22 March 1991 at the geography department building of the University of Jaffna, Tirunelvely. The paper was presented by Professor S. Suseendirarajah.

2. *Pundit* is an honorific conferred on those deemed learned according to the traditional/religious scholarly system in Hindu society. One has to pass a series of evaluation procedures set up for the purpose of granting this title.

3. The writing of that paper and the ensuing public debate occurred when I was away on study leave in the United States for my doctoral research. According to my informants, the author criticized the *pundit's* stature in that paper partly because the author's father and the *pundit* had taught together in a local school and didn't get along too well. Some people saw this background as explaining the critical attitude of the author (A. J. Canagaratne, personal communication, May 2001).

4. Saivism is the religious faith based on the worship of the Hindu god Shiva. In Jaffna society Saivism constitutes the dominant religious and social ideology (Sivatamby 1992; Gnanakumaran 1991/1992).

5. This is not the place to recount the origins of Enlightenment science or the establishment

of the values that constitute positivistic assumptions. For a critical review of the Enlightenment movement, see Hess 1995, 54–86.

6. I am synthesizing here views articulated by diverse theorists in this evolving tradition. Those who wish to grapple with the primary texts should read the historian of science Kuhn (1962); poststructuralists Foucault (1972) and Derrida (1981); feminists Haraway (1989) and Harding (1991); and postcolonialists Said (1978) and Spivak (1990).

7. To give some examples, Lave and Wenger (1991) prefer the term *communities of practice* and Pratt (1991) the term *contact zone*. I integrate the useful insights of these scholars into my definition of discourse communities.

8. Swales (1990) objects to the notion of a discourse community as defined by a shared worldview or ideology because he thinks that members can belong to different discourse communities and therefore must hold different subjectivities. But this view assumes that subjects always hold a unitary worldview. This perspective also assumes a unitary subjectivity—that we are always in possession of a single sense of identity. It is not difficult for subjects to adopt the required values and identities of the multiple discourse communities they shuttle between.

9. Though telephones, audio recordings, TV, and video may now carry speech to geographically distant communities, this occurs with considerable mediation. These media still don't serve to constitute speakers of English in Sri Lanka, Nigeria, and England, for example, into one speech community. The values and attitudes they hold in relation to the language may perhaps make them a discourse community.

10. But we must note that Knorr-Cetina's (1981) perspective is a bit too deterministic and reductive. Nonmaterial concerns—such as ideological and cultural motivations for knowledge construction—need to be also integrated into this materialistic model. For instance, the opposition of periphery communities to Enlightenment principles in favor of their indigenous knowledge is also motivated by cultural identity, pride, and integrity, not solely by market considerations. It is in this way that we can explain the preoccupation at UJ with celebrating the pundit and his knowledge tradition.

11. There is an emergent scholarship of analyzing the academy that confirms the materialist and conflictual orientation provided here. Cheryl Geisler (1994) has made an insightful contribution to theorizing the politics of academic communities by explaining the formation of the American university system in the context of sociohistorical forces. She situates the process of academic professionalization in the rise of the middle class, industrialization, and market forces in the nineteenth century. The expanding domains of economy and production required forms of knowledge that could not be handled by the church, law, or medicine—the prevailing elite professional groups. In the place of the previous system of apprenticeship, the academy provided a more objective, institutionalized, and formal training for the new professions. This process of professionalization provided social mobility freed from the constraints of aristocratic birth, thus spawning a new sociocultural group. But the vested interests of this emergent class had to be protected in turn. The academy functioned as a gatekeeper to see that this professional status and class membership were distributed selectively. What we see then is that the discourse-producing activity of the American university system is implicated in class-based ideological and material interests.

12. A classic example of this is the area of second language acquisition (SLA). The constructs formed in clinical settings in center communities do not take into account the amazingly creative processes of mixing and switching codes that occur in everyday communication in multilingual communities. As a consequence, SLA perceives these processes pejoratively as signs of linguistic incompetence (Sridhar 1994; Singh 1998).

Chapter 3

1. This discussion is indebted to Atkinson (1991), who provides a useful account of different approaches to conventions in written discourse.

2. Bazerman (1988) explains the origins of the review process in similar ways. He says that publishability decisions in the early days of scientific journals led to personal problems between writers and the editor. Animosity would develop when authors considered the editor to have rejected the paper for personal reasons. The subsequent conventions of anonymous/collective refereeing set up a more impersonal, institutionalized way of resolving such decisions.

3. I define and illustrate these moves in detail in chapter 4.

4. All this doesn't rule out the importance of oral interactions in academic communities. Conferences and seminars do play a role in the construction of knowledge and professional identity. But literacy provides far greater resources and options for these purposes.

Chapter 4

1. The books referred to are Eastman 1992, Heller 1988, and Myers-Scotton 1992.

2. I am not arguing that the findings of L2 composition studies on composing strategies can be rejected out of hand. I am only pointing to another layer of explanation that can place in context the deficiencies usually attributed to "non-native" writers of English.

3. I must grant that these composition studies are mostly done with students and not advanced scholars. Though it might be unfair to relate the claims from these studies to advanced scholars, whose linguistic and discursive proficiency might be different, we must note that journal editors in the center are influenced by the explanations and constructs provided by L2 composition scholars. Conversely, a consideration of the challenges faced by periphery scholars enables us to rethink our explanations of the practices of ESL student writers as well (as I go on to demonstrate in this chapter).

4. In recent publications, some center scholars have begun making an argument for taking material determinants more seriously in composition studies—see Lu and Horner 1998; Reynolds 1998.

5. A center critic has suggested that since these papers don't follow Swales's conventions, they are not RAs. But this is a circular explanation that is detrimental to periphery writers: in other words, RAs have x structure; the papers under consideration don't have x structure; therefore, they are not RAs. What is important is that the papers analyzed here appear in journals that are classified as research publications and are treated as such by the writers themselves. These journals are different from more midbrow or popular journals in the local context, even if they may appear nonspecialized to center scholars in terms of the latter's academic culture.

6. We have to treat local scholars trained in the West differently. They can be expected to undertake research for its own sake, though they usually don't get much respect from the local community for their academic work.

7. This term is borrowed from SLA research. It refers to deviations from the rule that result when learners apply a rule too strictly (without consideration of exceptions) or attempt to avoid typical mistakes by overapplying a rule.

8. Although the journal was published in 1993, its publication date appears as 1991/1992 to maintain the sequence. I have left out of this analysis my paper, which also appeared in this journal. As my article was written within two years of arriving from doctoral work abroad, it contains many recent references that were not available locally, making the paper quite different from the typical articles that appear in the journal.

9. The mainstream editors interviewed by Flowerdew (2001) make a similar observation about inappropriate citations given to boost the authority of the periphery submission. But they are critical of this practice.

10. I will discuss in the final chapter how periphery writers can do this borrowing more creatively and effectively. Howard (1995) makes a distinction between a "creative plagiarism" that transmutes the borrowed material into a new whole and a less independent practice of plagiarism.

11. Perhaps center reviewers can be more charitable about this rhetorical feature in periphery RAs because descriptions of methods are getting deemphasized in center RAs themselves (Atkinson 1999).

12. Science scholars in the local community are in a slightly different situation as they can still claim to be using certain standard procedures and instruments in their labs—even if those are not very recent.

13. See for a definition of these terms of analysis Atkinson 1999, 75–109.

14. I acknowledge that in center RAs, too, scholars conclude by pointing to work that needs to be done. But in local RAs the authors could go further, to apologize to the readers or seek forgiveness for any offensive statements (as I will illustrate later).

15. There are of course many *other* complex reasons—discussed in this book—why my paper was better known in the center and less known in the periphery and the reverse situation applied for Suseendirarajah's paper.

16. I am borrowing this term from sociolinguistics to use it analogously for the switches writers make in rhetoric when they write for different audiences and linguistic contexts. Although this term is rarely used in writing research, I have discussed the heuristic value of this term in Canagarajah 2000.

17. These terms refer to politeness strategies. Some communities/contexts require an effort by the speaker to display politeness to the interlocutor through suitable discourse strategies (i.e., positive face); other communities/contexts prefer more detachment and restraint from the speaker in expressions of politeness.

18. See Belcher 1997 on the nonagonistic discourse of non-native graduate students; Mauranen 1993b on the end-weighted, implicit RAs of Finnish scholars; and Cmejrkova 1996 on similar forms of discourse among Czech scholars.

Chapter 5

1. For those not aware of American or European postage/exchange rates—and lacking the possibility of calling the publisher to get more information—this can be an added nuisance.

2. *World Englishes* seems to have learned from this experience. When I submitted another paper a few months later, the editorial letter clearly stated that they had "accepted the paper for publication" even though they requested revisions based on a reviewer's comments.

3. As we know, editors from refereed journals often invite closely acquainted scholars to submit papers for publication. The review process for them is largely confirmatory. While less known scholars go through the rigors of the review process, better-known scholars have an easier ride. In this sense, those who have published previously, and are respected in the disciplinary circles, get to publish more easily than obscure scholars do.

4. *SLJSAS* is published by the Faculty of Arts of the University of Jaffna, comprising an editorial board elected from among the teaching staff. *Navasilu* (New flame) is the official journal of the English Association of Sri Lanka and is usually published from Colombo. *Thatched Patio* is published by the Institute of Contemporary Race and Ethnicity in Colombo. *Panpaadu* (Cul-

ture) is published by the Department of Hindu Cultural Affairs, which is a branch of the Sri Lankan government in Colombo.

Chapter 6

1. This event took place on 12 September 1991, at the Faculty of Arts, University of Jaffna. What follows is from my observation notes on this event.

2. What is valued in this RA structure is a polemical approach that distinguishes the writer's position from the rival positions of other philosophers on the same subject. In the more strategic of such approaches, the writer piggybacks on the claims of rival philosophers by negotiating a superior or more balanced third position that plays off those of rivals.

3. Though there are certainly more informal presentations in American colloquia, they are still focused and objective, eschewing the spontaneous and conversational nature of oral presentations in the periphery.

4. The following are the transcription conventions used:

italics:	utterance made originally in Tamil
underlined:	English gloss for Tamil utterance
regular script:	utterance originally uttered in English
UPPER CASE:	emphasis
//	pause of .5 seconds or more
=	latched utterance
[ ]	overlapping utterance
,	sustained intonation
?	rising intonation
.	falling intonation

5. The "Renaissance man" or "gentleman scholar" archetype was also popular among European scholarly communities, and they probably encouraged this ideal during colonialism in South Asia. Though this ideal has substantially disappeared in the West, it is still found here and there (as in the writing of structuralist and poststructuralist philosophers/literary critics Barthes, Derrida, Foucault, etc.).

6. As typical of our practice in Jaffna, some of us still have the typed copy of the article. Since the typist left out the bibliographical information, we don't have the name of the author or the issue number. It is not difficult for me to get the full information now as I am based in the West. But many of my colleagues at UJ will simply have this typed piece of paper and won't be able to use the article for citation purposes.

7. We should not generalize oral communicative practices to all local community members. The academics in the local community do manifest modes of expertise that are different from those of the laypeople. Laypeople employ vernacular discourses (e.g., narrative and personal) in all contexts, whereas professionals can codeswitch between vernacular and academic discourses. There is in fact the widely held view among laypeople that scholarly ways of talking are "difficult." This view can be fed by many features—the use of jargon, complex syntax, English syntactic constructions and terminology, and the general abstraction and detachment of discourse. Therefore it is possible to distinguish within Tamil itself between academic and lay discourses.

8. There are changes underway in this regard in the center. Schwebke and Medway (2001) argue that everyday concerns and civic interests are gradually getting more integrated into academic discourses since the shift to isolation around the 1960s.

Chapter 7

1. Sometimes a knowledge tradition developed in the periphery becomes fashionable in the center at a time when the discourses of the center are dominant in the periphery. Consider the case of indigenous medicinal practices like *Ayurvedha*. After systematic denigration by the colonial administrations and their educational system, the positivistic tradition has become the mainstream approach for local scholars and professionals. In fact there is evidence that some of the missionaries considered such indigenous medical systems as quack medicine or heathenish superstition. Currently, however, "alternative medicine" has become a catchword in the West. Streets in New York and London are sprawling with small offices offering Chinese, Indian, Spanish, and African modes of cure for eager American patients. There are pharmacists selling herbs and concoctions as alternatives to chemical substances. But, alas, while this has become a money-spinning venture in the West, the cream of periphery scholars is working hard to master the rudiments of Western medicine!

2. While I point out these ironies, which are quite common in many fields in the academy, the mention of these scholars' names here should not be construed as an attempt to disparage their work. Phillipson, Pennycook, and Holliday are brilliant scholars who have initiated politically informed research in the field of ELT. In fact, these scholars would be the first to acknowledge the scholarly inequalities in the discipline; they are themselves working to make a space for periphery discourses in the academy.

3. Wickramasuriya 1976 illustrates the many subtle forms of local protest against English education in Sri Lanka. Chelliah 1922, a history of English education written by a local teacher while the British were still ruling Sri Lanka, unwittingly reveals some of the local oppositional discourses.

4. Though there are colored people like African Americans and Hispanic Americans who are L1 speakers of English, other standards are used to discriminate against them according to dialect and label them inferior.

5. A look at recent advertisement for ESL teachers in Korea, Japan, or Taiwan will bear this out.

6. The World Development Report of the World Bank states that a study of 121 rural water supply projects in forty-nine countries found that 7 out of every 10 projects succeeded when the intended beneficiaries participated in project design. But only 1 in 10 succeeded when they did not (World Bank 1999, 14). This finding shows how important it is to take account of local knowledge when engaging in development work.

7. This information was originally obtained at <http://afr.worldbank.org/aft2/poverty>. Current information is available at <http://www.afriline.net/welcome.html> and <http://www.worldbank.org/poverty/index.htm>.

Chapter 8

1. *Lanka's* ISSN number is 1100-0082.

2. Despite rising tuition costs, the United States continues to attract the most foreign students. According to figures offered by the United States Information Agency (USIA), in the 1996–1997 academic year 458,000 foreign students studied in the United States, followed by 170,000 in France (Honan 1998, A32). Although the United States is losing students to less costly universities in Australia and other nations, the number still represents 32 percent of all foreign students (down from 40 percent five years earlier).

3. There are of course exceptional scholars in the center who continue to mentor their students after graduation. But this benefit is not always available to periphery scholars who return

home because of the practical difficulties in maintaining contact with their mentors from technologically backward locations.

4. *Jaffna* is the Anglicized form of *Yalppanam*. Uppsala University documents use the local form for reasons of linguistic and ideological affirmation.

5. I am thinking here of the workshops held for junior faculty members to help them write for publication or apply for grants.

6. Bazerman (1988) discusses how Newton resorted to writing books in order to sidestep the challenges and debates with readers in early journals of the Royal Society of London. As periphery scholars cannot keep in touch with and participate in the ongoing debates in the scholarly circles, as they receive the journals late, they too find it convenient to write books rather than journal articles.

7. Though the *TESOL Quarterly* was discontinued after the 1989 issue due to funding problems, the available journals were sufficient for my purposes when I wrote my paper in 1992.

8. There are other African American scholars like hooks (1989) who use the vernacular quite boldly in their academic writing. In *Talking Back* she also makes an argument for why such language use would function as a form of resistance to the partisan ideologies informing academic knowledge.

9. The "would" in this sentence has been pointed to by some American referees as an incorrect usage that needs correcting. For my fellow Sri Lankan speakers and me, this is so much part of our "standard" that we don't treat this even as a local peculiarity. It is possible that the form was used as a politeness feature (with added humility) by the locals during the colonial period (as my colleague Dwight Atkinson points out). Readers can treat this modal as an example of the complexities of dialect usage in mainstream writing. Does this modal affect their understanding of my ideas? What ethos does this usage give me, the writer? Is this humility something I should embrace or resist?

10. I am indebted to Hess (1995) for many of these examples.

Works Cited

Academic exchange between Yalppanam and Uppsala. 1996. Uppsala: Uppsala University Religious Studies.

Adas, Michael. 1989. *Machines as the measure of men.* Ithaca: Cornell University Press.

Alvarez, Claude. 1990. "Science, colonialism and violence: A Luddite view." In *Science, hegemony, and violence,* ed. Ashish Nandy, 68–112. Delhi: Oxford University Press.

Amarou, M., A. Suresh Canagarajah, Pat Killian, and Tim Robinson. 1998. "Connecting the global community through conduit scholars." Symposium at the thirty-second annual TESOL convention, 17–21 March, Seattle, Wash.

Anderson, Benedict. 1984. *Imagined communities: Reflections on the origins and spread of nationalism.* London: Verso.

Anderson, Robert S. 1991. "The origins of the International Rice Research Institute." *Minerva* 29/1: 61–89.

Anderson, Robert S., and Barrie M. Morrison. 1982. Introduction to *Science, politics, and the agricultural revolution in Asia,* ed. Robert S. Anderson, Barrie M. Morrison, Paul Brass, and Odwin Levy. Boulder: Westview.

Appadurai, Arjun. 1994. "Disjuncture and difference in the global cultural economy." In *Colonial discourse and post-colonial theory,* ed. P. Williams and L. Chrisman, 324–39. New York: Columbia University Press.

———. 1996. *Modernity at large: Cultural dimensions of globalization.* Minneapolis: University of Minnesota Press.

Apple, Michael. 1986. *Teachers and texts: A political economy of class and gender relations in education.* New York: Routledge and Kegan Paul.

Arumugam, V. 1993. "AayiraTTu ToLayiraTTu eLupaTukaLukku pin ilankai kalviyil puTiya pookkukaL—eTirpaRpum niraiveRRamum (New Trends in Sri Lankan Education since 1970—Expectation and fulfilment)." Prof. S. Selvanayagam Memorial Lecture 9, University of Jaffna, Sri Lanka. Mimeograph.

Arvanitis, Rigas, and Yvon Chatelin. 1988. "National scientific strategies in tropical soil sciences." *Social Studies of Science* 18:113–46.

Asad, T, ed. 1973. *Anthropology and the colonial encounter.* London: Ithaca Press.

Atkinson, Dwight. 1991. "Discourse analysis and written discourse conventions." *Annual Review of Applied Linguistics* 11:57–76.

———. 1996. "The Philosophical Transactions of the Royal Society of London, 1675–1975: A sociohistorical discourse analysis." *Language in Society* 25/1: 333–72.

———. 1999. *Scientific discourse in sociohistorical context.* Mahwah, N.J.: Lawrence Erlbaum.

Bahri, Deepika. 1997. "Marginally off-center: Postcolonialism in the teaching machine." *College English* 59/3: 277–98.

Bailey, K. M., and R. Ochsner. 1983. "A methodological review of the diary studies: Windmill tilting or social science?" In *Second language acquisition studies,* ed. K. M. Bailey, M. Long, and S. Peck, 188–98. Rowley, Mass.: Newbury House.

Bajaj, Jatinder K. 1990. "Francis Bacon, the first philosopher of modern science: A non-Western view." In *Science, hegemony, and violence,* ed. Ashish Nandy, 24–67. Delhi: Oxford University Press.

Baldauf, Richard B. 1986. "Linguistic constraints on participation in psychology." *The American Psychologist* 41:220–24.

Baldauf, Richard B., and B. H. Jernudd. 1983. "Language of publications as a variable in scientific communication." *Australian Review of Applied Linguistics* 6:97–108.

Barber, Benjamin. 1995. *Jihad vs. McWorld: How the planet is both falling apart and coming together—and what this means for democracy.* New York: Times Books.

Barton, David, and Mary Hamilton. 1998. *Local literacies: Reading and writing in one community.* London and New York: Routledge.

Bauman, Richard, and Joel Sherzer, eds 1974. *Explorations in the ethnography of speaking.* New York: Cambridge University Press.

Bazerman, Charles. 1984. "Modern evolution of the experimental report in physics: Spectroscopic articles in *Physical Review,* 1893–1890." *Social Studies of Science* 15:163–96.

———. 1987. "Codifying the social scientific style: The APA publication manual as behaviorist rhetoric." In *The rhetoric of the human sciences,* ed. J. S. Nelson, A. Megill, and D. N. McCloskey, 125–44. Madison: University of Wisconsin Press.

———. 1988. *Shaping written knowledge: The genre and activity of the experimental article in science.* Madison: University of Wisconsin Press.

Belanger, M. 1982. "A preliminary analysis of the structure of the discussion sections in ten neuroscience journal articles." Mimeograph. Cited in John Swales. 1990. *Genre analysis: English in academic and research settings.* Cambridge: Cambridge University Press.

Belcher, Diane D. 1997. "An argument for nonadversarial argumentation: On the relevance of the feminist critique of academic discourse to L2 writing pedagogy." *Journal of Second Language Writing* 6/1: 1–21.

———. 1999. "Stories we live by: Co-constructing the literacy narratives of highly successful L2 writers." Paper presented at thirty-third annual TESOL convention, 9–12 March, New York.

Berkenkotter, Carol, and Thomas Huckin. 1995. *Genre knowledge in disciplinary communication.* Mahwah, N.J.: Lawrence Erlbaum.

Bhabha, Homi K. 1994. *The location of culture.* New York: Routledge.

Bizzell, Patricia. 1982. "Cognition, convention and certainty: What we need to know about writing." *PRE/TEXT* 3:213–43.

———. 1992. *Academic discourse and critical consciousness.* Pittsburgh: University of Pittsburgh Press.

Bloomfield, Leonard. 1933. *Language.* London: Allen and Unwin.

Bollinger, Dwight. 1964. "Around the edge of language: intonation." *Harvard Educational Review* 34:282–96.

Bourdieu, Pierre. 1977. "The economics of linguistic exchanges." *Social Science Information* 16: 645–68.

Bourdieu, Pierre, and Jean-Paul Passeron. 1977. *Reproduction in education, society and culture.* London: Sage.

Braine, George, ed. 1998. *Non-native educators in English language teaching.* Mahwah, N.J.: Lawrence Erlbaum.

Brandt, Deborah. 1990. *Literacy as involvement: The acts of writers, readers and texts.* Carbondale: Southern Illinois University Press.

Brodkey, Linda. 1987. *Academic writing as social practice.* Philadelphia: Temple University Press.

Brown, Penelope, and Stephen Levinson. 1987. *Politeness: Some universals of language usage.* Cambridge: Cambridge University Press.

Bruffee, Kenneth. 1983. "Writing and reading as collaborative or social acts." In *The writer's mind,* ed. J. N. Hays. Urbana: National Council of Teachers of English.

Canagarajah, A. Suresh. 1992. "English in Jaffna Tamil society: Towards a sociolinguistic and applied linguistic appraisal." Paper presented at the Academic Forum, 10 December, University of Jaffna, Sri Lanka. Mimeograph.

———. 1993a. "American textbooks and Tamil students: A clash of discourses in the ESL classroom." *Language, Culture and Curriculum* 6/2: 143–56.

———. 1993b. "Critical ethnography of a Sri Lankan classroom: Ambiguities in opposition to reproduction through ESOL." *TESOL Quarterly* 27/4: 601–26.

———. 1993c. "Up the garden path: Second language writing approaches, local knowledge, and pluralism." *TESOL Quarterly* 27/2: 301–6.

———. 1994a. "Competing discourses in Sri Lankan English poetry." *World Englishes* 13/3: 361–76.

———. 1994b. tamiL ilakkiya vimarsanam: amaippiyal vaatamum piRa viyaakiyaana muRaikaLum paRRiya oor matippiiTu (Literary criticism in Tamil: An appraisal of structuralist and later interpretive methods). *Panpaadu* 4/1: 32–40.

———. 1995a. "Challenges in English literacy for African-American and Lankan Tamil learners: Towards a pedagogical paradigm for bidialectal and bilingual minority students." *Language and Education* 11/1: 15–36.

———. 1995b. "Functions of code switching in the ESL classroom: Socialising bilingualism in Jaffna." *Journal of Multilingual and Multicultural Development* 16/3: 173–96.

———. 1995c. "The political-economy of code choice in a revolutionary society: Tamil/English bilingualism in Jaffna." *Language in Society* 24/2: 187–212.

———. 1995d. "Use of English borrowings by Tamil fish vendors: Manipulating the context." *Multilingua* 14/1: 5–24.

———. 1996a. "From critical research practice to critical research reporting." *TESOL Quarterly* 29/2: 320–30.

———. 1996b. "Non-discursive requirements in academic publishing, material resources of periphery scholars, and the politics of knowledge production." *Written Communication* 13/4: 435–72.

———. 1999. *Resisting linguistic imperialism in English teaching.* Oxford: Oxford University Press.

———. 2000. "Understanding L2 academic writing as codeswitching." Paper presented at the thirty-fourth annual TESOL convention, 14–18 March, Vancouver.

———. 2001. "The fortunate traveler: Shuttling between communities and literacies by economy class." In *Reflections on Multiliterate Lives,* ed. D. Belcher and U. Connor, 23–37. Clevedon, U.K.: Multilingual Matters.

Chelliah, John V. 1922. *A century of English education.* Vaddukoddai: Jaffna College.

Clandinin, D. J., and F. M. Connelly, F. M. 1991. "Narrative and story in practice and research." In *The reflective turn: Case studies in and on educational practice,* ed. D. Schon, 258–81. New York: Teachers College Press.

Clay, Jason. 1990. "Editorial: Genes, genius, and genocide." *Cultural Survival Quarterly* 14/4: 1.

Cmejrkova, Svetla. 1996. "Academic writing in Czech and English." In *Academic writing: Intercultural and textual issues,* ed. A. Ventola and A. Mauranen, 137–52. Amsterdam and Philadelphia: John Benjamins.

Connor, Ulla. 1996. *Contrastive rhetoric: Cross cultural aspects of second language writing.* Cambridge: Cambridge University Press.

————. 1999. "Learning to write academic prose in a second language: A literacy autobiography." In *Non-native educators in English language teaching,* ed. G. Braine, 29–42. Mahwah, N.J.: Lawrence Erlbaum.

Crossette, Barbara. 2001. "Move to curb biotech crops ignores poor, U.N. finds." *New York Times,* 8 July, A4.

Currey, J., Alan Hill, Keith Sambrook, and Kirsten Petersen. 1990. "Working with Chinua Achebe: The African writers series." *Kunapipi* 7:149–59.

Daniell, B. 1999. "Narratives of literacy: Connecting composition to culture." *College Composition and Communication* 50/3: 393–410.

David, Kenneth. 1974. *The new wind: Changing identities in South Asia.* Hague: Mouton.

de Beaugrande, Robert, and Wolfgang Dressler. 1981. *Introduction to text linguistics.* London: Longman.

de Lima, Roberto Kant. 1992. "The anthropology of the academy." In *Knowledge and Society,* vol. 9, *The anthropology of science and technology,* ed. David Hess and Linda Layne. Greenwich, Conn: JAI Press.

Denny, Peter J. 1991. "Rational thought in oral culture and literate decontextualization." In *Literacy and orality,* ed. David Olson and Nancy Torrance, 66–89. Cambridge: Cambridge University Press

Derrida, Jacques. 1981. *Positions.* Trans. Alan Bass. Chicago: University of Chicago Press.

Doheny-Farina, Stephen. 1996. *The wired neighborhood.* New Haven: Yale University Press.

Dube, Siddharth. 1995a. "Higher education a key issue in Sri Lankan conflict." *The Chronicle of Higher Education,* 28 April, A66.

————. 1995b. "The prospect of peace: Sri Lanka's universities welcome growing calm as civil conflicts wind down." *The Chronicle of Higher Education,* 28 April, A65.

Dubois, B. L. 1986. "From *New England Journal of Medicine* and *Journal of the American Medical Association* through the Associated Press to the local newspaper: Scientific translation for the laity." In *Wissenschaftssprachen und Gesellschaft: Aspekte der Kommunikation und des Wissenstranfers in der heutigen Zeit,* ed. T. Bungarten, 243–53. Hamburg: Akademion.

Eastman, Carol M., ed. 1992. *Codeswitching.* Clevedon, U.K.: Multilingual Matters.

Eisenstein, E. 1979. *The printing press as an agent of change.* Cambridge: Cambridge University Press.

Elkin, A. P. 1977. *Aboriginal men of high degree.* New York: St Martin's.

Fahnestock, Jeanne. 1986. "Accommodating science: The rhetorical life of scientific facts." *Written Communication* 3/2: 275–96.

Faigley, Lester. 1985. "Nonacademic writing: The social perspective." In *Writing in nonacademic settings,* ed. Lee Odell and Dixie Goswami, 231–48. New York and London: Guilford Press.

————. 1997. "Literacy after the revolution." *College Composition and Communication* 48/1, 30–43.

Fairclough, Norman. 1995. *Critical discourse analysis: The critical study of language.* London: Longman.

Feldman, Carol Fleicher. 1991. "Oral metalanguage." In *Literacy and orality,* ed. David Olson and Nancy Torrance, 47–65. Cambridge: Cambridge University Press.

Flowerdew, John. 2001. "Attitudes of journal editors to nonnative speaker contributions." *TESOL Quarterly* 35/1: 121–50.

Flowerdew, John, and T. Dudley-Evans. 1999. "Genre analysis of editorial correspondence to journal contributors." Paper presented at the convention of the American Association of Applied Linguistics, 7 March, Stamford, Conn.

Foucault, Michel. 1972. "The discourse on language." In *The Archeology of Knowledge,* 215–37. New York: Pantheon.

Fox, Helen. 1994. *Listening to the world: Cultural issues in academic writing,* Urbana, Ill.: National Council of Teachers of English.

Franco, Jean. 1988. "Beyond ethonocentrism: Gender, power and the Third World intelligentsia." In *Marxism and the interpretation of culture,* ed. C. Nelson and C. Grossberg, 503–15. Basingstoke, U.K.: Macmillan.

Frank, A. Gundar. 1969. *Latin America: Underdevelopment or revolution.* New York: Monthly Review Press.

Galtung, Johann. 1971. "A structural theory of imperialism." *Journal of Peace Research* 8/2: 81–117.

———. 1980. *The true worlds: A transnational perspective.* New York: Free Press.

Garfield, Eugene. 1978. "The Science Citation Index as a quality information filter." In *Coping with the bio-medical literature explosion: A qualitative approach,* ed. Kenneth Warren, 68–77. New York: Rockefeller Foundation.

———. 1983. Talking science. *Nature* 303:354.

Geertz, Clifford. 1983. *Local knowledge: Further essays in interpretive anthropology.* New York: Basic Books.

Geisler, Cheryl. 1994. *Academic literacy and the nature of expertise: Reading, writing, and knowing in academic philosophy.* Mahwah, N.J.: Lawrence Erlbaum.

Gibbs, Wayt W. 1995. "Information have-nots." *Scientific American,* May, 12B–14B.

Giddens, Anthony. 1990. *The consequences of modernity.* Stanford: Stanford University Press.

Gilbert, G. N., and M. Mulkay. 1984. *Opening Pandora's box: A sociological analysis of scientific discourse.* Cambridge: Cambridge University Press.

Giroux, Henry A. 1979. "Writing and critical thinking in the social studies." *Curriculum Inquiry* (March): 291–310.

———. 1983. *Theory and resistance in education: A pedagogy for the opposition.* South Hadley: Bergin.

———. 1992. *Border crossings: Cultural workers and the politics of education.* New York: Routledge.

Glanz, James. 2001. "The world of science becomes a global village." *New York Times,* 1 May, F1–2.

Gnanakumaran, N. 1991/1992. "Concept of Brahman according to Sankaracarya." *Sri Lanka Journal of South Asian Studies* 3 (new series): 72–79.

———. 1993/1994. "Studies in Caiva Cittantam." *Lanka* 8–9:36–59.

Goffman, Erving. 1961. *Asylums: Essays on the social situation of mental patients and other inmates.* New York: Anchor.

Govardhan, Anam K., Bhaskaran Nayar, and Ravi Sheorey. 1999. "Do U.S. MATESOL programs prepare students to teach abroad?" *TESOL Quarterly* 33/1: 114–25.

Grice, H. P. 1975. "Logic and conversation." In *Syntax and semantics,* vol.3, *Speech acts,* ed. P. Cole and J. Morgan, 41–58. New York, London: Academic Press.

Guha, Ranajit, and Gayatri Spivak, eds. 1988. *Selected subaltern studies.* New York: Oxford University Press.

Gumperz, John J. 1982a. *Discourse strategies.* Interactional Sociolinguistics Series, vol. 1. Cambridge: Cambridge University Press.

———. 1982b. *Language and social identity.* Interactional Sociolinguistics Series, vol. 2. Cambridge: Cambridge University Press.

Haraway, Donna. 1989. *Primate visions: Gender, race, and nature in the world of modern science.* New York: Routledge.

Harding, Sandra. 1991. *Whose science? Whose knowledge? Thinking from women's lives.* Ithaca: Cornell University Press.

Harland, Richard. 1987. *Superstructuralism: The philosophy of structuralism and post-structuralism.* London: Methuen.

Harris, Joseph. 1989. "The idea of community in the study of writing." *College Composition and Communication* 40/1: 11–22.

Harwood, Jonathan. 1993. *Styles of scientific thought: The German genetics community, 1930–1933.* Chicago: University of Chicago Press.

Heath, Shirley Brice. 1983. *Ways with words.* Cambridge: Cambridge University Press.

Heller, Monica. 1988. *Codeswitching.* Berlin: Mouton de Gruyter.

Herzberg, Bruce. 1986. "The politics of discourse communities." Paper presented at the thirty-seventh annual College Composition and Communication Convention, March, New Orleans.

Hess, David J. 1995. *Science and technology in a multicultural world.* New York: Columbia University Press.

Hessen, Boris. 1971. *The social and economic roots of Newton's Principia.* New York: Howard Fertig.

Hinds, J. 1983. "Contrastive rhetoric: Japanese and English." *Text* 3:183-196.

Hitt, Jack. 2001. "Building a better blood sucker." *New York Times Magazine,* 6 May, 92–96.

Hockett, Charles F. 1958. *A course in modern linguistics.* New York: Macmillan.

Holliday, Adrian. 1994. *Appropriate methodology and social context.* Cambridge: Cambridge University Press.

Holloway, W., and T. Jefferson. 1997. "Eliciting narrative through the in-depth interview." *Qualitative Inquiry* 3:53–70.

Honan, William H. 1998. "For many foreign students, American colleges cost too much." *New York Times,* 28 September, A32.

hooks, bell. 1989. *Talking back: Thinking feminist, thinking black.* Boston: South End Press.

hooks, bell. 1990. "Choosing the margin as a space for radical openness." In *Yearning: Race, gender and cultural politics,* 145–54. Boston: South End Press.

Hornberger, Nancy. 1994. "Ethnography." *TESOL Quarterly* 28/4: 688–90.

Howard, Rebecca Moore. 1995. "Plagiarisms, authorships, and the academic death penalty." *College English* 57/7: 788–806.

Huff, Toby. 1993. *The rise of early modern science: Islam, China, and the West.* Cambridge: Cambridge University Press.

Hymes, Dell, ed. 1969. *Reinventing anthropology.* New York: Pantheon.

———. 1972. "Models of the interaction of language and social life." In *Directions in sociolinguistics: The ethnography of communication,* ed. John J. Gumperz and Dell Hymes, 35–71. New York: Holt, Rinehart and Winston.

Jacob, Margaret. 1976. *The Newtonians and the English Revolution, 1689–1720.* Ithaca: Cornell University Press.

Jernudd, B. H., and R. B. Baldauf Jr. 1987. "Planning science communication for human resource development." In *Language education in human resource development,* ed. B. K. Das, 144–89. Singapore: RELC.

Kachru, Braj B. 1986. *The alchemy of English: The spread, functions and models of non-native Englishes.* Oxford: Pergamon.

Kailasapathy, K. 1968. *Tamil heroic poetry.* Oxford: Oxford University Press.

———. 1981. *Ilakkiyamum tiRanaaivum* (Literature and criticism). Madras: Madras Book House.

Kaplan, Robert B. 1966. "Cultural thought patterns in intercultural education." *Language Learning* 16:1–20.

————. 1976. "A further note on contrastive rhetoric." *Communication Quarterly* 24:12–19.

————. 1986. "Culture and the written language." In *Culture bound,* ed. J. M. Valdes, 8–19. Cambridge: Cambridge University Press.

Killingsworth, M. J., and M. K. Gilbertson. 1992. *Sign, genres, and communities in technical communication.* Amityville, N.Y.: Baywood Publishing.

Kirkpatrick, David D. 2000. "As publishers perish, libraries feel the pain." *New York Times,* 3 November, C1, C5.

Knorr-Cetina, Karin D. 1981. *The manufacture of knowledge: An essay on the constructivist and contextual nature of science.* Oxford: Pergamon.

Kochman, Thomas. 1981. *Black and white styles in conflict.* Chicago: University of Illinois Press.

Kress, Gunther. 1985. "Ideological structures in discourse." In *Handbook of discourse analysis,* vol. 4, ed. Tuan van Dijk, 27–42. London: Academic Press.

Kristof, Nicholas D. 1999. "Alien abduction? Science calls it sleep paralysis." *New York Times,* 6 July, F1.

Kubota, Ryuko. 1999. "Japanese culture constructed by discourses: Implications for applied linguistics research and ELT." *TESOL Quarterly* 33/1: 9–35.

Kuhn, Thomas S. 1962. *The structure of scientific revolutions.* Chicago: University of Chicago Press.

Labov, William. 1972. *Sociolinguistic patterns.* Philadelphia: University of Pennsylvania Press.

Larsen, Neil. 1990. *Modernism and hegemony.* Minneapolis: University of Minnesota Press.

Latour, B., and S. Woolgar. 1979. *Laboratory life: The social construction of scientific facts.* Princeton: Princeton University Press.

Lave, J., and E. Wenger. 1991. *Situated learning: Legitimate peripheral participation.* Cambridge: Cambridge University Press.

Lewis, D. 1969. *Convention: A philosophical study.* Cambridge: Harvard University Press.

Li, Xiao-Ming. 1999. "Writing from the vantage point of an outsider/insider." In *Non-native educators in English language teaching,* ed. G. Braine, 43–56. Mahwah, N.J.: Lawrence Erlbaum.

Loomba, Ania. 1994. "Overworlding the 'Third World.'" In *Colonial discourse and post-colonial theory: A reader,* ed. Patrick Williams and Laura Chrisman, 305–23. New York: Columbia University Press.

Lu, Min-Zhan, and Bruce Horner. 1998. "The problematic of experience: Redefining critical work in ethnography and pedagogy." *College English* 60/2: 257–77.

Luke, C. 2000. Cyber schooling and technological change: Multiliteracies for new times. In *Multiliteracies: Literacy learning and the design of social futures,* ed. B. Cope and M. Kalantzis, 69–91. London and New York: Routledge.

Lunn, Eugene. 1982. *Marxism and modernism.* Berkeley: University of California Press.

Lyotard, Jean-Francois. 1984. *The postmodern condition: A report on knowledge.* Minneapolis: University of Minnesota Press.

MacDonell, Diane. 1986. *Theories of discourse: An introduction.* Oxford: Blackwell.

Manivasakar, V. 1991/1992. "Intellectual colonialism vis-a-vis pseudo developmentalism: Irony and agony of the Third World." *Sri Lanka Journal of South Asian Studies* 3 (new series): 51–59.

Marcus, G., and M. M. J. Fischer. 1986. *Anthropology as cultural critique: An experimental moment in the human sciences.* Chicago: University of Chicago Press.

Mauranen, Anna. 1993a. "Contrastive ESP rhetoric: Metatext in Finnish-economic texts." *English for Specific Purposes* 12:3–22.

————. 1993b. *Cultural differences in academic rhetoric.* Frankfurt am Main: Peter Lang.

McGilvray, Dennis. 1982. *Caste: Ideology and interaction.* Cambridge: Cambridge University Press.

Mehan, Hugh. 1985. "The structure of classroom discourse." In *Handbook of Discourse Analysis,* vol. 3, ed. Tuan A. van Dijk, 119–31. New York: Academic Press.

Merton, Robert. 1970. *Science, technology, and society in seventeenth-century England.* New York: Howard Fertig.

Michaels, Sarah, and James Collins. 1984. "Oral discourse styles: Classroom interaction and the acquisition of literacy." In *Coherence in spoken and written discourse,* ed. Deborah Tannen, 219–44. Norwood, N.J.: Ablex.

Milroy, Lesley, and James Milroy. 1992. "Social network and social class: Toward an integrated sociolinguistic model." *Language in Society* 21/1: 1–26.

Mohanty, Chandra. 1988. "Under western eyes: Feminist scholarship and colonial discourses." *Feminist Review* 30:65–88.

Moravcsik, M. J. 1985. *Strengthening the coverage of Third World science.* Eugene, Oreg.: Institute of Theoretical Science.

Muchiri, Mary N., Nshindi G. Mulamba, Greg Myers, and Deoscorous B. Ndoloi. 1995. "Importing composition: Teaching and researching academic writing beyond North America." *College Composition and Communication* 46/2: 175–98.

Murray, D. 2000. "Protean communication: The language of computer-mediated communication." *TESOL Quarterly* 34/3: 397–422.

Myers, Greg. 1985. "Texts as knowledge claims: The social construction of two biology articles." *Social Studies of Science* 15:583–630.

————. 1990. *Writing Biology: Texts in the social construction of scientific knowledge.* Madison: University of Wisconsin Press.

Myers-Scotton, C. 1992. *Social motivations for codeswitching: Evidence from Africa.* Oxford: Oxford University Press.

Nadarajasundaram, M. 1991/1992. "The cultural differences and their impact on management decision making: An overview of Japan and Sri Lanka." *Sri Lanka Journal of South Asian Studies* 3 (new series): 15–33.

Nandy, Ashish, ed. 1990. *Science, hegemony, and violence.* Delhi: Oxford University Press.

Narasimhan, R. 1991. "Literacy: Its characterization and implications." In *Literacy and orality,* ed. David R. Olson and Nancy Torrance, 177–97. Cambridge: Cambridge University Press.

Ngugi wa Thiong'o. 1983. *Barrel of a pen.* London: New Beacon Books.

Olson, David. 1991. "Literacy and objectivity: The rise of modern science." In *Literacy and orality,* ed. David Olson and Nancy Torrance, 149–65. Cambridge: Cambridge University Press.

Olson, David, and Nancy Torrance, eds. 1991. *Literacy and orality.* Cambridge: Cambridge University Press.

Osborne, Lawrence. 2001. "Regional disturbances." *New York Times Magazine,* 6 May. 98–102.

Paranirupasingham, S. 1991. "tiru poo kailasapaty avarkaLum poRuLaaraaiciyum" (Mr. P. Kailasapathy and the search for Truth). Paper presented at the Academic Forum, 2 October, University of Jaffna, Sri Lanka.

Paul, Dannette. 1996. "Introducing chaos into scientific discourse: A study of reception and effect of rhetorical devices in revolutionary science." Ph.D. diss., Pennsylvania State University.

Pear, Robert. 1999. "N.I.H plan for journal on the web draws fire." *New York Times,* 8 June, F1, F6.

Peirce, Bronwyn N. 1989. "Towards a pedagogy of possibility in teaching of English internationally." *TESOL Quarterly* 23/3: 401–20.

Pennycook, Alastair. 1989. "The concept of 'method,' interested knowledge, and the politics of language teaching." *TESOL Quarterly* 23/4: 589–618.

————. 1994. *The cultural politics of English as an international language.* London: Longman.

————. 1996. "Borrowing others' words: Text, ownership, memory, and plagiarism." *TESOL Quarterly* 30/2: 201–30.

Peters, Douglas P., and Stephen J. Ceci. 1982. "Peer-review practices of psychological journals: The fate of published articles, submitted again." *The Behavioral and Brain Sciences* 5:187–255.

Pfaffenberger, Bryan. 1982. *Caste in Tamil culture.* New Delhi:Vikas.

Phillipson, Robert. 1992. *Linguistic imperialism.* Oxford: Oxford University Press.

Pickering, A. 1995. *The mangle of practice:Time, agency, and science.* Chicago: University of Chicago Press.

Porter, T. M. 1995. *Trust in numbers: The pursuit of objectivity in science and public life.* Princeton: Princeton University Press.

Pratt, Mary Louise. 1987. "Linguistic utopias." In *The linguistics of writing: Arguments between language and literature,* ed. Nigel Fabb, Derek Attridge, Alan Durant, and Colin MacCabe, 48–66. Manchester: Manchester University Press.

———. 1991. "Arts of the contact zone." *Profession* 91:33–40.

Prior, Paul. 1998. *Writing/disciplinarity: A sociohistoric account of literate activity in the academy.* Mahwah, N.J.: Lawrence Erlbaum.

Purves, A. C., ed. 1988. *Writing across languages and cultures: Issues in contrastive rhetoric.* Newbury Park, Calif.: Sage.

Raj, J. 1982. "WASP ideology: the kernel of the American Kernel Lessons." *Lanka Guardian* 5/11: 15–18.

Relman, Arnold. 1978. "Are journals really quality filters?" In *Coping with the bio-medical literature explosion: A qualitative approach,* ed. Kenneth Warren, 54–60. New York: Rockefeller Foundation.

Reutten, Mary K. 1998. "Abidjan journal." *College English* 60/1: 51–56.

Reynolds, Nedra. 1998. "Composition's imagined geographies:The politics of space in the frontier, city, and cyberspace." *College Composition and Communication* 50/1: 12–35.

Rohter, Larry. 2001. "Brazil bounding forward as genomics powerhouse." *New York Times,* 1 May, F1–2.

Rosenthal, Elisabeth. "Chairman Mao's cure for cancer." *New York Times Magazine,* 6 May, 70–73.

Ross, M., and R. Buehler. 1994. "On authenticating and using personal recollections." In *Autobiographical memory and validity of retrospective reports,* ed. N. Schwarz and S. Sudman, 55–69. New York: Springer-Verlag.

Rymer, Jone. 1988. "Scientific composing processes: How eminent scientists write journal articles." In *Writing in academic disciplines,* ed. D. Joliffe, 211–50. Norwood, N.J.: Ablex.

Said, Edward W. 1978. *Orientalism.* Harmondsworth, U.K.: Penguin.

———. 1983. "Travelling theory." In *The world, the text, and the critic,* 226–47. Cambridge: Harvard University Press.

———. 1993. *Culture and imperialism.* New York: Alfred A. Knopf.

Salager-Meyer, Francoise. N.d. "Scientific multilingualism and 'lesser languages.'" Facultad de Medicina, Universidad de los Andes.Typescript.

Sanmugadas, A. 1984. "Modern Tamil literature of Sri Lanka." In *Commemorative Souvenir: Jaffna Public Library,* 15–20. Jaffna: Catholic Press.

Saunders, Frances Stonor. 1999. *The cultural cold war: The CIA and the world of arts and letters.* New York: New Free Press.

Schenke, Arleen. 1991. "The 'will to reciprocity' and the work of memory: Fictioning speaking out of silence in ESL and feminist pedagogy." *Resources for Feminist Research* 20:47–55.

Scheurich, James J., and Michelle D. Young. 1997. "Coloring epistemologies: Are our research epistemologies racially biased?" *Educational Researcher* 26/4: 4–17.

Schwebke, Linda, and Peter Medway. 2001. "The reader written: Successive constructions of self and text in encounters with everyday writing." *Written Communication* 18/3: 350–89.

Scollon, R. 1991. "Eight legs and one elbow: Stance and structure in Chinese English composition." Paper presented at the International Reading Association, Second North American Conference on Adult and Adolescent Literacy, 21 March, Banff.

Scott, James C. 1985. *Weapons of the weak: Everyday forms of peasant resistance.* New Haven: Yale University Press.

Selfe, Cynthia, and Richard J. Selfe Jr. 1994. "The politics of the interface: Power and its exercise in electronic contact zones." *College Composition and Communication* 45/4: 480–504.

Seshagiri, S., and M. Chitra. 1983. *Biodynamic horticulture: Improvements and extensions.* Monograph Series on Engineering of Photosynthetic Systems, vol. 15. Madras: Shri AMM Murugappa Chettiar Research Center.

Shapin, Steven. 1984. "Pump and circumstance: Robert Boyle's literary technology." *Social Studies of Science* 14:481–520.

Shen, F. 1989. "The classroom and the wider culture: Identity as a key to learning English composition." *College Composition and Communication* 40/4: 459–66.

Shiva, Vandana. 1990. "Reductionist science as epistemological violence." In *Science, hegemony, and violence,* ed. Ashish Nandy, 232–56. Delhi: Oxford University Press.

Silva, Tony. 1993. "Toward an understanding of the distinct nature of L2 writing: The ESL research and its implications." *TESOL Quarterly* 27/4: 657–78.

Singh, Rajendra, ed. 1998. *The native speaker: Multilingual perspectives.* New Delhi: Sage.

Sitrampalam, S. K. 1991/1992. "The form Velu of Sri Lankan Brahmi inscriptions: A reappraisal." *Sri Lanka Journal of South Asian Studies* 3 (new series): 60–72.

Sivatamby, K. 1984. "Towards an understanding of the culture and ideology of the Tamils of Sri Lanka." In *Commemorative Souvenir: Jaffna Public Library,* 49–56. Jaffna: Catholic Press.

———. 1990. "The ideology of Saiva-Tamil integrality: Its sociohistorical significance in the study of Yalppanam Tamil society." *Lanka* 5:176–82.

———. 1992. "YaaLpaaNa camuuka tai viLanki koLLal—atan uruvaakkam asaiviyakkam paR-Riya oru piraarampa usaaval" (Understanding Jaffna society: A preliminary inquiry into its "formation" and "dynamics"). Professor S. Selvanayagam Memorial Lecture 8, University of Jaffna, Sri Lanka. Mimeograph.

Smith, Dinitia. 1999. "Hoping the web will rescue young scholars: In the publish-or-perish world, can they live on the Internet?" *New York Times,* 12 June, B7, B9.

Smitherman, Geneva. 1999. "CCCC's role in the struggle for language rights." *College Composition and Communication* 50/3: 349–76.

Spivak, Gayatri. 1990. *The post-colonial critic.* New York: Routledge.

Sridhar, S. N. 1994. "A reality check for SLA theories." *TESOL Quarterly* 28/4: 800–805.

Stolberg, Sheryl Gay. 2001. "The estrogen alternative." *New York Times Magazine,* 6 May, 108–10.

Suseendirarajah, S. 1978. "Caste and language in Jaffna society." *Anthropological Linguistics* 20:312–19.

———. 1980. "Religion and language in Jaffna society." *Anthropological Linguistics* 22:345–62.

———. 1991. "PanTitamaNiyin peerum pukaLum vanta vaaRu" (Accounting for the name and prestige of Panditamani). Paper presented at the Academic Forum, 22 March, University of Jaffna, Sri Lanka. Mimeograph.

———. 1992. "English in our Tamil society: A sociolinguistic appraisal." Paper presented at the Academic Forum, 28 October, University of Jaffna, Sri Lanka. Mimeograph.

Swales, John. 1985. "English language papers and authors' first language: Preliminary explorations." *Scientometrics* 8:91–101.

———. 1990. *Genre analysis: English in academic and research settings.* Cambridge: Cambridge University Press.

———. 1996. "Occluded genres in the academy: The case of the submission letter." In *Academic writing: Intercultural and textual issues,* ed. Eija Ventola and Anna Mauranen, 45–58. Amsterdam and Philadelphia: John Benjamins.

———. 1998. *Other floors, other voices: A textography of a small university building.* Mahwah, N.J.: Lawrence Erlbaum.

Tannen, Deborah. 1982. *Spoken and written language: Exploring orality and literacy.* Norwood, N.J.: Ablex.

Tierney, J. 1997. "Our oldest computer, upgraded." *New York Times Magazine,* 28 September, 46.

Traweek, Sharon. 1988. *Beamtimes and lifetimes.* Cambridge: Harvard University Press.

Turkle, Sherry. 1978. *Psychoanalytic politics.* New York: Basic Books.

Velupillai, A. 1991/1992. "Patterns of basic sentences in Tamil and some semantic observations." *Sri Lanka Journal of South Asian Studies* 3 (new series): 1–14.

Ventola, Eija, and Anna Mauranen, eds. 1996. *Academic writing: Intercultural and textual issues.* Amsterdam and Philadelphia: John Benjamins.

Viswanathan, Gauri. 1989. *Masks of conquest.* New York: Columbia University Press.

Vithiananthan, S. 1984. "Folk dramatic traditions of the Tamils of Sri Lanka." In *Commemorative Souvenir: Jaffna Public Library,* 21–28. Jaffna: Catholic Press.

Wallerstein, Immanuel. 1974. *The modern World-System, 1: Capitalist agriculture and the origins of the European world-economy in the sixteenth century.* New York: Academic Press.

———. 1991. *Geopolitics and geoculture.* Cambridge: Cambridge University Press.

Warschauer, M. 2000. "The changing global economy and the future of English teaching." *TESOL Quarterly* 34/3: 511–36.

Weiner, Tim. 1997. "You spy? Let's talk." *New York Times,* 8 June, section 4, 5.

Wenger, Etienne. 1998. *Communities of practice.* Cambridge: Cambridge University Press.

Wickramasuriya, S. 1976. "Strangers in their own land: The radical protest against English education in colonial Ceylon." *Navasilu* 1:15–31.

Widdowson, H. G. 1994. "The ownership of English." *TESOL Quarterly* 28/2: 377–88.

Williams, Jane, ed. 1989. *Tambimuttu: Bridge between two worlds.* London: Peter Owen.

World Bank. 1996. *Taking action to reduce poverty in sub-Saharan Africa: An overview.* Washington, D.C.: World Bank.

———. 1999. *World development report: Knowledge for development, 1998/1999 summary.* Washington, D.C.: World Bank.

Index

A. J. *See* Canagaratne ("A. J.")

academia, 60, 71, 218, 233; center / periphery collaboration in, 289–93; center scholars using work of periphery, 235, 243–47; competition within, 66–68, 141, 193; democratization of, 293, 304–5; democratization of, center's role, 277–83; democratization of, periphery's role, 283–89; disciplines of, 33, 89–91; effects of ethnic conflict on, 8–10, 26, 102–4; effects of material resources, 106–7; exchange programs in, 279–80, 282–83; faculty relations in, 191–94, 217; foreign students in, 312*nn2–3;* freedom of postcolonial scholars, 303–4; importance of publishing in, 33, 115, 190–93, 246; influence of center on periphery scholars, 26, 28–29, 268–69; as multidisciplinary, 178, 189, 194–95, 208, 210; periphery, 51–53, 75, 115, 118, 187, 287–88; relation of periphery scholars to center, 193–94, 208, 267–68; response to traditional scholarship, 183–86; rhetorics of, 90, 204–5; role in knowledge dissemination, 5, 203–4; security of faculty positions in, 190–91, 197; specialization in, 33, 89–90, 114–15, 161–62; status in, through publication, 27, 33, 244; uses of literacy in center, 97–100; valuing talking, 218–24. *See also* academic communities; University of Jaffna

academic communication, 309*n4;* center's role in democratization of, 277–83; democratization through changing discourses, 293–302; periphery's role in democratization of, 283–89

academic communities, 37, 305, 308*n11,* 309*n4,* 311*n5;* of center *vs.* periphery, 70, 228–29; factionalism within, 195–96; inequalities between, 238–40; literary practices of, 13–16,

97–100; outside ideas in, 225, 291–93; of periphery, 231, 286–88. *See also* disciplinary communities; discourse communities

academic culture, 197–200, 226; based on reading not writing, 210, 243; conflicting, 197–200; periphery and center, 11, 231; of UJ, 26, 187–96, 216–25

Academic Forum, at University of Jaffna, 50–53, 75, 94, 307*n3;* context for, 56–57; discussion at, 80–81, 140, 219; membership of, 64–65; presentations at, 77–79, 183–86

academic publishing, 69, 304, 309*n2;* accommodating periphery authors, 29–30, 170, 175–76, 277, 285–86; center dominance in, 22–23, 27–29, 42–43, 131–32, 238–40, 247–51; center dominance through, 33–34, 168–69, 300–302; center / periphery relations in, 13–16, 19, 25–28, 42–43, 268–69; consequences of center dominance, 37, 140, 235–36, 238–40, 243–47, 260–61; conventions of, 20–25, 85–86, 93, 140–41, 150, 158, 171–73; democratization of, 275, 302–3; exclusion of periphery from, 11–12, 49, 107–8, 230, 235–36; factors in getting published, 206–7, 214; fields of opportunity for, 299–300; importance in knowledge construction, 5, 59–60, 226–28, 244; importance of, 6, 287–88; nonconventional approaches to, 269–72; in periphery, 17, 115, 177–81, 225, 256, 275; reform efforts in, 31, 264, 275, 293–94; and research, 33, 93; resistance to center hegemony over, 30, 302; role in disciplinary discourse, 225–26; status through, 161, 237, 241. *See also* journals; publishing conventions

academic writing, 19, 44; analysis of journals,